Endorsements

"*The Bible Teacher's Guide* ... will help any teacher study and get a better background for his/her Bible lessons. In addition, it will give direction and scope to teaching of the Word of God. Praise God for this contemporary introduction to the Word of God."

—Dr. Elmer Towns
Co-founder of Liberty University
Former Dean, Liberty Baptist Theological Seminary

"Expositional, theological, and candidly practical! I highly recommend The Bible Teacher's Guide for anyone seeking to better understand or teach God's Word."

—Dr. Young–Gil Kim
Founding President, Handong Global University

"Helpful to both the layman and the serious student, The Bible Teacher's Guide, by Dr. Greg Brown, is outstanding!"

—Dr. Neal Weaver
President, Louisiana Baptist University

"Whether you are preparing a Bible study, a sermon, or simply wanting to dive deeper into a personal study of God's Word, these will be very helpful tools."

—Eddie Byun
Missions and Teaching Pastor, Venture Christian Church, Los Gatos, California
Author of Justice Awakening

"I am happy that Greg is making his insights into God's truth available to a wider audience through these books. They bear the hallmarks of good Bible teaching: the result of rigorous Bible study and thoroughgoing application to the lives of people."

—Ajith Fernando
Teaching Director, Youth for Christ
Author of A Call to Joy and Pain

"The content of the series is rich. My prayer is that God will use it to help the body of Christ grow strong."

—Dr. Min Chung
Senior Pastor, Covenant Fellowship Church, Urbana, Illinois
Adjunct Professor, Urbana Theological Seminary

"Knowing the right questions to ask and how to go about answering them is fundamental to learning in any subject matter. Greg demonstrates this convincingly."

—Dr. William Moulder
Professor of Biblical Studies, Trinity International University

"Pastor Greg is passionate about the Word of God, rigorous and thorough in his approach to the study of it... I am pleased to recommend The Bible Teacher's Guide to anyone who hungers for the living Word."

—Dr. JunMo Cho
Professor of Linguistics, Handong Global University
Contemporary Christian Music Recording Artist

"I can't imagine any student of Scripture not benefiting by this work."

—Steven J. Cole
Pastor, Flagstaff Christian Fellowship, Flagstaff, Arizona
Author of the Riches from the Word series

Handwritten notes at top of page:

TUE JULY 23 EYE 9:30

MCAUTO.COM

EMMEY Wed ?
OS A 11:00

SVP COPAY

Contents

Preface

And entrust what you heard me say in the presence of many others as witnesses to faithful people
2 Timothy 2:2 (NET)

Paul's words to Timothy still apply to us today. The church needs teachers who clearly and fearlessly teach the Word of God. With this in mind, The Bible Teacher's Guide (BTG) series was created. This series includes both expositional and topical studies that help teachers lead small groups, pastors prepare sermons, and individuals increase their knowledge of God's Word.

Each lesson is based around the hermeneutical principle that the original authors wrote in a similar manner as we do today—with the intention of being understood. Each paragraph and chapter of Scripture centers around one main thought, often called the Big Idea. After finding the Big Idea for each passage studied, students will discuss the Big Question, which will lead the small group (if applicable) through the entire text. Alongside the Big Question, note the added Observation, Interpretation, and Application Questions. The Observation Questions point out pivotal aspects of the text. The Interpretation Questions facilitate understanding through use of the context and other Scripture. The Application Questions lead to life principles coming out of the text. Not all questions will be used, but they have been given to help guide the teacher in preparing the lesson.

As the purpose of this guide is to make preparation easier for the teacher and study easier for the individual, many commentaries and sermons have been accessed in the development of each lesson. After meditating on the Scripture text and the lesson, the small group leader may wish to follow the suggested teaching outline:

(1) Introduce the text and present the Big Question.
(2) Allow several minutes for the members to discuss the question, search for the answers within the text, and listen to God speak to them through His Word.
(3) Discuss the initial findings, then lead the group through the Observation, Interpretation, and Application Questions.

On the other hand, the leader may prefer to teach the lesson in part or in whole, and then give the Application Questions. He may also choose to use a "study group" method, where each member prepares beforehand and shares teaching responsibility (see Appendices 1 and 2). Some leaders may find it most effective to first read the main section of the lesson corporately, then to follow with a brief discussion of the topic and an Application Question.

Again, The Bible Teacher's Guide can be used as a manual to follow in teaching, a resource to use in preparation for teaching or preaching, or simply as an expositional devotional to enrich your own study. I pray that the Lord may bless your study, preparation, and teaching, and that in all of it you will find the fruit of the Holy Spirit abounding in your own life and in the lives of those you instruct.

Introduction

Authorship

Though some liberal scholars question Pauline authorship based on Ephesians' unique vocabulary, style, and "advanced" doctrine, both internal and external evidence clearly support Paul's authorship. The internal evidence is twofold: The author says that he is Paul twice (1:1 and 3:1), and Colossians, which is widely accepted as a Pauline epistle, is very similar to Ephesians—suggesting both the same author and the same time frame of writing. These epistles contain around 32 verses that are essentially the same,[1] and both claim to be written from prison (cf. 6:20, 3:1, 4:1; Col 4:3, 10). In addition, Tychicus carried both letters to Asia (Col 4:7-9; Eph 6:21-22). Most scholars believe Paul wrote Ephesians the first time he was imprisoned by the Romans (around 60-62 AD).

As for external evidence, the case is equally strong. William MacDonald, author of the Believer's Bible Commentary, says this:

> No other Pauline Epistle has such an early and continuous stream of witnesses, starting with Clement of Rome, Ignatius, Polycarp, and Hermas, and going on with Clement of Alexandria, Irenaeus, and Hippolytus. Marcion included it in his "canon," though calling it "Laodiceans." The Muratorian Canon also lists Ephesians as by Paul.[2]

There is some controversy over the recipients. Ephesians 1:1 says "to the saints [in Ephesus]"; however, some of the earliest, most trusted manuscripts lack this phrase. Therefore, many believe Ephesians was originally a circular letter intended for "all Christians in Asia Minor, with Ephesus being the primary or first recipient."[3] Further arguments for this include the fact that Ephesians is missing personal greetings and information about the receiving church, which are normal for Paul's letters. Also, in Ephesians 3:1-7, Paul writes as if the Ephesians do not know him personally. He says in verse 2: "if indeed you have heard of the stewardship of God's grace that was given to me for you." This sounds strange since Paul had spent three years ministering in Ephesus (Acts 20:31). Therefore, it is likely that the epistle was meant for the church in general.

Background

Ephesus was a port city located at the mouth of the Cayster River, on the east side of the Aegean Sea—making it rich for commercial trade. Emperor Augustus declared it the capital of Asia Minor (modern day Turkey) in 27 BC[4]; therefore, it was a political center as well. But it was probably best known for religion. The temple of Artemis (or Diana) was located in Ephesus. The statue of Diana was a multi-breasted, crowned woman, symbolizing fertility. It had close links to local commerce and was a major tourist attraction.[5] R. C. Sproul adds,

> The temple of Diana was one of the seven wonders of the world. It was 425 feet in length and 220 feet in breadth. Architecturally it was composed of 127 white marble columns, each 62 feet high. It was opulently decorated with ornate carvings and priceless paintings. Its chief attraction, however, was an image of Diana said to have fallen directly from heaven to earth. The temple was so popular among pagans that Ephesus emerged as the religious centre of all Asia.[6]

The temple employed hundreds of prostitutes[7], and was therefore a haven for deplorable and perverse sexual acts in honor of Diana. Worshipers believed that participating in profane intercourse ensured them of increased financial prosperity.[8]

Ephesus also contained the largest Greek open-air theater, which seated 25,000 spectators. It hosted chariot races and fights with animals.[9] People flocked to Ephesus, which was a "melting pot of nations and ethnic groups. Greek and Roman, Jew and Gentile mingled freely in its streets."[10] It probably had a population of over 250,000.[11] All this made it a perfect place for Paul to plant a church and send a circular letter.

In Acts 18:19, Paul briefly visited Ephesus on his second missionary journey and left Priscilla and Aquila there. This exceptionally gifted couple probably planted the first seeds of the gospel in Ephesus.[12] In Acts 19, Paul returned and spoke boldly in the synagogue for three months (v. 8). When some rejected him and publicly maligned the gospel, Paul took his disciples to the hall of Tyrannus and taught them there (v. 9). This went on for two years, and all the Jews and Greeks residing in Asia heard the gospel (v. 10). In fact, God began to perform miraculous works through Paul, so much so, that when handkerchiefs and aprons touched him and were taken to the sick, they were healed and evil spirits left them (v. 12). The results of his ministry were staggering. Those practicing witchcraft repented and burned their books. The cost was calculated at fifty thousand drachmas (v. 19)—equivalent to $500,000 in today's currency.[13]

Because the craftsmen of idols lost money, a great uproar began in the city. A mob shouting, "Great is Artemis of the Ephesians!" (v. 28) abducted Paul's travel companions and dragged them into the theatre amidst great confusion. Finally, the city clerk quieted the crowd, encouraged the craftsmen to press formal charges, warned the crowd of potential consequences for rioting, and dismissed them all. Soon after that, Paul left Ephesus (Acts 20:1).

He left Timothy to pastor the Ephesian church for approximately a year and half—primarily confronting false teachers in the congregation (1 Tim. 1:3, 20). "Thirty or so years later, Christ gave the apostle John a letter for this church, indicating that the people had left their first love for Him (Rev. 2:1–7)."[14] Tradition teaches that John later pastored the Ephesian church after his release from Patmos.[15] In fact, he wrote 1 John to this church.

Purpose

Ephesians is written in a "bifid" pattern common to many of Paul's letters. The first three chapters are doctrinal, and the last three focus on practical living. Paul writes to teach God's purpose for the church and to give instructions on right conduct in light of this teaching. As this is done, several themes emerge.

The first theme is the "mystery" of the church. Here, "mystery" means a truth not revealed in the past, but now made fully known. The primary mystery Paul focuses on is the fact that believing Jews and Gentiles are now one in Christ (Eph 3:6). The Old Testament taught that Abraham's seed would be a blessing to all nations (Gen 22:18), and it prophesied that the Jews would bring many ethnic groups to God (Zech 8:3). However, it never taught that Jews and Gentiles would have equal standing or explained their position "in Christ"—a phrase mentioned twelve times in Ephesians.[16] "In fact, Paul refers to the mystery in each of the six chapters of this book."[17] He teaches that Jews and Gentiles are fellow members of the church, that they are raised and seated with Christ in the heavenly places, that Christ is the head of the body, that the ascended Christ gifts leaders to equip the church and help it grow, that the church is the Bride of Christ and is engaged in spiritual warfare, and much more.

Another theme seen throughout Ephesians is the blessings believers receive in Christ. "The word 'riches' is used five times in this letter; 'grace' is used twelve times; 'glory' eight times; 'fullness' or 'filled' six times; and the key phrase 'in Christ' (or 'in Him') some twelve times."[18] Paul begins Chapter 1 by declaring that believers have every spiritual blessing in Christ (v. 3). He then names some of these blessings: Believers are chosen, predestined, redeemed, forgiven, lavished with wisdom and understanding, and heirs (2:6) in Christ. The blessings are innumerable (1:2, 5–9; 2:7; 3:8, 16, 19; 4:13; 5:18; 6:10–13). This would have struck a chord with the Ephesians, as they were in a prosperous, wealthy city, with the temple of Diana and all its treasures. However, these believers needed to understand and reckon their immeasurable wealth in Christ, and so do we today.

Love is also a major theme in Ephesians. Agape, a Greek word used to refer to God's love, is primarily an act of the will rather than an emotion. Paul declares that God predestined the believers in love (1:3-4), and that he (Paul) heard about the Ephesians' love for all the saints (1:15). Even when they were dead in trespasses and sins, God raised them up and seated them in Christ because of his great love for them (2:3-5). In Ephesians 3:17-18, Paul prays for the Ephesians to be rooted and established in love, and to be able to comprehend with all saints Christ's great love for them. It is by speaking the truth in love that the body grows (4:15-16). Believers are called "dearly loved children," and commanded to imitate God by living lives of love (5:1-2). Husbands are called to love their wives as Christ loved the church (5:25). Ephesians 6:23-24 closes the epistle with Paul's benediction prayer for God to gift believers with love. Love saturates this epistle! William MacDonald adds,

> Paul starts and ends his Epistle with this concept (1:4; 6:24), and uses the verb and noun more in Ephesians than anywhere else in his Letters. This may show the Holy Spirit's foreknowledge, because while thirty years in the future the large and active congregation would still be obeying the command to fight false doctrine, our Lord tells them in His Letter to Ephesus that He held it against them that they had left their first love (Rev. 2:4).[19]

Finally, a major theme of Ephesians is spiritual warfare. In Chapter 1, Paul talks about how Christ was raised far above every power and principality (v. 20-22)—referring to the hierarchy of demons. In Christ's ascension, he conquered the demonic world and now rules over it (cf. Col 2:15). In addition, Paul shares how believers are seated in the heavenly places with Christ (Eph 2:6), which implies that they have a position of power over the demonic world through Christ. This would have been important for the Ephesians to hear. Many of them were saved out of the occult (cf. Acts 19:19-20). They had previously reveled in demonic power, and maybe some feared retribution from these spirits. However, there was no need to fear because Christ had conquered them and believers are seated over them.

Paul continues the theme of spiritual warfare in Ephesians 6:10-20. He calls believers to be strong in the power of the Lord and to put on the full armor of God, so they can stand against the powers and principalities. When believers are born again, they enter a spiritual battle against Satan and his demons. Paul calls believers to put on God's armor—representing godly actions and attitudes—so they can stand in the evil day.

In considering this magnificent epistle, some say it can not only be divided between doctrine (1-3) and duty (4-6), but also sit (1-3), walk (4-6:9), and stand (6:10-24). In chapters 1-3, believers must learn their new position—seated in the heavenly places with Christ and recipients of divine blessings. In chapters 4-6:9, believers must begin to walk in consideration of their heavenly position and blessings. Finally, in 6:10-24, believers must stand against the evil forces in the heavenly places. As you study Ephesians, may you better understand God's purpose for the church. Thank you, Lord! Amen!

How to Live in Praise, Even in Trials

Blessed is the God and Father of our Lord Jesus Christ, who has blessed us with every spiritual blessing in the heavenly realms in Christ. For he chose us in Christ before the foundation of the world that we may be holy and unblemished in his sight in love. He did this by predestining us to adoption as his sons through Jesus Christ, according to the pleasure of his will – to the praise of the glory of his grace that he has freely bestowed on us in his dearly loved Son.
Ephesians 1:3 (NET)

How can we live a life of constant praise? First Thessalonians 5:18 calls for us to give thanks in all things for this is God's will for our lives. Ephesians 5:18-20 calls for us to be filled with the Spirit, to sing psalms and hymns and spiritual songs, making a melody in our hearts to the Lord, always giving thanks to God for everything. Christians are meant to be a people of praise and worship.

Why do we often fail at this? Why is our praise often so shallow? Some people only worship at church. Others praise God only in good times, but not when things are bad or difficult.

In this text we see the beginning of Paul's letter to the Ephesians, which starts with praise to God. Chapter 1:3-14 is one long run-on sentence in the Greek. But not only is it one sentence, it is one long praise to God. In verse 3, Paul says, "Blessed is the God and Father of our Lord Jesus Christ." In verse 6 he says, "to the praise of the glory of his grace," and finally in verse 14, he says, "to the praise of his glory." Many theologians believe that Paul is actually singing a song that models a Hebrew blessing song in verses 3-14.[20] These blessing songs always began with "Blessed are You, Lord God." Similarly, Paul here declares, "Blessed is the God and Father of our Lord Jesus Christ" (v.3).

At this time, Paul was imprisoned in Rome for preaching the gospel, but his heart was not in prison. While chained next to a Roman soldier, his heart was free and lost in worship. And he seeks to draw the Ephesians and us into continual worship as well—worship not dependent upon our circumstances.

In this song, Paul praises God for the great riches given to believers in Christ (v. 3). This would have resonated with the Ephesians, as Ephesus was considered the bank of Asia. The Temple of Diana, one of the Seven Wonders of the World, was there. It was not only a center for idolatrous worship, but also a depository for wealth, housing some of the greatest art treasures of the ancient world.[21]

However, Paul is saying that the wealth of believers is even greater than that of the city. Therefore, they should praise God no matter their circumstances. This is true for us as well.

How can we live a life of ever resounding praise regardless of our circumstances? How can we develop consistency in our worship?

Jesus says in John 4:23 that the Lord seeks worshipers who worship in spirit and truth. In this, I believe we see why we often do not worship God. One of the components necessary for worship is truth, or doctrine. We cannot truly worship what we do not know or understand. We cannot worship someone if we don't know how worthy he is.

Sadly, many Christians lack true worship and true joy because they lack doctrine. They lack theology. Often people say, "Don't give me doctrine! Give me Jesus!" However, they are one and the same. John's favorite title for Christ was the "Word" (John 1:1). He was the communication of God, as he taught the words of God (John 12:49). If we do not know God's words, if we do not know theology, then we cannot truly worship him.

To compound this situation, 2 Timothy 4:3-4 (NIV) describes how in the last days people will not be able to stand "sound doctrine", but "instead, to suit their own desires, they will gather around them a great number of teachers to say what their itching ears want to hear." We are in a season of church history where people don't want doctrine. Therefore, the teaching in the church is often weak and our worship suffers.

Paul's praise is full of theology; it is full of doctrine. His focus is not on his circumstances, but on the wonderful grace of God. This is worship that an immature Christian can never really offer; it is rich in doctrine. As we study this text, my hope is that we also may worship more fully as we understand what God has done for us and what he is doing in us, and begin to focus on those things.

Big Questions: What does Paul praise God for in his blessing song? How can we implement worship in our daily lives, especially when going through trials?

In Order to Live in Praise, Believers Must Focus on Their New Home—the Heavenly Realms

Blessed is the God and Father of our Lord Jesus Christ, who has blessed us with every spiritual blessing in the heavenly realms in Christ.
Ephesians 1:3

Interpretation Question: What does the term "heavenly realms" refer to, and how are believers related to it?

The first aspect of Paul's praise that must stand out is the believers' new home. He says that we have been blessed in the heavenly realms; this can be literally translated as "the heavenlies." This is the first of five times this term is used in Ephesians, and it is not used anywhere else in Paul's letters.[22]

What does he mean by the heavenlies? In Ephesians 1:20, he says God raised Christ from the dead and seated him in the heavenlies. In Ephesians 2:6, he says we are seated with him in the heavenlies. In Ephesians 6:12, he says we battle with powers and principalities in the heavenlies.

This is the paradox of the believer's existence. Even as we are right now literally on the earth, we are also literally in heaven. This is because of our position in Christ (Eph 1:3). We are there with God our Father and Christ our Lord. We are dual citizens of earth and heaven (Phil 3:20-21).

While in prison, Paul contemplated this reality and worshiped God the Father because of it. How this positional reality really works, I don't think we can be sure. However, if we are going to worship as Paul did, we must first believe it. We must accept it as true. It's not figurative; it's not metaphorical. Not only is Christ there, but we are there with him. Hebrews 12:22-24 says this:

> But you have come to Mount Zion, the city of the living God, the heavenly Jerusalem, and to myriads of angels, to the assembly and congregation of the firstborn, who are enrolled in heaven, and to God, the judge of all, and to the spirits of the righteous, who have been made perfect, and to Jesus, the mediator of a new covenant, and to the sprinkled blood that speaks of something better than Abel's does.

The writer of Hebrews says this is our position and company now, not sometime in the future. We are seated in the heavenly realms with the angels, the church, the saints of the Old Testament, God and Christ.

Secondly, we must focus on it. Colossians 3:1-2 says, "Therefore, if you have been raised with Christ, keep seeking the things above, where Christ is, seated at the right hand of God. Keep thinking about things above, not things on the earth."

Our hearts must seek things above. Sadly, most Christians have shallow worship because their hearts are set on money, on the treasures of this world, on the trials that distract them, etc. If we are going to worship, we must be consumed with heaven and the King of heaven—God (Matt 6:9-10). We must be consumed with the agenda of heaven, building the kingdom on this earth (Matt 20:18-19). We must be consumed with the law of heaven—God's Word. We must be consumed with developing the character of heaven. Romans 14:17 says, "For the kingdom of God does not consist of food and drink, but righteousness, peace, and joy in the Holy Spirit." We must be consumed with the coming Savior from heaven. Philippians 3:20 says, "But our citizenship is in heaven – and we also await a savior from there, the Lord Jesus Christ".

Is your mind consumed with the heavenlies? Have you set your mind on things above and not on earthly things? Or are you consumed with the things of this world? If you're consumed with the things of this world, your praise will be weak.

If we are going to live in praise even while going through trials, we must be consumed with our heavenly home.

Application Questions: How can we focus more on our heavenly citizenship instead of our earthly home? What disciplines will help us with this endeavor?

In Order to Live in Praise, Believers Must Focus on Their Spiritual Blessings

> Blessed is the God and Father of our Lord Jesus Christ, who has blessed us with every spiritual blessing in the heavenly realms in Christ.
> Ephesians 1:3

Interpretation Questions: What does the phrase "every spiritual blessing" refer to? And what is the practical application for believers?

The next aspect of Paul's praise to God (while in prison) focuses on every spiritual blessing of believers in the heavenly realms. What does Paul mean by "every spiritual blessing"? "In the New Testament pneumatikos (spiritual) is always used in relation to the work of the Holy Spirit."[23] In fact, it can be translated "all the blessings of the Spirit"—referring to the Holy Spirit of God.[24]

While in prison, Paul was probably not only hungry, but also lacking in basic comfort, freedom, and other physical blessings. But that did not stop him from praising God for his blessings! Being a follower of Christ does not exempt us from pain and suffering in this world. In fact, many times it increases pain and suffering. However, God does promise innumerable blessings from the Spirit.

What do these blessings from the Spirit include? We will consider many of them as we go through Ephesians 1:4-13, election, predestination as sons, redemption, etc. However, this list is not exhaustive. There is much, much more. Spiritual blessings include the fruit of the Spirit. Galatians 5:22-23 says, "But the fruit of the Spirit is love, joy, peace, patience, kindness, goodness, faithfulness, gentleness and self-control."

Paul worshiped in prison because the Holy Spirit gave him joy, regardless of his circumstances. The Spirit gave him love for the churches. The Spirit gave him patience to faithfully endure his trials and deal with difficult people. The blessings of the Spirit are legion, and we should rejoice in them daily. Christ describes those who believe in him as having rivers of living water flowing "from within" them (John 7:38-39). He describes them as those who will never thirst again (John 4:14). That sounds like people who should be rejoicing!

Interpretation Questions: What about physical blessings? Does God promise to give us physical blessings as well?

In light of the above, does this mean God will not supply our physical needs as well? Contrary to the tenets of the prosperity gospel, God does not promise us earthly wealth and health. But, he does promise to meet our needs according to his riches in glory (Phil 4:19). Christ declares that we have a Father who knows our needs, and that we shouldn't worry about what we will eat, drink, or wear (Matt 6:25-34). Paul says that since God has already given us his best—his Son—surely he will give us all things (Rom 8:32). Yes, we can be sure God will meet all our needs on this earth. Charles Spurgeon says,

> "He that gives us heaven will surely give us all that is needful on the road thither." And, "We shall have enough spending money on the road to glory; for he who has guaranteed to bring us there will not starve us along the way."[25]

With that said, how do we receive these spiritual blessings in the heavenly places? How can we access the wealth that the Spirit of God supplies to believers?

Application Question: How can we access the blessings of the Spirit in our lives?

1. We access the blessings of the Spirit by abiding in Christ.

Paul said all these blessings are "in Christ" (1: 3). This means we have them positionally because of our union with him, but the Spirit applies them as we abide in this relationship. Christ says, "'I am the vine; you are the branches. The one who remains in me – and I in him – bears much fruit, because apart from me you can accomplish nothing" (John 15:5).

We must abide in Christ through being in his Word, prayer, and the gathering of the saints in order to receive joy, peace, love, and patience. Are you remaining in Christ? Or are you simply visiting him on occasion?

2. We access the blessings of the Spirit by persevering in prayer for them.

Certainly, asking God for them in prayer is part of abiding, but it will benefit us to consider this aspect of abiding separately. Christ says this about the Holy Spirit to his disciples in Luke 11:11-13:

> "What father among you, if your son asks for a fish, will give him a snake instead of a fish? Or if he asks for an egg, will give him a scorpion? If you then, although you are evil, know how to give good gifts to your children, how much more will the heavenly Father give the Holy Spirit to those who ask him!"

When Christ says God will give the Holy Spirit to those who ask him, he is talking to the disciples, who are believers. They already had the Holy Spirit. Therefore, what is he talking about? He is talking about God blessing the disciples with the ministries of the Holy Spirit. One commentator says this about verse 13:

> In the original Greek, verse 13 does not say that God will give the Holy Spirit, but rather He will "give Holy Spirit" (without the article). Professor H. B. Swete pointed out that when the article is present, it refers to the Person Himself, but when the article is absent, it refers to His gifts or operations on our behalf. So in this passage, it is not so much a prayer for the Person of the Holy Spirit, but rather for His ministries in our lives.[26]

Do you lack peace in the midst of your storm? Ask. Do you lack joy in your trial? Ask. Do you lack love for someone whose behavior is unlovable? Ask. Luke 11:9-10 says,

> "So I tell you: Ask, and it will be given to you; seek, and you will find; knock, and the door will be opened for you. For everyone who asks receives, and the one who seeks finds, and to the one who knocks, the door will be opened."

This literally means to ask and keep asking, seek and keep seeking, knock and keep knocking, and the door will be opened to you. We must not only ask, but we must persevere in asking.

Some don't receive because they don't ask. James 4:2 says, "You do not have because you do not ask." Some don't have because they give up asking. They don't persevere like the widow who approached the unjust judge (Luke 18:1-8).

Don't stop asking God! Don't stop praying! And God will give you the blessings of the Spirit that are already yours in Christ.

This is the reason worship can arise from within prison walls. Every spiritual blessing was Paul's, and they're ours as well.

Application Questions: How should the reality of this wealth of spiritual blessings encourage you daily, especially during trials? What spiritual blessing is God currently calling you to persevere in seeking?

In Order to Live in Praise, Believers Must Focus on Their Union with Christ

Blessed is the God and Father of our Lord Jesus Christ, who has blessed us with every spiritual blessing in the heavenly realms in Christ.
Ephesians 1:3

The next thing we must focus on if we are going to live in praise is our union with Christ. This is the sphere of our blessing—the reason we receive them. Scripture teaches that when we were born again, we were united with Christ. First Corinthians 12:13 says, "For in one Spirit we were all baptized into one body. Whether Jews or Greeks or slaves or free, we were all made to drink of the one Spirit." When we were saved, we were united with Christ and became members of his body.

Now God no longer sees us in our sins, but he sees us in Christ. We are not accepted because of anything we have done; we are accepted because of Christ. Second Corinthians 5:21 says, "God made the one who did not know sin to be sin for us, so that in him we would become the righteousness of God." We are the righteousness of God because God sees us in the Son. First Corinthians 6:17 says, "But the one united with the Lord is one spirit with him." Commentator William MacDonald adds:

When a person is converted, God no longer looks upon him as a condemned child of Adam. Rather He sees him as being in Christ, and He accepts him on that basis. It is important to see this. The believing sinner is not accepted because of what he is in himself, but because he is in Christ. When he is in Christ, he stands before God clothed in all the acceptability of Christ Himself. And he will enjoy God's favor and acceptance as long as Christ does, namely, forever.[27]

This is our new position; we are in Christ. And Paul's focus on this is seen in how he refers to our positon in Christ, in various ways, eleven times just in Chapter 1.[28] Here are a few examples:

> From Paul, an apostle of Christ Jesus by the will of God, to the saints [in Ephesus], the faithful in Christ Jesus.
> Ephesians 1:1

> Blessed is the God and Father of our Lord Jesus Christ, who has blessed us with every spiritual blessing in the heavenly realms in Christ.
> Ephesians 1:3

> For he chose us in Christ before the foundation of the world that we may be holy and unblemished in his sight in love.
> Ephesians 1:4

> In him we have redemption through his blood, the forgiveness of our trespasses, according to the riches of his grace
> Ephesians 1:7

> And when you heard the word of truth (the gospel of your salvation) – when you believed in Christ – you were marked with the seal of the promised Holy Spirit
> Ephesians 1:13

Why should we continue to praise God? We should praise him because he chose us in Christ before the foundation of the world. We should praise him continually because we have been redeemed from sin. We should rejoice because we have every spiritual blessing in Christ. In Adam, we had sin, condemnation, and shame. But in Christ we have forgiveness, honor, and power—every spiritual blessing.

This must be our focus and our joy while on this earth. We must rejoice in our position in Christ. Are you still rejoicing in your position in Christ?

Application Questions: How can we discipline ourselves to focus on our new position in Christ? How should this reality affect our daily lives?

In Order to Live in Praise, Believers Must Focus on Their Election

> For he chose us in Christ before the foundation of the world that we may be holy and unblemished in his sight in love.
> Ephesians 1:4

The next reason we should continually praise God is for our election—his choosing us for salvation. This doctrine has often been a source of anger and dispute; however, this is not the way it is handled in Scripture. Rather, it is a source of continual rejoicing. In this text, Paul praises God for the election of himself and other saints. Similarly, in Peter's letter to the persecuted Christians in Asia Minor, he simply calls them those "who are chosen" (1 Peter 1:1) or "God's elect" as in the NIV. This was a common title for Christians in the early church.

This tells us something. If it was a cause for singing for the early church and a title they called one another, then it must be something tremendously good. If it is a source of bitterness and tension in the modern church, it is only because we don't truly understand it or have corrupted it.

Interpretation Question: What does Paul mean by the teaching that God chose us before the creation of the world?

It can mean one of two things.

1. First, some believe it means God selected us because he saw we would believe in the future. They say God looked down the corridor of time and saw we would have faith and therefore chose us. However, this really negates God's selection of us. Salvation then becomes based on man's initiative—man's choosing—instead of God's.

2. Second, others believe that God chose us based solely on his sovereignty. As God, he has the right to choose, and he did.

Which is correct? I believe the second view has more scriptural support.

Interpretation Question: What are some scriptural supports for God's election based solely on his sovereignty and grace?

- Scripture teaches that because of his sin, man cannot choose God, apart from grace.

Even though many boast in free will, the reality is that sin makes us a slave. And as slaves, we need someone to redeem us, to set us free. Consider what Paul says about man's condition because of sin.

Romans 8:7 says, "the outlook of the flesh is hostile to God, for it does not submit to the law of God, nor is it able to do so." The natural mind cannot submit to God's will. It is at enmity with God.

Romans 3:10-11 says, "just as it is written: 'There is no one righteous, not even one, there is no one who understands, there is no one who seeks God." Sin affects man in such a way that he will not seek God. He will not come after him. God had to take the initiative. Christ came to seek and to save those who were lost (Luke 19:10). We cannot seek him and couldn't find him if we did—we are lost.

First Corinthians 2:14 says, "The unbeliever does not receive the things of the Spirit of God, for they are foolishness to him. And he cannot understand them, because they are spiritually discerned." Apart from the Holy Spirit, we cannot accept or even understand the Word of God.

This leaves only one possible way for man to be saved. Salvation has to be wholly from God. Man's eyes are blinded and his mind is clouded. His will is bound by sin, and he cannot accept the things of God. Election does not mean that God foresaw faith in us before he created the world. It means he foresaw how sin would so ravage mankind that we would be eternally lost. If any were going to be saved, God had to take the initiative. He had to choose some. He reached down into the slave market of men where all were bound by sin, and saved a few.

What other evidence is there for this view?

- Scripture teaches that our faith is a gift from God, apart from any work of our own.

Consider Ephesians 2:8-9. "For by grace you are saved through faith, and this is not from yourselves, it is the gift of God; it is not from works, so that no one can boast." Sometimes this verse is misquoted. Sometimes people say we are saved by faith. No, we are not. We are saved by grace—God's unmerited favor. In fact, this verse says that the very faith we put in Christ is a gift of God. Because man could not respond to God, God had to give some—the elect—faith. Therefore, no man can boast in their salvation or even in their faith. It is a gift from the sovereign God, who elects some to salvation.

Interpretation Question: What about those who never get saved? Were they elected to damnation?

Well, this creates a further complication. What about the lost—those who never will be saved? Did God elect them to damnation? No. Scripture never teaches God's election of the lost. He doesn't need to elect the lost, because our own sin condemns and separates us from him. He needs to elect some to salvation.

Certainly, this is a complicated and difficult doctrine. One professor says, "Try to explain election and you may lose your mind. But try to explain it away and you may lose your soul!" [29] Yes, election is a difficult doctrine, but it does show God's mercy. As a just God, he could justly allow everybody to go to hell for their sin. But in his mercy, he chooses to save a few.

Interpretation Question: How does election fit with human responsibility?

What about human responsibility? Why do we preach the gospel if God has already elected some to salvation? This is the mystery of election. Scripture teaches these two seemingly conflicting doctrines together. It says God elected, and yet, at the same time, it says man is responsible—he is responsible to respond to the gospel. In fact, we see them both in one verse. John 6:37 says, "Everyone whom the Father gives me will come to me, and the one who comes to me I will never send away."

Do you see that? All that the Father gave Christ (the elect) will come to Christ (human responsibility). Even though they are elected, they will choose of their own "free will" to come to God. This is how we know they are elected. Human responsibility and God's sovereignty somehow fit together. The mystery is in our minds—not God's. I believe we fall into wrong doctrine by emphasizing one over the other. Some emphasize God's sovereignty to the point where man makes no decision. Others emphasize man's responsibility and lower God's sovereignty. We must teach them side by side, for in some way or another, they are both true.

Purpose of Election

Interpretation Question: What is the purpose of election?

Now, what is the purpose of election? Ephesians 1:4 says, "For he chose us in Christ before the foundation of the world that we may be holy and unblemished in his sight in love." God elected us so we could be holy and unblemished, or it can be translated blameless; he elected us for sanctification.

"Positively it is 'to be holy' — that is, set apart from the world, separate, different. And negatively it is to be 'blameless' — literally, without spot or blemish, a sacrifice to be presented to God."[30] God elected us to be separate from the world. We must be different. He also elected us to be pure and righteous before him. Believers were elected for the purpose of sanctification— to become more like Christ (Rom 8:29).

If we think we are saved, but we are not different--our language and desires haven't changed, we don't desire the Word of God or want to worship God and know him better, and we still live in sin and enjoy it--then maybe we are not really elected. In 2 Peter 1:5-10, we are commanded to make our election sure by growing in godliness.

Are you sure about your election? Are you growing in godliness?

If we are elect, our lives will be continually changing. Yes, it may be a slow process, but it is a process every believer is engaged in. God has promised to complete the work he began in us (Phil 1:6).

Those professing faith in Matthew 7:21-23 called Christ "Lord," but their lives were not holy. Here is what Christ says about such people:

> "Not everyone who says to me, 'Lord, Lord,' will enter into the kingdom of heaven – only the one who does the will of my Father in heaven. On that day, many will say to me, 'Lord, Lord, didn't we prophesy in your name, and in your name cast out demons and do many powerful deeds?' Then I will declare to them, 'I never knew you. Go away from me, you lawbreakers!'"

What was their problem? They were living sinful lives—their "faith" had not led to change, so there was no election. Election leads us into holiness and blamelessness.

Has your profession of faith changed your life? If not, you might not be elected. Salvation is not just positional (cf. 2 Cor 5:21), it is actual—it actually changes us (cf. James 2:17).

Application Question: What are some ways the doctrine of election should affect us?

1.   The doctrine of election should create humility.

Salvation is by grace, and there is no place for boasting in our wisdom and knowledge; even our faith is a gift of God.

2.   The doctrine of election should lead us to worship.

Our only boasting should be in God. As mentioned, understanding theology—doctrine—should increase our worship. Why did God set his loving affection on us? The answer lies in his sovereignty—simply because he chose to do so. It had nothing to do with us. It was amazing grace. This should lead us to worship.

3.   The doctrine of election should motivate us to evangelize.

Some think this doctrine hinders evangelism. However, they are wrong. Rightly understood, election should motivate us to preach the gospel.

Fear of rejection often hinders believers from sharing their faith, but it shouldn't. God has chosen the elect, and they will come to Christ (John 6:37). I can preach with confidence because I know that before time God chose some to be saved, and they will eventually respond. Listen to what Acts 13:48 says: "When the Gentiles heard this, they began to rejoice and praise the word of the Lord, and all who had been appointed for eternal life believed."

Consider Paul's words to Timothy: "So I endure all things for the sake of those chosen by God, that they too may obtain salvation in Christ Jesus and its eternal glory" (2 Timothy 2:10). Paul was indeed motivated to reach the elect.

4.   The doctrine of election is evidence that Scripture is divine.

If Scripture were man made, these types of contradictions might not be present. However, if it is truly divine, then we would expect there to be many things we cannot fully comprehend. How can God be three separate persons and yet one? How can Christ be fully God and fully man? How can God be sovereign and yet man have human responsibility? These doctrines simply attest to the divine origin of Scripture. Finite man cannot and should not expect to fully comprehend an infinite God.

Application Questions: Why is election such a controversial doctrine? What view do you take on the subject and why?

In Order to Live in Praise, Believers Must Focus on Their Adoption as Sons

He did this by predestining us to adoption as his sons through Jesus Christ, according to the pleasure of his will
Ephesians 1:5

Interpretation Question: What is the difference between election and predestination?

The next thing we should focus on to live a life of praise is our adoption as sons. God predestined us to be in his family. But what is the difference between predestination and election? Aren't they the same thing?

The word [predestination] simply means "to ordain beforehand, to predetermine." Election seems to refer to people, while predestination refers to purposes. The events connected with the crucifixion of Christ were predestined (Acts 4:25–28). God has predestined our adoption (Eph 1:5), and our conformity to Christ (Rom 8:29–30), as well as our future inheritance (Eph. 1:14).[31]

God's purpose in electing and predestining us was to make us his sons—his children. God could have just saved us; he didn't need to make us part of his family. How can we apply this truth?

Application Question: What applications can we take from our adoption as sons?

1. Adoption means that we are absolutely new people—our past is behind and our identity is in Christ.

   Commentator William Barclay says this:

   In Roman law, "When the adoption was complete it was complete indeed. The person who had been adopted had all the rights of a legitimate son in his new family and completely lost all rights in his old family. In the eyes of the law he was a new person. So new was he that even all debts and obligations connected with his previous family were abolished as if they had never existed."[32]

   The people who Paul wrote to would have immediately thought of this. A person adopted into a wealthy family was completely new. All debts and ties to his old life were canceled. And this is true for us as well. We are new in Christ.
   We are no longer obligated to live in sin—no longer obligated to follow the ways of the world. We are free to follow Christ and enjoy fellowship with him, and we can leave our past lives behind—which includes our sin. Therefore, even when we fall, we should remember our adoption, confess, repent, and continue to follow Christ (cf. Rom 6:11).
   Are you bound to some sin? Let it go—for you have been adopted into God's family. You are new.

2. Adoption means we receive God's inheritance.

   No doubt this was a cause of much rejoicing and praise on Paul's part. Under Roman law an adopted son would receive the rights and privileges of a biological son—including an inheritance—and we receive every spiritual blessing in Christ (Eph 1:3). Romans 8:17 says: "And if children, then heirs (namely, heirs of God and also fellow heirs with Christ) – if indeed we suffer with him so we may also be glorified with him."
   Whatever Christ has is ours as well. God has committed all judgment to him (John 5:22), and Scripture says that when he returns, we will reign and judge with him. Scripture teaches we will judge the world and the angels with him (1 Cor 6:2-3). Is this not something to praise God for? Adoption means we receive Christ's inheritance.

3. Adoption means we have a new family.

Christ says, "My mother and brothers are those who hear God's word and put it into practice." We are now part of the family of God. We have brothers, sisters, moms, and dads all around the world. And one day, we will all be together in heaven.

In fact, Paul taught that even here on earth we should treat people in the church as family. First Timothy 5:1-2 says, "Do not address an older man harshly but appeal to him as a father. Speak to younger men as brothers, older women as mothers, and younger women as sisters – with complete purity."

To add to this, Scripture teaches that though Christ is our God, he is also our brother. Romans 8:29 says, "because those whom he foreknew he also predestined to be conformed to the image of his Son, that his Son would be the firstborn among many brothers and sisters." Christ is the firstborn, the chief amongst the family of God and all creation (Col 1:15)—and we have been adopted into the family of God.

4. Adoption means we get a new nature.

Now, this reality is foreign to the practice of human adoption. Adoptive parents can make a child part of their family, and give him wealth and many other benefits, but they cannot impart their DNA into that child. However, this is exactly what God does with us. We are adopted not by legal action but by a new birth (John 3:3). God has given us his nature through the Spirit. Romans 8:15 says, "For you did not receive the spirit of slavery leading again to fear, but you received the Spirit of adoption, by whom we cry, "Abba, Father.""

We have been given his Spirit. The Spirit draws us to call God "Abba"—"Daddy dearest." He also gives us a desire to read the Word and to see souls saved. As he gives us holy affections, we start to hate sin and love righteousness. In adoption, we receive the nature and characteristics of our Father.

How could Paul not sing while in prison? He had been adopted into the family of God. He was a new person; he had received a new inheritance, a new nature, and a new family. As we contemplate these realities, it should draw us into worship as well. Praise God for our wonderful adoption into his family! Thank you, Lord!

Application Question: In what ways is God calling you to apply this reality of being an adopted son and having a new family in Christ?

In Order to Live in Praise, Believers Must Focus on God's Abundant Grace

> to the praise of the glory of his grace that he has freely bestowed on us in his dearly loved Son.
> Ephesians 1:6

Next, Paul worships God for his glorious grace. Every gift mentioned—the spiritual blessings in the heavenly places—have come to us because of God's grace. It was by unmerited favor we were elected, predestined, and adopted. It is unmerited favor that daily changes us and sustains us. In Christ, we have received abundant grace. And this grace is the very thing Paul prays for in the beginning of his letter: "Grace and peace to you from God our Father and the Lord Jesus Christ!" (1:2).

And just as wonderful as the grace we have received is the fact that God wants to give us more. James 4:6 says, "he gives greater grace." How can we not praise God as well? He is the fount from whom all blessings flow—from him come blessings evermore.

Are you contemplating the Lord's wonderful grace? Are you petitioning him for more? The worshiping believer is one who stands in awe of God's overflowing and abundant grace, even in the midst of trials, and drinks deeply from it.

In verses 7-14, we will see further works of God's grace.

Application Questions: Paul praised God for his grace while in prison; have you found any other disciplines helpful in cultivating a lifestyle of worship? What things tend to distract you from worshiping God for his glorious grace?

Conclusion

How can we live a life of praise, even during trials? How can we sing songs of praise even when wrongly accused and in prison? We must have doctrine that draws us to sing. We must not only worship in spirit (with the right heart), but in truth. We must know the truth about God. We must know his Word. Let us leave this portion of our study with this challenge in mind: If we don't have theology, then we won't have doxology—worship. If we don't study him—his mysteries and his works in us—then we won't know how worthy he is of our worship and praise.

Are you worshiping him with truth throughout the day like Paul did, even during trials?

1. In order to live in praise, believers must focus on their new home—the heavenly realms.
2. In order to live in praise, believers must focus on their spiritual blessings.
3. In order to live in praise, believers must focus on their union with Christ.
4. In order to live in praise, believers must focus on their election.
5. In order to live in praise, believers must focus on their adoption as sons.
6. In order to live in praise, believers must focus on God's abundant grace.

How to Live in Praise, Even in Trials—Part Two

In him we have redemption through his blood, the forgiveness of our trespasses, according to the riches of his grace that he lavished on us in all wisdom and insight. He did this when he revealed to us the secret of his will, according to his good pleasure that he set forth in Christ, toward the administration of the fullness of the times, to head up all things in Christ – the things in heaven and the things on earth.
Ephesians 1:7-10 (NET)

How can we live a life of praise, even while going through trials? Ephesians 1:3-14 is the longest sentence in the Bible, and it seems to be one continuous song. Paul begins his instructions to the Ephesians with, "Blessed is the God and Father of our Lord Jesus Christ, who has blessed us with every spiritual blessing in the heavenly realms in Christ" (Ephesians 1:3).

Paul was imprisoned in Rome awaiting a possible death sentence, but even then, he praised God. His ability to praise came from his focus. Paul was not focused on his unfortunate circumstances, but on the heavenly realms, where believers are seated in Christ. He focused on all the spiritual blessings believers have—blessings that come from the Spirit. They include our seat in the heavenly realms, our position in Christ, our election, and our adoption as sons into the family of God (v. 3-6)

In Ephesians 1:7-10, he continues his praise for the spiritual blessings believers received in Christ. As we continue this study, we will learn about how to live a life of praise by living a life of focus.

Big Questions: What other riches does Paul praise God for in this blessing song? How can we focus on these riches in order to implement worship in our daily lives, especially during trials?

In Order to Live in Praise, Believers Must Focus on Their Redemption

> In him we have redemption through his blood, the forgiveness of our trespasses, according to the riches of his grace
> Ephesians 1:7

Interpretation Question: What does redemption mean?

Paul praises God for the believer's redemption in Christ. "To redeem means 'to purchase and set free by paying a price.'"[33] There were probably over 60 million slaves in the Roman Empire, and buying and selling them was big business. Slaves occupied many positions: teachers, doctors, metalsmiths, carpenters, poets, etc. If a person wanted to set a friend or relative free, they would have to buy the slave's freedom. This is the situation to which Paul is alluding.

However, we must ask, "Who were these Christians (and people in general) enslaved to?" Jesus says, "I tell you the solemn truth, everyone who practices sin is a slave of sin" (John 8:34). Similarly, Paul says, "For we know that the law is spiritual – but I am unspiritual, sold into slavery to sin" (Romans 7:14). This is the state of every person before they accept Christ: enslaved to sin.

Sin had so enslaved us that we could not respond to God or understand his Word. As Romans 8:7-8 says, "because the outlook of the flesh is hostile to God, for it does not submit to the law of God, nor is it able to do so. Those who are in the flesh cannot please God." Our minds were hostile to God. Our wills could not submit to God's law. In fact, sin had so bound us that we would not even seek God (Rom 3:11).

However, God looked down the corridors of time, saw man's future enslavement, and predestined to send his Son to die for our sins (Acts 4:27-28). Christ died because that was the just payment for our sins. Romans 6:23 says, "For the payoff of sin is death." Christ died to appease God's just wrath, and to redeem us from our slave master. When he died on the cross, he said, "It is completed" (John 19:30), which literally means "paid in full." Christ paid the price for our sins so we would no longer be slaves of sin and under the wrath of God. As John 8:36 says, "So if the son sets you free, you will be really free."

When Paul says believers have redemption through Christ's blood, he is using a "metonym" (a form of figurative language) for Christ's death.[34] It was Christ's death that set us free from our bondage. Christ says, "For even the Son of Man did not come to be served but to serve, and to give his life as a ransom for many'" (Mark 10:45). Romans 5:8-9 says,

> But God demonstrates his own love for us in this: While we were still sinners, Christ died for us. Since we have now been justified by his blood, how much more shall we be saved from God's wrath through him!

While imprisoned, chained up to a Roman soldier, Paul reflected on his previous spiritual enslavement. Bound to sin and blinded by the devil, he had persecuted the early church. But Christ had mercy on him and set him free from this bondage.

No doubt many of the Christians hearing Paul's letter were slaves, and though they might never receive their earthly freedom, they were free in Christ. Christ had redeemed them; he was their ultimate Master and one day they would be free from every hindrance to fully serve him.

We should worship because of our freedom. We are free to serve and worship Christ.

Application Question: How can we, as believers, continually apply our redemption in Christ?

1. To apply our redemption, we must consider ourselves dead to sin, free from its slavery.

Paul says to think about this reality often, and to allow it to guide our actions: "So you too consider yourselves dead to sin, but alive to God in Christ Jesus" (Romans 6:11). "Consider yourselves dead to sin" means to think of ourselves as dead to sin but alive to God. Even when we stumble, we should not think of ourselves as bound to sin and lust—for we are not. We are new in Christ and free to serve God. We must fight from this vantage point.

Thinking on this reality is important because the enemy often lies to believers. He tells them that they will never be free, that they are too addicted and bound. This is a lie. We are free in Christ, and we must fight our battles in light of this reality. When we truly understand it, it will set us free. Christ says the truth will set us free (John 8:32) and that he whom the Son sets free is free indeed (v. 36). When we truly adopt this mindset, we cannot help but sing.

There is a story about Augustine, a church father, who lived from 358-430 AD. Before accepting Christ, he was very promiscuous. While walking through the market one day, he ran into an old fling. When he saw her, he immediately turned and ran in the opposite direction. The lady was shocked. She said, "My love! My love! Where are you going? It is I!" He responded, "I know! But it is not I any longer!" Augustine counted himself dead to sin, but alive to Christ. He saw himself as a new creation, and no longer a slave. We must reckon this to be true about ourselves as well. As Paul says, "I have been crucified with Christ, and it is no longer I who live, but Christ lives in me. So the life I now live in the body, I live because of the faithfulness of the Son of God, who loved me and gave himself for me" (Galatians 2:20).

Similarly, focusing on this reality helps many believers break an addiction or stronghold in their lives. They start to really think on what Christ completed on the cross: he broke the chains of sin. They just need to believe it and fight to live according to this reality.

2. To apply our redemption, we must consider ourselves alive to Christ—slaves of God and righteousness.

Not only did Christ pay the price to free us from slavery, but he also purchased us for himself. This means that we are slaves of God, owned by him, and free to serve him. When rebuking the Corinthians for sexual immorality, Paul refers to this truth:

> Or do you not know that your body is the temple of the Holy Spirit who is in you, whom you have from God, and you are not your own? For you were bought at a price. Therefore glorify God with your body.
> 1 Corinthians 6:19-20

We should not live in sexual immorality or any other sin because our bodies are not our own. Paul says this in Romans 6:17-19:

> But the one united with the Lord is one spirit with him. Flee sexual immorality! "Every sin a person commits is outside of the body"– but the immoral person sins against his own body. Or do you not know that your body is the temple of the Holy Spirit who is in you, whom you have from God, and you are not your own?

As slaves of sin, we displeased God by offering our minds and bodies over to various evil desires. But now, as slaves of God and righteousness, we should offer our minds and bodies continually to righteousness.

Is there an opportunity to serve? Let us offer ourselves. Is there an opportunity to encourage someone? Let us offer ourselves. Is there an opportunity to worship? Let us offer ourselves. After all Christ has done for us, we should offer our bodies as living sacrifices, which is our reasonable act of worship (Romans 12:1).

In fact, this reality of no longer being a slave to sin but rather a slave of Christ and righteousness was so ingrained in Paul's theology that he often referred to himself as a "slave" of Christ. Consider these verses:

> From Paul and Timothy, slaves of Christ Jesus, to all the saints in Christ Jesus who are in Philippi, with the overseers and deacons
> Philippians 1:1

> From Paul, a slave of Christ Jesus, called to be an apostle, set apart for the gospel of God

Romans 1:1

The word "slave" means a "bond slave, without any ownership rights of their own."[35] Essentially, Paul was saying, "I don't own anything anymore—not even my body! I am a slave of Christ! I was purchased with a price, and now I'm a slave of righteousness!"

If God set us free from slavery to sin, how can we go back to our old slave master? Let us devote ourselves to seeking his face, worshiping him, and serving others, since that is why he purchased us. When we were bound by sin we couldn't do these things—we were antagonistic to God and couldn't submit to his law (Rom 8:7). But now we are free. Former slaves who focus on this reality cannot help but praise God regardless of their circumstances.

Application Questions: How does the concept of redemption encourage or challenge you in your faith? How do you feel God is calling you to further apply this reality to your life or ministry?

In Order to Live in Praise, Believers Must Focus on Their Forgiveness in Christ

In him we have redemption through his blood, the forgiveness of our trespasses, according to the riches of his grace
Ephesians 1:7

Another spiritual blessing believers receive is forgiveness. In response to Christ's death for our sins, God forgave us. The word forgive means "to carry away."[36] This cannot but remind us of the prescribed ritual on the Jewish Day of Atonement (Lev 16). The priest took two goats. He killed one and sprinkled its blood on the mercy seat in the Holy of Holies. He laid his hands on the other goat and confessed the sins of Israel. The second goat was then taken far into the wilderness and let go. This symbolized the sins of Israel being carried away, never to return.

While in prison, Paul rejoiced in this truth. Because of Christ's death and payment for our sins, they have been taken far away, never to be brought back again. Psalm 103:12 says, "As far as the eastern horizon is from the west, so he removes the guilt of our rebellious actions from us." Hebrews 10:17 says, "Their sins and their lawless deeds I will remember no longer."

Romans 8:1-2 says, "There is therefore now no condemnation for those who are in Christ Jesus. For the law of the life-giving Spirit in Christ Jesus has set you free from the law of sin and death." When instituting the Lord's Supper, Christ said, "this is my blood, the blood of the covenant, that is poured out for many for the forgiveness of sins" (Matt 26:28). Christ's blood was poured out for our forgiveness—so our sins could be carried away.

Interpretation Question: Why do we still need to confess our sins if they are already forgiven?

The truth is that on the cross, God forgave our sins judicially. If we are believers, then we will never be judged for our sins because Christ paid the penalty. However, there is still a need to confess for familial forgiveness. For example, if I do or say something that hurts my wife and we're not talking, it doesn't change the fact that she is legally my wife; however, I still need to confess to restore intimacy—familial forgiveness.

Christ compares this type of forgiveness to cleansing when talking to Peter about the need for foot washing. He says, "The one who has bathed needs only to wash his feet, but is completely clean. And you disciples are clean, but not every one of you" (John 13:10).

Peter was already clean because God had forgiven his sins judicially on the cross. However, he still needed cleansing from his daily failings. He still needed familial forgiveness, and it's the same with us. We need to daily bring our sins and failures before the Father so we can be wiped clean.

Interpretation Questions: What does Paul mean by "in accordance with the riches of God's grace"? What does this teach us about the extent of this cleansing—this forgiveness?

"According to the riches of his grace that he lavished on us" (Eph 1:7-8) means that God lavishly forgave us. It has often been said if a millionaire gives ten dollars to charity, he gives "out of his riches." But if he gives a million dollars, he gives "in accordance" with his riches. Similarly, God abundantly lavished forgiveness on us in accordance with the riches of his grace.

We learn something about this in 1 John 1:9: "But if we confess our sins, he is faithful and righteous, forgiving us our sins and cleansing us from all unrighteousness." When we confess our sins to God, not only does he forgive us, but he cleanses us from "all" unrighteousness. This means he forgives us even of sins we are not aware of.

The greatest command in the Bible is to love God with our whole heart, mind, and soul (Matt 22:37-38). However, at no time have I loved God that way, and it's the same for every other person. This is often called the depravity of man. In a real sense, I am always failing God—not loving him or others as I should. However, God's grace is so abundant that he is always lavishing forgiveness on me. When I confess my known sins, he forgives me of all unrighteousness. This is "according to the riches of his grace."

That is the kind of forgiveness God lavishes on his children. Paul sang because he was forgiven. He sang because God cleansed him daily in accordance with the riches of his grace and forgiveness.

Application Question: Why is it that so many choose not to accept God's lavish grace in forgiveness?

Sadly, many believers miss this lavish grace.

1. They miss it because they refuse to confess their sins and repent.
2. Or, they miss it because they allow themselves to be bound in condemnation, which keeps them from accepting God's forgiveness.

What Christ died for and God forgave, they continue to look back on, not recognizing it as covered by Christ's blood and "carried away." They often mistake condemnation by the devil as conviction by the Holy Spirit. The enemy of our souls tempts believers to sin and then says, "Feel bad! Feel really, really bad! Now, don't read your Bible! Don't go to church!" Conviction draws us towards God and away from sin, but condemnation draws us away from God and towards sin. The believer who is under condemnation often falls into depression, locks himself in his room, and isolates himself from other believers and opportunities to worship. He thinks God cannot and should not forgive. Or he thinks he must linger in depression as some form of penance—as though he could ever earn his forgiveness.

Listen, Christ did everything for a believer to come boldly to the throne room of God, to enjoy his presence, and to receive his grace. "Therefore let us confidently approach the throne of grace to receive mercy and find grace whenever we need help" (Hebrews 4:16). This is why we can sing.

If we are to live in praise, we must focus on our forgiveness—God's carrying away of our sins. Like Paul, we must continually forget what is behind (as God has, Heb 10:17) and press forward to what is ahead (Phil 3:13).

Application Questions: In what ways have you experienced condemnation for sin? How do you typically react to it? How can we recognize the difference between condemnation and conviction in order to help ourselves and others?

In Order to Live in Praise, Believers Must Focus on Their Spiritual Discernment

that he lavished on us in all wisdom and insight. He did this when he revealed to us the secret of his will, according to his good pleasure that he set forth in Christ, toward the administration of the fullness of the

times, to head up all things in Christ – the things in heaven and the things on earth.
Ephesians 1:8-10

Interpretation Question: In what way has God lavishly given believers "wisdom and understanding" (v. 8)?

Another of the spiritual riches Paul rejoices in is spiritual discernment. God gives wisdom (knowledge) and insight (what to do with this knowledge) into the mystery of his will. This means God gives believers understanding of ultimate things like "life and death, God and man, righteousness and sin, heaven and hell, eternity and time."[37] Included in this is the mystery Paul writes about in Ephesians 1:9.

The phrase "secret of his will," or it can be translated "mystery," is common terminology in the book of Ephesians. In Ephesians 3:6, we see the mystery of God's bringing Jews and Gentiles together in one body. In Ephesians 5:32, we see the mystery of Christ, and the church as his bride. "Mystery" means a "sacred secret, once hidden but now revealed to God's people."[38] Believers have been let into God's inner circle.

Christ says in John 15:15 that he no longer calls the disciples "servants," but "friends," because he has revealed to them the master's business. This is also our reality. One of the spiritual blessings God gives us is the ability to know his will and his plans. In fact, this is one of the reasons God gave us the Holy Spirit. Paul says this in 1 Corinthians 2:6-10:

> Now we do speak wisdom among the mature, but not a wisdom of this age or of the rulers of this age, who are perishing. Instead we speak the wisdom of God, hidden in a mystery, that God determined before the ages for our glory. None of the rulers of this age understood it. If they had known it, they would not have crucified the Lord of glory. But just as it is written, "Things that no eye has seen, or ear heard, or mind imagined, are the things God has prepared for those who love him." God has revealed these to us by the Spirit. For the Spirit searches all things, even the deep things of God.

Paul says God has given believers "secret wisdom." If the rulers of the age (ruling men and ruling demons) had had this wisdom, they would not have crucified our Savior. God reveals this truth to his followers through the Holy Spirit. This is one of our spiritual blessings.

Observation Question: What is the mystery that God reveals to believers (Ephesians 1:9)?

The "mystery," the "secret wisdom," is that God plans "to bring all things in heaven and on earth together under one head, even Christ" (v. 10).

Interpretation Question: What does the mystery that God is going to bring all things "together" under Christ tell us about "all things" (1:10)?

1. This mystery implies that "all things" are in a state of disorder.

Adam's sin created discord in the relationship between God and himself (Genesis 3). Adam immediately hid from God, and man is still hiding from God today. Then Adam and Eve hid from each other. People today have shallow relationships. We hide behind our fig leaves—our jobs, nationalities, possessions, religious trappings, etc. to hide our insecurity, pain, and sin. We hide from God and from others.

In addition, man is prone to discord. God says the woman will desire her husband and the husband will rule over his wife (Gen 3:16). Clearly, there will be discord in marriage. When Adam and Eve had their first two sons, Cain killed his younger brother, Abel. Man is in a state of discord—even family relationships often aren't safe.

Not only was man affected, but all creation was as well. God cursed the ground because of man's sin: "Cursed is the ground because of you" (Gen 3:17). The ground bears not only thorns and thistles, but droughts, floods, hurricanes, tsunamis, and earthquakes. Romans 8:20-21 says,

> For the creation was subjected to frustration, not by its own choice, but by the will of the one who subjected it, in hope that the creation itself will be liberated from its bondage to decay and brought into the glorious freedom of the children of God.

Even the heavens are in disorder. Before man fell, angels fell in heaven—negatively affecting it (cf. Rev 12:4). Hebrews says that even the heavens had to be cleansed by Christ's blood (cf. Hebrews 9:23).

2. This mystery teaches that in the fullness of time Christ will restore "all things."

One day, all things will be restored as they come under the headship of Christ. "When the times reach their fulfillment" or, as translated in the KJV, "the fulness of times" is when Christ brings his kingdom on earth (v. 10). He will remove the curse from nature. Isaiah 11:6-9 says,

> A wolf will reside with a lamb, and a leopard will lie down with a young goat; an ox and a young lion will graze together, as a small child leads

them along. A cow and a bear will graze together, their young will lie down together. A lion, like an ox, will eat straw. A baby will play over the hole of a snake; over the nest of a serpent an infant will put his hand. They will no longer injure or destroy on my entire royal mountain. For there will be universal submission to the Lord's sovereignty, just as the waters completely cover the sea.

There will be no more war. They will make their weapons into farm implements (Isaiah 2:4), and the knowledge of the Lord will cover the earth as water. That is the mystery God has revealed to his people. Colossians 1:19-20 says, "For God was pleased to have all his fullness dwell in the Son and through him to reconcile all things to himself by making peace through the blood of his cross – through him, whether things on earth or things in heaven."

With that said, some have taken "all things" to mean universal salvation. They would say even rebellious men, the devil, and the demons will be forgiven. However, that is not what Scripture teaches. At Christ's coming, he will divide those on the earth into sheep and goats (Matt 25). The sheep will enter into his kingdom (v. 34), and the goats will go into the everlasting destruction prepared for the devil and his angels (v. 41).

However, there is still a sense in which the devil and unbelievers will be brought into submission to Christ. They will submit to Christ because they must. Psalm 2:9 says he will rule them with "an iron scepter," meaning they will be forced to submit. The Lamb who was slain will return to the earth as a Lion, and all will submit. Philippians 2:9-11 says,

> As a result God exalted him and gave him the name that is above every name, so that at the name of Jesus every knee will bow – in heaven and on earth and under the earth – and every tongue confess that Jesus Christ is Lord to the glory of God the Father.

How can the believer rejoice when the world is in a state of disarray? How can he rejoice when things are difficult in his life? He can rejoice because God has given him wisdom and understanding—he knows the mysteries of this earth. His redeemer lives and all things will ultimately be made right. The Lion of Judah is coming! He will reign on the earth, and we will reign with him. Only a believer with this perspective can rejoice and sing while in a prison cell, or when life seems like a dungeon. He sees the light of the Son of God (John 8:12). God gave believers wisdom and understanding into the mystery of God's will, and this causes them to rejoice. Amen!

Application Question: How should we apply the fact that God has given us this secret wisdom?

First Corinthians 4:1-2 says, "One should think about us this way – as servants of Christ and stewards of the mysteries of God. Now what is sought in stewards is that one be found faithful." The wisdom God gives believers is a stewardship, and we must be faithful stewards of it. As stewards, one day we will give an accounting to God. "Make every effort to present yourself before God as a proven worker who does not need to be ashamed, teaching the message of truth accurately" (2 Tim 2:15). As we consider this reality, we must ask ourselves these questions:

- Are we doing our best to study God's Word?
- Are we doing our best to rightly interpret God's Word?
- Are we doing our best to faithfully share God's Word?

Only those who do their best with the stewardship of God's mysteries will be approved by God. And meditating on these mysteries will draw us into worship. Those who are not faithful with God's mysteries will find no room for worship, especially during trials.

Application Question: In what ways is God challenging you to be a faithful steward of his Word?

Conclusion

How can we live a life of praise, even during trials? In Ephesians 1:3-14, we see Paul's song while in prison. He could sing because of his focus on Christ and his blessings. In verses 3-10, we are challenged to focus on these aspects of our spiritual blessings:

1. In order to live in praise, believers must focus on their new home—the heavenly realms.
2. In order to live in praise, believers must focus on their spiritual blessings.
3. In order to live in praise, believers must focus on their union with Christ.
4. In order to live in praise, believers must focus on their election.
5. In order to live in praise, believers must focus on their adoption as sons.
6. In order to live in praise, believers must focus on God's abundant grace.
7. In order to live in praise, believers must focus on their redemption.
8. In order to live in praise, believers must focus on their forgiveness.

9. In order to live in praise, believers must focus on their spiritual discernment.

How to Live in Praise, Even in Trials—Part Three

> In Christ we too have been claimed as God's own possession, since we were predestined according to the one purpose of him who accomplishes all things according to the counsel of his will so that we, who were the first to set our hope on Christ, would be to the praise of his glory. And when you heard the word of truth (the gospel of your salvation) – when you believed in Christ– you were marked with the seal of the promised Holy Spirit, who is the down payment of our inheritance, until the redemption of God's own possession, to the praise of his glory.
> Ephesians 1:11-14 (NET)

How can we live a life of praise, even when going through trials?

While Paul was imprisoned in Rome awaiting a possible death sentence, he wrote the book of Ephesians. In Ephesians 1:3-14 specifically, he appears to be singing a praise song to God. It begins with, "Praise be to the God and Father of our Lord Jesus Christ, who has blessed us in the heavenly realms with every spiritual blessing in Christ" (Ephesians 1:3).

How could Paul praise God while in prison—in the midst of great difficulty? No doubt his ability to praise came from his focus. Paul was not focused on his unfortunate circumstances, but on the heavenly realms, where believers are seated in Christ (v. 3). In verses 3-10, he details many of the believer's spiritual blessings. These include election and adoption as sons into the family of God, redemption, forgiveness of sins, and wisdom and discernment (v. 4-10).

In Ephesians 11-14, he continues this song about the spiritual blessings believers receive in Christ. As we continue this study, we will learn more about living a life of praise by focusing on the blessings of God.

Big Questions: What does Paul praise God for in this part of his blessing song? How can we implement worship in our daily lives, especially during trials?

In Order to Live in Praise, Believers Must Focus on God's Sovereignty

> In Christ we too have been claimed as God's own possession, since we were predestined according to the one purpose of him who accomplishes all things according to the counsel of his will so that we, who were the first to set our hope on Christ, would be to the praise of his glory. And when you heard the word of truth (the gospel of your salvation) – when you believed in Christ– you were marked with the seal of the promised Holy Spirit.
> Ephesians 1:11-13

Another aspect that we must focus on if we are going to live a life of praise is God's sovereignty. Paul again mentions that believers were chosen and predestined (cf. v. 4-5), but he adds "according to the one purpose of him who accomplishes all things according to the counsel of his will" (v.11).

Paul not only sees God in control of salvation, as he chooses to elect some, but also in complete control of all things. He says God works "all things"— according to (or "in conformity with," as in the NIV) the counsel of his will. The word "accomplishes" is the Greek word 'energeo,' from which we get the English words "energy" and "energize."[39] Scripture teaches that God is energizing all things for his purposes and is therefore in control of everything. Nothing happens apart from his sovereign will. No doubt this was a tremendous comfort to Paul while he was in prison.

Interpretation Question: In what ways do we see God's sovereignty over "all things" taught throughout Scripture?

1. Scripture teaches God's ordination of all man's days, as they were planned out beforehand.

David says, "Your eyes saw me when I was inside the womb. All the days ordained for me were recorded in your scroll before one of them came into existence" (Psalm 139:16).

2. Scripture teaches God's control over natural events.

Christ tells the disciples that God feeds the birds and clothes the lilies of the field (Matthew 6:26, 30). We would all say these happen by natural processes; however, Scripture teaches that events can have multiple causes and yet God be the ultimate cause. Theologians have called this the "law of concurrence."

3. Scripture teaches God's control of chance events.

"The dice are thrown into the lap, but their every decision is from the Lord" (Proverbs 16:33).

4. Scripture teaches God's control over the hearts of men.

In the case of Pharaoh and the enslaved Israelites, Scripture teaches both that Pharaoh hardened his own heart and that God hardened it (Ex 8:15, 14:8). In support of this, Proverbs 21:1 says, "The king's heart is in the hand of the Lord like channels of water; he turns it wherever he wants."

5. Scripture teaches God's control over all disasters.

"If disaster overtakes a city, is the Lord not responsible?" (Amos 3:6). Note that Amos does not qualify this as "some disasters," but disaster in general.

6. Scripture teaches God's control over Satan and evil.

In the story of Job, Scripture shows Satan getting permission from God to attack all Job had, including his family (Job 1:12).
As water poured into a plastic bottle "conforms" to the bottle, everything "conforms" to God's will and is in some way foreordained (cf. Ephesians 1:11 NIV). In fact, he is energizing everything towards his purpose. This is indeed a mystery!

Interpretation Question: How can God be in control of everything—including man's choices and the evil in the world—and yet still be just?

One Scripture that may help us understand God's sovereignty is Colossians 1:17: "He himself is before all things and all things are held together in him." Christ holds our bodies together, as well as the angels and demons, atoms, and everything else. Nothing can function without his energy. Therefore, nothing can act apart from his control. God is not like a watchmaker, who makes something that operates on its own, apart from its creator. Scripture teaches God's total control of creation at all times (Eph 1: 11).
With all that said, though Scripture teaches God's sovereignty, it also teaches that God cannot be blamed for sin, he does not tempt man, and that man is responsible for his own choices. "Let no one say when he is tempted, 'I am tempted by God,' for God cannot be tempted by evil, and he himself tempts no one" (James 1:13). Again, this is a mystery.

The "Two Wills" of God

Another concept that might help us reconcile this difficult truth of God's sovereignty over man's choices and his sovereignty over evil is to consider the will of God. Many theologians parse God's will into two parts: his moral, or perfect, will, and his sovereign will. Not everything in God's moral will happens. For instance, Scripture says God isn't willing that "any should perish but that all should come to repentance," and he desires that all men be saved (2 Peter 3:9, KJV, 1 Tim 2:4). However, not all will be saved. Some will perish, even though that is not God's perfect will (cf. Matt 25:41). God's moral, or perfect, will does not always happen.

Is it God's will for little children to be abused? No. Is it his will that we fall into sin? No. It is not God's perfect will. But somehow, in God's sovereign will, it is. Even the death of his Son was predestined (Acts 2:23). God works in all things and uses all "for good for those who love God" (Romans 8:28). He energizes all things according to the purpose of his will (Eph 1:11), and does so in such a way that he cannot be blamed for evil, justly holding men and angels responsible for their actions. Again, this is a mystery in Scripture—but it is a necessary mystery for us to accept in order to rejoice in trials. God is in control, and he works all things for our good—even evil things.

Paul was able to rejoice and sing in prison because he focused on God's sovereignty. He saw God in control of his election to salvation, and he also saw God in control of his unfortunate circumstances. He had peace and joy while in prison awaiting a possible death sentence because he saw God as totally in control—not the devil, and not evil men. As he says in Romans 8:28, "And we know that all things work together for good for those who love God, who are called according to his purpose."

It was this theology that gave Joseph peace in the presence of those who had sold him into slavery. He said to his brothers, "What you meant for bad, God meant for good" (Gen 50:20, paraphrase). It was the same with Job. Instead of being angry at those who robbed him or about the death of his children, he simply said, "The Lord gives and he takes away. Blessed be the name of the Lord" (Job 1:21, paraphrase). Those who don't understand or focus on God's sovereignty only see the devil and people. They instead focus on these, and it takes away their joy— their song. But Job and Joseph focused on the sovereignty of God, and so did Paul.

With all of that said, Paul didn't just see God's sovereignty, he also saw human responsibility. In continuing his praise over the believer's election, he says:

so that we, who were the first to set our hope on Christ, would be to the praise of his glory. And when you heard the word of truth (the

gospel of your salvation) – when you believed in Christ – you were marked with the seal of the promised Holy Spirit, who is the down payment of our inheritance, until the redemption of God's own possession, to the praise of his glory.
Ephesians 1:12-14

Interestingly, in this section he speaks first to the Jews and then to the Gentiles. He says, "so that we [Jews], who were the first to set our hope on Christ" (v.12) and "you [Gentiles] heard the word of truth (the gospel of your salvation) – when you believed in Christ – you were marked with the seal" (v. 13). In speaking to the Jews who first put their hope in Christ and then to the Gentiles who heard the word of truth and believed, Paul is recognizing human responsibility—though it is secondary to God's sovereignty. The Jews and Gentiles responded because they were first chosen and predestined according to the purpose of him who works everything according to the purpose of his will. This is a balanced view. Focusing on God's sovereignty is not a denial of human effort or responsibility, or even the work of the evil one. Rather, it is a recognition of who is ultimately in control.

Yes, we recognize our sin, the failures of others, and the work of the evil one—but not apart from the sovereign rule of God, who works everything for the good of those who love him. In God's sovereignty, he can even use my sin, the failures of others, and the temptation of the evil one to make me into the image of his Son, which he predestined before time (Rom 8:28-29). This is how we can live in praise while suffering. We must see God as sovereign, and in control over the events of our lives.

Do you see God as sovereign? Or do you tend to focus on men and the devil rather than God? It's the one who focuses on God's sovereignty who can sing in a prison cell.

Application Question: Why is an understanding of God's sovereignty important for our spiritual lives?

1. It is important for prayer.

If God is not in control, why pray? Why pray to a God who doesn't control everything? How can you have faith that your prayers will be answered if God isn't absolutely in control?

2. It is important for comfort.

How can you have comfort in a world that is ungodly—full of demons and evil men—unless you have supreme confidence that God is ultimately in control? If you don't believe in God's sovereignty, you will probably be a bitter, angry person, or at least a complainer. When Shimei cursed David as he fled from Absalom, David's soldiers wanted to kill Shimei. David responded, "God has told him to curse, let him curse (paraphrase)" (2 Sam 16:11). David saw God in control of the curses of evil men, and he trusted God's purposes. Instead of becoming bitter, angry, and vengeful as his men did, David trusted God.

Job was the same. When he lost his family and career, he said, "The Lord gives and he takes away; blessed be the name of the Lord (paraphrase)." Those without this doctrine will lack comfort.

3. It is important for faith.

We can live and minister in confidence because the Sovereign God will provide for us, protect us, and empower us. He is our Shepherd and we will not lack (Psalm 23). He provides for the lilies of the field and the birds of the air, and he will certainly provide for us (Matt 6:25-34).

Application Questions: How does an understanding of God's sovereignty comfort or encourage you? How can we maintain a proper balance as we consider events in light of God's sovereignty, man's responsibility, and the work of the evil one?

In Order to Live in Praise, Believers Must Focus on the Ministry of the Holy Spirit

> when you believed in Christ– you were marked with the seal of the promised Holy Spirit, who is the down payment of our inheritance, until the redemption of God's own possession, to the praise of his glory.
> Ephesians 1:13b-14

Observation Questions: What terms does Paul use to describe the Holy Spirit in Ephesians 1:13b-14, and what do they mean?

Paul's next cause for rejoicing is the ministry of the Holy Spirit in the believer's life. God has given each believer the Holy Spirit, and he has many roles in the believer's life. We learn a great deal about these roles by the words Paul uses for the Spirit: "seal" and "down payment."

Interpretation Question: What does the word "seal" tell us about the Holy Spirit's work in the believer's life?

1. As a seal, the Holy Spirit represents authenticity—he proves that the believer's salvation is real.

John MacArthur says this:

> The sealing of which Paul speaks here refers to an official mark of identification that was placed on a letter, contract, or other important document. The seal usually was made from hot wax, which was placed on the document and then impressed with a signet ring. The document was thereby officially identified with and under the authority of the person to whom the signet belonged.[40]

The Holy Spirit authenticates the believer. Romans 8:9 says, "if anyone does not have the Spirit of Christ, this person does not belong to him." The Holy Spirit bears witness with our spirit that we are children of God (Rom 8:16). He authenticates us by changing us, making us more into Christ's image. He gives us new desires—desires to pray, serve, love God and others, and to read his Word. If a professing believer doesn't have these holy affections, he is not truly saved—he is missing the seal of the Holy Spirit.

2. As a seal, the Holy Spirit represents God's ownership.

In those days, slaves and cattle bore the seals of their owners. The Holy Spirit not only authenticates the believer, but also demonstrates God's ownership.

3. As a seal, the Holy Spirit represents the security of the believer.

Seals also were used as a form of security. Often kings or others in authority would seal something to say that it should not be touched or tampered with. John MacArthur's comments are helpful here as well:

> In ancient times the seal of a king, prince, or noble represented security and inviolability. When Daniel was thrown into the lion's den, King Darius, along with his nobles, placed their seals on the stone placed over the entrance to the den, "so that nothing could be changed with regard to Daniel" (Dan. 6:17). Any person but the king who broke or disturbed that seal would likely have forfeited his life. In a similar way the tomb where Jesus was buried was sealed. Fearing that Jesus' disciples might steal His body and falsely claim His resurrection, the Jewish leaders obtained Pilate's permission to place a seal on the stone and to guard it with soldiers (Matt. 27:62–66).[41]

This is one of the reasons we know that the true believer's salvation is secure. The Holy Spirit seals him. Consider what Paul says in Ephesians 4:30,

"And do not grieve the Holy Spirit of God, by whom you were sealed for the day of redemption." Even though we have been redeemed from slavery to sin, our ultimate redemption awaits our resurrected bodies. The Holy Spirit seals us until that final work happens, and so do Jesus and the Father:

> "My sheep listen to my voice, and I know them, and they follow me. I give them eternal life, and they will never perish; no one will snatch them from my hand. Father, who has given them to me, is greater than all, and no one can snatch them from my Father's hand. The Father and I are one."
> John 10:27-30

God the Father, God the Son, and God the Holy Spirit secure and protect the believer's salvation.

4.   As a seal, the Holy Spirit represents authority.

To have a king's signet ring or seal meant to hold his power and authority (cf. Esther 8:8-12). In the same way, God's seal on believers represents their authority to teach the Word of God, to defend it, to use their spiritual gifts to build God's kingdom, etc. Christ said this when he ascended to heaven:

> "All authority in heaven and on earth has been given to me. Therefore go and make disciples of all nations, baptizing them in the name of the Father and the Son and the Holy Spirit, teaching them to obey everything I have commanded you. And remember, I am with you always, to the end of the age."
> Matthew 28:18-20

Because we have been sealed with the Holy Spirit, we have the authority of the King to do his ministry.

Interpretation Question: What does it mean to be given the Holy Spirit as a "down payment"?

Not only did Paul say the Holy Spirit was a seal, but also a "down payment of our inheritance, until the redemption of God's own possession" (Eph 1:14). The Holy Spirit secures our inheritance.

It must be noted that "our inheritance" can also be translated as "were made an inheritance." [42] It could mean either that God has given us an inheritance or that we are God's inheritance. In Ephesians 1:18, he focuses on believers being an inheritance to God: "since the eyes of your heart have been enlightened – so that you may know what is the hope of his calling, what is the wealth of his glorious inheritance in the saints." However, the context here (Ephesians 1:3—"blessed us with every spiritual blessing in the heavenly realms") points to interpreting verse 14 as "our inheritance," as in the NET.

Now, in what ways is the Holy Spirit a down payment?

1. As a down payment, the Holy Spirit guarantees our future inheritance.

The word "down payment" can be translated as "earnest," or even "engagement ring."[43] An engagement ring is a promise for future marriage. An earnest is "the down payment to guarantee the final purchase of some commodity or piece of property."[44] When a person bought a piece of property in those times, he put down earnest money. This guaranteed that the rest of the money was coming. If he failed to pay, he would lose his earnest. We call this a "down payment" today.

The Lord gave us the Holy Spirit as our guarantee that we will receive every spiritual blessing in Christ in full.

2. As a down payment, the Holy Spirit is a foretaste of our inheritance in heaven.

An earnest was part of a future payment. In the same way, the Holy Spirit is a foretaste of our future heavenly inheritance. "For the kingdom of God does not consist of food and drink, but righteousness, peace, and joy in the Holy Spirit" (Romans 14:17). Heaven will be full of righteousness, peace, and joy, all blessings the Holy Spirit wants to give us now. He wants to get rid of the sin in our lives and fill us with righteousness, and to give us peace and joy—no matter what trials we encounter. Our current experience in the Holy Spirit is a taste of our heavenly reward.

How can we sing during our trials? We can sing because God has given us an inheritance. He sealed us and is protecting us. He has given us his authority to use for his glory. He has confirmed that we are his. He has given us a taste and a guarantee of heaven. While Paul was in prison, he enjoyed a taste of his inheritance in heaven through the work of the Holy Spirit. Though he had lost everything else, he had everything in Christ and through the work of the Holy Spirit. This is true for us as well. Let us sing because of our heavenly inheritance, which we can enjoy even now.

Application Questions: In what ways does the Holy Spirit's role as a seal and a deposit comfort or encourage you? How can we better apply these realities to our lives and ministry?

In Order to Live in Praise, Believers Must Focus on the Glory of God

> so that we, who were the first to set our hope on Christ, would be to the praise of his glory. And when you heard the word of truth (the gospel of your salvation) – when you believed in Christ – you were marked with the seal of the promised Holy Spirit, who is the down payment of our inheritance, until the redemption of God's own possession, to the praise of his glory.
> Ephesians 1:12-14

Finally, Paul focuses on the glory of God. "Glory" refers to the weight of something, or the greatness of a person or thing. In verses 12 and 14, he says that the ultimate reason God saves us is for the praise of his glory. Salvation is not ultimately about man; it is about God and his glory. God is glorified through our salvation because it could only happen through his initiative in electing and saving man. Salvation glorifies God because it was through his wisdom and power that this plan was made and carried out.

In fact, this is mentioned several times throughout the letter. One of the ways man's salvation glorifies God is by demonstrating God's grace and wisdom to the angels in heaven. Look at these verses:

> And he raised us up with him and seated us with him in the heavenly realms in Christ Jesus, to demonstrate in the coming ages the surpassing wealth of his grace in kindness toward us in Christ Jesus.
> Ephesians 2:6-7

> The purpose of this enlightenment is that through the church the multifaceted wisdom of God should now be disclosed to the rulers and the authorities in the heavenly realms.
> Ephesians 3:10

Who is God demonstrating his grace and wisdom to? The angels. When the demonic angels fell in heaven, the angels had never seen God's grace. They saw God's perfect judgment and wrath on the demons. But in man, they see God's grace—unmerited favor—as he saves an undeserving people. They also see his wisdom, as this was planned before time. Salvation is ultimately a work that glorifies God. Sometimes churches preach the gospel as though salvation is the ultimate purpose of God and Scripture. No—the glory of God is. Saving man is a means to glorify God and reveal his characteristics to all, including the angels.

Paul was able to sing in prison because he saw that the ultimate purpose of his life was to glorify God. Listen, if the ultimate purpose of your life is comfort, happiness, and joy, you will not be able to sing during your trials; instead, you will worry, complain, and become bitter.

Only those who realize that God is ultimately in control, and that everything is conforming to God's plan to bring glory to himself, praise him even during trials. They say, "If my suffering brings glory to God, so be it. If my persevering brings glory to God, so be it. If my prospering brings glory to God, so be it. But let everything in my life be for the glory of God." That is the type of heart and the type of focus that can praise God in every trial.

What is your focus? Is it your happiness, your success, and your glory? If so, you won't be able to sing during your trials, as Paul did. "So whether you eat or drink, or whatever you do, do everything for the glory of God" (1 Cor 10:31).

Amen. Let this be so.

Application Question: How can we live for the glory of God?

1. We live for God's glory by doing our best at the endeavors he has called us to.

    "Whatever you are doing, work at it with enthusiasm, as to the Lord and not for people" (Col 3:23).

2. We live for God's glory by trusting him in everything.

    "Trust in the Lord with all your heart, and do not rely on your own understanding" (Prov 3:5).

3. We live for God's glory by submitting to him in everything.

    Like Christ, we must pray, "Not my will, but thy will be done" (Luke 22:42, paraphrase).

4. We live for God's glory by seeking to reflect him in everything we do.

    "Be imitators of God as dearly loved children" (Eph 5:1). When we imitate God, we glorify him.

5. We live for God's glory by thanking him in everything and by worshiping him, even as Paul did.

"In everything give thanks. For this is God's will for you in Christ Jesus" (1Thess 5:18).

Application Questions: What makes it hard to live a life that is totally focused on the glory of God? Why is it so easy to get distracted from this? How is God challenging you to make his glory your focus in everything, even trials?

Conclusion

How can we live a life of praise, even while in trials? In Ephesians 1:3-14, we see Paul's praise song while in prison. From it, we learn:

1. In order to live in praise, believers must focus on their new home—the heavenly realms.
2. In order to live in praise, believers must focus on their spiritual blessings.
3. In order to live in praise, believers must focus on their union with Christ.
4. In order to live in praise, believers must focus on their election.
5. In order to live in praise, believers must focus on their adoption as sons.
6. In order to live in praise, believers must focus on God's abundant grace.
7. In order to live in praise, believers must focus on their redemption.
8. In order to live in praise, believers must focus on their forgiveness.
9. In order to live in praise, believers must focus on their spiritual discernment.
10. In order to live in praise, believers must focus on God's sovereignty.
11. In order to live in praise, believers must focus on the ministry of the Holy Spirit.
12. In order to live in praise, believers must focus on the glory of God.

Developing an Apostolic Prayer Life

For this reason, because I have heard of your faith in the Lord Jesus and your love for all the saints, I do not cease to give thanks for you when I remember you in my prayers. I pray that the God of our Lord Jesus Christ, the Father of glory, may give you spiritual wisdom and revelation in your growing knowledge of him, – since the eyes of your heart have been enlightened – so that you may know what is the hope of his calling, what is the wealth of his glorious inheritance in the saints, and what is the incomparable greatness of his power toward us who believe, as displayed in the exercise of his immense strength. This power he exercised in Christ when he raised him from the dead and seated him at his right hand in the heavenly realms
Ephesians 1:15-20 (NET)

Selected by God to build the foundation of the church, the apostles did so by bearing witness to the resurrected Christ, by their teaching, and by prayer.

The apostles were noted for prayer. When there was a need to provide for the widows in the early church, the apostles couldn't do it because they had to devote themselves to "prayer and to the ministry of the word" (Acts 6:4). When the leaders of the church at Antioch were fasting and praying, the Holy Spirit told them to set apart Paul and Barnabas for the ministry God had called them to (Acts 13:1-3). This was the beginning of Paul's missionary journeys.

In addition, in the majority of the apostle Paul's epistles to churches, he starts off sharing how he has been praying them (Rom 1:9-10, Phil 1:4, Col 1:9, etc.). Praying for God's church was an important component of laying the foundation.

Although the foundation of the church has been laid and the original apostles have passed away, we can still have an apostolic ministry, specifically in the area of prayer. God wants to use us to build his church through prayer.

As we consider Ephesians 1:15-20, we learn principles of apostolic prayer—prayer that builds up God's church.

Big Questions: How can we develop an apostolic prayer life? What principles can be discerned from Ephesians 1:15-20?

Apostolic Prayer Comes from a Right Heart—an Informed, Caring, and Consistent One

> ✶ For this reason, because I have heard of your faith in the Lord Jesus and your love for all the saints, I do not cease to give thanks for you when I remember you in my prayers.
> Ephesians 1:15-16

While Paul was in prison, someone informed him about the faith of the Ephesians and their love for all the saints. It must be noted that faith and love are essential marks of genuine conversion. Those who truly have faith in Christ are new creations, old things are passed away, all things become new (2 Cor 5:17). One of the new things in the life of a true believer is love for other believers. Jesus says, "They will know you are my disciples by the way you love one another" (John 13:35, paraphrase). If we do not love our fellow believers, then we have not passed from death to life. "We know that we have crossed over from death to life because we love our fellow Christians. The one who does not love remains in death" (1 John 3:14). And as Paul says in Romans 5:5, "the love of God has been poured out in our hearts through the Holy Spirit who was given to us."

The believers in Ephesus had experienced this outpouring, and therefore loved "all the saints"—not just the saints in their local congregation or city, but saints everywhere. They had been radically changed by God.

One of the things that should be noted about Ephesians 1:15 is how Paul says, "because I have heard of your faith in the Lord Jesus." It seems to be spoken as though he had never met these believers. The problem with this is that he had spent at least three years in Ephesus (Acts 20:31). For this reason, along with the fact that "in Ephesus" (Eph 1:1) is not in the early manuscripts, many scholars believe this letter was written not only to the Ephesians, but also to several other congregations in Asia Minor.[45]

Observation Question: What aspects of apostolic prayer can be discerned from Ephesians 1:15-16? Giving thanks

1. Apostolic prayer is informed.

Paul prays with gratitude because he has heard about the faith and love of these saints. It is hard to pray for things we know nothing about.

In order to cultivate our prayer lives, we must seek to be informed. This might include asking others for their prayer requests so we can constantly lift them up. It could include reading and watching the news so we can know how to pray for our nation and for the world in general. No doubt Paul is implying the

pray for the Church - worldwide

need to be informed in Ephesians 6:18: "be alert, with all perseverance and requests for all the saints." We must be alert to problems, events in general, and instances of spiritual warfare so that we can pray for all the saints.

If we do not stay informed, we will not be able to pray as we ought.

thankful to Church & Chris for Revelation Study & current Eph. study

2. Apostolic prayer is caring.

Another aspect of Paul's apostolic prayer is his care for the Ephesians—he has "not stopped giving thanks" for them. He is thankful for the Ephesians' spiritual attainments and successes, which shows a great deal about his heart. Many do not rejoice when others succeed, whether spiritually, socially, or vocationally. Rather, a spirit of jealousy or anger creeps in, making them incapable of true prayer. We must have a selfless, caring heart in order to pray.

We must truly want the best for others. We must want them to know God, and to excel at work, church, school, and in their relationships. This is the type of heart needed to pray. Sadly, this is the reason many of us do not pray. We do not care about others as we should, but are much more concerned about ourselves. *oh me!*

3. Apostolic prayer is consistent.

Paul's own prayers were consistent, and he commands all believers to "constantly pray" (1 Thessalonians 5:17). We see this consistency in his prayers for the Colossians and the Romans as well as the Ephesians.

For this reason we also, from the day we heard about you, have not ceased praying for you and asking God to fill you with the knowledge of his will in all spiritual wisdom and understanding.
Colossians 1:9

For God, whom I serve in my spirit by preaching the gospel of his Son, is my witness that I continually remember you and I always ask in my prayers, if perhaps now at last I may succeed in visiting you according to the will of God. *every prayer*
Romans 1:9-10 *according to the will of God.*

Paul was constantly praying for the church, and this should be true of us as well. But how can we practice constant prayer—prayer without ceasing? Does this mean that we never stop praying all day long?

Not necessarily. The Greek word translated as "constantly" in ancient literature was used of a "hacking cough."[46] When a person has a bad cough, it is not that he never stops coughing. It's that he coughs all day—the cough keeps coming back. We must do the same with our prayers. Throughout the day, we must constantly remember the church, our neighbors, our co-workers, our leaders, and the lost in general before God. Prayer must be our constant endeavor and focus throughout the day.

Apostolic prayer is informed, caring, and consistent.

Application Questions: How would you rate your prayer life on a scale of 1-10? What are some practical tips that can help us to be more faithful in prayer, and specifically in intercession?

Apostolic Prayer Focuses on Knowing God More

> I pray that the God of our Lord Jesus Christ, the Father of glory, may give you spiritual wisdom and revelation in your growing knowledge of him.
> Ephesians 1:17

Next, we begin to see the petitions within Paul's prayer; he wants the believers to grow in understanding God, and in other spiritual truths. We see this in the use of the word "knowledge" in verse 17, where he prays for the believers to have the Spirit of wisdom and revelation so that they may know God better.

Commentator Kent Hughes points out some useful information about the word "knowledge" as used in this text:

> The regular Greek word for personal knowing is gnosis, but here the word is intensified with the preposition epi. Paul is asking for an epignosis—a "real, deep, full knowledge"—a "thorough knowledge"[47]

Paul wants these believers to have a deep and thorough knowledge of God. When we are first saved, we come to know God. As Christ says in his high priestly prayer to the Father, "Now this is eternal life – that they know you, the only true God, and Jesus Christ, whom you sent." (John 17:3). In speaking to the false professors in Matthew 7:23, he says, "I never knew you." To be saved is to know God.

Paul wasn't praying for these believers to know God, for they all did. He was praying for a deep and experiential knowledge of God which would continue until they got to heaven. In speaking about Christ's coming and the eternal state, Paul says, "For now we see in a mirror indirectly, but then we will see face to face. Now I know in part, but then I will know fully, just as I have been fully known" (1 Corinthians 13:12).

In the eternal state, we will have an intimate knowledge of God which is currently unattainable for us. However, this should be our goal here on earth. Paul says this in Philippians 3:10, "My aim is to know him, to experience the power of his resurrection, to share in his sufferings, and to be like him in his death."

After leaving everything for Christ, Paul said his continual endeavor for the rest of his life was knowing God, and it should be ours as well. In Latin, there is a phrase "summum bonum" which means, "the greatest good out of which all good flows." For them, the greatest good was knowing God, and it was from this knowledge that everything good flowed—peace, love, joy, service, justice, and mercy all flow from this knowledge. And therefore, this must be our continual pursuit in life.

Interpretation Question: How can believers get to know God better?

We can learn several insights about getting to know God better from Paul's prayer in Ephesians 1:17.

1. Believers can know God better by praying for this knowledge.

Paul prays for this church to come to a deeper knowledge of God. He prayed because that was one of the ways it would happen. We must pray for it as well. We must pray this for ourselves and others. We must ask God to make himself known. This is exactly what Moses did. He prayed to God, "Show me your glory" (Ex 33:18). And God did.

We must pray this way as well. We must pray that he will reveal himself through the Word of God, worship, service, and our daily jobs. This must be our continual petition as we go throughout the day: Lord, help me and others to know you more. Those who pray these types of prayers will grow in intimacy with God.

2. Believers can know God better by relying on the ministry of the Holy Spirit.

Paul prays for spiritual wisdom and revelation (Eph 1:17). There is some controversy over what he means by the word "spirit." Is he referring to the Holy Spirit, the human spirit, or something else? The NIV translators interpret it as the Holy Spirit—"Spirit of wisdom and revelation."

This is because it is impossible to know God or have revelation about him apart from the Holy Spirit. In John 16:13, the Holy Spirit is called the Spirit of truth, meaning that his job is to lead us into truth about God.

First Corinthians 2:14 says this, "The unbeliever does not receive the things of the Spirit of God, for they are foolishness to him. And he cannot understand them, because they are spiritually discerned." Apart from the Holy Spirit, we cannot understand anything about God. He is the one who reveals truth to us.

Now with that said, since Paul is writing to believers, he is not praying for them to have the Holy Spirit. In Ephesians 1:13-14, he says that believers are sealed by the Holy Spirit and that he is a deposit in them guaranteeing their inheritance. How can he then pray for them to have the Spirit?

Paul is clearly referring to the Holy Spirit's ministry. He prays that the Holy Spirit would give these believers revelation about God through the Word of God, creation, events, and the witness of other believers. And he also prays for wisdom to apply this knowledge.

Christ says something similar to his disciples in Luke 11:11-13:

> What father among you, if your son asks for a fish, will give him a snake instead of a fish? if he asks for an egg, will give him a scorpion? If you then, although you are evil, know how to give good gifts to your children, how much more will the heavenly Father give the Holy Spirit to those who ask him!"

Again, in speaking to believers, he is not telling them to pray for the Holy Spirit but rather for the ministry of the Spirit. He encourages them to ask and trust that God will give it to them. God wants to give believers every good gift that comes from the Holy Spirit.

3. We come to know God better by having the right disposition.

However, others think Paul is referring to a right disposition, instead of the Holy Spirit. That is why the NET translates this "spiritual wisdom and revelation." John MacArthur says:

> But like our English spirit, pneuma sometimes was used of a disposition, influence, or attitude—as in "He is in high spirits today." Jesus used the word in that sense in the first beatitude: "Blessed are the poor in spirit" (Matt. 5:3). He was not referring to the Holy Spirit or to the human spirit but to the spirit, or attitude, of humility.[48]

The reason people have different views on the word "spirit" is because both are true. We need the Holy Spirit to know God, but we also need the right disposition to know God.

A person with a disposition of wisdom and revelation is a person who desires to grow in the wisdom and knowledge of God. He hungers for God. Without a hunger to know God, we won't ever get to know him deeply. Many Christians are simply content with their spiritual lives and their knowledge of God. They don't have an inner disposition pushing them to pursue God and to know his voice and Word more. This type of disposition will never know God intimately.

Jeremiah 29:13 says, "When you seek me in prayer and worship, you will find me available to you. If you seek me with all your heart and soul." We must have a heart that draws near God to find him. Matthew 5:6 says, "Blessed are those who hunger and thirst for righteousness, for they will be satisfied."

If we really hunger to know God more, then he will reveal himself to us. Do you hunger and thirst for his Word? Do you hunger and thirst for his presence? Listen to the prayer in Psalm 42:1-2: "As a deer longs for streams of water, so I long for you, O God! I thirst for God, for the living God. I say, 'When will I be able to go and appear in God's presence?'"

Is this your disposition—famished apart from the knowledge of God? This is the disposition we must have. This is the disposition we must ask God for—for ourselves and for others.

If we are going to know God, we must labor constantly in prayer, as Paul did. We must pray for the Holy Spirit to reveal God, and we must also pray that God will give us the right disposition to receive and know him more.

Application Questions: How would you rate your hunger to know God more? What things temper your hunger for the greatest good—God? How can we increase our hunger to know God more?

Apostolic Prayer Focuses on Knowing the Hope of God's Plan for the Saints

> since the eyes of your heart have been enlightened – so that you may
> know what is the hope of his calling,
> Ephesians 1:18

Next, Paul prays for these believers to know the hope to which God called them. Hope is very important because it guides our lives. If a person hopes to be a doctor, he focuses on the sciences and studies diligently. Hope drives the direction of his life.

If Christians don't have the right hope, they will live for this world and thus often find themselves discouraged and depressed. This is why Paul prays for these believers to have their hearts enlightened so they will know the hope to which God called them.

When he says "heart," he is using a figurative expression for the mind, will, and emotions. Unlike the contemporary use of "heart," it is not primarily emotional. He wants their inner man to be completely enlightened to the hope of their calling.

Interpretation Question: What type of calling is Paul referring to?

Scripture typically refers to two types of calls. There is the general call of the gospel which goes to all people. Romans 10:13 says, "Whosoever shall call upon the name of the Lord shall be saved" (KJV). Everybody is offered the gospel—this is the general call. Theologians call the second one the effectual call—the call that is effective and results in a person's salvation. Look at how Paul uses this word in Romans 8:29-30:

> because those whom he foreknew he also predestined to be conformed to the image of his Son, that his Son would be the firstborn among many brothers and sisters. And those he predestined, he also called; and those he called, he also justified; and those he justified, he also glorified.

In talking about those God foreknew and predestined to be like Christ, Paul says that God called them, justified them, and glorified them. In this passage, he refers to the effectual call—the call that leads to salvation. When God effectually called us, it wasn't just about salvation—it was for so much more. It spans God's work before creation, in us now, and throughout eternity.

This call motivated Paul, and it should motivate us as well. He says this in Philippians 3:13-14:

> Brothers and sisters, I do not consider myself to have attained this. Instead I am single-minded: Forgetting the things that are behind and reaching out for the things that are ahead, with this goal in mind, I strive toward the prize of the upward call of God in Christ Jesus

He pressed forward to win the prize for which God 'called' him heavenward. Paul put his hope in the call, and it drove his life.

The very reason so many Christians live such earthly lives is because they have a very low understanding of their call and how God wants to use them.

Interpretation Question: What does the hope of our calling include?

1. The hope of God's calling includes righteous works on earth.

Ephesians 2:10 says, "For we are his workmanship, having been created in Christ Jesus for good works that God prepared beforehand so we may do them." God saved us to serve him. To Jeremiah he says, "Before I formed you in your mother's womb I chose you. Before you were born I set you apart. I appointed you to be a prophet to the nations" (Jeremiah 1:5). God called him to be a prophet before he was born. Paul, similarly, was called to be an apostle (1 Cor 1:1).

Each one of us has a call to serve God and glorify him on earth. We are his workmanship. This means the trials and difficulties we encounter are not haphazard or pointless. They are like the work of a craftsman chipping away at a rock—creating a masterpiece that brings glory to himself.

We need to hear this, especially as the enemy constantly lies to us and tries to tell us we are purposeless and evolutionary accidents. No, God has a specific calling—with specific works—for each individual.

2. The hope of God's calling includes Christ's coming and our resurrected bodies.

First John 3:2-3 says,

> Dear friends, we are God's children now, and what we will be has not yet been revealed. We know that whenever it is revealed we will be like him, because we will see him just as he is. And everyone who has this hope focused on him purifies himself, just as Jesus is pure.

John says that those who truly hope in this reality purify themselves. The fact that Christ is coming, that we will be resurrected, and that we will be like him when we see him is a motivation to live holy and righteous lives. Those who have no hope in Christ's second coming and resurrection live secular, earthly lives. Yes, we must pray for our hearts to be enlightened to this so we can live the pure lives God called us to.

3. The hope of his calling includes the restoration of creation at our resurrection.

Romans 8:19-21 says,

> For the creation eagerly waits for the revelation of the sons of God. For the creation was subjected to futility – not willingly but because of God who subjected it – in hope that the creation itself will also be set free from the bondage of decay into the glorious freedom of God's children.

When Adam sinned, God cursed the ground. Creation is connected to humanity. In fact, when humanity is living in sin, creation still reacts. In Leviticus 18:28, God commands Israel to not practice sexual immorality, homosexuality, bestiality, and the offering of their children to Molech lest the land vomit them up. The land would react to sin, as it did at the fall.

But, when God restores humanity to righteousness, when the sons of God are resurrected, all creation will be restored as well. This is a tremendous hope. Even though Christians are persecuted and mocked for their beliefs and the way they live, they are the salt of the earth. They are tremendously valuable to all of creation. One day, creation will be set free into the glorious freedom of the children of God. We must continually hope in this, and this hope must drive us.

4. The hope of his calling includes ruling and serving with Christ in the kingdom.

When the Corinthian church was arguing and suing one another, Paul said this in 1 Corinthians 6:1-4:

> When any of you has a legal dispute with another, does he dare go to court before the unrighteous rather than before the saints? Or do you not know that the saints will judge the world? And if the world is to be judged by you, are you not competent to settle trivial suits? Do you not know that we will judge angels? Why not ordinary matters! So if you have ordinary lawsuits, do you appoint as judges those who have no standing in the church?

In essence, Paul is saying, "Why are you hiring the world to judge your disputes? Don't you know that one day you will judge angels? So, how much more should you judge the temporary things of this life? If you really have this hope, it should change how you interact with one another. After all, one day you will rule and judge with Christ!" Romans 8:17 says we are "heirs" with Christ. Whatever belongs to Christ is also ours.

If we really have this hope, we will stop being so consumed with the temporary kingdom of this world. Why live for what's temporary when the eternal is surpassingly better? Why live to rule on this earth, when we are called to rule in the new heaven and the new earth? Christ says, "Blessed are the meek, for they will inherit the earth" (Matt 5:5).

What is your hope in? Is your hope earthly or heavenly? In the same way people with an earthly hope are motivated and driven by it, the hope of our calling in Christ should motivate us. Let us pray for the eyes of our heart to be enlightened and understand the hope of our calling in Christ. Let us pray to be driven by eternal hope.

Application Questions: What hopes drive your life? Why is it so hard to be motivated by our eternal calling? How can we make sure that the hope of our eternal calling is really directing us?

Making it through the day

Apostolic Prayer Focuses on Knowing God's Inheritance in the Saints

> since the eyes of your heart have been enlightened – so that you may know what is the hope of his calling, what is the wealth of his glorious inheritance in the saints,
> Ephesians 1:18

Next, Paul pray for these believers to understand the riches of God's glorious inheritance in the saints. This reality was continually taught about Old Testament Israel. God chose them from all the nations of the earth to be his special inheritance. Deuteronomy 32:9 says, "For the Lord's allotment is his people, Jacob is his special possession."

However, in Ephesians, Paul wrote to both Jews and Gentiles in the church (Eph 3:6). Just as Old Testament Israel was God's great inheritance, so now is the church. This is taught in many New Testament verses:

> As we wait for the happy fulfillment of our hope in the glorious appearing of our great God and Savior, Jesus Christ. He gave himself for us to set us free from every kind of lawlessness and to purify for himself a people who are truly his, who are eager to do good.
> Titus 2:13-14

> But you are a chosen race, a royal priesthood, a holy nation, a people of his own, so that you may proclaim the virtues of the one who called you out of darkness into his marvelous light.
> 1 Peter 2:9

To Titus, Paul said God was purifying for himself a people that were "his very own," eager to do what is good. Peter said the church was "a people belonging to God." I'm not sure that we can fully grasp this reality with our limited minds. Listen to what several commentators said about this:

William MacDonald says:

> It is certainly an exhibition of unspeakable grace that vile, unworthy sinners, saved through Christ, could ever occupy such a place in the heart of God that He would speak of them as His inheritance.[49]

Kent Hughes adds:

> Think of it: he owns all the heavens and numberless worlds, but we are his treasures. The redeemed are worth more than the universe. We ought to be delirious with this truth! Paul prays that we will see this with our heart's eyes.[50]

Application Question: How should we apply this deep reality of believers being God's inheritance?

1. As believers we must remember how much God delights in us and cares for us.

    Zephaniah 3:17 says, "The Lord your God is in your midst; he is a warrior who can deliver. He takes great delight in you; he renews you by his love; he shouts for joy over you."
    God delights in us, he sings over us, and he wants us to have peace in knowing how much he cares for us. As a father, it would hurt my heart for my daughter to be running around frantic and worried about what she will eat, drink, and wear. As her father, I am committed to providing for her. In an even greater way, we are God's, and he will take care of us (cf. Matt 6:26).
    This is especially important to understand when the enemy comes to tempt and make us doubt God's goodness and love for us. This is what he did with Eve in the Garden—tempting her to doubt God and then sin against him. Our enemy still does this today. We must trust that God delights in us and cares for us.

2. As believers we must seek to give God pleasure through our lives.

    As we consider that we are God's inheritance, we must continually seek to please God in everything, for that is why he created us. Consider what Paul prayed for the Colossians:

    > For this reason we also, from the day we heard about you, have not ceased praying for you and asking God to fill you with the knowledge of his will in all spiritual wisdom and understanding, so that you may live worthily of the Lord and please him in all respects – bearing fruit in every good deed, growing in the knowledge of God,
    > Colossians 1:9-10

    Paul desired for the Colossians to please God in every way. In addition, the Psalmist prayed, "May my words and my thought be acceptable in your sight, O Lord, my sheltering rock and my redeemer" (Psalm 19:14). Understanding that we are God's inheritance should motivate us to please him in our every action and attitude.

Application Question: What does the concept of believers being God's inheritance make you think of? How does this reality encourage or challenge you?

Apostolic Prayer Focuses on Knowing God's Great Power in the Saints

> and what is the incomparable greatness of his power toward us who believe, as displayed in the exercise of his immense strength. This power he exercised in Christ when he raised him from the dead and seated him at his right hand in the heavenly realms
> Ephesians 1:19-20

Finally, Paul wants us to comprehend God's great power towards us who believe. It can actually be translated "in us" (cf. Jubilee Bible 2000, Aramaic Bible in Plain English).[51] In fact, in verse 19, he uses "four different Greek synonyms to emphasize the greatness of that power". [52] Kent Hughes' comments are helpful. He says:

> With the Greek synonyms inserted, verse 19 reads like this: "... and his incomparably great power [dunamis] for us who believe. That power [kratos] is like the working [energia] of his mighty strength [ischus]." Paul has layered these synonyms to express as best he can the highest power possible. He exhausted his language describing this power of the resurrection (see v. 20).[53]

Paul is trying to help us comprehend how great the power of God working in us is. It is the same power God used to raise Christ from the dead. Believers need this power for many reasons.

Application Question: Why has God given us this power and why is it necessary for us to access it?

1. This great power is necessary for us to grow in holiness.

    Second Peter 1:3-4 says:

    > I can pray this because his divine power has bestowed on us everything necessary for life and godliness through the rich knowledge of the one who called us by his own glory and excellence. Through these things he has bestowed on us his precious and most magnificent promises, so that by means of what was promised you may become partakers of the divine nature, after escaping the worldly corruption that is produced by evil desire.

This great power is available to both help us escape the corruption in the world and also to continually grow into the image and character of God.

2.   This great power is necessary for us to minister to others.

Paul says:

Toward this goal I also labor, struggling according to his power that powerfully works in me
Colossians 1:29

I am able to do all things through the one who strengthens me.
Philippians 4:13

Whatever God has called us to do, he has given us the power to accomplish. We must realize this.

3.   This great power is necessary to keep our salvation.

First Peter 1:5 says, "who by God's power are protected through faith for a salvation ready to be revealed in the last time." God's power is shielding us until the completion of our salvation—which is when we will look just like Christ. Those who are truly born again will not lose their salvation because God's power keeps them. Christ puts believers in his Father's hand and he places them in his own hand as well. No one will be able to snatch them out of their hands (John 10:28-29).

4.   This great power is necessary to complete our salvation, as we will one day be resurrected.

Romans 8:11 says, "Moreover if the Spirit of the one who raised Jesus from the dead lives in you, the one who raised Christ from the dead will also make your mortal bodies alive through his Spirit who lives in you." The same Spirit and power that raised Christ from the dead will one day raise us from the dead. Thank you, Lord!

The final aspect of apostolic prayer is interceding for ourselves and others to know God's great power within us. Are you interceding to know and experience God's power? Are you asking God to allow others to know and experience it in their home life, marriage, work, and ministry?

In Ephesians 1:20-23, Paul describes how great this power is. God used it to raise Christ from the dead, to seat him in the heavens over the demonic realm, and to make Christ the head of the church. This incomparable great power is at work in us. In the next study, we will give attention to the incomparable greatness of God's power towards us.

Application Question: Why do most Christians live powerless lives? What keeps us from commonly accessing God's power?

Conclusion

How can we develop an apostolic prayer life? What principles can we discern from Paul's prayer in Ephesians 1:15-20?

1. Apostolic prayer comes from a right heart—an informed, selfless, consistent one.
2. Apostolic prayer focuses on knowing God more.
3. Apostolic prayer focuses on knowing the hope of God's plan for the saints.
4. Apostolic prayer focuses on knowing God's inheritance for the saints.
5. Apostolic prayer focuses on knowing God's great power in the saints.

God's Incomparably Great Power

since the eyes of your heart have been enlightened – so that you may know what is the hope of his calling, what is the wealth of his glorious inheritance in the saints, and what is the incomparable greatness of his power toward us who believe, as displayed in the exercise of his immense strength. This power he exercised in Christ when he raised him from the dead and seated him at his right hand in the heavenly realms far above every rule and authority and power and dominion and every name that is named, not only in this age but also in the one to come. And God put all things under Christ's feet, and he gave him to the church as head over all things. Now the church is his body, the fullness of him who fills all in all.
Ephesians 1:18-23 (NET)

How great is God's power at work in the lives of believers?

In Ephesians 1:18-19, Paul prayed for the Ephesians to comprehend how great God's power was in their lives. In fact, he says the power is "incomparably great," meaning that there is no power like it (v. 19). There is no power greater—not the atomic bomb, not love, not hate, nor anything else. Paul tries to describe this power by heaping up synonyms for it in verses 19 and 20. Kent Hughes comments are helpful:

That is why Paul stacked all those power synonyms upon one another in verses 19 and 20 as he prayed that we might experience "his [God's] incomparably great power for us who believe. That power is like the working of his mighty strength, which he exerted in Christ when he raised him from the dead" (italics added). The stupendous power Paul is describing can be glimpsed in the nuances of the synonyms he used: 1) "[P]ower." Dunamis is the word we get dynamite from and is used over 100 times in the New Testament. It indicates raw power or strength. 2) "[W]orking." Energeia, from which we derive our word energy, means "inworking" and suggests the inward propulsion of power. 3) "[M]ighty" (kratos) means "ability to conquer," as when Caesar conquered Cleopatra. Autocrat comes from this word. 4)

"[S]trength" (ischus) refers to physical force. These graphic synonyms in the Pauline bouquet depict the awesome extent of God's power.[54]

The implication of Paul's prayer and description of this power was that these believers were living below the power available to them. This no doubt showed up in an inability to conquer sin, to have joy in Christ, and to persevere through trials.

It's no different for us. We often live lives that are sub-Christian—missing God's best. However, the reality is that God through his divine power has given us everything we need for life and godliness (2 Peter 1:3). There is no legitimate reason why we should lack God's abundant life and holiness—for God has given us his power and resources.

Therefore, in Ephesians 1:20-23, Paul goes to great lengths to describe this power. He says that God publicly displayed this power in Christ, and it is now operating in us.

In this study, we will consider the greatest power the world has ever seen in order to better comprehend what is available to us. And the reason we need to comprehend it is so that we will begin to daily operate in this power.

Big Question: In what ways does Paul describe the extent of God's incomparable great power at work in us in Ephesians 1:20-23? How should we daily access this power?

Christ's Resurrection Displayed God's Incomparably Great Power

and what is the incomparable greatness of his power toward us who believe, as displayed in the exercise of his immense strength. This power he exercised in Christ when he raised him from the dead and seated him at his right hand in the heavenly realms
Ephesians 1:19-20

The greatness of God's power to us was displayed in Christ's resurrection. In the Old Testament, people often measured God's power by the creation of the earth. Isaiah 40:28 says, "Do you not know? Have you not heard? The Lord is an eternal God, the creator of the whole earth. He does not get tired or weary; there is no limit to his wisdom." However, in the New Testament, it is measured by the miracle of the resurrection.

Why is this miracle so great? It is simply because nobody other than Christ has defeated death. Kings, presidents, heroes, and spiritual leaders all die and none have experienced this resurrection. Man has not and cannot conquer death regardless of the great scientific and medical advancements made. No one has or will ever figure out how to stop death. This power is only in God and was displayed in Christ.

Some might say, "Well, Christ was not the first person raised from the dead. There were others." This is true. However, Christ's resurrection was unique. He was the first to be raised from the dead and to never die again.

The first resurrection recorded in the Bible was when Elijah raised the widow's son (1 Kings 17); however, this child eventually died again. Christ raised Lazarus from the dead (John 11), but he also died again later. And every other resurrected person in history eventually died again. Essentially, one could say, "Death, though delayed, eventually got the victory." But this was not true of Christ. He rose from the dead, never to die again. God through his power conquered death. First Corinthians 15:20 says this about Christ: "But now Christ has been raised from the dead, the firstfruits of those who have fallen asleep."

The firstfruits are the first of a harvest, and the firstfruits tell a farmer something about the coming fruits. Christ is the firstfruits of the dead. He was the first resurrected of those who will never die. He is the beginning of what will happen to the church. This was the greatest power ever seen on the earth.

Application Question: What are the applications of this resurrection power for the church?

1. The church has already experienced a spiritual resurrection at salvation through this power.

Ephesians 2:1, 4-5 says this,

And although you were dead in your transgressions and sins ... But God, being rich in mercy, because of his great love with which he loved us, even though we were dead in transgressions, made us alive together with Christ – by grace you are saved!

One of the ways this resurrection power worked in us was by our spiritual resurrection. The word "death" really just means "separation." When Adam sinned in the Garden, he died spiritually. Then when God came to meet with him, Adam hid. In the same way, man now hides from God. He is spiritually dead towards God. His mind is in a state of hostility towards him, and he cannot submit to God's law (Rom 8:7). In fact, God's Word is foolishness to him (1 Cor 2:14).

But when we were resurrected (saved) from spiritual death, this power removed the blindness from our eyes and opened our hearts and minds towards Christ. Now we are alive to God. The Word of God and prayer, which were once dead to us, are now very much alive. We are alive to righteousness and good works. This is God's power at work in us—we have experienced a spiritual resurrection.

2. The church will experience a physical resurrection through this power when Christ returns.

First Corinthians 15:51-57 says,

Listen, I will tell you a mystery: We will not all sleep, but we will all be changed –in a moment, in the blinking of an eye, at the last trumpet. For the trumpet will sound, and the dead will be raised imperishable, and we will be changed. For this perishable body must put on the imperishable, and this mortal body must put on immortality. Now when this perishable puts on the imperishable, and this mortal puts on immortality, then the saying that is written will happen, "Death has been swallowed up in victory." "Where, O death, is your victory? Where, O death, is your sting?" The sting of death is sin, and the power of sin is the law. But thanks be to God, who gives us the victory through our Lord Jesus Christ!

Paul teaches the mystery of the physical resurrection. Some who are alive when Christ returns will never die—they will be changed "in the twinkling of an eye." Their bodies will be transformed into heavenly bodies. And those who previously died will be resurrected from the dead. This is our future if we are truly born again followers of Christ. One day, through God's power, we will be resurrected from the dead.

And no doubt, like Paul, we will sing, "Where, O death, is your victory? Where, O death, is your sting? But thanks be to God who gives us the victory through our Lord Jesus Christ!"

Application Question: How should the reality of the resurrection from dead challenge and encourage believers?

Christ's Ascension and Enthronement in Heaven Displayed God's Incomparably Great Power

and what is the incomparable greatness of his power toward us who believe, as displayed in the exercise of his immense strength. This power he exercised in Christ when he raised him from the dead and seated him at his right hand in the heavenly realms far above every rule and authority and power and dominion and every name that is

named, not only in this age but also in the one to come. And God put all things under Christ's feet ...
Ephesians 1:19-22

Just as man cannot conquer death, he cannot conquer evil. Man has tried education. They say, "If we educate people then the crime rate will go down." Or, "If we place people in a different environment, it will change them." However, these methods do not work. An educated person just commits more intelligent crimes, and a change of environment cannot change man's heart. Man cannot ultimately conquer evil—but evil was conquered in Christ's ascension and seating at the right hand of God. Ephesians 4:8 says, "Therefore it says, 'When he ascended on high he captured captives; he gave gifts to men.'"

This is a picture of a conquering general marching through the city in a parade. Behind him in this parade are those he conquered—his captives—marching in chains with their heads bowed. And as the general marches, he gives gifts to his people. This is what happened with Christ in his ascension. He conquered the devil and gave spiritual gifts to his church (cf. Eph 4:11).

In addition, Colossians 2:15 says, "Disarming the rulers and authorities, he has made a public disgrace of them, triumphing over them by the cross." In Christ's ascension, he disarmed the rulers and authorities. When Paul says, "far above all rule and authority, power and dominion" (v. 21), he seems to be primarily referring to a hierarchy of ruling demons. Just as human armies have generals, colonels, sergeants, and privates, it seems to be that way with demons. Paul also addresses this when he describes the church's spiritual battle in Ephesians 6:12, "For our struggle is not against flesh and blood, but against the rulers, against the powers, against the world rulers of this darkness, against the spiritual forces of evil in the heavens." Christ conquered the devil in his resurrection and ascension. The evil forces gathered against him in his crucifixion were defeated in his resurrection and ascension.

But not only was Christ exalted to the right hand of God over the demonic realm, but over all of creation as King. God put him over "every title that can be given, not only in the present age but also in the one to come" (v.21). Psalm 2, a messianic Psalm, says this:

Why do the nations rebel? Why are the countries devising plots that will fail? The kings of the earth form a united front; the rulers collaborate against the Lord and his anointed king. They say, "Let's tear off the shackles they've put on us! Let's free ourselves from their ropes!" The one enthroned in heaven laughs in disgust; the Lord taunts them. Then he angrily speaks to them and terrifies them in his rage, saying, "I myself have installed my kingon Zion, my holy hill." The king says, "I will announce the Lord's decree. He said to me: 'You are my son! This very day I have become your father! Ask me, and I will give you the nations as your inheritance, the ends of the earth as your personal property. You will break them with an iron scepter; you will smash them like a potter's jar!'" So now, you kings, do what is wise; you rulers of the earth, submit to correction! Serve theLord in fear! Repent in terror! Give sincere homage! Otherwise he will be angry, and you will die because of your behavior, when his anger quickly ignites. How blessed are all who take shelter in him!

In Psalm 2, David prophesied that God would install his Son, the Messiah, over all the kings of the earth. Christ was the Davidic king prophesied about throughout the Old Testament. Paul, while speaking in a synagogue in Antioch, said Christ's installment as the Davidic king was fulfilled at Christ's resurrection. Acts 13:33-34 says,

> ... that this promise God has fulfilled to us, their children, by raising Jesus, as also it is written in the second psalm, 'You are my Son; today I have fathered you.' But regarding the fact that he has raised Jesus from the dead, never again to be in a state of decay, God has spoken in this way: 'I will give you the holy and trustworthy promises made to David.'

Christ now rules in heaven at God's right hand as the Davidic King, but one day he will fully exercise his rule on this earth. Every knee will bow and every tongue will confess that Jesus Christ is Lord (Phil 2:10-11). Amen!

Application Question: What applications can we take from God's power displayed in Christ's ascension and enthronement in heaven?

1. God's power displayed in Christ's ascension and enthronement reminds us that one day we will not only be resurrected but also ascend to heaven as Christ did.

The power of God not only raised Christ from the dead but also took him to heaven. In Acts 1:8-9, we see Christ talking to the apostles and then ascending to heaven in a cloud. Similarly, we will ascend to heaven to be with Christ.

Christ says this in John 14:1-3:

> "Do not let your hearts be distressed. You believe in God; believe also in me. There are many dwelling places in my Father's house. Otherwise, I would have told you, because I am going away to make ready a place for you. And if I go and make ready a place for you, I will

come again and take you to be with me, so that where I am you may be too."

Christ promised his disciples that they would be where he is in heaven. One day he is coming again to take us to heaven. This will be done by the power of God already at work in us.

2. God's power displayed in Christ's ascension and enthronement reminds us that we will one day rule with him.

Scripture already says that we are positionally seated with Christ in the heavenly realms (Ephesians 2:6). This is a present reality because of our union with Christ. However, one day we will rule with him in heaven and on earth, as his co-heirs. Romans 8:17 says, "And if children, then heirs (namely, heirs of God and also fellow heirs with Christ) – if indeed we suffer with him so we may also be glorified with him." We are co-heirs with Christ, and we will share in his glory. Paul teaches that we will even judge the world and angels with Christ (1 Cor 6:2-3).

This is the power operating in us. This power raised and seated us in the heavenly places with Christ. It is through this power that we will rule with Christ eternally on earth and in heaven. Paul wants believers to comprehend the present reality of this power in our lives.

3. God's power displayed in Christ's ascension and enthronement reminds us that we also can conquer sin, Satan, and all powers of the enemy.

This is the very reason that Paul commands the church in Ephesians 6:10-11: "Finally, be strengthened in the Lord and in the strength of his power. Clothe yourselves with the full armor of God so that you may be able to stand against the schemes of the devil." The same power that conquered the devil and his schemes in Christ's ascension and enthronement is working in us to stand against the devil and his schemes. In fact, we are seated with Christ in a position of authority over the enemy (Eph 2:6). God's power has given us everything we need for life and godliness (2 Peter 1:3)—including power to conquer sin and the enemy.

Application Question: How can we operate in Christ's power to conquer sin and the devil in our lives?

Christ's Headship over the Church Displayed God's Incomparably Great Power

> And God put all things under Christ's feet, and he gave him to the church as head over all things. Now the church is his body, the fullness of him who fills all in all.
> Ephesians 1:22-23

The last aspect of the incomparable greatness of God's power Paul emphasizes is Christ's headship over the church. Paul says that God "appointed him to be head over everything for the church which is his body" (v. 22 and 23).

This means that Christ is not only the ruler of angels, demons, and people but also the church. However, the difference is that Christ will rule the powers and principalities and the unredeemed by force with an iron scepter (Psalm 2:9). On the other hand, he will rule with the church in an organic relationship as their head.

In Ephesians Chapter 2, Paul talks about God's formation of a new entity through Christ's death and resurrection. He states that believing Jews and Gentiles were created into a third race—the church (v. 14-15)—and this race has become the body of Christ. God's power is not only displayed in Christ's rulership over the church, but in the church becoming Christ's body—inextricably linked forever.

In verse 23, Paul says, "Now the church is his body, the fullness of him who fills all in all." This verse has stimulated great discussion amongst commentators.

 Interpretation Question: What does the "the fullness of him who fills all in all" refer to?

 1. Some commentators believe this verse refers to Christ being the fullness of God who fills all in all.

"Him" would then refer to God instead of Christ. John Stott explains the first view this way:

> The first explanation takes the phrase as a description not of the church (the body) but of Christ (the head), i.e. '… the church, which is the body of him who is the fullness of him who fills all in all'. In this case Paul is saying not that the church is the fullness of Christ, but that Christ is the fullness of God, who fills Christ as indeed he fills all things.[55]

This view presents several problems: "For one thing the syntax is awkward, requiring God to be both subject and object of the same sentence ('God … gave as head to the church Christ who is the fullness of God')."[56]

Another potential problem is that Scripture never explicitly says Christ is the fullness of God. It does say that God's fullness dwells in Christ (Col 2:9).

However, Scripture does teach that God fills "all in all." It says he fills the heavens and the earth (Jeremiah 23:24) and that the highest heavens cannot contain him (1 Kings 8:27).

2. Some commentators believe this verse refers to the church being the fullness of Christ and yet Christ filling all in all.

The problem with this view is that it would imply that Christ is incomplete without the church. If this is a correct interpretation, Paul obviously meant it in a paradoxical sense. [57] The God who needs nothing and is independent has chosen to depend upon his church. In the same way that a body cannot function without a head, a head cannot function without the body. Christ has chosen to work through his church on the earth and throughout eternity, and if the church does not work, then his work does not get done. This is a great mystery. In view of this, John Calvin proclaimed:

This is the highest honor of the church that, unless He is united to us, the Son of God reckons Himself in some measure imperfect. What an encouragement it is for us to hear, that not until He has us as one with Himself is He complete in all His parts, or does He wish to be regarded as whole![58]

3. Some commentators believe this verse refers to Christ being the fullness of the church and yet filling all in all.

Christ filling the church is taught throughout Scripture. Believers are the temple of the Holy Spirit (1 Cor 6:19) and Christ indwells them (Eph 3:17).

In further support of this view, Paul says in Ephesians 4:10, "He, the very one who descended, is also the one who ascended above all the heavens, in order to fill all things." Since Paul connects Christ's ascension with filling "all things," it's very plausible that he is doing the same thing in Ephesians 1:23. This interpretation has the fewest difficulties and is most likely the correct interpretation.[59]

Application Question: What applications can we take from the concept of Christ being the head and the church being his body?

1. The church must submit to Christ, even as a body submits to its head. Without submitting to Christ, we can do nothing good; in fact, we harm ourselves when we operate outside of his will. Therefore, it is a necessity for us to abide in Christ and hear his voice.

2. The church need one another, even as the members of a body need one another. Paul says the eye can't say to the hand, "I do not need you" (1 Cor 12:21). We need each other because God's power has made us one body, and therefore dependent upon one another. To try to be independent, as many in the church do, is to spiritually impoverish ourselves.

3. The church shares the glory of Christ—the Head. Whatever glory bestowed upon a head is also bestowed upon the body, for they are one and the same. It is the same with us, as the body of Christ. Christ has given us his glory and we will one day rule with him (cf. John 17:22, Rom 8:17).

As the ascended Christ is the conqueror of the powers and principalities, he is also the honored Head of the church. God's great power has made Christ the head and us his body. Thank you, Lord! Amen.

Application Question: How is God calling you to honor Christ as your head in your daily life and also by working with and serving his body?

Application

Certainly, Paul did not want the Ephesians to just comprehend this power, but also to experience it daily. He himself desired this, as seen in Philippians 3:10: "My aim is to know him, to experience the power of his resurrection, to share in his sufferings, and to be like him in his death." He also prays for the Ephesians to experience more of God's power in Ephesians 3:16: "I pray that according to the wealth of his glory he may grant you to be strengthened with power through his Spirit in the inner person."

Application Question: How can we daily experience the power of the resurrection in our lives?

1. In order to daily experience the power of the resurrection, we must pray for it.

As Paul prays for the Ephesians to be strengthened with power in the inner being (3:16), we must also pray this for ourselves and others. Through prayer, we access God's power. To fail to pray is to walk without it—in our own strength.

2. In order to daily experience the power of the resurrection, we must have faith.

Christ says that if we have faith the size of a mustard seed, we can move mountains (Matthew 17:20). Some Christians never experience this power because they believe God for too little. They want to get to heaven, but they have no real desire to be used by God on earth. When God calls them to step out in faith, they have every excuse to not believe or obey him (cf. Judges 6:15). Christ said he couldn't do many miracles in his home town because of their lack of faith (Mk 6:5), and no doubt, this is also true for many believers and churches today.

3. In order to daily experience the power of the resurrection, we must allow God to use us in our weakness.

Second Corinthians 12:9-10 says,

But he said to me, "My grace is enough for you, for my power is made perfect in weakness." So then, I will boast most gladly about my weaknesses, so that the power of Christ may reside in me. Therefore I am content with weaknesses, with insults, with troubles, with persecutions and difficulties for the sake of Christ, for whenever I am weak, then I am strong.

It is in our weakness that God shows himself strong. Many times he allows us to go through trials and become weak just so we can experience the power of the resurrection in our lives and ministries (cf. 2 Cor 1:9). Sometimes he calls us to serve outside of our giftedness—outside of where we are comfortable—so we can experience his power. And when we experience it, we start to learn that we can't live without it.

How is God making you weak so you can experience his power?

4. In order to daily experience the power of the resurrection, we must abide in Christ.

John 15:5 says, "I am the vine; you are the branches. The one who remains in me – and I in him – bears much fruit, because apart from me you can accomplish nothing." Remaining in Christ, or "abiding," as it can be translated, is a discipline. It includes reading the Word of God, prayer, worship, church fellowship, and serving. By making our home in Christ, we experience the power of the vine in and through our lives. Those who fail to abide—those who fail to live a life of discipline—will lack power and therefore fruitfulness in their lives.

Are you experiencing God's power in your life and ministry?

Application Questions: Are there any areas in your life where you especially need to experience God's power? How is God calling you to more faithfully appropriate it?

Conclusion

How great is God's power in the life of a believer? God's divine power has given us everything we need for life and godliness (2 Pet 1:3). This power is at work in us (Eph 1:18-19), and we must comprehend it and appropriate it daily.

1. Christ's resurrection displayed God's incomparably great power.
2. Christ's ascension and enthronement in heaven displayed God's incomparably great power.
3. Christ's headship over the church displays God's incomparably great power.

Characteristics of True Believers

And although you were dead in your transgressions and sins, in which you formerly lived according to this world's present path, according to the ruler of the kingdom of the air, the ruler of the spirit that is now energizing the sons of disobedience, among whom all of us also formerly lived out our lives in the cravings of our flesh, indulging the desires of the flesh and the mind, and were by nature children of wrath even as the rest... But God, being rich in mercy, because of his great love with which he loved us, even though we were dead in transgressions, made us alive together with Christ – by grace you are saved! –and he raised us up with him and seated us with him in the heavenly realms in Christ Jesus, to demonstrate in the coming ages the surpassing wealth of his grace in kindness toward us in Christ Jesus.
Ephesians 2:1-7 (NET)

What are characteristics of true believers?

In Ephesians 1:19, Paul prays for believers to comprehend God's great power at work in them. He then describes how this same power resurrected Christ from the dead and seated him in heavenly places, far above all rule and authority (Eph 1:20-21). God's power in Christ conquered the grave and evil in Christ's resurrection, ascension, and rule. This same power is at work in believers.

In Ephesians 2:1-7, Paul demonstrates how God's power works in us by describing the believer's past, present, and future. He describes what God's power has done in our lives, what it is doing, and what it will do. Therefore, he is giving characteristics of true believers, those who have experienced God's power.

This is one of the problems with the contemporary church. It is full of people who declare, "I know God," and "I am a Christian." But their lives bear no marks of his power—of a saving relationship with him.

If the power that raised Christ from the dead and seated him above all authorities is at work in us, there will be evidence. As we consider these characteristics of true believers, we must consider whether we possess them.

For if the past and present reality of a true believer are not ours, we can be sure the future reality of a believer (mainly heaven) is not ours as well.

Christ said that in the last days many will declare, "Lord, Lord" but he will reply, "I never knew you." (Matt 7:23). Are the characteristics of a true believer in your life? Have you experienced the incomparable power of God that is at work in those who believe (Eph 1:19)?

Big Questions: What are the characteristics of true believers—their past, present, and future? What applications should we take from these truths?

True Believers Were Delivered from Spiritual Death

> And although you were dead in your transgressions and sins,
> Ephesians 2:1

The first thing God's power does in the life of every true believer is deliver him from death. Paul says, "And although you were dead in your transgressions and sins" (v.1). Since one of Paul's major aims in this book is to teach the unification of Gentile and Jew in God's church (cf. Eph 2:14-15), he often addresses one group, then the other. When he says "you" in verse 1, he is referring to the Gentiles. Before coming to Christ, the Gentiles were dead in their transgressions and sins. Then Paul includes the Jews as well in Ephesians 2:3, when he says, "all of us also formerly lived out our lives in the cravings of our flesh," and "were by nature children of wrath even as the rest..." This was not just a reality for the Gentiles, but for all mankind.

Before Christ, all are dead in their transgressions and sins.

Interpretation Question: What does Paul mean by mankind being "dead" in their transgressions and sins?

Obviously, he was not referring to physical death for they were all alive—reading or listening to this letter. He was referring to spiritual death. "Death" really just means separation. When a person dies, his body is separated from his spirit. But when a person dies spiritually, he is separated from God.

When Adam sinned in the Garden, the first thing he did was hide from God. Sin affected his relationship with God. Adam no longer desired to walk and talk with him in the Garden. In fact, he hid from God. Adam's sin caused this desire to hide, and it is now in his offspring.

When Paul says "transgression," he is referring to an action or thought "committed in open violation of a known law."[60] In the Garden, Adam committed a transgression when he broke the law God gave him. He also committed a "sin," which means "to miss the mark." This term was used of hunting with a bow and arrow.[61] Adam missed the mark of God's holiness (cf. Rom 3:23).

When God created Adam and all mankind, he made them in the image of God (Gen 1:27). And this is what all mankind has missed—they have missed the mark of God's holiness in thought, speech, and action. Therefore, all men are dead in their transgressions and sins. Romans 6:23 says, "For the payoff of sin is death." This is what transgressions and sins earned mankind—separation from God.

One characteristic of being dead is not responding to stimuli. If you play music to a corpse, it cannot hear it, feel it, or enjoy it, and therefore will not respond. A corpse cannot relate to someone because it is dead. This is the state of mankind spiritually. They are dead to God and the things of God. They cannot respond to God.

Paul says, "The unbeliever does not receive the things of the Spirit of God, for they are foolishness to him. And he cannot understand them, because they are spiritually discerned" (1 Corinthians 2:14). The natural man cannot accept the things that come from the Spirit, nor can he understand them. It is impossible because they are spiritually discerned. Spiritually dead men cannot accept the Word of God; they cannot accept the worship of God. There is a natural antagonism towards the things of God.

What about other religions and how people seek other gods?

Scripture says this is actually a rejection of the true God. Since man will not accept the true God, they make up idols in their own image or the images of other creatures (Rom 1:21-23). But they will not seek the true God. They cannot. Romans 3:11-12 says, "there is no one who understands, there is no one who seeks God. All have turned away."

This is the state of mankind—dead to God. They cannot understand God, have turned away from him, and won't seek him. They are dead in transgressions and sins.

Interpretation Question: Does this mean that man can do no good?

Man is still made in the image of God, even though he is damaged by sin and has a fallen nature (Gen 9:6). Therefore, he has a tremendous capacity to do good, as he naturally reflects God. However, man can do nothing good that pleases God, nor can he contribute to his salvation. Romans 3:12 says, "there is no one who shows kindness, not even one." Even man's righteous deeds are like filthy rags in God's eyes (Isaiah 64:6). This is true because man's works come from a wrong heart—a heart full of pride, selfish ambition, envy, and jealousy—a heart lacking love (cf. 1 Cor 13:1-3). This is often called the "depravity of man."

In considering both man's good works and man's state of spiritual death, John MacArthur's comments are helpful:

Man's common state of sin has often been compared to a diverse group of people standing on the bank of a wide river, perhaps a mile across. Each of them is trying to jump to the other side. The little children and old people can jump only a few feet. The larger children and agile adults can jump several times that far. A few athletes can jump several times farther still. But none of them gets near the other side. Their degrees of success vary only in relation to each other. In relation to achieving the goal they are equal failures.

Throughout history people have varied greatly in their levels of human goodness and wickedness. But in relation to achieving God's holiness they are equal failures. That is why the good, helpful, kind, considerate, self–giving person needs salvation as much as the multiple murderer on death row. The person who is a good parent, loving spouse, honest worker, and civic humanitarian needs Jesus Christ to save him from the eternal condemnation of hell as much as the skid row drunk or the heartless terrorist. They do not lead equally sinful lives, but they are equally in the state of sin, equally separated from God and from spiritual life.[62]

Warren Wiersbe adds:

All lost sinners are dead, and the only difference between one sinner and another is the state of decay. The lost derelict on skid row may be more decayed outwardly than the unsaved society leader, but both are dead in sin—and one corpse cannot be more dead than another! This means that our world is one vast graveyard, filled with people who are dead while they live (1 Tim. 5:6).[63]

This is the state of all believers before they come to Christ. We "were" dead in our transgressions and sins, and every true believer understands their sinful state before God, even as the Ephesians did. First John 1:8 says, "If we say we do not bear the guilt of sin, we are deceiving ourselves and the truth is not in us." When John says the truth is not in us, he is probably referring to the gospel. Assurance of salvation is one of the themes of 1 John. He writes to those who believe in the Son of God so that they may know they have eternal life (1 John 5:13). Without recognition of our sin, depravity, and deadness to God, nobody can be saved. In order to understand the gospel—the good news—one must first understand the bad news—man's spiritual death and need for a savior. If one does not recognize and accept it, he cannot be saved. He cannot trust in his good works, baptism, the prayers of the saints, etc., and be saved.

This is important to understand, for there are those who think they are without sin or that their sins aren't that bad, and that they can be saved apart from grace. It was especially important for the Jews to hear this, for many Jews believed they could keep the law perfectly and thus merit salvation. Even the rich man who approached Christ believed he had kept the law, and therefore was kept from salvation—though he desired it (Matt 19:20).

True believers recognize their sin. Paul said he was the chief or worst of sinners (1 Tim 1:15). When Peter met Christ, he declared "I am a sinful man!" (Luke 5:8). Isaiah declared that he had unclean lips, and so did his people (Isaiah 6:5). True believers recognize their deadness in sin and call out to Christ. Without understanding this reality, one cannot be saved.

Have you called out to Christ for salvation? Romans 10:13 says, "Everyone who calls on the name of the Lord will be saved."

What are other characteristics of true believers?

Application Question: Briefly share your salvation story. How did you come to a conscious understanding of your sin and deadness before God so you could accept Christ?

True Believers Were Delivered from a Life of Disobedience

in which you formerly lived according to this world's present path, according to the ruler of the kingdom of the air, the ruler of the spirit that is now energizing the sons of disobedience, among whom all of us also formerly lived out our lives in the cravings of our flesh, indulging the desires of the flesh and the mind, and were by nature children of wrath even as the rest....
Ephesians 2:2-3

Observation Question: What powers control and lead people into disobedience, as seen in verses 2-3?

Next, in verses 2-3, Paul describes how believers previously lived a lifestyle of disobedience. Ephesians 2:2 calls unbelievers "children of disobedience" (KJV). Before Christ, we followed the world, Satan, and the flesh into disobedience towards God. It is not that believers are no longer tempted by these three forces, because they are. However, true believers no longer follow these three forces as a lifestyle. A lifestyle of disobedience and captivity to these forces no longer characterizes them because of God's power in salvation. First John 3:9-10 says this:

Everyone who has been fathered by God does not practice sin, because God's seed resides in him, and thus he is not able to sin, because he has been fathered by God. By this the children of God and the children of the devil are revealed: Everyone who does not practice righteousness – the one who does not love his fellow Christian – is not of God.

A true believer no longer lives a lifestyle of disobedience by following these forces.

Now we will consider these three influences which control the lives of unbelievers and still tempt believers.

1. Before Christ, believers followed the ways of this world.

When Paul says "world," he is not referring to the physical world but to the social value-system in the world, which is against God.[64] The world is a system of thoughts and beliefs that contradict God and his Word. It is a system of groupthink, where everybody is expected to think the same. John Stott calls it "cultural bondage."[65] It includes how people view success, beauty, family, riches, power, and life in general.

The world is trying to conform everybody into the same image and draw people away from following God. Romans 12:2 says, "Do not be conformed to this present world, but be transformed by the renewing of your mind, so that you may test and approve what is the will of God – what is good and well-pleasing and perfect."

The world is trying to mold people into the same pattern. This shows up in many forms and ideologies. One of the major patterns in this world today is pluralism and relativism. It says, "You can believe anything you want to believe, and if it's good for you it's OK, as long as it doesn't hurt anybody else." The problem with this is that you lose absolutes. There is no real right or wrong—except for believing in absolute truth. Sexual immorality is OK. Homosexuality is OK. Adultery is OK. Divorce is acceptable. But anything that claims to be absolute truth is wrong. In a society like this, Christianity becomes more and more marginalized and persecuted because it teaches "absolutes." One should not lie, steal, or cheat. Sexual immorality is wrong. Homosexuality is wrong. Christ is the only way to heaven. This claws at the world system and stirs it to anger because the world constantly aims to mold people, even believers, into its form.

However, those who have been truly saved, though still affected by the world, are not characterized by it. Again, Paul says, "in which you formerly lived [in disobedience] according to this world's present path" (Eph 2:2). This means true believers no longer live according to the groupthink and cultural bondage of the world. They are different, and this will heap up persecution towards them. First Peter 4:3-4 says,

For the time that has passed was sufficient for you to do what the non-Christians desire. You lived then in debauchery, evil desires, drunkenness, carousing, drinking bouts, and wanton idolatries. So they are astonished when you do not rush with them into the same flood of wickedness, and they vilify you.

A true Christian will commonly find himself mocked, considered strange, or even persecuted. Others will say, "You don't want to get drunk on the weekend." "You don't have sex before marriage." "You won't help us cheat on this test." "You won't lie." "You don't curse." "What's wrong with you?" Believers will continually be considered strange because they no longer follow the ways of this world. In fact, John said this reality is a test of true salvation. First John 2:15 says, "Do not love the world or anything in the world. If anyone loves the world, the love of the Father is not in him."

When John says, "the love of the Father is not in him," he is saying this person is not saved. He does not love God. In fact, assurance of salvation is the very theme of the book (cf. 1 John 5:13).

Are you still following the ways of this world? Or has God changed you? Those who are born again no longer follow the ways of this world. As Paul says in Galatians 6:14, "the world has been crucified to me, and I to the world."

2.   Before Christ, believers followed the ways of the devil.

Not only did believers follow the way of the world before they knew Christ, but they also followed the ways of the devil. Paul said the Ephesians followed "the ruler of the kingdom of the air, the ruler of the spirit that is now energizing the sons of disobedience" (Eph 2:2). Now when Paul talks about "the ruler of the spirit that is now energizing the sons of disobedience," he is not saying that every unbeliever is possessed. Scripture teaches that Satan is not omnipresent like God. He cannot be in more than one place at once. The way he works in unbelievers is by tempting them through the world system, demons, and the flesh to be disobedient to God.

Interpretation Question: What types of temptation does Satan use?

• Satan tempts people through lies.

In the first temptation, he lied to Eve, saying that if she ate of the tree she would be like God. He also implied that God lied to her and didn't want the best for her. This is true of Satan's work in the world system as well. It is a system built on lies. It says, "People must do this; they must do that; they must think this way; they must dress that way." It is a system based on the lies of the devil.

- Satan tempts people through fear.

Scripture says he is a roaring lion seeking whom he may devour (1 Peter 5:8). Lions roar to provoke fear in their prey. Satan tempts through fear—fear of the future, fear of the past, fear of what other people think. Proverbs 29:25 says, "The fear of people becomes a snare." Through fear Satan handicaps people and keeps them from following God and doing his will.

- Satan tempts people through the love of money and power.

When he tempted Jesus, he appeared to him and said, "If you bow down to me, I will give you all the kingdoms of this world" (Matt 4:9, paraphrase). This is exactly what the majority of the world is running after. They are seeking money and fame, and it keeps them away from following God. First Timothy 6:10 says, "For the love of money is the root of all evils. Some people in reaching for it have strayed from the faith and stabbed themselves with many pains."

Certainly, there are many other ways the enemy tempts people including "the lust of the flesh, the lust of the eyes, and the pride of life" (1 John 2:16, KJV).

Interpretation Question: What does Paul mean by the "ruler of the kingdom of the air"?

When Paul says this, he seems to be talking about something in the heavenly realms. Scripture teaches that Satan has innumerable demons following his bidding, and they have some type of rule in the heavenly realms. We get a clear picture of this in Daniel 10. Daniel, a Jewish administrator in Babylon, was fasting for three weeks, and during that time, he saw a vision of an angel. The angel told Daniel that he initially came to answer his prayer when he first prayed, but he was resisted by the Prince of Persia, referring to a demon ruling in that country (v. 13). The angel gave Daniel revelation, and then said he was leaving to fight with the Prince of Persia and that the Prince of Greece would come as well (v. 20).

Scripture teaches that Satan is the prince of this world (John 12:31) and the prince of demons (Matt 9:34). He works to control this world and the people in it, not only through the world system but through a hierarchy of demons. Their place of rule is the heavenly realms—the air.

Paul talks about this further in Ephesians 6:12 when he says, "For our struggle is not against flesh and blood, but against the rulers, against the powers, against the world rulers of this darkness, against the spiritual forces of evil in the heavens."

Before Christ, we were not only following the world, but we were following the influence of the devil through his demons.

3.   Before Christ, believers followed the lusts and desires of the flesh.

The final way believers were controlled and influenced to disobey God is through the flesh. When Paul said the flesh, he is not referring to the body. The body itself is neutral—it can be used for good or bad. However, within our bodies, we have a "fallen nature" passed on from Adam. We have a nature full of lusts and desires for evil things. MacArthur says this about lusts and desires:

> Epithumia (lusts) refers to strong inclinations and desires of every sort, not simply to sexual lust. Thelēma (desires) emphasizes strong will-fullness, wanting and seeking something with great diligence. As with trespasses and sins, lusts and desires are not given to show their distinctiveness but their commonness. They are used synonymously to represent fallen man's complete orientation to his own selfish way.[66]

We lust for sex outside of marriage, for wealth and power, for excessive food and sleep, etc. However, if we are now following Christ, we are no longer controlled by these desires because the power and control of the flesh was broken by Christ. Romans 6:6-7 says, "We know that our old man was crucified with him so that the body of sin would no longer dominate us, so that we would no longer be enslaved to sin. (For someone who has died has been freed from sin)." These desires no longer control us, but they still tempt us and can become strongholds in our lives.

Application Question: How can a believer walk in daily victory over these forces?

Believers maintain this victory by battling. They battle to no longer be conformed to this world, but to be transformed by the renewing of their minds (Romans 12:2). They transform their minds by continually meditating on and practicing Scripture. They buffet their bodies and make them slaves through continual discipline (1 Cor 9:27). Paul says, "train yourself for godliness" (1 Tim 4:7). Through rigorous spiritual disciplines like meditating on Scripture, prayer, church fellowship, repentance and serving others, we control our flesh. Paul says, "live by the Spirit and you will not carry out the desires of the flesh" (Gal 5:16). Finally, we defeat the devil by relying on God's power. Nothing in our flesh will work. Paul tells these believers to be strong in the Lord and his mighty power to stand against the devil. They must put on the full armor of God—a daily righteous lifestyle—to have victory (Eph 6:10-18).

Application Questions: In what ways did the world, Satan, and the flesh control your unregenerate life? In what ways have you experienced freedom from the control of these forces? In what ways do you still find yourself tempted by them?

True Believers Were Delivered from Wrath

> were by nature children of wrath even as the rest...
> Ephesians 2:3b

Next, Paul says the Ephesians were objects of wrath before they accepted Christ. When he says "we," he includes the Jews with the Gentiles (v. 3). Though raised in the Jewish faith, they were objects of wrath before they were saved.

Interpretation Question: What does Paul mean when he calls unbelievers objects of wrath?

Objects of wrath could mean one of two things:

1. Unbelievers have a natural disposition towards "anger, malice, bitterness, and hot temper."[67]

Before Christ, we are naturally prone towards anger and wrath to various degrees. This anger is demonstrated towards both God and man. Romans 8:7 says, "the outlook of the flesh is hostile to God, for it does not submit to the law of God, nor is it able to do so." The natural man is hostile towards God, his Word, and many times also his people. Jesus says, "If the world hates you, be aware that it hated me first" (John 15:18). In fact, the end times will be characterized by hostility towards Christians. Matthew 24:9 says, "Then they will hand you over to be persecuted and will kill you. You will be hated by all the nations because of my name."

This is part of the reason John teaches that love for the brethren is a proof of salvation. "We know that we have crossed over from death to life because we love our fellow Christians. The one who does not love remains in death" (1 John 3:14). Paul himself knew this well. Before Christ, he persecuted believers—he arrested and even consented to their death. But after Christ, he loved the brothers and even willingly suffered for them.

But not only were we prone towards anger at God, his Word, and believers, but also people in general. Anger and unforgiveness often characterize our relationships with others and sometimes even our families. Some of the characteristics of the sin nature within us are hatred, discord, fits of rage, and dissensions (Gal 5:20). However, when we are saved and walking in the Holy Spirit, we show love, peace, and patience towards God and others.

Before Christ, people are antagonistic towards God and his Word, and often towards both believers and people in general. But in Christ, these same people are now the meek who will inherit the earth (Matt 5:5). We are the merciful who will receive mercy (Matt 5:7), and the peacemakers who will be called sons of God (Matt 5:9).

Application Questions: In what ways did wrath characterize you before Christ? How did Christ change you? How do you still struggle with a tendency towards anger?

2.   Unbelievers are objects of God's wrath.

Not only do unbelievers have a disposition towards wrath, but they are under the wrath of God. John 3:36 says, "The one who believes in the Son has eternal life. The one who rejects the Son will not see life, but God's wrath remains on him."

Because God is a holy God, he cannot look upon sin. Therefore, mankind—who is characterized by sin— is under his just wrath.

Interpretation Question: In what ways is the unbelieving world under the wrath of God?

This wrath is seen in at least two ways.

- The wrath of God is seen in God handing the world over to sin and disobedience and allowing mankind to reap the consequences of rebellion.

Romans 1:18 says, "For the wrath of God is revealed from heaven against all ungodliness and unrighteousness of people who suppress the truth by their unrighteousness."

Throughout the rest of Romans 1, Paul describes how the world has chosen not to acknowledge God, and therefore, he has handed them over to idolatry, sexual immorality, homosexuality, and all types of sin. Essentially, God says, "Fine, you don't want to acknowledge me. Reap the consequences of your sin."

When we look at the world, we see the wrath of God. His wrath is seen in his handing man over to his own devices. God allows people to turn away from him and reap the consequences: division in families, discord in relationships, wounds and sickness from sexual immorality, government corruption, etc. All these sins and consequences reflect God's wrath on unbelievers. When people refuse to acknowledge him, God hands them over to sin and its consequences

- But ultimately, the wrath of God will be seen in eternal separation from him and judgment in hell.

Revelation 20:15 says, "If anyone's name is not found written in the book of life, that person was thrown into the lake of fire."

In hell there will be various degrees of punishment based on the amount/degree of sin committed and one's knowledge of God and his Word. The one who knew the Master's will and was still disobedient will be beaten with many blows. But he who did not know shall be beaten with few blows (Lk 12:47-48). In either case, hell is a place where unbelievers bear God's eternal wrath for their sins.

Application Question: In what ways do you see the wrath of God clearly displayed in society (cf. Rom 1:18-32)?

True Believers Have Experienced a Spiritual Resurrection

But God, being rich in mercy, because of his great love with which he loved us, even though we were dead in transgressions, made us alive together with Christ – by grace you are saved!
Ephesians 2:4-5

In verse 4, there is a dramatic change in the direction of the passage. In verses 1-3, we see the depth of our sin and our depravity before Christ, and then in verse 4, we see God who saves us. Paul essentially says our salvation had nothing to do with us. Dead men and women can't save themselves. It is totally a work of God based on his character. Paul doesn't say that one day man decided to try harder; he says that God saved us.

Observation Question: What characteristics of God led him to save us?

1. God saved us because of his great love.

The word used for "love" here is agape in the Greek. It is a volitional love—an act of the will. God looked upon us as we were dead in sin and decided to bestow his love on us. One of the major characteristics of God is love. First John 4:8 simply says, "God is love." It defines who he is. In fact, before he created man, he was not bored in heaven. He was living in a perfect love relationship with the Son and the Holy Spirit. His character is love.

John 3:16 says, "For God so loved the world, that he gave his only begotten Son, that whosoever believeth in him should not perish, but have everlasting life" (KJV).

John 15:13 says, "No one has greater love than this – that one lays down his life for his friends." While in our sin, God loved us and moved to save us.

What other characteristics intrinsic to God's nature led him to save us?

2.   God saved us because of his mercy.

Mercy is "feelings of pity, compassion, affection, kindness. It is a desire to succor, to tenderly draw to oneself and to care for."[68]

Because of his mercy, he withholds the wrath we deserve and provided a way for us to be saved through his Son, Jesus Christ.

3.   God saved us because of his grace.

Mercy means he withholds the wrath we deserve. Grace means he gives us what we don't deserve—unmerited favor. Salvation is a gift of grace. It means that we can do nothing to merit or earn it. It is nothing we can work for.

This is the fallacy of all the religions in the world: they teach that people can earn salvation. But the gospel tells us that we are not good enough to receive God's favor. We are objects of God's wrath because of our sin. Our only hope is grace—unmerited favor—which comes through Jesus Christ.

Ephesians 2:8-9 says, "For by grace you are saved through faith, and this is not from yourselves, it is the gift of God; it is not from works, so that no one can boast." No one can boast of their salvation, for even the ability to believe—faith—is a gift of God. We were too dead in our sin to believe, and therefore God gave us the grace to respond to him.

Interpretation Question: What does this new life—this spiritual resurrection—look like in the life of a believer?

In the same way that spiritually dead people are characterized by a lack of responsiveness to spiritual stimuli, spiritually alive people are characterized by responsiveness to spiritual stimuli. For example:

1.   People who have been spiritually resurrected love God.

Instead of being hostile to God and Christ (Rom 8:7), these people love God and continually want to know him more. Consider these verses:

My aim is to know him, to experience the power of his resurrection, to share in his sufferings, and to be like him in his death, and so, somehow, to attain to the resurrection from the dead.
Philippians 3:10-11

As a deer longs for streams of water, o I long for you, O God! I thirst for God, or the living God. say, "When will I be able to go and appear in God's presence?" I cannot eat, I weep day and night; all day long they say to me, "Where is your God?"
Psalm 42:1-3

2.   People who have been spiritually resurrected love the people of God.

First John 3:14 says, "We know that we have crossed over from death to life because we love our fellow Christians. The one who does not love remains in death."

3.   People who have been spiritually resurrected are drawn to prayer.

Romans 8:15 says, "For you did not receive the spirit of slavery leading again to fear, but you received the Spirit of adoption, by whom we cry, 'Abba, Father.'"

4.   People who have been spiritually resurrected study and obey the Word of God.

John 14:21 and 24 say this:

The person who has my commandments and obeys them is the one who loves me. The one who loves me will be loved by my Father, and I will love him and will reveal myself to him... The person who does not love me does not obey my words.

5.   People who have been spiritually resurrected continually put to death sin in their lives.

Romans 8:13-14 says,

(for if you live according to the flesh, you will die), but if by the Spirit you put to death the deeds of the body you will live. For all who are led by the Spirit of God are the sons of God.

When Paul describes those who live according to the sinful nature, he is talking about unbelievers. However, those who by the Spirit put sin to death are those who are alive—they are sons of God.

Is there a continual decreasing of sin in your life? If you are saved, the Holy Spirit continually works in your life to convict you of sin, to help you hate it and overcome it. Believers are continually putting sin to death in their lives.

Praise God for saving us because of his love, mercy, and grace! Praise God for his power which gave us new life! Thank you, Lord! Amen.

Application Questions: In what ways are you continually experiencing the fruits of the spiritual resurrection in your life? How should a person respond if he is lacking these fruits?

True Believers Have Been United with Christ

> But God, being rich in mercy, because of his great love with which he loved us, even though we were dead in transgressions, made us alive together with Christ – by grace you are saved! and he raised us up with him and seated us with him in the heavenly realms in Christ Jesus, to demonstrate in the coming ages the surpassing wealth of his grace in kindness toward us in Christ Jesus.
> Ephesians 2:4-7

Another present reality of all believers is their unity with Christ. Paul mentions this reality throughout the epistle in many different ways. He begins the epistle with the greeting, "From Paul, an apostle of Christ Jesus by the will of God, to the saints [in Ephesus], the faithful in Christ Jesus" (Ephesians 1:1). These believers were physically located in Ephesus, and at the same time spiritually located "in Christ Jesus." He goes on to say how they have every spiritual blessing "in Christ" (v. 3). He says believers were chosen "in Christ" (v. 4). In verse 7, "in him" we have redemption through his blood and forgiveness of sins. Paul is enraptured with the theology of believers being in Christ, and we should be as well. This is what happened to us at salvation—we were spiritually united with Christ.

Observation Question: In what ways is our spiritual union with Christ reckoned in verses 4-7?

1.   Believers were made alive with Christ in his resurrection (v. 4).

When Paul says, God "made us alive with Christ," he is referring to our death and resurrection in Christ. When Christ died on the cross, God reckoned us as being with him. All our sins were with him on the cross. When he was put into the grave, we were with him. When he was resurrected, we were with him. Our sins and our old nature were left in the grave in order for us to live a new life in Christ. Paul focuses on this same reality when telling the Romans why they should no longer live in sin. Consider what he says in Romans 6:1-6:

> What shall we say then? Are we to remain in sin so that grace may increase? Absolutely not! How can we who died to sin still live in it? Or do you not know that as many as were baptized into Christ Jesus were baptized into his death? Therefore we have been buried with him through baptism into death, in order that just as Christ was raised from the dead through the glory of the Father, so we too may live a new life. For if we have become united with him in the likeness of his death, we will certainly also be united in the likeness of his resurrection. We know that our old man was crucified with him so that the body of sin would no longer dominate us, so that we would no longer be enslaved to sin.

This is why we should no longer live as slaves to sin—because we died to it and were raised to live a new life with Christ.

2. Believers ascended with Christ to the heavenly realms and now are seated with him (v. 6).

Paul says, "And he [God] raised us up with Christ and seated us with him in the heavenly realms in Christ Jesus." When Christ ascended to heaven (Acts 1), we ascended with him. He is now seated at the right hand of God, far above all rule and authority (including the demonic rule, Eph 1:20-21). This means we rule with him and also have authority over the enemy with him. This is our new position in Christ—whatever is his is ours.

Application

As an application, this union must continually identify us. Paul says this in Galatians 2:20: "I have been crucified with Christ, and it is no longer I who live, but Christ lives in me. So the life I now live in the body, I live because of the faithfulness of the Son of God, who loved me and gave himself for me." Paul didn't even see himself as living any more. Christ was living through him. It must be the same for us. We died with Christ and were resurrected and ascended with him. We are ruling with him in the heavenly realms. We are seated over all power and rule of the devil because of our union to our resurrected and ascended Lord.

This reality must grasp us, and it must become our identity, as it was Paul's.

Application Question: How should our identity in Christ affect our daily lives? How can we become more consumed with this reality, even as Paul was?

True Believers Will Glorify God's Grace in the Coming Ages

> and he raised us up with him and seated us with him in the heavenly realms in Christ Jesus, to demonstrate in the coming ages the surpassing wealth of his grace in kindness toward us in Christ Jesus.
> Ephesians 2:6-7

Finally, we see the future of believers. Though they are presently seated and ruling with Christ in the heavenly realms, this reality will not be fully consummated until the redemption of our bodies at Christ's second coming.

In the future, we will physically rule with Christ in the heavens and on earth. With that said, our ascension and ruling with Christ was not God's ultimate purpose in our salvation. God's ultimate purpose was to "to demonstrate in the coming ages the surpassing wealth of his grace in kindness toward us in Christ Jesus" (v. 7).

Our salvation and union with Christ will be a testimony to all throughout eternity. It will bring glory to God's grace. Paul has been emphasizing God's purpose to glorify his grace in salvation from early in chapter 1. He says this in verses 1:6, 12, 14:

> to the praise of the glory of his grace that he has freely bestowed on us in his dearly loved Son.
> Ephesians 1:6

> so that we, who were the first to set our hope on Christ, would be to the praise of his glory.
> Ephesians 1:12

> who is the down payment of our inheritance, until the redemption of God's own possession, to the praise of his glory.
> Ephesians 1:14

In fact, we see the angels and all the people in heaven glorifying God for his great salvation in Revelation 7:10-12:

> They were shouting out in a loud voice, "Salvation belongs to our God, to the one seated on the throne, and to the Lamb!" And all the angels stood there in a circle around the throne and around the elders and the four living creatures, and they threw themselves down with their faces
> to the ground before the throne and worshiped God, saying, "Amen!

Praise and glory, and wisdom and thanksgiving, and honor and power and strength be to our God for ever and ever. Amen!"

God's grace in salvation will be our focus in worship throughout eternity. In fact, Paul shares how it was especially a part of God's plan to demonstrate this grace and wisdom to the angels, who have never experienced God's grace and mercy in salvation. Paul says this in Ephesians 3:10: "The purpose of this enlightenment is that through the church the multifaceted wisdom of God should now be disclosed to the rulers and the authorities in the heavenly realms." First Peter 1:12 says the angels long to look into the gospel. They desire to understand it. We are their teachers now and throughout eternity. This is God's ultimate purpose in salvation—the glory of God.

With that said, this should not just be our focus in heaven, but also on earth. God saved us to bring glory to himself. Therefore, this must be our constant endeavor. Paul said, "Whether you eat or drink, do all things to the glory of God" (1 Cor 10:31, paraphrase).

Are you living to glorify God on a daily basis?

Application Question: How has God been challenging you to bring glory to him in your daily endeavors?

Conclusion

As we consider Ephesians 2:1-7, we see characteristics of true believers. We see their past, their present, and their future. If we have not experienced the realities of true believers in our past and present, we can be sure that the future of true believers—heaven, ruling with Christ, and bringing glory to his grace—will not be our reality.

What are characteristics of true believers?

1. True believers were delivered from spiritual death.
2. True believers were delivered from a life of disobedience.
3. True believers were delivered from wrath.
4. True believers have experienced a spiritual resurrection.
5. True believers have been united with Christ.
6. True believers will glorify God's grace in the coming ages.

Characteristics of True Believers—Part Two

> For by grace you are saved through faith, and this is not from
> yourselves, it is the gift of God; it is not from works, so that no one can
> boast. For we are his workmanship, having been created in Christ
> Jesus for good works that God prepared beforehand so we may do
> them.
> Ephesians 2:8-10 (NET)

What are characteristics of true believers? How does God save those he loves?

In Ephesians 2:1-7, Paul describes the Ephesians' salvation experience—past, present, and future. They were dead in transgressions and sins; they followed the ways of the world, the devil, and the flesh. They were objects of wrath, but God, through his power, made them alive with Christ. He seated them in heavenly places. And his eternal purpose in their salvation is to display the glory of the riches of his grace. The believer's salvation is for God—to bring glory to him.

These realities are true of every believer because of God's power (cf. Eph 1:18-19). True believers have experienced the power of God in their lives. If we have not experienced these radical changes, we must ask whether or not we have truly been born again.

In Ephesians 2:8-10, Paul further describes characteristics of a true believer's salvation.

Big Question: What are the characteristics of true believers? What is the process of salvation?

True Believers Are Saved by Grace Alone

> For by grace you are saved
> Ephesians 2:8

Interpretation Question: What does "grace" mean, and how are believers saved by it?

Salvation is by grace because dead men cannot save themselves (Eph 2:1). Salvation comes through the unmerited favor of God on sinful people. It is by God's initiative alone, not man's. After the fall, man naturally began to hide from God, as Adam did. God had to seek after Adam to find him. This is the message of the Bible; it is the gospel—God seeking after man.

"For God so loved the world, that he gave his only begotten Son, that whosoever believeth in him should not perish, but have eternal life" (John 3:16, KJV). Salvation is by God's initiative.

In fact, Paul says, "And if it is by grace, it is no longer by works, otherwise grace would no longer be grace" (Romans 11:6). This means that one cannot be saved by church attendance, being born into a Christian family, baptism, observance of the Lord's Supper, or any other "good work."

It is a work totally of God. And for this reason, only those who recognize this can be saved. Listen to what Christ teaches in Matthew 5:3, "Blessed are the poor in spirit, for the kingdom of heaven belongs to them."

When he says, "poor in spirit," he is referring to those who recognize their spiritual poverty. They recognize that they can do nothing to merit salvation. They are spiritually bankrupt, and therefore need the riches of God's grace. This is very similar to what Christ teaches in Matthew 18 about the kingdom of heaven. He held a child and said this to his disciples, "I tell you the truth, unless you turn around and become like little children, you will never enter the kingdom of heaven!" (v. 3).

The word used for "child" was used of a very small child—an infant or toddler. Christ was saying, "Unless you recognize your weakness and inability to help yourself like an infant does, then you cannot be saved." Salvation is only by grace.

Who or what are you trusting for salvation? Anything other than God's grace will not work.

 Application Questions: What are some common works that people trust in for their salvation? Why must salvation be by grace and not works?

True Believers Are Saved through Faith

> For by grace you are saved through faith, and this is not from yourselves, it is the gift of God; it is not from works, so that no one can boast.
> Ephesians 2:8-9

Not only is a person saved by grace, every person who will be saved must put his faith in Christ. We see this taught throughout Scripture.

In Acts 16:31, Paul said this to a jailer about how to be saved, "Believe in the Lord Jesus and you will be saved, you and your household." Similarly,

John says, "But to all who have received him – those who believe in his name – he has given the right to become God's children" (John 1:12).

✤ John MacArthur tells a helpful story:

> The story is told of a man who came eagerly but very late to a revival meeting and found the workmen tearing down the tent in which the meetings had been held. Frantic at missing the evangelist, he decided to ask one of the workers what he could do to be saved. The workman, who was a Christian, replied, "You can't do anything. It's too late." Horrified, the man said, "What do you mean? How can it be too late?" "The work has already been accomplished," he was told. "There is nothing you need to do but believe it."[69]

Some people struggle with the concept of putting faith in Christ. However, faith is a crucial part of life and society. John MacArthur says,

> Every person lives by faith. When we open a can of food or drink a glass of water we trust that it is not contaminated. When we go across a bridge we trust it to support us. When we put our money in the bank we trust it will be safe. Life is a constant series of acts of faith. No human being, no matter how skeptical and self–reliant, could live a day without exercising faith.[70]

Interpretation Question: What are the characteristics of true saving faith?

1. True faith believes the content of the gospel.

Paul declares that in order for a person to be saved, he must have belief, or faith (Eph 2:8). However, faith is only as good as the object of our faith. We don't believe in faith; we believe in the object or the content of our faith.
What is the content of true saving faith?

- The content includes an admission that we cannot save ourselves. We cannot work for our salvation, nor can we earn it. Everyone is totally lost because of sin. And as Romans 6:23 says, "For the payoff of sin is death."

Because of our sins, we are separated from a holy God, and we will ultimately be separated from him eternally in a burning fire that will not be quenched. The writer of Hebrews says, "without it [holiness] no one will see the Lord" (Heb 12:14).
It is this reality that drives a person to come to Christ and be saved. He realizes that he needs a savior.

- The content includes belief in the death, burial, and resurrection of Christ for the sins of the world. Paul says,

> by which you are being saved, if you hold firmly to the message I preached to you – unless you believed in vain. For I passed on to you as of first importance what I also received – that Christ died for our sins according to the scriptures, and that he was buried, and that he was raised on the third day according to the scriptures
> 1 Corinthians 15:2–4

The content is both bad news and good news. The bad news is that we are both separated from and under the wrath of a just God because of our sins. But the good news is that God's Son came to earth and died for our sins, was buried, and rose again on the third day so that one day those who believe in him will rise again. This is the content of the gospel.

However, it must be noted that intellectual belief in the gospel alone is not sufficient for salvation.

2. True faith is committed to the Lord of the Gospel.

The word "faith" used here in Ephesians 2:8 is more than just intellectual belief. In Greek this word can be translated as "trust," "commit," or even "obedience." The word in classical Greek was used of those in a contractual relationship.[71] There is a commitment of the will and not just the mind.

This is important to say because there are some who say that intellectual belief alone is enough for salvation. However, James tells us that even the demons believe and shudder—and they're obviously not saved (James 2:19). Simple belief that Jesus is God and Savior isn't enough. We must also choose to follow and obey him. In Luke 14:26-27, Jesus says this:

> "If anyone comes to me and does not hate his own father and mother, and wife and children, and brothers and sisters, and even his own life, he cannot be my disciple. Whoever does not carry his own cross and follow me cannot be my disciple."

To have faith means to accept Jesus Christ as Lord of our lives (cf. Rom 10:9-10). It includes repentance as a person turns away from his former life and begins to follow Christ. A transfer of leadership must take place. This is important to understand because many make false confessions. Christ warns us about this in the Sermon on the Mount. He says,

"Not everyone who says to me, 'Lord, Lord,' will enter into the kingdom of heaven – only the one who does the will of my Father in heaven. On that day, many will say to me, 'Lord, Lord, didn't we prophesy in your name, and in your name cast out demons and do many powerful deeds?' Then I will declare to them, 'I never knew you. Go away from me, you lawbreakers!'
Matthew 7:21–23

Many in the church have only belief—only profession. They have right doctrine. They know that Christ is Lord, and they even serve him in the church, but they are not truly saved. Christ says true faith leads to doing the "will" of the Father in heaven (v. 21).

   3. True faith is a gift of God.

Warren Wiersbe says, "The word 'that' in Eph. 2:8 [this in the NIV], in the Greek, is neuter; while 'faith' is feminine. Therefore 'that' cannot refer to 'faith.' It refers to the whole experience of salvation, including faith."[72] Faith is a gift that God gives believers by his grace. Consider these verses:

For it has been granted to you not only to believe in Christ but also to suffer for him,
Philippians 1:29

When they heard this, they ceased their objections and praised God, saying, "So then, God has granted the repentance that leads to life even to the Gentiles."
Acts 11:18

True faith is a gift from God, and for this reason no one can boast about saving themselves. In heaven, there will not be a bunch of people beating their chests over achieving salvation. All will be humbled before God's great grace.

Application Questions: Why do you believe false faith is so common in the church (cf. Matt 7:21-23)? What are some characteristics of false faith?

True Believers Are Saved Eternally

For by grace you are saved
Ephesians 2:8

Not only is salvation by grace and through faith, salvation is also eternal. We can see this in the Greek tense used in "you are saved" (Eph 2:8). "The tense of the Greek participle shows that salvation has happened in the past with continuing results. It's a done deal."[73] Salvation is eternal and cannot be lost.

John 3:16 says, "For this is the way God loved the world: He gave his one and only Son, so that everyone who believes in him will not perish but have eternal life." Eternal life by nature is life that never ends. If a person could lose this life or if it stopped, it would have never been eternal.

Interpretation Question: How does Scripture teach that salvation is eternal and cannot be lost?

1.   Salvation is eternal because Christ keeps believers eternally.

Listen to what Christ says about the salvation of those who come to him:

> "For I have come down from heaven not to do my own will but the will of the one who sent me. Now this is the will of the one who sent me – that I should not lose one person of every one he has given me, but raise them all up at the last day. For this is the will of my Father – for everyone who looks on the Son and believes in him to have eternal life, and I will raise him up at the last day."
> John 6:38-40

Christ came down to earth to do his Father's will, and his Father's will was that he would lose none of those given to him. Who are the ones given to him? They are the elect, chosen before the foundation of the earth, as Paul talks about in Ephesians 1:4. "For he chose us in Christ before the foundation of the world that we may be holy and unblemished in his sight."

All those who were chosen before the foundation of the earth, all those who come to Christ, shall have eternal life and be raised up on the last day. If Christ could fail at this, how could he be God—for God cannot fail?

Interpretation Question: How does Christ keep those who are saved?

•   In heaven, Christ prays for the believers. Hebrews 7:25 says, "So he is able to save completely those who come to God through him, because he always lives to intercede for them." He prays for those who come to him so he can save them "completely." This is exactly what Christ did for Peter when he was tempted by Satan to deny Christ. He said, "I have prayed for your faith so that it will not fail" (Lk 22:32, paraphrase).

- Christ never allows believers to be tempted beyond what they are able to bear (1 Cor 10:13). In John 18, when Jesus was betrayed, he protected the disciples from being taken by the soldiers. John says, "He said this to fulfill the word he had spoken, 'I have not lost a single one of those whom you gave me.'" (John 18:9). Christ did this because he knew the disciples' faith was too weak. They would have ultimately fallen away from God if they had to give their lives for Christ at that point. He protected their faith in the trial.

- Christ keeps believers secure in his hand. In John 10:28, he says, "I give them eternal life, and they will never perish; no one will snatch them from my hand."

2. Salvation is eternal because the Holy Spirit keeps believers eternally.

Ephesians 4:30 says, "And do not grieve the Holy Spirit of God, by whom you were sealed for the day of redemption." He seals and keeps believers until eternal redemption.

3. Salvation is eternal because God, the Father, keeps believers eternally.

John 10:29 says, "My Father, who has given them to me, is greater than all, and no one can snatch them from my Father's hand."

Salvation is eternal because God does it. He saves his people by grace. It is not based on anything they did or will do. It is based totally on the unmerited favor of God. Therefore, salvation is eternal. It was completed in the past and has continuing results in the future. The entire Trinity keeps the salvation of believers through grace.

Application Questions: Many believers believe that one can lose his salvation. Why? What is the evidence for this position? Which view do you believe is most supported by Scripture?

True Believers Are Saved for Good Works

For we are his workmanship, having been created in Christ Jesus for good works that God prepared beforehand so we may do them. Ephesians 2:10

Interpretation Question: What does it mean for believers to be God's "workmanship"?

One of the reasons God created us was for the purpose of doing good works. Titus 2:13-14 says,

> as we wait for the happy fulfillment of our hope in the glorious appearing of our great God and Savior, Jesus Christ. He gave himself for us to set us free from every kind of lawlessness and to purify for himself a people who are truly his, who are eager to do good.

Christ is making a unique people on the earth who are eager for good works. Paul calls believers God's workmanship. Kent Hughes said this:

> The word "workmanship" comes from the Greek word poiema, from which we derive our English word "poem." The Greek literally means, "that which has been made — a work — a making," and sometimes it is even translated as "poem." [74]

This word can also be translated "masterpiece," as in the New Living Translation. MacDonald adds:

> In other words, God has a blueprint for every life. Before our conversion He mapped out a spiritual career for us. Our responsibility is to find His will for us and then obey it. We do not have to work out a plan for our lives, but only accept the plan which He has drawn up for us. This delivers us from fret and frenzy, and insures that our lives will be of maximum glory to Him, of most blessing to others, and of greatest reward to ourselves. [75]

God has a calling on each of our lives. In the same way God called Jeremiah to be a prophet even before he was born, he calls us for his purpose as well (cf. Jer 1:5). There are two things we must consider about this. (1) God works in us to prepare us for good works. (2) God works through us to complete the good works. Philippians 2:13 says, "for the one bringing forth in you both the desire and the effort – for the sake of his good pleasure – is God."

However, the order is important. Before God works through us, he must first work in us. How does God work in those he saves? How does he prepare his masterpieces?

Interpretation Question: How does God prepare his masterpieces? How does he work in those he has saved to prepare them for good works?

1. God prepares his masterpieces through giving them the Holy Spirit.

Ezekiel 36:27 says, "I will put my Spirit within you; I will take the initiative and you will obey my statutes and carefully observe my regulations." God gives us his Spirit to change us, to empower us, and to guide us into the good works he prepared for us. Romans 8:14 says that those who are sons are led by the Holy Spirit. God leads believers into good works as they submit to him.

2.   God prepares his masterpieces through the Word of God.

Second Timothy 3:16-17 says, "Every scripture is inspired by God and useful for teaching, for reproof, for correction, and for training in righteousness, that the person dedicated to God may be capable and equipped for every good work."

Through studying Scripture, God conforms us into his image and equips us for every good work. If we aren't studying his Word, we cannot complete the works God prepared for us. It is by his Word that he makes us grow. First Peter 2:2 says, "And yearn like newborn infants for pure, spiritual milk, so that by it you may grow up to salvation."

Are you allowing God to prepare you for good works through his Word?

3.   God prepares his masterpieces through prayer.

Before Christ began his ministry, he spent forty days praying and fasting in the wilderness (cf. Lk 4:1-14). When he left the wilderness, he was filled with the power of the Holy Spirit in order to do his ministry (v. 14).

In addition, there was a time when the disciples could not cast out a demon, even though Christ had given them the power to do so. When they asked why they couldn't cast it out, Christ responded, "This kind can come out only by prayer" (Mark 9:29). This probably meant that the disciples had ceased to live a lifestyle of prayer, and therefore were powerless to do God's work. Often, we can't complete God's work because we also have ceased to pray.

Moreover, God prepares his masterpieces through the prayers of others. Paul commonly asked for prayer in order to do the works God called him to accomplish. In Ephesians 6:19, Paul petitioned, "Pray for me also, that I may be given the message when I begin to speak – that I may confidently make known the mystery of the gospel."

Are you dwelling in prayer and asking others to continually pray for you? God prepares men and women for good works through prayer.

4.   God prepares his masterpieces through waiting seasons.

Abraham was prepared through years of waiting in the promised land. Moses was trained by forty years of waiting in the wilderness. God prepared

David through waiting. God prepared Paul through years in Arabia and then in Tarsus before he began his ministry in Antioch. Christ waited thirty years for his ministry. While waiting, God works in our hearts and teaches us how to trust him to fulfill his call on our lives.

Are you willing to patiently wait?

5. God prepares his masterpieces through trials.

    Hebrews 12:7 and 11 say this:

    Endure your suffering as discipline; God is treating you as sons. For what son is there that a father does not discipline?... Now all discipline seems painful at the time, not joyful. But later it produces the fruit of peace and righteousness for those trained by it.

God prepares his saints for a harvest of righteousness and peace through trials. God prepared Joseph while he served as a slave and a prisoner in Egypt. God prepared David by giving him an employer, King Saul, who constantly hunted and tried to kill him. God prepared Christ through the wilderness, temptation, and suffering (cf. Heb 5:8). God prepares his people for good works through trials. Paul says this:

    Blessed is the God and Father of our Lord Jesus Christ, the Father of mercies and God of all comfort, who comforts us in all our troubles so that we may be able to comfort those experiencing any trouble with the comfort with which we ourselves are comforted by God.
    2 Corinthians 1:3-4

Paul says the very reason God allowed him and his associates to suffer was so that they could comfort others with the comfort received from God. God prepares his ministers through trials.

Are you submitting to God in your trials so he can prepare you for greater ministry?

6. God prepares his masterpieces through the discipleship of other mature Christians.

    Elisha was trained by Elijah. Samuel was trained by the priest Eli. The apostles were trained by Jesus. Mark was trained by Barnabas and Peter. Timothy was trained by Paul. In fact, Paul said this to Timothy: "Because of this I remind you to rekindle God's gift that you possess through the laying on of my hands" (2 Timothy 1:6). Through this relationship, God imparted a spiritual gift to Timothy. This was probably very similar to how Elisha received a double portion from Elijah.

In the same way, when one is discipled by a mature Christian, God will often impart the gifts of the discipler to the disciple. He gifts people in evangelism, counseling, helps, administration, leadership, etc. I personally have watched the gifts of others materialize in my life as I was poured into by them.

Proverbs 27:17 says, "As iron sharpens iron, so a person sharpens his friend." God prepares his masterpieces for good works by the sharpening of other godly masterpieces.

Who is sharpening you? Who are you sharpening?

Let us remember that in order for God to work through us, we must allow him to work in us. He has given us his Spirit to guide this process. Are you allowing him to continually prepare you for good works?

Application Questions: In what ways has God prepared you for specific works? In what ways is God continually preparing you? Are there any ministry visions that God has given you?

True Believers Should Have Assurance of Salvation

> For by grace you are saved through faith, and this is not from yourselves, it is the gift of God; it is not from works, so that no one can boast. For we are his workmanship, having been created in Christ Jesus for good works that God prepared beforehand so we may do them.
> Ephesians 2:8-10

The final thing that we must notice is that Paul knew the Ephesians were saved, with the implication—that the Ephesians knew it as well. The doctrine of assurance of salvation is unique to Christianity. In other religions, there can be no assurance because salvation is based on one's works. If people are saved by their works, how can they know if they attained salvation or are good enough to be accepted by God? Even Catholicism does not teach assurance of salvation. I recently read that when Pope Benedict XVI died, Pope Francis called for the faithful to pray him into heaven.[76] If the Pope can't have assurance of heaven, how can anybody else?

This is because Catholicism teaches that faith plus works is needed for salvation, and therefore, one cannot have assurance. However, Paul teaches that the Ephesians had "been saved". Again, the perfect tense means something completed in the past with continuing results. And the rest of Scripture teaches this as well. Because we are saved by grace alone and not our works, lest any man should boast, we can have assurance of salvation.

In fact, Scripture teaches that every Christian should seek assurance. Assurance is different from eternal security. Eternal security teaches that if a person is truly saved, he will never lose his salvation because God will keep him. God knows those who are his (2 Tim 2:19); however, assurance is the believer knowing that he is saved. And this is something the believer must seek. Consider these passages:

> Therefore, brothers and sisters, make every effort to be sure of your calling and election. For by doing this you will never stumble into sin.
> 2 Peter 1:10

> but I declared to those in Damascus first, and then to those in Jerusalem and in all Judea, and to the Gentiles, that they should repent and turn to God, performing deeds consistent with repentance.
> Acts 26:20

> Put yourselves to the test to see if you are in the faith; examine yourselves! Or do you not recognize regarding yourselves that Jesus Christ is in you – unless, indeed, you fail the test!
> 2 Corinthians 13:5

Peter says that believers must make their calling and election sure. Paul says that after they repented, believers must prove their repentance by their deeds. In 2 Corinthians 13:5, he commands believers to test the reality of their salvation.

This is how one gains assurance. Believers are God's workmanship, created for good works. These good works prove one's salvation. If we are without them, then we are probably not saved. John Calvin wrote, "It is faith alone that justifies, but faith that justifies can never be alone."[77] Similarly, consider what Christ declares in Matthew 7:21 about some who profess salvation. He says, "Not everyone who says to me, 'Lord, Lord,' will enter into the kingdom of heaven – only the one who does the will of my Father in heaven."

These are the ones who are saved—those who faithfully do God's will.

Interpretation Question: How can we test our salvation so we can have assurance?

1. Assurance of salvation comes from a changed relationship to sin.

First John 3:9-10 says,

> Everyone who has been fathered by God does not practice sin, because God's seed resides in him, and thus he is not able to sin,

because he has been fathered by God. By this the children of God and the children of the devil are revealed: Everyone who does not practice righteousness – the one who does not love his fellow Christian – is not of God.

The believers' relationship to sin changes because God placed his divine nature within them. They don't desire to sin and can't enjoy it as they used to. When they fail, that failure leads to conviction and mourning. Has God changed your relationship to sin? This is one of the proofs of salvation.

2. Assurance of salvation comes from a changed relationship with other believers.

First John 3:14-15 says,

We know that we have crossed over from death to life because we love our fellow Christians. The one who does not love remains in death. Everyone who hates his fellow Christian is a murderer, and you know that no murderer has eternal life residing in him.

Christ says this in John 13:35, "Everyone will know by this that you are my disciples – if you have love for one another.'"

Has God given you a love for other believers? If so, you love to be with them. You love to serve them with your spiritual gifts. You love to pray for them. You love to sacrifice for them. This radical love for believers will identify you as a Christian to others, and it also will help assure you of your salvation.

3. Assurance of salvation comes from obedience to God's Word.

Consider these texts:

On that day, many will say to me, 'Lord, Lord, didn't we prophesy in your name, and in your name cast out demons and do many powerful deeds?' Then I will declare to them, 'I never knew you. Go away from me, you lawbreakers!' "Everyone who hears these words of mine and does them is like a wise man who built his house on rock. The rain fell, the flood came, and the winds beat against that house, but it did not collapse because it had been founded on rock. Everyone who hears these words of mine and does not do them is like a foolish man who built his house on sand. The rain fell, the flood came, and the winds beat against that house, and it collapsed; it was utterly destroyed!" Matthew 7:22-27

But be sure you live out the message and do not merely listen to it and so deceive yourselves.
James 1:22

The church is full of those who listen to the Word every Sunday but do not obey it. They are deceiving themselves about their salvation. One day the judgment will come and prove that the foundation of their house was not on God and his Word. Only those who do the Father's will are saved (Matt 7:21).

It is God's will for you to have not only salvation, but also assurance of salvation. Paul says, "Repent and prove your repentance by your deeds." Peter says, "Make your election sure." The way we do this is by growing. We are not saved by good works, but true salvation will always produce good works. Those who are truly saved are new creations in Christ; old things have passed away, all things have become new (2 Cor 5:17).

Do you have assurance of salvation?

Application Questions: Some have said that assurance of salvation is a lost doctrine—most churches don't teach it and most Christians don't understand it. Do you think this is true? Why or why not? Do you have assurance of salvation? If so, how? If not, why not?

Conclusion

1. True believers are saved by grace alone.
2. True believers are saved through faith.
3. True believers are saved eternally.
4. True believers are saved for good works.
5. True believers should have assurance of salvation.

Remembering Christ the Peacemaker

Therefore remember that formerly you, the Gentiles in the flesh – who are called "uncircumcision" by the so-called "circumcision" that is performed on the body, by human hands – that you were at that time without the Messiah, alienated from the citizenship of Israel and strangers to the covenants of promise, having no hope and without God in the world. But now in Christ Jesus you who used to be far away have been brought near by the blood of Christ. For he is our peace, the one who made both groups into one and who destroyed the middle wall of partition, the hostility, when he nullified in his flesh the law of commandments in decrees. He did this to create in himself one new man out of two, thus making peace, and to reconcile them both in one body to God through the cross, by which the hostility has been killed. And he came and preached peace to you who were far off and peace to those who were near, so that through him we both have access in one Spirit to the Father.
Ephesians 2:11-18 (NET)

How can we live in peace with one another and with God?

After the fall, a great division entered the world. Adam and Eve hid from one another, and they both hid from God. From that moment, Eve would always try to usurp her husband and Adam would try to dominate his wife (Gen 3:16). Sin caused separation among people and between God and man. We now live in a world marked by division. The world is full of racism, ethnocentrism, elitism, agnosticism, atheism, and many other views that separate.

However, in the midst of this darkness, God promised to send a seed that would crush the head of the serpent—Satan—who started the conflict (Genesis 3:15). This seed would mend the division that was in the world and bring peace and unity. Here in Ephesians 2:11-18, Paul emphasizes how Christ is this peacemaker.

The major theme of this passage is peace; it is mentioned four times (14, 15, and twice in 17). When Christ was born on earth, the angels announced, "Glory to God in the highest, and on earth peace among people with whom he is pleased!" (Lk 2:14). Christ came to the earth to bring peace to men—peace with one another and with God. Therefore, the answer to the division in the world is Christ—the peacemaker.

Sadly, even those who know Christ are still prone to division. Churches split, couples divorce, and believers harbor deep seated unforgiveness towards one another and sometimes even towards God. How then can believers operate in the peace that Christ brought?

Moreover, Matthew 5:9 says, "Blessed are the peacemakers, for they will be called the children of God." Those who have experienced Christ's peace should be peacemakers in this world. How can we live in peace and be those who bring peace?

These questions were important to the Ephesians, as discord seemed to be a problem in this mixed congregation of Jews and Gentiles. The Jews and the Gentiles had conflict over culture, and deep-seated animosity from their past. In this passage, Paul speaks to these Christians struggling with division and reminds them of their peace in Christ. We often need reminders of this as well, so we can live in peace instead of the discord which often mars our contemporary churches.

Big Questions: How does Christ provide peace for the world? How can believers continually live in peace with God and with one another?

In Order to Have Peace, Believers Must Remember Their Sad State Before Christ

> Therefore remember that formerly you, the Gentiles in the flesh – who are called "uncircumcision" by the so-called "circumcision" that is performed on the body by human hands – that you were at that time without the Messiah, alienated from the citizenship of Israel and strangers to the covenants of promise, having no hope and without God in the world.
> Ephesians 2:11-12

In targeting the Ephesian discord, Paul calls the Gentiles to remember their sad state before they met Christ. He gives six characteristics of their pre-Christian life.

Observation Question: How does Paul characterize the Gentiles before they met Christ?

1. The Gentiles had a hostile relationship with the Jews.

He says, "Therefore remember that formerly you, the Gentiles in the flesh – who are called "uncircumcision" by the so-called "circumcision" that is performed on the body by human hands" (Eph 2:11).

The Jews called Gentiles "uncircumcised" as a racial slur. David called Goliath an "uncircumcised Philistine" before slaying him (1 Sam 17:26). Circumcision was the sign of God's covenant with the Jews, which he originally gave to Abraham (Gen 17:11). On the eighth day, Jews surgically removed the foreskin of their male children's reproductive organ.

Circumcision was always meant to represent an inward circumcision—a change of heart. Moses said this to Israel in Deuteronomy 10:16, "Therefore, cleanse [circumcise] your heart and stop being so stubborn!"

In fact, Paul says that to have a circumcised flesh and not a circumcised heart was uncircumcision—it counted for nothing. Romans 2:28-29 says,

> For a person is not a Jew who is one outwardly, nor is circumcision something that is outward in the flesh, but someone is a Jew who is one inwardly, and circumcision is of the heart by the Spirit and not by the written code. This person's praise is not from people but from God.

Unfortunately, the Jews, who were called to be God's priests to the world (Ex 19:6), hated the Gentiles and ceased to be missionaries to them. Instead, they despised the Gentiles and exalted themselves. A good example of this is the story of Jonah. God called Jonah to preach repentance to the Ninevites, but instead of speaking to them, he ran from God. And when he repented and did preach to the Ninevites, he was angry at God for saving them.

The ancient division between Jews and Gentiles is comparable to that between blacks and whites in America during slavery and immediately after. It's comparable to the war between the Shiites and Sunni Muslims. One commentator says the "enmity between Jews and Gentiles was the greatest racial and religious difference the world has ever known."[78] It was deep-seated, and it is still prominent throughout the world, as seen in anti-Semitism.

William Barclay helps us understand this ancient hostility, especially on the Jewish side. He writes:

> The Jew had an immense contempt for the Gentile. The Gentiles, said the Jews, were created by God to be fuel for the fires of hell. God, they said, loves only Israel of all the nations that he had made ... It was not even lawful to render help to a Gentile mother in her hour of sorest need, for that would simply be to bring another Gentile into the world. Until Christ came, the Gentiles were an object of contempt to the Jews. The barrier between them was absolute. If a Jewish boy married a Gentile girl, or if a Jewish

girl married a Gentile boy, the funeral of that Jewish boy or girl was carried out. Such contact with a Gentile was the equivalent of death.[79]

Paul called for the Gentiles to remember the great hostility they once had with their (now) Jewish brothers in Christ.

2. The Gentiles were without Christ.

Paul also says, "that you were at that time without the Messiah" (v. 12). How were they separate from Christ? The promise of the messiah was given to Israel (cf. Gen 22:18). Most Gentiles knew nothing of it. In fact, when Christ came to the earth, he came first to the lost sheep of Israel (Matt 15:24). The Gentiles were without the messiah.

3. The Gentiles were without citizenship in Israel.

The Gentiles were excluded from citizenship in Israel. Why did this matter? God gave the Jews his commandments and his temple—where his presence dwelled. God gave Israel priests who were called to minister before him day and night. In order to worship God, Gentiles had to become Jewish converts like Ruth and Rahab, but even then, they were still excluded from many aspects of worship because they lacked citizenship.

4. The Gentiles were without covenants.

When people disobeyed God at the tower of Babel, God chose to redeem the earth through a new way—through Abraham. Therefore, God made covenants with his children—Israel. Consider what Paul says about the Jews in Romans 9:4-5:

who are Israelites. To them belong the adoption as sons, the glory, the covenants, the giving of the law, the temple worship, and the promises. To them belong the patriarchs, and from them, by human descent, came the Christ, who is God over all, blessed forever! Amen.

God made covenants with Abraham, Isaac, Jacob, David, and the nation of Israel. He promised to give them a land, to give them the messiah, and to use them to spread the knowledge of God throughout the earth. God said this through Jeremiah:

"I, Lord, make the following promise: 'I have made a covenant with the day and with the night that they will always come at their proper times.

Only if you people could break that covenant could my covenant with my servant David and my covenant with the Levites ever be broken. So David will by all means always have a descendant to occupy his throne as king and the Levites will by all means always have priests who will minister before me.
Jeremiah 33:20-21

The Gentiles had no such covenants. They were without them.

5. The Gentiles were without hope.

How were they without hope? John MacArthur's comments are helpful:

Most Gentiles of Paul's day either thought that death ended all existence or that it released the spirit to wander aimlessly in some nether world throughout the rest of eternity. Death brought only nothingness or everlasting despair. The Greek philosopher Diogenes said, "I rejoice in sport in my youth. Long enough will I lie beneath the earth bereft of life, voiceless as a stone, and shall leave the sunlight which I love, good man though I am. Then shall I see nothing more. Rejoice, O my soul, in thy youth." [80]

Since there was no true hope in the afterlife, many lived for pleasure. Like Paul, they said, "If the dead are not raised, let us eat and drink, for tomorrow we die'" (1 Cor 15:32).
Even those who worshiped the gods of the ancient world lived in fear, not hope. Since their gods were made in the image of men, they were evil, jealous, lustful, and wicked. They often warred with people. Theirs was truly a life without hope, even if they lived a religious life.

6. The Gentiles were without God.

As mentioned, most believed in many gods; however, they didn't believe in the one true God. This speaks to those today who believe that to worship Buddha, Allah, Yahweh, etc., is to worship the same God. Scripture does not teach such a view. The pagans were polytheistic, and yet, they were without God. There is only one God—the God of Scripture.
In fact, Scripture teaches that to worship other gods is a result of denying the true God. Romans 1:21-23 says,

For although they knew God, they did not glorify him as God or give him thanks, but they became futile in their thoughts and their senseless hearts were darkened. Although they claimed to be wise, they became fools and exchanged the glory of the immortal God for an image resembling mortal human beings or birds or four-footed animals or reptiles.

The Gentiles were in discord with the Jews, without Christ, without citizenship, without the covenants, without hope, and without God. And this was true for all of us as well, in a sense. Apart from Christ, our life was full of discord—often with those we saw as different from ourselves. We were without hope and without God.

Application Question: Why was it important for the Gentiles and why is it important for us to remember the past?

1. Remembering the past is important for remaining thankful.

Many times we live unthankful lives because we have forgotten what we used to be, and how God has changed us. Paul reminds them and us so that we can remain thankful for God's grace in our lives. God delivered us from lives full of division and unified us with himself and one another. He gave us peace through Christ. Thank you, Lord!

2. Remembering the past is important so we never fall back into old patterns—discord with one another and distance from God.

Sadly, discord was rampant in the early church, especially between Jews and Gentiles. In Galatians, we read that even the apostle Peter would at times still not eat with Gentiles because of pressure from other Jews (Gal 2:12). In Romans 14, it seems that Jews and Gentiles were dividing over eating food offered to idols, the practice of the Sabbath, and other aspects of the law. In addition, Acts 6 records that the Grecian Jewish widows were neglected by the Hebraic Jews in the daily food distribution. There was even discord between Jews of different cultures. This division continued to reap animosity and discord in the early church. No doubt some separated into totally Jewish congregations and totally Gentile congregations to avoid discord. But that wasn't God's perfect will. As revealed next, God called for them to be one body (Eph 2:14-15). And this is true for us today as well.

The church is meant to be multicultural, multiracial, and multiethnic in order to bring glory to God. We must remember what we came from so that we will not go back to living a life full of discord, anger, and unforgiveness.

Christians who have forgotten their previous state and what God has done for them will be prone towards racism, ethnocentrism, elitism, and even denominationalism. We see this all the time. In fact, Sunday has often been called the most divided day in the world. On Sundays, various races and denominations gather together in places separate from one another to "worship God." We must remember our previous state so we won't return to the division which marks the world, and also so we can continually praise God for his transformational work in us.

Application Questions: In what ways do we still see hostility between races, classes, genders, etc., among Christians today? In what ways have you been delivered from this type of hostility through Christ?

In Order to Have Peace, Believers Must Remember that Christ Brought Us Reconciliation with One Another

> But now in Christ Jesus you who used to be far away have been brought near by the blood of Christ. For he is our peace, the one who made both groups into one and who destroyed the middle wall of partition, the hostility, when he nullified in his flesh the law of commandments in decrees. He did this to create in himself one new man out of two, thus making peace
> Ephesians 2:13-15

Next, Paul addresses how Christ united these two hostile people groups—the Jews and the Gentiles.

Observation Question: How has Christ united Jews and Gentiles?

1. Christ united Jews and Gentiles by bringing both groups near God.

Paul says, "But now in Christ Jesus you who used to be far away have been brought near" (v. 13). When he says they were brought near, he means near God. Unity has been developed by both Jew and Gentile being brought closer to God.

A great illustration of this is a triangle. At the peak is God and on the two sides are people. The closer we get to God, the closer we will naturally get to one another. This was Christ's method of unifying people—he brings them closer to God.

And this is true for all division—division in friendships, family, marriage, etc.—the closer we get to God, the closer and more unified we become with one another. However, the farther we get from God, the more we will find division and discord in our relationships.

In fact, this also works in reverse. If we are right with others (walking in righteous relationships with them), then we will naturally become closer to

God. Our horizontal relationships always reflect our vertical relationship and vice versa. Christ says this in Matthew 5:23-24:

> "So then, if you bring your gift to the altar and there remember that your brother has something against you, leave your gift there in front of the altar. First go and be reconciled to your brother and then come and present your gift."

If we are in discord with others, we must first make those relationships right so we can properly worship God. Our horizontal relationships affect our vertical relationships and our vertical relationship affects our horizontal.

Are you in discord with anybody? Many times the answer to fixing that relationship is as simple as drawing near God. When we draw near God, he changes our hearts so we can better work for reconciliation.

Are you distant from God? Many times the answer to fixing that relationship is drawing near others—having proper fellowship with his body. I have often experienced times of dryness in my spiritual life simply because I was not in proper fellowship. The more isolated we are from believers—God's family—the more we will find ourselves isolated from him.

2. Christ brought unity through his death for sin.

Paul says the way we are brought near God is "by the blood of Christ" (Eph 2:13). The blood of Christ is a "euphemism" (a mild expression substituted for a harsh one) for Christ's death. Christ died for the sins of the world. Romans 4:25 says, "He was given over because of our transgressions and was raised for the sake of our justification."

For Christ to bring unity among people, he had to deal with the very thing that separated them, which was sin. Again, when man sinned in the Garden, it naturally brought separation both in human relationships and our relationship with God. Therefore, Christ died for our sin to deliver us from its power so we could be united.

Romans 6:6 says, "We know that our old man was crucified with him so that the body of sin would no longer dominate us, so that we would no longer be enslaved to sin." When Christ died for our sins, our old self—our sin nature—died with him. It died in the sense that the power of sin over us was broken.

The root of division is sin—our pride, our selfishness, our insecurity, our anger, our jealousy, our envy, etc. We argue and fight because we want our own way. But through Christ's death, believers are now no longer bound to follow the sinful urges that result in discord.

Are you in discord? Then, how is God calling you to practically live out your death to sin? In Romans 6:11, Paul says, "So you too consider yourselves dead to sin, but alive to God in Christ Jesus." Humble yourself—reckon your pride and anger dead. As one person said, "Dead people don't get offended." Stop living in that old nature since Christ set you free from it. It died on the cross with Christ, and you must reckon it so.

3. Christ brought unity by becoming our peace.

Ephesians 2:14 says, "For he is our peace." It must be noted that Christ did not simply bring peace, he became our peace. John MacArthur shares this story about World War II to illustrate how Christ is our peace:

> During World War II a group of American soldiers was exchanging fire with some Germans who occupied a farm house. The family who lived in the house had run to the barn for protection. Suddenly their little three–year–old daughter became frightened and ran out into the field between the two groups of soldiers. When they saw the little girl, both sides immediately ceased firing until she was safe. A little child brought peace, brief as it was, as almost nothing else could have done.[81]

Similarly, Jesus Christ came to the earth as a baby so that he could bring peace between those who were warring and divided. However, this peace is not temporary; it is an eternal peace. Christ became peace for us. And therefore, he must be the reason we labor for peace in our relationships. Consider what Paul said to two ladies fighting in the Philippian congregation: "I appeal to Euodia and to Syntyche to agree in the Lord" (Phil 4:2).

How were they supposed to work things out? They needed to agree with each other in the Lord. They needed to resolve their conflict on the basis of Christ having brought peace. They needed to resolve their conflict on the basis of Christ's character. They needed to resolve their conflict by being like Christ—the one who humbled himself to serve and unify others (Phil 2:5). This is true for us as well. Christ is our peace.

4. Christ brought unity by abolishing the Mosaic law that separated Jews and Gentiles.

Ephesians 2:14-15 says: "For he is our peace, the one who made both groups into one and who destroyed the middle wall of partition, the hostility, when he nullified in his flesh the law of commandments in decrees."

One of the things that divided Jews and Gentiles was the Mosaic law, which God originally gave to the Jews. According to this law, the Jews were to be separate. They were not allowed to intermarry with other nations. They had to wear different clothes and eat different foods. However, God's purpose in the Jews being separate was to prevent contamination by the sinful pagan cultures.

The hope was that pagans would notice the righteousness of the Jews and be drawn to God (cf. Deut 4:6-8). The law commanded separation for this purpose.

In fact, the temple itself had several courts. East of the temple was the Court of Priests, then the Court of Jews (for laymen), then the Court of Women, and then the Court of Gentiles. And between the Court of Gentiles and the rest of the temple was a wall with inscriptions in Greek and Latin saying: "No foreigner may enter within the barricade which surrounds the sanctuary and enclosure. Anyone who is caught doing so will have himself to blame for his ensuing death."[82]

It was this wall that the Jews claimed Paul and his Gentile friend, Trophimus, crossed, when they attacked and threatened to kill Paul—leading to his first imprisonment (Acts 21:28-33). However, Christ abolished, literally annulled, the regulations in the Jewish law so that believers are no longer under it (Eph 2:15). Jews and Gentiles are no longer called to be separate.

Interpretation Question: In what ways did Christ abolish the law?

- Christ abolished the law by paying the penalty required by it for our sins. Romans 6:23 says, "For the wages of sin is death; but the gift of God is eternal life through Jesus Christ our Lord" (KJV).

- Christ abolished the law by fulfilling the perfect righteousness required by it that we could not fulfill. Second Corinthians 5:21 says, "God made the one who did not know sin to be sin for us, so that in him we would become the righteousness of God."

- Christ abolished the law by his death, and our death with him, to the law—delivering us from its governance.

  Romans 7:1-4 says,

  Or do you not know, brothers and sisters (for I am speaking to those who know the law), that the law is lord over a person as long as he lives? For a married woman is bound by law to her husband as long as he lives, but if her husband dies, she is released from the law of the marriage. So then, if she is joined to another man while her husband is alive, she will be called an adulteress. But if her husband dies, she is free from that law, and if she is joined to another man, she is not an adulteress. So, my brothers and sisters, you also died to the law through the body of Christ, so that you could be joined to another, to the one who was raised from the dead, to bear fruit to God

Paul compares our union with Christ to the marriage union. When one spouse dies, the other is free to remarry—he or she is no longer bound by the law of marriage. In the same way, we died with Christ on the cross, and therefore our previous marriage to the law was broken. We are now married to Christ and called to submit to him instead of the law. In fact, Paul later says that although as believers we are not under the Mosaic law, we are under the law of Christ. First Corinthians 9:21 says, "To those free from the law I became like one free from the law (though I am not free from God's law but under the law of Christ) to gain those free from the law."

The law of Christ is his teachings in the New Covenant (i.e. the New Testament) coming through both Christ himself and his apostles. Many of the teachings in the New Covenant are the same as those in the Old Covenant. Do not lie, do not steal, do not cheat, etc.; however, the governance is different. It's like being punished by Korean law while residing there instead of in the United States. Similarly, we are now married to Christ, and we are under his governance and not that of the Mosaic law. It should be noted that while many teachings in Christ's law are the same as in the Mosaic law, others are different. For instance, under the New Covenant we are not under the food, Sabbath, and festival laws and rituals (cf. Col 2:16-17).

Christ destroyed the law to unite us as one. The Jew is not nearer to God than the Gentile, and the Gentile is not nearer than the Jew. We are all on equal standing in the New Covenant. Colossians 3:11 says, "Here there is neither Greek nor Jew, circumcised or uncircumcised, barbarian, Scythian, slave or free, but Christ is all and in all."

5.   Christ brought unity by creating a new man.

Ephesians 2:15 says, "He did this to create in himself one new man out of two, thus making peace." Christ brought unity by creating something new—a new race. Kent Hughes' illustration and comments on this are helpful:

> Bishop John Reed tells about driving a school bus in Australia which carried whites and aborigines. Tired of all the squabbling, one day far out in the country he pulled over to the side of the road and said to the white boys, "What color are you?" "White." He told them, "No, you are green. Anyone who rides in my bus is green. Now, what color are you?" The white boys replied, "Green." Then he went to the aborigines and said, "What color are you?" "Black." "No, you are green. Anyone who rides on my bus is green." All the aborigines answered that they were green. The situation seemed resolved until, several miles down the road, he heard a boy in the back of the bus announce, "All right, light green on this side, dark green on that side." Bishop Reed had the right idea. What was needed was a new race, "the greens," but he couldn't

pull it off! Our text says that Jesus created a new man, a new humanity, a new race.[83]

In the New Covenant, a Gentile doesn't have to become a Jew to worship God, and a Jew doesn't have to become a Gentile. When we are saved, God essentially shatters the racial and ethnic barriers that divide us as we are united in the church. We are not black, white, Jew, Gentile, Asian, African, or any other race or ethnicity. We are all part of the church—citizens of heaven living on the earth (Phil 3:20). It is for this reason that the church should not be divided by racial, social, or economic distinctions—for we are all one in Christ. Galatians 3:28 says, "There is neither Jew nor Greek, there is neither slave nor free, there is neither male nor female– for all of you are one in Christ Jesus."

Christ unites us, drawing us near God and each other by breaking the power of sin through his death, by becoming our peace, and by removing the barrier of the Mosaic law—making us a new people. Therefore, we must labor to keep the unity God has given us (cf. Eph 4:3).

Application Question: How should we as Christians apply Christ's work of unifying people in our lives, churches, and communities?

In Order to Have Peace, Believers Must Remember that Christ Brought Us Reconciliation with God

> and to reconcile them both in one body to God through the cross, by which the hostility has been killed. And he came and preached peace to you who were far off and peace to those who were near, so that through him we both have access in one Spirit to the Father.
> Ephesians 2:16-18

Finally, Paul talks about how Christ reconciled both Jews and Gentiles to God through the cross. To reconcile means to "renew a friendship." Christ did this in many ways.

Observation Question: In what ways did Christ reconcile both Jewish and Gentile believers to God?

1.   Christ reconciled believers to God through his death (v. 16).

Paul says that Christ reconciled us to God through the cross. Before salvation, we were separated from God because we weren't like him—we weren't holy. Hebrews 12:14 says, "without it [holiness] no one will see the Lord" Holiness is a separation from sin to righteousness. And Christ accomplished this for us by his death. He made us holy by taking our sin on the cross with him and giving us his perfect righteousness (2 Cor 5:21). The righteousness of Christ imputed to our account allows us to come into God's presence and have a relationship with him.

2.   Christ reconciled believers to God through preaching the gospel of peace (Eph 2:17).

The Greek word for "preached" is euangelizō, and it "literally means to bring or announce good news, and is almost always used in the New Testament of proclaiming the gospel, the good news of salvation through Jesus Christ." [84] It is the same term from which we get the English words "evangelize," "evangelist," and "evangelical."

As seen by the context, this preaching happened after the cross (cf. 16-17); therefore, it does not primarily refer to his pre-resurrection ministry but to his post-resurrection ministry. After Christ's resurrection, he appeared to his apostles and said, "Peace be with you" (John 20:19). This also probably refers to Christ's gospel ministry through the apostles and subsequent generations of Christians. Jesus still preaches today through his followers. It is wonderful to consider that when Christians preach the gospel, Christ preaches through them. Romans 10:15 says, "How beautiful are the feet of them that preach the gospel of peace, and bring glad tidings of good things!" (KJV).

Do you have beautiful feet? Are you allowing Christ to preach through you and reconcile people to God?

3.   Christ reconciled believers to God by giving them access by one Spirit.

Ephesians 2:18 says, "so that through him we both have access in one Spirit to the Father." One cannot but notice the Trinitarian work involved in this reconciliation. Christ gives Jews and Gentiles access to God by the Holy Spirit. John MacArthur's comments are helpful in considering the word "access." He says,

Prosagōgē (access) is used only three times in the New Testament, in each case referring to the believer's access to God (see also Rom. 5:2; Eph. 3:12). In ancient times a related word was used to describe the court official who introduced persons to the king. They gave access to the monarch. The term itself carries the idea not of possessing access in our own right but of being granted the right to come to God with boldness, knowing we will be welcomed. [85]

We often think of Christ as once and for all giving us access to God through the cross, but according to Scripture we still go through Christ in approaching God. Hebrews 13:15 says, "Through him then let us continually offer up a sacrifice of praise to God, that is, the fruit of our lips, acknowledging his name."

In the Old Testament, the priest and the people of Israel could only approach God through the blood of a lamb. Every year the people sacrificed a lamb so they could approach God and be accepted by him. It is the same for us, except that our Lamb was slain once and for the sins of the entire world. Every time we enter into God's presence, God still sees the perfect sacrifice and righteous life of the Lamb. It is for this reason that we have access.

In fact, this somewhat reflects Christ's teaching in John 10:1-14 about him being the Good Shepherd and the Gate for the sheep. John 10:9 says, "I am the door. If anyone enters through me, he will be saved, and will come in and go out, and find pasture." In John 10:11, Christ says, "I am the good shepherd. The good shepherd lays down his life for the sheep." It almost seems like he is mixing metaphors, but he is not. The Palestinian shepherd gathered all the sheep into a pen or erected a temporary fence at night—leaving a narrow opening for a door. The shepherd then laid across the narrow opening, as the door to the pen.[86] Christ, the Good Shepherd, is still the doorway to God, not just for salvation, but daily. He is the way, the truth, and the life (John 14:6). Therefore, as believers we can "confidently approach the throne of grace to receive mercy and find grace whenever we need help" (Heb 4:16).

And it is by the Holy Spirit that we continually approach God (Eph 2:18). The Holy Spirit works in our hearts to draw us near God and to seek his face. Romans 8:15 says, "For you did not receive the spirit of slavery leading again to fear, but you received the Spirit of adoption, by whom we cry, 'Abba, Father.'"

Are you still drawing near God? Christ paved the way for us to have continual access to God. Christ gave us the Holy Spirit to encourage us and draw into God's presence (cf. John 16:7, Eph 2:18). The Holy Spirit enables us to cry out, "Abba, Father"— "Daddy Dearest."

Why is this important? Often Christians deem themselves unworthy to come into God's presence because of some failure or sin. However, God never accepts us because of our righteousness. We weren't saved because of our righteousness, and it is not our current righteousness that gives us access to God. It is still Christ's.

God doesn't accept us because we did our daily devotions or went to church on Sunday. We are always accepted on the basis of Christ's righteousness. Christ is still our doorway; he is our public official that brings us into the court of God. Therefore, we can always come with boldness. We are righteous in Christ and accepted because of him.

Christ removed the hostility between us and God—reconciling us to the Father. He is truly the seed that would crush the head of the serpent and make all things right (Gen 3:15). He is our peacemaker.

Application Questions: How has Christ, through the Holy Spirit, been drawing you to deeper intimacy with God? Describe your experiences in evangelism. How has Christ been challenging you to participate in reconciling others to God?

Conclusion

How can we maintain the peace Christ, our peacemaker, has given us with one another and also with God?

1. In order to have peace, believers must remember their sad state before Christ.
2. In order to have peace, believers must remember that Christ brought reconciliation with one another.
3. In order to have peace, believers must remember that Christ brought reconciliation with God.

Three Metaphors of the Church: How to Be the Church and Not Just Attend It

> So then you are no longer foreigners and noncitizens, but you are fellow citizens with the saints and members of God's household, because you have been built on the foundation of the apostles and prophets, with Christ Jesus himself as the cornerstone. In him the whole building, being joined together, grows into a holy temple in the Lord, in whom you also are being built together into a dwelling place of God in the Spirit.
> Ephesians 2:19-22 (NET)

What is the church? How can believers be the church instead of just attending the church?

The problem with most Christians is that they have a low "ecclesiology"—a low understanding of what the church is and their role in it. For most, being the church simply means that they call themselves Christians and attend church on a regular or semi-regular basis. But outside of that, they have no real commitment to or investment in the church.

If we don't fully understand the purpose of something, it is destined for misuse. And that is exactly what is happening in Christ's church today. Most Christians don't really understand it; therefore, they misuse it.

There was something of this happening in the early church, and Paul addresses it in Ephesians 2:19-22. In the previous verses (11-18), Paul calls for the Gentiles to consider their past—they were hated by the Jews, called "the uncircumcision," without citizenship in Israel, without covenants, without hope, without Christ, and without God.

The Jews were called to be a holy nation that drew the other nations to God. However, they became prideful in their lofty position as God's people, and instead of ministering to the Gentiles, they hated them. There was tremendous animosity between the two groups. But through his death, Christ brought these two hostile groups near God. He made them one man—one body; he made them his church.

It seems that Paul addressed this, because there was still division happening in the early church. Though they were saved and part of Christ's body, they weren't being the church. In Romans 14, Paul writes of division over eating meat offered to idols, practicing the Sabbath day, and other things that divided Jew and Gentile Christians. Even the apostle Peter would not eat with Gentiles when certain Jews were around (Galatians 2). No doubt, they started to form separate congregations—Jewish churches and Gentile churches. The early church did not fully understand what Christ had done for them, and therefore they were not being the church.

The same is true today. Many Christian don't understand the church and therefore are not living as the church. Church is often something simply attended—with few ramifications other than that.

What is the church and how can we be the church and not just attend it? In this text, Paul gives three metaphors to help us "Be the Church."

Big Question: What three metaphors does Paul use for the church, and how can we live out these realities?

To Be the Church, We Must Live as Heavenly Citizens

> So then you are no longer foreigners and noncitizens, but you are fellow citizens with the saints and members of God's household
> Ephesians 2:19

The first metaphor Paul uses is that of citizens in the kingdom of heaven. He says, "you are no longer foreigners and aliens." William Barclay's comments are helpful in understanding the terms "foreigners" and "aliens":

> Paul uses the word xenos for foreigner. In every Greek city there were xenoi, and they did not lead an easy life. One wrote home: 'It is better for you to be in your own homes, whatever they may be like, than to be in a strange land.' The foreigner was always regarded with suspicion and dislike. Paul uses the word paroikos for stranger. The paroikos was one step further on. A person described in this way was a resident alien, someone who had taken up residence in a place but who had never become a naturalized citizen; such people paid a tax for the privilege of existing in a land which was not their own. Both the xenos and the paroikos were always on the fringe. Paul uses the word xenos for foreigner. In every Greek city there were xenoi, and they did not lead an easy life. One wrote home: 'It is better for you to be in your own homes, whatever they may be like, than to be in a strange land.' The foreigner was always regarded with suspicion and dislike. Paul uses the word paroikos for stranger. The paroikos was one step further on. A person described in this way was a resident alien, someone who had taken up residence in a place but who had never become a naturalized citizen; such people paid a tax for the privilege of existing

in a land which was not their own. Both the xenos and the paroikos were always on the fringe.[87]

Foreigners and aliens were often looked at with suspicion and discriminated against, and this is how the Gentiles were treated before Christ formed the church. They were like second class citizens as far as worshiping God. They could not enter the temple; they could not be priests and, in most cases, were despised by Israel. However, in Christ, Gentile Christians are now full citizens of the kingdom of heaven.

Among Christians there is some disagreement over what the kingdom of heaven is. John the Baptist preached the kingdom of heaven and so did Christ and his apostles (cf. Matt 3:2, 10:7). However, in studying texts on the kingdom of heaven, it clearly has both a present and future reality. For instance, Luke 17:20-21 says:

Now at one point the Pharisees asked Jesus when the kingdom of God was coming, so he answered, "The kingdom of God is not coming with signs to be observed, nor will they say, 'Look, here it is!' or 'There!' For indeed, the kingdom of God is in your midst."

Christ says the kingdom of God is within you, or it can be translated "in your midst." The kingdom of heaven is present, and yet, we still wait for it. In the Lord's Prayer, we pray, "Thy kingdom come. Thy will be done in earth, as it is in heaven" (Matt 6:10, KJV). Therefore, the kingdom of heaven is wherever people proclaim submission to God. It is in our hearts, and yet it is a coming reality. One day, at Christ's coming, he will literally rule on this earth as in heaven. And as the church, we should currently live as citizens of this kingdom.

Application Question: How should believers live out the reality that they are citizens of heaven?

1. Heavenly citizens have different cultural norms than those of the earth.

These different cultural norms include different speech, dress, values, etc. Ephesians 4:29 says, "You must let no unwholesome word come out of your mouth, but only what is beneficial for the building up of the one in need, that it may give grace to those who hear." Citizens of heaven should only let words come out of their mouths that will be helpful and build others up. They should not be known for sexual jokes, cursing, or other language that defiles.

First Timothy 2:9 says, "Likewise the women are to dress in suitable apparel, with modesty and self-control. Their adornment must not be with braided hair and gold or pearls or expensive clothing." Though Paul speaks to women in this text, the principles apply to all Christians. Christians should be known for their modest dress, avoiding extremes in clothing. In the world, clothes are often used to show one's wealth and to draw attention and glory to the wearer. But the Christian should want all glory to go to God, and therefore avoid lavish, sexually alluring, or ragged clothing (often another way of seeking attention).

Not only should Christians be different in their talk and their clothing, but also in the way they think. Romans 12:2 says, "Do not be conformed to this present world, but be transformed by the renewing of your mind." The world culture trains people how to think about beauty, success, life, and death. However, citizens of heaven should think very differently about these things, because their views are based on Scripture. Citizens of heaven should be continually transforming their minds through the Word of God.

2. Heavenly citizens should continually practice the righteousness of the kingdom.

Romans 14:17 says, "For the kingdom of God does not consist of food and drink, but righteousness, peace, and joy in the Holy Spirit." These are all present realities that should be growing in our lives. We should be growing in righteousness and helping others to do so as well. We should be growing in peace with God, peace with others, and peace of heart. We should also be growing in joy regardless of our circumstances because our joy is in God. Philippians 4:4 says, "Rejoice in the Lord always. Again I say, rejoice!"

3. Heavenly citizens should continually proclaim the kingdom to others.

Acts 28:31 says this about Paul: "proclaiming the kingdom of God and teaching about the Lord Jesus Christ with complete boldness and without restriction." Paul continually proclaimed the kingdom of God—preaching the gospel and the return of Jesus Christ.

This should be true for us as well. As citizens of heaven, we must continually proclaim the gospel to all who will hear. The gospel is that this present world is not it—there is more. The sin, discord, death, and decay of this world are not it. God has more. There is a kingdom coming, and those who repent and follow Christ shall enter it.

4. Heavenly citizens should long for the kingdom of heaven.

Hebrews 11:16 says this about Abraham and the other patriarchs of the faith: "But as it is, they aspire to a better land, that is, a heavenly one. Therefore, God is not ashamed to be called their God, for he has prepared a city for them." Though living on the earth, Abraham and the patriarchs longed for their heavenly home—and God is not ashamed to be called their God. No doubt God is ashamed of some Christians. Why? Because they don't really desire the city he prepared for them; instead, they love and worship the things of this world (1 John 2:15). However, God is pleased with those who long for the coming kingdom.

One of the ways we long for this coming kingdom is by praying for it. Again, the Lord's Prayer is "Thy kingdom come. Thy will be done." We should long for it especially as we see the sin and destruction happening daily in our world.

Another way we long for the kingdom is by longing for our King—our Savior—to come. Paul says this in Philippians 3:20-21:

> But our citizenship is in heaven – and we also await a savior from there, the Lord Jesus Christ, who will transform these humble bodies of ours into the likeness of his glorious body by means of that power by which he is able to subject all things to himself.

Are you being the church? Are you living as a citizen of the kingdom of heaven? Is your language, your behavior, your priorities, and your hopes different? To be the church, we must live as citizens of heaven.

Application Questions: What aspect of being a heavenly citizen is most challenging to you and why? How is God calling you to grow in this area? What keeps us from longing for his kingdom? How can we foster a longing for his kingdom and its righteousness?

To Be the Church, We Must Live as Family Members

> So then you are no longer foreigners and noncitizens, but you are fellow citizens with the saints and members of God's household
> Ephesians 2:19

The next way that Christians can be the church is by living as family members. Not only has Christ made us heavenly citizens, but also members of the same family. There is greater unity and intimacy between family members than between citizens.

This should be something that characterizes Christians. Christ says this about his followers in Matthew 12:48-50:

> "Who is my mother and who are my brothers?" And pointing toward his disciples he said, "Here are my mother and my brothers! For whoever does the will of my Father in heaven is my brother and sister and mother."

Christ regarded his disciples as family members and God as their Father. He taught the disciples to pray, "Our Father in heaven, may your name be honored" (Matt 6:9). When we began following Christ, we became family. This family includes people from different socio-economic backgrounds, races, and ethnic groups, and it includes believers both in heaven and on earth. Ephesians 3:14-15 says, "For this reason I kneel before the Father, from whom every family in heaven and on the earth is named."

In 1 Timothy 5:1-2, Paul says this about how believers should treat one another: "Do not address an older man harshly but appeal to him as a father. Speak to younger men as brothers, older women as mothers, and younger women as sisters – with complete purity." We should treat one another as family. Christ said, "Everyone will know by this that you are my disciples – if you have love for one another" (John 13:35). We are to be known by this intimate familial love.

Application Question: How should we practically apply the reality of the church being family?

1. As family, believers should consider using familial terms.

    Paul calls Timothy his "genuine child in the faith" (1 Tim 1:2). He refers to himself as a "father" to the Corinthians (1 Cor 4:15), and calls the Romans "brothers" (Rom 12:1). We should consider using these familial terms as well.

2. As family, believers must make the church their priority.

    Galatians 6:10 says, "So then, whenever we have an opportunity, let us do good to all people, and especially to those who belong to the family of faith." Yes, we should do good to all, but especially to believers. They must be our priority. When something is your priority, you invest your time, money, and energy in it, and you give up other things to focus on it. This should be true of our investment in the Body of Christ.

    Sadly, for most, job, schooling, and housing are the main priorities instead of their church. Believers often uproot their families from a great church where God is using them and move for career and other opportunities. This often leads to spiritual struggles. They find a new church, but often struggle to get involved—and it never feels like home. Their spiritual life suffers because they didn't prioritize their church home—their Christian family.

    Where has God planted you? How is God calling you to make church your priority?

3. As family, believers must develop intimate relationships with one another.

Family is a place where we share intimate secrets and struggles, and this should be true of the church as well. James 5:16 says, "So confess your sins to one another and pray for one another so that you may be healed. The prayer of a righteous person has great effectiveness." Sadly, many have no transparency in their church relationships. Everybody in the church is kept at arm's length, if not an entire body's length.

We must develop intimate relationships within the body of Christ. We must learn to confess our sins and share our successes with one another, and also to seek the prayers of the saints. These are practical aspects of being family.

4. As family, believers must encourage one another in their spiritual growth.

In families, parents invest their lives, money, and time in helping their children grow as individuals. Church members should help one another grow as well, especially in their relationship with Christ. This is the priority of people who are "being" the church. As the writer of Hebrews says, "And let us take thought of how to spur one another on to love and good works" (Hebrews 10:24).

Are you considering how you can help your church—your brothers and sisters in Christ? Are you considering how you can serve and help them reach their potential in Christ? If we are going to be the church and not just attend it, we must live as family members.

Application Question: In what ways is God calling you to apply the reality of the church being a family?

To Be the Church, We Must Live as God's Temple

because you have been built on the foundation of the apostles and prophets, with Christ Jesus himself as the cornerstone. In him the whole building, being joined together, grows into a holy temple in the Lord, in whom you also are being built together into a dwelling place of God in the Spirit.
Ephesians 2:20-22

Next, Paul teaches that the Gentiles are being built into a holy temple where God dwells. No doubt this conjured up images of the Jewish temple, which Gentiles could never fully enter. However, they were now God's temple.

Application Question: How can we apply the reality of the church being God's temple?

- As God's temple, we must constantly worship God.

That was the primary purpose of the temple. There, people gathered to worship and offer sacrifices pleasing to God. Hebrews 13:15-16 says: "Through him then let us continually offer up a sacrifice of praise to God, that is, the fruit of our lips, acknowledging his name. And do not neglect to do good and to share what you have, for God is pleased with such sacrifices."

Here the author says praise, good works, and giving are sacrifices that please God. This must be our continual endeavor as God's temple. We must ask ourselves daily, "How can I please and worship God today both individually and with other believers?"

Similarly, Paul says in 1 Corinthians 10:31, "So whether you eat or drink, or whatever you do, do everything for the glory of God." Everything we do can and should be worship.

- As God's temple, we must live carefully—in a God-honoring manner.

In one of Watchman Nee's books, he says that if you have a little bit of change in your pocket, you can walk around carefree. However, if you have a large sum of money in your pocket, you will walk very carefully lest you lose it. Not that we can lose God, but he who dwells in us is so valuable that his indwelling should drastically change how we walk.[88] We should be different. Let us walk carefully in order not to dishonor God with our mouths and our meditations. Let us always remember that our individual bodies, and also we as the church, are his temple.

- As God's temple, we must practice holiness.

The priests and Levites made sure that God's temple never became defiled. There were ceremonial washings and cleansings even for the plates in the temple. In the same way, as the temple of God, we must keep ourselves from anything that might defile. First Thessalonians 5:22 says, "Stay away from every form of evil." When Jesus went into the temple, he made a whip and turned over tables because God's house was being defiled. We must have that same type of zeal for God's temple—our bodies and the church. We must get rid of all sin and anything that does not honor God.

Paul further expands on this idea of God's temple by considering three critical elements.

Observation Question: What are the three elements of the temple that Paul refers to in Ephesians 2:20-21?

1. The apostles and prophets are the foundation of the temple.

Interpretation Question: Who were the apostles and prophets and in what way are they the foundation of the temple?

Ephesians 2:20 says the temple is built on the "foundation of the apostles and prophets." There is some controversy over this. Is Paul referring to the Old Testament prophets and the New Testament apostles? Or is he referring to New Testament apostles and prophets? Most likely he is referring only to those who ministered in the New Testament. The primary support for this view is the order in which he lists the two groups. If he is referring to the Old Testament prophets, then it would make sense that the prophets would be listed first. Instead, he is probably referring to those who ministered with the apostles in building the foundation of the church. Ephesians 3:4-5 also supports this:

> When reading this, you will be able to understand my insight into this secret of Christ. Now this secret was not disclosed to people in former generations as it has now been revealed to his holy apostles and prophets by the Spirit.

The apostles were specifically a "small and special group whom Jesus chose, called and authorized to teach in his name, and who were eyewitnesses of his resurrection, consisting of the Twelve plus Paul and James and perhaps one or two others."[89]

How are the apostles and prophets the foundation of the church, especially since Scripture says Christ is the foundation of the church (1 Cor. 3:11)? The primary way the apostles and the prophets are the foundation of the church is through their teaching. They wrote the New Testament Scripture on which the church is built, and they founded local churches based on these truths. Paul says this in 1 Corinthians 3:10-11:

> According to the grace of God given to me, like a skilled master-builder I laid a foundation, but someone else builds on it. And each one must be careful how he builds. For no one can lay any foundation other than what is being laid, which is Jesus Christ.

The apostles and prophets laid the foundation of the church through their teachings, and their emphasis on the resurrected Christ. There are several principles that we can learn from this about being the church.

Application Question: How can we apply the reality that the church is built on apostolic teaching?

- Since the church is built on apostolic teaching, we, as members of the church, must be devoted to apostolic teaching.

The early church was "devoting themselves to the apostles' teaching and to fellowship, to the breaking of bread and to prayer" (Acts 2:42). We must be devoted to daily studying God's Word, memorizing it, teaching it, and sharing it with others.

- Since the church is built on apostolic teaching, when seeking a church, we should look for one that faithfully preaches the Word of God.

Many churches no longer preach the Bible. They say it is too antiquated, full of errors, and irrelevant to the needs of the people. Instead, they preach psychology, history, stories, and jokes. Second Timothy 4:3-4 says:

For there will be a time when people will not tolerate sound teaching. Instead, following their own desires, they will accumulate teachers for themselves, because they have an insatiable curiosity to hear new things. And they will turn away from hearing the truth, but on the other hand they will turn aside to myths.

Because Satan realizes the Word of God is the foundation of the church, he always attacks it to bring the church down. Even at the beginning of time, Satan attacked the Word. He asked Eve, "Did God really say?" When seeking a church to raise your family in, find one that unashamedly preaches the Word of God.

Application Questions: In what ways have you seen churches stop preaching the Word of God, particularly the gospel? What effect does it have on believers? How is God calling you to be more devoted to apostolic teaching?

2. Christ is the cornerstone of the temple.

Ephesians 2:20-21 says: "you have been built on the foundation of the apostles and prophets, with Christ Jesus himself as the cornerstone. In him the whole building, being joined together, grows into a holy temple in the Lord." The cornerstone was a messianic picture of Christ in the Old Testament. Isaiah 28:16 says, "Therefore, this is what the sovereign master, the Lord, says: "Look,

I am laying a stone in Zion, an approved stone, set in place as a precious cornerstone for the foundation. The one who maintains his faith will not panic."

Interpretation Question: What is a cornerstone and how does Christ fulfill that role?

> James Boice says this:
>
> A cornerstone was important for two reasons. It was part of the foundation, and it also fixed the angle of the building and became the standard from which the architect traced the walls and arches throughout.[90]

- Since Christ is the cornerstone of the church, it is on him that the church is built.

When Jesus asked Peter who he was, Peter replied, "You are the Christ, the Son of God." And Jesus replied, "On this rock, I will build my church" (Matt 16:16-18, paraphrase). Christ is this rock. He is the cornerstone on which the church is built. Only those who accept Christ and his teachings are part of the church (cf. Matt 7:24-27).

Is your life built on Christ—his life, death, resurrection, and teaching? Any other foundation will fail.

- Since Christ is the cornerstone of the church, it is through him that the church is unified.

Paul says this in Ephesians 2:21, "In him the whole building, being joined together." As mentioned in Ephesians 2:14, "For he is our peace, the one who made both groups into one." He is the one who joins the Jew and Gentile together, abolishing the ancient hostility. And he is the one who brings the church together today. We can be unified because of him, whether we are Jew, Gentile, rich, poor, male, or female.

In fact, Paul pleaded with two women fighting in Philippi to be unified because of Christ. Consider what he says in Philippians 4:2, "I appeal to Euodia and to Syntyche to agree in the Lord."

It must be noticed that he doesn't say, "Work out your differences." He says, "Agree with each other in the Lord." They were to agree based on their commonality, which was bigger than any difference they had. In the same way, we can only have unity based on Christ. If our unity is based on culture, affinity, gender, socio-economic status, hobbies or anything else, it will not stand. Only Christ can unify the church and keep it unified.

Are you walking in unity with the rest of the church? Yes, certain people's personalities may get on your nerves. They may think differently than you, and they may even hurt you. However, you can seek unity because of Christ—he is the unifier. Let that commonality trump all differences. Christ is our cornerstone.

- Since Christ is the cornerstone of the church, it is through him that we grow.

Ephesians 2:21 says, "In him the whole building, being joined together, grows into a holy temple in the Lord." It was upon the foundation, the cornerstone, that the rest of the building was built. In the same way, both our individual and our corporate spiritual growth come through Christ. Christ says, "'I am the vine; you are the branches. The one who remains in me – and I in him – bears much fruit, because apart from me you can accomplish nothing" (John 15:5). It is only by abiding in Christ, our cornerstone, that we can we grow and ultimately fulfill our purpose.

We abide in Christ and therefore grow spiritually through studying Scripture, prayer, fellowship with other believers, and serving. Many are not growing because they are not abiding in Christ—they are not staying connected to the cornerstone. Therefore, they are useless in building up the temple of God.

What is the next aspect of the temple that Paul refers to?

3. The people of God are bricks in the temple.

Again, Ephesians 2:22 says, "in whom you also are being built together into a dwelling place of God in the Spirit." Though Paul does not actually say so, the implication is that he is referring to individual believers as bricks or stones in the temple of God. Peter uses this same analogy in 1 Peter 2:5 when he says, "you yourselves, as living stones, are built up as a spiritual house to be a holy priesthood and to offer spiritual sacrifices that are acceptable to God through Jesus Christ."

Yes, Scripture teaches that individual believers are the temple of God. First Corinthians 6:19-20 says, "Or do you not know that your body is the temple of the Holy Spirit who is in you, whom you have from God, and you are not your own? For you were bought at a price. Therefore glorify God with your body."

However, Scripture also teaches that when believers gather together, God is with us. First Corinthians 3:16 says, "Do you not know that you are God's temple and that God's Spirit lives in you?" The word "you" in this passage is plural, referring to the church. Similarly, Christ says in Matthew 18:20, "For where two or three are assembled in my name, I am there among them" When believers are present together, there is a special way in which God meets with them. In fact, there are some things he does in a corporate gathering that he does not do when we are alone.

Application Question: How can we apply the reality that individual believers are bricks in the temple of God?

- As bricks in the temple of God, we need one another.

A brick is not good for much by itself. But when it is with other bricks, it goes into making a beautiful building. In the same way, apart from the body of Christ, we may miss God's best.

Are you living in union with the body of Christ—the beautiful bricks that make up God's temple?

- As bricks in the temple of God, God is constantly adding other bricks until the temple is complete, and we must aid in that process.

One day the temple will be complete. God will add the final Jews and Gentiles to the church, and the temple will be finished. He has called us to aid in that process by faithfully sharing the gospel with others. As Matthew 28:19 says, we must go throughout the earth and make disciples of all nations.

Are you being the church and not just attending it? In order to do that, we must remember that we are God's temple.

Application Questions: In what ways is God calling you to live out the reality that the church is the temple of God—built on the foundation of apostolic teaching, with Christ as the cornerstone and believers as bricks? In what ways is this teaching new or challenging to you?

Conclusion

How can believers be the church instead of simply attending it?

1. To be the church, we must live as heavenly citizens.
2. To be the church, we must live as family members.
3. To be the church, we must live as God's temple.

Marks of Faithful Servants

For this reason I, Paul, the prisoner of Christ Jesus for the sake of you Gentiles – if indeed you have heard of the stewardship of God's grace that was given to me for you, that by revelation the divine secret was made known to me, as I wrote before briefly. When reading this, you will be able to understand my insight into this secret of Christ. Now this secret was not disclosed to people in former generations as it has now been revealed to his holy apostles and prophets by the Spirit, namely, that through the gospel the Gentiles are fellow heirs, fellow members of the body, and fellow partakers of the promise in Christ Jesus. I became a servant of this gospel according to the gift of God's grace that was given to me by the exercise of his power. To me – less than the least of all the saints – this grace was given, to proclaim to the Gentiles the unfathomable riches of Christ and to enlighten everyone about God's secret plan – a secret that has been hidden for ages in God who has created all things. The purpose of this enlightenment is that through the church the multifaceted wisdom of God should now be disclosed to the rulers and the authorities in the heavenly realms. This was according to the eternal purpose that he accomplished in Christ Jesus our Lord, in whom we have boldness and confident access to God because of Christ's faithfulness. For this reason I ask you not to lose heart because of what I am suffering for you, which is your glory.
Ephesians 3:1-13 (NET)

What are marks of faithful servants—those who will hear God say, "Well done!"?

In Ephesians 2:11-22, Paul teaches how Jews and Gentiles, who were formerly antagonistic towards one another, were now both part of Christ's body. God made the two one. This teaching was tremendously controversial in the early church. In fact, the Jews had Paul arrested, in part, for teaching it (cf. Acts 21:29).

In Ephesians 3:1-13, Paul explains his authority to teach this mystery. He emphasizes that it is a stewardship from God. Ephesians 3:2-3 says, "if indeed you have heard of the stewardship of God's grace that was given to me for you, that by revelation the divine secret was made known to me, as I wrote before briefly." Paul calls himself a steward of God's grace and later a servant of the gospel (3:7).

It appears that Ephesians 3:2-13 is a parenthesis to his original thought. In verse 1, he says, "For this reason." Then, almost abruptly, he explains his authority as a steward and servant of the gospel, as if some were not aware of it. Then he returns to his original thought in verse 14 with "For this reason," as he shares his prayer for God's church.

In Paul's parenthesis, we learn about his stewardship, or servanthood, of God's mystery. Not only do we learn about Paul's servanthood, but also, through his example, we learn about how we can be faithful servants.

In the Parable of the Talents, God describes each believer as a servant, or steward, given various gifts and responsibilities. He will bless the faithful and declare to them, "Well done, good and faithful slave! You have been faithful with a few things. I will put you in charge of many things. Enter into the joy of your master" (Matt 25:23). As we serve our Master, God, it should be our desire to be faithful and honored by him.

Similar to Paul, God gave us his gospel, his power, and his gifts to serve him and others. And, as stewards, we must be faithful. First Corinthians 4:2 says, "Moreover it is required in stewards, that a man be found faithful" (KJV). One day, at Christ's second coming, he will survey our stewardship. Were we faithful stewards of all he gave us? The faithful will be commended and rewarded, and the unfaithful will be rebuked and lose their reward (Matt 25:24-30).

While considering Paul's parenthesis about his stewardship, we discern marks of a faithful servant—and these should both encourage and challenge us.

Big Question: What marks of faithful servants can be discerned from Paul's description of himself and his ministry?

Faithful Servants Suffer Willingly for Christ and Others

> For this reason I, Paul, the prisoner of Christ Jesus for the sake of you Gentiles
> Ephesians 3:1

In verse 1, Paul says he is a prisoner of Christ Jesus for the sake of the Gentiles. Paul suffered for Christ and also for the Gentiles. The very reason Paul was in prison was because he taught that Gentiles now shared the same spiritual privileges as Jews. While in Jerusalem, he was accused of bringing an Ephesian, Trophimus, into the temple (cf. Acts 21:29). This was an accusation the Jews fabricated because of their animosity towards him and his teachings. Paul was not only in prison for the Gentiles, but for the Ephesians specifically.

Paul willingly taught the truth even if it offended others and caused him suffering. He was willing to be persecuted for Christ. When Christ originally appeared to Paul in a vision, he showed Paul how much he would suffer for his name. Acts 9:15-16 says:

> But the Lord said to him, "Go, because this man is my chosen instrument to carry my name before Gentiles and kings and the people of Israel. For I will show him how much he must suffer for the sake of my name."

In 2 Corinthians 11:23-28, Paul describes much of his suffering. He says,

> Are they servants of Christ? (I am talking like I am out of my mind!) I am even more so: with much greater labors, with far more imprisonments, with more severe beatings, facing death many times. Five times I received from the Jews forty lashes less one. Three times I was beaten with a rod. Once I received a stoning. Three times I suffered shipwreck. A night and a day I spent adrift in the open sea. I have been on journeys many times, in dangers from rivers, in dangers from robbers, in dangers from my own countrymen, in dangers from Gentiles, in dangers in the city, in dangers in the wilderness, in dangers at sea, in dangers from false brothers, in hard work and toil, through many sleepless nights, in hunger and thirst, many times without food, in cold and without enough clothing. Apart from other things, there is the daily pressure on me of my anxious concern for all the churches.

One of the problems with much of the church today is its unwillingness to suffer. The church wants its "Best Life Now," and therefore is not willing to suffer for Christ and others. Faithful servants will experience suffering. Matthew 5:10 says, "Blessed are those who are persecuted for righteousness, for the kingdom of heaven belongs to them." Suffering for righteousness marks those who are part of God's kingdom. In fact, Christ says that if one is not willing to take up his cross and follow him, he cannot be his disciple (Luke 14:27).

Therefore, there will be aspects of suffering in the life of every true believer. Faithfulness has a cost, and every true servant bears it. Sometimes it means being considered weird or different because of our views or beliefs. Sometimes it results in physical suffering. First Peter 4:3-4 says,

> For the time that has passed was sufficient for you to do what the non-Christians desire. You lived then in debauchery, evil desires, drunkenness, carousing, drinking bouts, and wanton idolatries. So

they are astonished when you do not rush with them into the same flood of wickedness, and they vilify you.

Faithful servants will experience some form of suffering—some form of our Lord's cross—and Jesus promises blessings to those who do. He says,

"Blessed are you when people insult you and persecute you and say all kinds of evil things about you falsely on account of me. Rejoice and be glad because your reward is great in heaven, for they persecuted the prophets before you in the same way."
Matthew 5:11-12

Are you willing to suffer for your Master and for others? Those who do so will be blessed—approved—by God.

Application Questions: Would you say that persecution towards Christians is growing or lessening? In what ways have you experienced suffering for your faith?

Faithful Servants Trust God's Sovereignty

For this reason I, Paul, the prisoner of Christ Jesus for the sake of you Gentiles
Ephesians 3:1

Interestingly, Paul calls himself a prisoner of Christ Jesus. He didn't see himself as a prisoner of the Jews or of Rome. He was in prison because Christ allowed it—Christ was his captor.

We see this attitude in many of God's faithful servants. When Job's camels were kidnapped by raiders, he didn't blame them. He saw God as in control. He said, "The Lord gives, and the Lord takes away. May the name of the Lord be blessed!" (Job 1:21). When Joseph's brothers begged for mercy for selling him into slavery, he said, "What you meant for bad, God meant for good" (Gen 50:20, paraphrase).

These servants saw God as sovereign over everything, even the workings of evil men and Satan himself. This is important because if God's servants don't see him as sovereign, they often become bitter when bad things happen. They focus on their own failures, the evil works of men, and the evil works of the enemy, and their focus on God is lost.

Hebrews 12:15 says, "See to it that no one comes short of the grace of God, that no one be like a bitter root springing up and causing trouble, and through him many become defiled." Bitterness in the heart causes people to miss the grace of God, and it also causes trouble and defiles many. Instead of being bitter, faithful servants see God's sovereignty over everything. Paul knew he was a prisoner of Christ—not of Rome or the Jews.

Do you see God as in control of all things? Our God holds the king's heart in his hand like a watercourse (Prov 21:1). Even the roll of the dice is of him (Prov 16:33). Our God is sovereign, and he works all things for the good of those who love him (Rom 8:28).

Application Questions: In what ways do you find God's sovereignty even over evil comforting? How do you reconcile God's sovereignty with human and demonic responsibility?

Faithful Servants Seek to Understand God's Mysteries

> if indeed you have heard of the stewardship of God's grace that was given to me for you, that by revelation the divine secret was made known to me, as I wrote before briefly. When reading this, you will be able to understand my insight into this secret of Christ. Now this secret was not disclosed to people in former generations as it has now been revealed to his holy apostles and prophets by the Spirit, namely, that through the gospel the Gentiles are fellow heirs, fellow members of the body, and fellow partakers of the promise in Christ Jesus.
> Ephesians 3:2-6

Interpretation Question: What does Paul mean by the word "secret"?

Next, Paul teaches how he received grace to understand the "secret of Christ" or it can be translated "mystery of Christ" as in the NIV (v. 4). What is Paul referring to by the word "secret" or "mystery"? Unlike the English meaning of "mystery," which refers to something not understood, a biblical mystery refers to a secret previously hidden in the past but now revealed. This secret is that "through the gospel the Gentiles are fellow heirs, fellow members of the body, and fellow partakers of the promise in Christ Jesus" (v. 6). Of course, God's plan has always been to bless the Gentiles through Abraham's seed (Gen 12:3, 22:18), but the Old Testament doesn't specifically teach that Jews and Gentiles will become one body and co-heirs together.

It was this truth that the Jews found so hard to understand and accept. In the book of Acts, we see God begin to reveal this mystery. He reveals it first to Peter—leading him to preach the gospel to the Gentile Cornelius and his family (Acts 10). Then the Jerusalem church, with James, affirms that the Gentiles do not need to become Jews to follow God—they are co-heirs with the Jews (Acts 15). Christ reveals this truth more fully through Paul, the apostle to the Gentiles.

Paul says, "if indeed you have heard of the stewardship of God's grace that was given to me for you" (Eph 3:2). By God's grace, Paul received this mystery as a stewardship from God.

However, this is not only true of Paul but also of every believer. First Corinthians 4:1-2 says: "Let a man so account of us, as of the ministers of Christ, and stewards of the mysteries of God. Moreover it is required in stewards, that a man be found faithful" (KJV).

We are called to be stewards of everything taught in Scripture—to protect it and teach it to others. Now, I am not sure how Paul received this mystery. Galatians 1:17 indicates that he was taught by Christ for three years in Arabia, so he must have received most of it through special revelation. However, God unveils these mysteries to us through his Word, and therefore we must study it. Second Timothy 2:15 says, "Make every effort to present yourself before God as a proven worker who does not need to be ashamed, teaching the message of truth accurately." The servants that will be approved are the ones who study and correctly handle God's truth.

The Great Commission is to "make disciples of all nations ... teaching them to obey everything I have commanded you." (Matt 28:19-20). In order to teach people to obey everything he commands, we must by necessity know all of God's Word. The Great Commission is not just about sharing the gospel; it is about leading people to Christ and discipling them according to his Word.

Are you a faithful servant? Faithful servants devote themselves to studying and understanding God's mysteries, just as the early church, was "devoting themselves to the apostles' teaching" (Acts 2:42).

Are you devoted to God's Word? Are you seeking to understand its mysteries? Sadly, many Christians say, "Doctrine doesn't matter. All that matters is to love one another." This is not true; in fact, understanding God's Word directs and increases our capacity to love. It equips the man of God for all righteousness (2 Tim 3:17). Faithful servants study God's Word so they can understand its truths and live lives that are pleasing to God.

Application Questions: Why is it important to study God's Word and to understand its mysteries? What is your spiritual discipline like in studying the Word? How can you strengthen it?

Faithful Servants Are Made by God

> I became a servant of this gospel according to the gift of God's grace that was given to me by the exercise of his power.
> Ephesians 3:7

One of the things that stands out about Paul's testimony is that he says, "I became a servant of this gospel according to the gift of God's grace" (v. 7). The word "became" can also be translated "was made" (ESV). The verb is passive—meaning that God acted upon Paul to make him a servant of the gospel. It is hard not to think of Christ's words to his original disciples. "Follow me, and I will turn you into fishers of people" (Mk 1:17). Acts 26:16 records these words of Jesus to Paul, "But get up and stand on your feet, for I have appeared to you for this reason, to designate you in advance as a servant and witness to the things you have seen and to the things in which I will appear to you." When Paul was blinded on his way to Damascus, Christ appointed him to be a servant and a witness. God chose to make him into a faithful servant of the gospel.

Paul says that receiving the message—the mystery—was by grace (Eph 3:2-3), the calling to be a servant of the gospel was by grace (3:7), and the power to do the work came from God as well (3:7). Paul was made a servant by God. John MacArthur adds:

> It was not Paul's education, natural abilities, experience, power, personality, influence, or any other such thing that qualified him to be a minister of Jesus Christ. He was made an apostle, a preacher, and a servant by the will and power of His Lord.[91]

And this is true of every faithful servant of God. God makes his servants. Ephesians 2:10 says, "For we are his workmanship, having been created in Christ Jesus for good works that God prepared beforehand so we may do them."

Application Question: How does God make his faithful servants?

1. God makes faithful servants through trials.

James 1:4 says, "But let patience have her perfect work, that ye may be perfect and entire, wanting nothing" (KJV). We must allow patience, or "perseverance," to have her perfect work in us. God develops his servants through trials and difficulties. God allowed Joseph to be a slave and a prisoner in preparation for saving many as second in command in Egypt. God allowed Moses to spend forty years in the wilderness to prepare him to lead Israel. God allowed David to be persecuted by Saul in preparation for his ascent to the throne. In trials, God humbles his people and teaches them to depend solely on him—not their gifts or abilities. He makes his servants in the fire.

2. God makes faithful servants through waiting seasons.

God made Abraham wait for twenty-five years for his son, Isaac, and Abraham is still waiting for his seed, Jesus, to fully bless all the nations. Joseph had to wait years before his father and brothers bowed down before him as in his dream. David waited to become king. In waiting, we learn to trust God and not ourselves.

3. God makes faithful servants through his Word.

Second Timothy 3:16-17 says, "Every scripture is inspired by God and useful for teaching, for reproof, for correction, and for training in righteousness, that the person dedicated to God may be capable and equipped for every good work." When God prepares someone for good works, he trains him through the Word. He gives him an insatiable desire for it, and enables him to study it faithfully. Job says that he has treasured the Word of God more than his daily bread (Job 23:12). David says he praises the Lord seven times a day for his righteous laws (Psalm 119:164). God calls Joshua to meditate on the law day and night and to obey it, with the promise that he will prosper if he does so (Josh 1:7-8). Faithful servants are made through faithful study of the Word of God.

4. God makes faithful servants through discipleship.

Typically, God makes a faithful servant by training him through other faithful servants. Proverbs says, "As iron sharpens iron, so a person sharpens his friend" (Prov 27:17). Elijah discipled Elisha. Jesus discipled the twelve. Paul discipled Timothy, and Barnabas discipled Mark. God makes his servants through the discipleship of other faithful men and women of God.

Are you allowing God to prepare you to become a faithful servant?

Application Questions: In what ways have you seen God preparing you for servanthood? How can you more actively submit to this preparation?

Faithful Servants Work through God's Power

> I became a servant of this gospel according to the gift of God's grace that was given to me by the exercise of his power.
> Ephesians 3:7

Not only does Paul call himself a servant of the gospel by God's grace, but he also says that God's power works in him to serve (v.7). This is also true of every faithful servant of the gospel. They don't operate within their own power, but consciously strive to work through God's power.

In John 15:5, Jesus says, "I am the vine; you are the branches. The one who remains in me – and I in him – bears much fruit, because apart from me you can accomplish nothing." The faithful servant knows the difference between Christ's power and his own. Working in his own strength is marked by frustration, anxiety, and fruitlessness, but Christ's power brings peace and fruitfulness. The faithful servant knows the difference, and labors to continue in Christ's power alone.

Paul previously taught the Ephesians about this power. In Ephesians 1, he prays that they may comprehend the great power at work in them, the same power that raised Christ from the dead (v. 19-20). In Ephesians 3:16, he prays for them to "turn on" this power. "I pray that according to the wealth of his glory he may grant you to be strengthened with power through his Spirit in the inner person."

This is true of every faithful servant; they operate in the power of God. Listen to what Paul says of himself in Colossians 1:29: "Toward this goal I also labor, struggling according to his power that powerfully works in me."

Application Question: How can we allow God's power to work through us?

1. God's power works through believers as they recognize their weakness.

In 2 Corinthians 12:9, Paul tells how he prayed for God to take away his thorn in the flesh—a demon that was tormenting him. However, God replied, "My grace is enough for you, for my power is made perfect in weakness.'"

Many times God allows trials for this very purpose in our lives. He allows difficulties and hardships so we can recognize our weakness. Apart from trials and difficulties, we are often too independent—too "strong" for God to work through us. Therefore, he humbles us through difficulties and trials so his power can be made perfect in our lives. Sometimes, he may actually call us to serve in areas where we are weak or even incompetent, so his power can be clearly displayed. However, many times we must step out in faith to experience God's power—like Peter stepping out of the boat to walk on water (Matt 14:29).

2. God's power works through those who pray.

In Mark 9, we learn that the disciples failed to cast a demon out of a young boy. After Christ healed the boy, they asked, "Why couldn't we cast it out?" Christ replied, "This kind can come out only by prayer" (v. 29). Christ probably wasn't saying that the disciples hadn't prayed to cast out the demon. The problem seems to be that they had ceased to live a lifestyle of prayer. Christ had previously left the nine while he and Peter, James and John went up the mountain for his transfiguration (v. 2). While Jesus was on the mountain, nobody woke the disciples up early to read the Word and pray. Most likely they became spiritually lazy and therefore lacked power. Similarly, our lives must be marked by faithful prayer for God's power to work through us.

3. God's power works through those who have faith.

In a parallel passage, Christ told the disciples that if they had faith the size of a mustard seed, they could move mountains (Matt 17:20). It seems that not only had they ceased to pray faithfully, but they also had little faith. The power of this demon had created doubt in the hearts of the disciples, and therefore they didn't really believe God could work through them.

Most Christians are like this; they believe God for their salvation, but when it comes to their daily bread, their needs, or the needs of others, they doubt God's faithfulness. Christ said that he could not perform many miracles in his hometown because of their lack of faith (Mk 6:5). We often are like this as well. In order to have God's power work in us, we must believe the promises in God's Word.

4.   God's power works in those who abide in his Word.

We mentioned this earlier, but it is worth repeating. Scripture "equips" the man of God for all righteousness (2 Tim 3:17). It empowers us and strengthens us to do God's work. We must live in God's Word to minister in his power.

Are you allowing God's power to work through you? Christ says that apart from him you can do nothing (John 15:5). Faithful servants know the difference between God's power operating in their lives and their own power. Therefore, they ardently seek to live and serve through God's power alone.

Application Questions: In what ways is God challenging you to allow his power to work in your life? What steps will you take to become more of a channel of God's power?

Faithful Servants Are Humble

> To me – less than the least of all the saints – this grace was given, to proclaim to the Gentiles the unfathomable riches of Christ
> Ephesians 3:8

Next, Paul says something that is linguistically impossible but, at the same time, theologically possible, when he calls himself "less than the least of all God's saints." It literally means the "leaster" or "less than the least."[92]

This demonstrates another characteristic of a faithful servant: he is humble. James 4:6 says, "God opposes the proud, but he gives grace to the humble." When a servant is humble, God's gives him grace. Paul already mentioned how he received grace to understand and share the mystery. This is true for all who humble themselves before God and others; they receive grace.

This is not a false, conjured-up humility; rather it is a true humility that comes from being in the presence of God. Paul was keenly aware of his weakness and failures because of his walk with God. Similarly, when Isaiah saw God, he declared, "Woe to me! I am ruined for I have unclean lips, and I come from a people of unclean lips" (Isaiah 6:5, paraphrase). When Peter realized that Jesus was God, he cried out, "Go away from me, Lord, for I am a sinful man" (Lk 5:8). Being in God's presence humbles us, as we clearly see our sin and weakness displayed against his perfection. This was true of Paul. In fact, in 1 Timothy 1:15, he calls himself the chief of sinners.

However, when a servant ceases to be humble and starts to see his good works as coming from himself instead of God, he forfeits God's grace. God opposes the proud (cf. James 4:6)—he fights against them so that they will become humble.

Application Question: How can we develop the humility of a servant?

1. As mentioned, humility comes from continually living in God's presence.

This is done through prayer, fellowship, studying God's Word, and living a holy life.

2. Humility comes from not comparing ourselves with others.

In 2 Corinthians 10:12, Paul says, "For we would not dare to classify or compare ourselves with some of those who recommend themselves. But when they measure themselves by themselves and compare themselves with themselves, they are without understanding."
When we continually compare ourselves with others, we either become discouraged and insecure, or prideful. In order to become humble, we must focus solely on God and his work; this results in humility and receiving more of God's grace.

3. Humility comes as a result of discipline as we put others before ourselves.

In order to grow in humility, we must practice humility by submitting to others and putting them first. First Peter 5:5 says, "In the same way, you who are younger, be subject to the elders. And all of you, clothe yourselves with humility toward one another, because God opposes the proud but gives grace to the humble"
Humility is a discipline. Instead of demanding our rights and privileges from others, we must instead submit to them and seek their benefit over ours.

This is a continual discipline, but as we practice it, God's grace will be given abundantly to us.

Application Questions: Why are we so prone to pride? What makes it so difficult to grow in humility? How is God calling you to further develop humility in your life?

Faithful Servants Share God's Mysteries with Everybody

> To me – less than the least of all the saints – this grace was given, to proclaim to the Gentiles the unfathomable riches of Christ and to enlighten everyone about God's secret plan – a secret that has been hidden for ages in God who has created all things. The purpose of this enlightenment is that through the church the multifaceted wisdom of God should now be disclosed to the rulers and the authorities in the heavenly realms. This was according to the eternal purpose that he accomplished in Christ Jesus our Lord, in whom we have boldness and confident access to God because of Christ's faithfulness.
> Ephesians 3:8-12

Here, Paul says that grace was given to him to preach the unsearchable riches of Christ to the Gentiles and to everyone else (v. 8-9). The word "preach" is euangelizō, which means to "announce good news."[93] Paul was called to proclaim the gospel—the good news of Christ—to all who would listen.

When Paul describes the message as the "unfathomable riches of Christ," he uses an interesting coupling. The Believer's Commentary shares this (via Blaikie):

> Two attractive words, riches and unsearchable, conveying the idea of the things that are most precious being infinitely abundant. Usually precious things are rare; their very rarity increases their price; but here that which is most precious is also boundless— riches of compassion and love, of merit, of sanctifying, comforting and transforming power, all without limit, and capable of satisfying every want, craving, and yearning of the heart, now and evermore.[94]

"The unfathomable riches of Christ" includes everything we receive at salvation. Paul refers to much of this in the first chapters of Ephesians. Believers were elected before time; delivered from spiritual death and from following the world, Satan, and the flesh; forgiven; redeemed; made alive with Christ; and seated in the heavenly places with Christ. Paul continually teaches these truths to believers so they will know their identity in Christ. And he teaches them to unbelievers so they will follow Christ.

However, the good news Paul proclaims doesn't stop there. It includes unveiling God's eternal purpose of making his "multifaceted" (literally "multi-colored") wisdom known to the rulers and authorities in the heavenly realms (v. 10).

Interpretation Question: Who are the rulers and authorities God is teaching through the church?

This clearly refers to angels, both good and bad. Paul refers to them again here in Ephesians 6:12: "For our struggle is not against flesh and blood, but against the rulers, against the powers, against the world rulers of this darkness, against the spiritual forces of evil in the heavens."

Saving a people from out of the world and uniting Jew and Gentile in the church were planned before time in order to teach the angels. Even today the angels continually learn from the church. First Peter 1:12 says,

> They were shown that they were serving not themselves but you, in regard to the things now announced to you through those who proclaimed the gospel to you by the Holy Spirit sent from heaven – things angels long to catch a glimpse of.

Angels desire to look into and understand the gospel. Since their primary function is to worship God, they desire to learn and understand everything about him. And as they learn more, they worship more fully. God works in the church to display not only his multi-colored wisdom, as he takes two people groups at animosity with one another and makes them one in Christ, but also his grace. In Ephesians 2:6-7 Paul says,

> and he raised us up with him and seated us with him in the heavenly realms in Christ Jesus, to demonstrate in the coming ages the surpassing wealth of his grace in kindness toward us in Christ Jesus.

It has been said that before man, the angels knew very little about God's grace. The angels who rebelled didn't receive mercy—they received judgment. The angels understood God's righteousness, holiness, and wrath. But through the church, they learn about God's grace. They are involved in our worship services (cf. 1 Cor 11:10, Heb 1:14), and they peer in, trying to more fully understand the riches of the gospel. This has been God's plan from eternity. The church is essentially the angels' graduate school.

Paul was commissioned to share these truths not only with the Gentiles but with everybody, and this is true for us as well. We should study

God's Word so we can declare his multi-colored wisdom to everyone, and as we share it, even the angels learn (cf. 1 Peter 1:12).

Are you sharing the Word of God with everybody?

Some feel incompetent, and not knowledgeable enough to teach. However, there is always somebody who knows less than we do. We must find that person and teach him, even if he is an unbeliever. The great commission is to make disciples and to teach them to obey everything Christ commanded (Matt 28:20). Every Christian is called to be a teacher (cf. Heb 5:12). This is what God's faithful servants do.

Application Questions: Share your evangelism and Bible teaching experience. How is God calling you to share more faithfully with others?

Faithful Servants Are Selfless

> For this reason I ask you not to lose heart because of what I am suffering for you, which is your glory.
> Ephesians 3:13

Finally, we cannot but notice Paul's concern for the Ephesians in this verse. He says, "I ask you not to lose heart because of what I am suffering for you, which is your glory." Paul was in prison, yet he was worried about the Ephesians' happiness and glory.

This is the epitome of a servant. Servants don't serve for their own glory, but for the glory and satisfaction of others—and this was true of Paul. He suffered for the Ephesians, even risking his own life so they could hear the gospel and fulfill God's plan for them.

This must be true of us as well. Paul says this in Philippians 2:3-5:

> Instead of being motivated by selfish ambition or vanity, each of you should, in humility, be moved to treat one another as more important than yourself. Each of you should be concerned not only about your own interests, but about the interests of others as well. You should have the same attitude toward one another that Christ Jesus had

Faithful servants do nothing out of selfish ambition, but in humility consider others better than themselves. This was the attitude of Christ, who suffered and died so that we could know God and have eternal life. Our Lord was the ultimate servant.

How is God calling you to seek the glory of others? John the Baptist said this of Christ, "He must become more important while I become less important" (John 3:30). We must have this mindset as well, not only about Christ, but also others.

How is God calling you to develop this selfless mindset in order to be a faithful servant—one who will be honored and rewarded by him?

Application Questions: Who is God calling you to serve by seeking their glory over your own? How is God calling you to get rid of your selfishness?

Conclusion

What are marks of a faithful servant, one to whom God says, "Well done"?

1. Faithful servants suffer willingly for Christ and others.
2. Faithful servants trust God's sovereignty.
3. Faithful servants seek to understand God's mysteries.
4. Faithful servants are made by God.
5. Faithful servants work through God's power.
6. Faithful servants are humble.
7. Faithful servants share God's mysteries with everybody.
8. Faithful servants are selfless.

Becoming Spiritually Mature

Just as Moses lifted up the serpent in the wilderness, so must the Son of Man be lifted up, so that everyone who believes in him may have eternal life." For this is the way God loved the world: He gave his one and only Son, so that everyone who believes in him will not perish but have eternal life. For God did not send his Son into the world to condemn the world, but that the world should be saved through him. The one who believes in him is not condemned. The one who does not believe has been condemned already, because he has not believed in the name of the one and only Son of God. Now this is the basis for judging: that the light has come into the world and people loved the darkness rather than the light, because their deeds were evil. For everyone who does evil deeds hates the light and does not come to the light, so that their deeds will not be exposed. But the one who practices the truth comes to the light, so that it may be plainly evident that his deeds have been done in God.
Ephesians 3:14-21 (NET)

How can we grow spiritually? What steps must we take?

In Ephesians 3:14-21, Paul prays for the Ephesians to become spiritually mature. His prayer is like a pyramid—each successive petition builds upon the other.[95] As we study this passage, not only do we learn general principles of prayer, we also learn how to mature spiritually.

Big Questions: What are the successive steps to spiritual maturity as demonstrated by Paul's prayer? How can we apply these to our lives in order to grow?

In Order to Mature Spiritually, Believers Must Know Their Identity in Christ

For this reason I kneel before the Father
Ephesians 3:14

Interpretation Question: What "reason" is Paul pointing back to in verse 14 that now prompts this prayer?

Paul is referring to the previous passage where he teaches that God made believing Jews and Gentiles one in Christ, and that God's eternal plan has been to teach the angels about his multi-colored wisdom. However, Paul is probably not only pointing back to these truths, but to all the truths taught in Ephesians chapters 1 and 2 about the believer's identity in Christ. Believers have every spiritual blessing in the heavenly places. They were elected before time, redeemed by his blood, and forgiven of their sins. They were delivered from spiritual death and from following the world, the devil, and the flesh, and made alive with Christ.

When Paul considers all that God did for believers, he is prompted to pray for their spiritual maturity—he wants them to live out their identity in Christ. And this should be true for us as well. When we consider all that God has done, it should challenge us to pray for spiritual maturity in ourselves and others—and to actively seek spiritual maturity. It is the most reasonable thing we can do considering all that God has done in our lives.

Paul says something similar in Romans 12:1: "Therefore I exhort you, brothers and sisters, by the mercies of God, to present your bodies as a sacrifice – alive, holy, and pleasing to God – which is your reasonable service." "Therefore" points back to all that Paul teaches in chapters 1-11 about salvation.

When we truly understand what God has done for us, we are challenged and encouraged to grow up into our divine calling. But from these passages, we also understand why so many are not growing. They aren't growing because they don't understand who they are in Christ and what God has done for them. Therefore, they continue to look just like the world. Like the Corinthians, they continue to be worldly—living like "unregenerate people" (1 Cor 3:1-3). They are prone to materialism, division, lust, and even hopelessness.

If we are going to pursue spiritual maturity, we must understand the "reason" Paul desired it for the Ephesians. We must know our identity in Christ and all that God did for us. It has often been said that the Christian life is understanding our new identity in Christ and learning to live it out.

Do you know your identity in Christ? Do you know that on the cross, Christ broke the power of sin over your life (Rom 6:1-11)? Do you know that you are God's workmanship, created in Christ for good works (Eph 2:10)? God has good and wonderful things planned for your life. Do you know that God seated you in the heavenly places with Christ and that one day you will rule with Jesus and even judge angels (Eph 1:3, 1 Cor 6:3)?

The more you comprehend of your eternal destiny, the more you will be pulled out of worldliness and sin. You will be encouraged to offer your body as a living sacrifice unto God, and to pray for your spiritual growth and that of others.

Application Questions: Why is knowing our identity in Christ and what God did for us important for spiritual growth? How can we come to know and live out our identity in Christ? In what ways has learning your identity in Christ helped you to grow in grace, and to be set free from specific sins?

In Order to Mature Spiritually, Believers Must Pray

> For this reason I kneel before the Father, from whom every family in heaven and on the earth is named. I pray that according to the wealth of his glory he may grant you to be strengthened with power through his Spirit in the inner person
> Ephesians 3:14-16

As Paul considers all that God did for the church, he is prompted to pray for the church's spiritual maturity. This means that prayer is an essential part of the process of a believer's spiritual growth. Before Christ went to the cross, he prayed in a similar manner for the church (John 17). He prayed that God would sanctify them by the Word of God, that they would be kept from the evil one, and that they would be united. If we are going to grow spiritually, we must pray for ourselves and for others.

In fact, when considering Paul's prayers throughout his epistles, we don't see him pray for the church's material needs (physical healing, finances, etc.). His prayers focus on the spiritual condition of believers, and this must be our priority as well. This doesn't mean that we don't pray for physical healing or material needs, but it does mean that our own spiritual condition and that of others should be our focus.

Also, as we consider Paul's prayer we learn many characteristics of godly prayer. I say "godly prayer" because it is possible for our prayers to be ungodly. In Matthew 6, Christ warns the disciples not to pray like the Pharisees and pagans because they will not be heard by God (v. 5-8). Such prayer is unacceptable to God.

Observation Questions: What are some characteristics of Paul's prayer, and thus godly prayer in general? How can we incorporate these characteristics into our own prayer life?

1. Godly prayer is inspired by Scripture.

As already mentioned, Paul's prayer is informed and inspired by Scripture. As he considers what God does for believers, he is prompted to pray.

This should be true for us as well. Scripture and prayer always go together. When a need arose for the Grecian widows to be cared for, the apostles said they could not do it because they had to give themselves to the ministry of the Word of God and prayer (Acts 6:3-4). These two always go together.

Not only should the Word of God inspire and inform our prayer, believers should also consistently pray Scripture. When Christ was dying on the cross for our sins, he prayed two scriptural prayers: "My God, my God, why have you abandoned me?" and "Into your hand I entrust my life." These were both from the Psalms (22:1, 31:5). While Christ was being murdered on the cross, Scripture not only prompted his prayer— it was his prayer. We should constantly pray the Word of God, especially since it is God's revealed will.

Application Question: How do you use Scripture in your prayer life?

   2.   Godly prayer is humble.

While praying, Paul was kneeling. The normal way for Jews to pray was standing up (cf. Mark 11:25). [96] To pray on one's knees represented humbling oneself before someone greater (cf. Ps. 95:6) and also intensity or great passion, as seen when Christ fell to the ground while praying in Gethsemane (Mark 14:35-36; cf. 2 Chr 6:13, Ezra 9:5–6). This is how our prayers should be.

One might ask, "Is it possible to pray any other way before God?" Why, certainly. When the Pharisee and the publican prayed before God, the Pharisee's prayer was prideful. He said, "God, I thank you that I am not like other people: I fast twice a week; I give a tenth of everything I get" (Luke 18:11-12). His prayer was prideful and selfish. Selfish prayer says, "I am the focus— not God and not others."

Christ warns the disciples not to pray loud and long in order to be seen by others (Matt 6:5-8). Many people put on a show for others when they pray, making much "Christian" prayer a charade. In contrast, Christ tells the disciples to go into their closet and pray privately—to be seen only by God.

In fact, we probably get a picture of this with the issue of tongues at the church in Corinth. Many commentators believe that when Paul says a person who prays in a tongue edifies himself and he who prophesies edifies others (1 Cor 14:4), he is referring to people speaking out loud in tongues without interpretation. These people are glorifying themselves instead of thinking about the others who were present. However, Paul commands that everything in church worship be done for the edification of others (1 Cor 14:26). Many Christians are like that—their prayers are meant to be seen and heard by others rather than God. Be careful of prideful prayer.

When we pray, we must remember that God opposes the proud and gives grace to the humble (James 4:6). Only those who pray with humility receive grace. This certainly is implied by Paul's posture, though one can pray in any posture to the Lord.

3. Godly prayer is familial.

Paul says, "from whom every family in heaven and on the earth is named" (Eph 3:15). He not only recognizes God as his own Father, but also as the Father of all believers in heaven and on earth. In fact, when Christ taught the Lord's Prayer, he taught us to pray, "Our Father" (Matt 6:9). The prayer is not individual but familial, as it considers other family members God cares for. When praying, we must remember that we are part of a family. We must constantly remember others in our prayers. This does not mean that we shouldn't pray for ourselves, but that even these prayers should be offered in consideration of our family.

4. Godly prayer is God-sized.

Paul says, "I pray that according to the wealth of his glory" (Eph 3:16). This is important. It has been said that if a billionaire donates ten dollars, he gives out of his wealth, but if he donates one million, he gives according to his wealth. This is Paul's prayer for believers, that God will strengthen them with power according to the wealth of his glory. Macdonald adds:

> Since the Lord is infinitely rich in glory, let the saints get ready for a deluge! Why should we ask so little of so great a King? When someone asked a tremendous favor of Napoleon it was immediately granted because, said Napoleon, "He honored me by the magnitude of his request."
>
> Thou art coming to a King,
> Large petitions with thee bring;
> For His grace and power are such,
> None can ever ask too much.
> —John Newton[97]

When praying for ourselves or others, we should pray great petitions. We should pray for God to abundantly supply needs, to greatly use others for his kingdom, etc.

Application Questions: What are some other practical principles concerning prayer? What disciplines have you found helpful in your prayer life?

In Order to Mature Spiritually, Believers Must Strengthen Their Inner Being

> I pray that according to the wealth of his glory he may grant you to be strengthened with power through his Spirit in the inner person, that Christ may dwell in your hearts through faith.
> Ephesians 3:16-17

The next aspect of Paul's prayer is that the Ephesians will be strengthened through the Spirit in the inner being. In Ephesians 1, Paul prays for the believers to know God's great power working in them, the same power that raised Christ from the dead (v. 19-20). But here, he prays for that power to be "turned on"— to strengthen believers. Someone said, "If God took the Holy Spirit out of this world, most of what we Christians are doing would go right on—and nobody would know the difference!" [98] Sadly, this is true. Most Christians live without this power, and therefore live ineffective lives.

Application Question: How can we allow the Spirit to strengthen us?

1. Obviously, the Spirit empowers us as we pray.

    This is clear from the context of Paul praying for believers to be strengthened. Christ fasted and prayed for forty days, and left the wilderness empowered by the Holy Spirit (Lk 4:1, 14). In Acts 4:29, we read that the early church gathered to pray for God to give them boldness to proclaim the gospel even while under persecution. After they prayed, the building was shaken and they all left filled with the Spirit of God. The Spirit empowers believers when they pray.
    Are you living in prayer?

2. The Spirit empowers us as we abide in God's Word.

    Second Timothy 3:17 says Scripture "equips the man of God for every good work" (paraphrase). Scripture empowers believers to do the righteous works God called them to do. If we are to be empowered by the Spirit, we must live in the Word of God.
    Are you abiding in God's Word?

3. The Spirit empowers us as we worship.

There is a story in the Old Testament about Jehoshaphat, the king of the Judah, fighting a battle against a nation through worship. Second Chronicles 20:21-22 says:

> He met with the people and appointed musicians to play before the Lord and praise his majestic splendor. As they marched ahead of the warriors they said: "Give thanks to the Lord, for his loyal love endures." When they began to shout and praise, the Lord suddenly attacked the Ammonites, Moabites, and men from Mount Seir

Similarly, when Elisha was approached by Jehoshaphat and Ahab about whether to go to war against another nation, he asked for a harpist. The harpist played, and the Spirit of God came upon Elisha to prophecy (2 Kings 3:15). God inhabits the praises of his people (Psalm 22:3, paraphrase) and his Spirit empowers us when we worship. In fact, Paul commands us to "in everything give thanks. For this is God's will for you in Christ Jesus. Do not extinguish the Spirit" (1 Thessalonians 5:18-19). The implication is that when we worry, complain, and argue instead of giving thanks, we quench the Spirit's work in our lives. However, when we give thanks and praise to God, he empowers our inner being.

Are you living in worship and thanksgiving, or in bitterness and complaining?

Interpretation Question: What exactly is the inner being?

Wiersbe's comments are helpful:

> This means the spiritual part of man where God dwells and works. The inner man of the lost sinner is dead (Eph. 2:1), but it becomes alive when Christ is invited in. The inner man can see (Ps. 119:18), hear (Matt. 13:9), taste (Ps. 34:8), and feel (Acts 17:27); and he must be "exercised" (1 Tim. 4:7–8). He also must be cleansed (Ps. 51:7) and fed (Matt. 4:4). The outer man is perishing, but the inner man can be renewed spiritually in spite of outward physical decay (2 Cor. 4:16–18). It is this inner power that makes him succeed.[99]

Paul says, "For I delight in the law of God in my inner being" (Rom 7:22). We need to be strengthened in the inner being to desire God's Word, to conquer sin, and to worship God. If our inner being is weak, we will not desire the things of God. In fact, we will find that we desire worldly things more than the things of God.

Observation Question: What is the result of having one's inner being strengthened with power?

Paul says that when a believer is strengthened in his inner being, Christ dwells in his heart through faith (Ephesians 3:17). What does this mean?

Doesn't God indwell every believer? Certainly. In Ephesians 1:1, Paul calls the Ephesians "saints"—meaning that each of them were saved by Christ, set apart for righteousness, and indwelled by him. However, our position is often different from our practice. The Corinthians are also called "saints" in 1 Corinthians 1:2 (KJV), but in 1 Corinthians 3:3, Paul calls them "still influenced by the flesh"—mere infants in Christ (1 Cor 3:1). They practiced sexual immorality (chapters 5 and 6), were suing one another (chapter 6), and abusing spiritual gifts like tongues (chapter 14), but they were still saints—set apart by God and indwelled by him (1 Cor 6:19).

The word that Paul uses for "dwell" means to "to settle down and feel at home," in contrast to feeling like visitor.[100] The reality is that Christ cannot be at home in a believer who is not living an empowered life through the Spirit. When we are not empowered by the Spirit of God, we live as slaves of sin, instead of as free men (cf. 2 Cor 3:17, Romans 6:16). We talk and walk like the world, even though we are not of the world. In a life like that, Christ can never feel at home.

Is Christ at home in your heart? Or is he like a visitor? Is he comfortable with your entertainment and how you spend your free time? Is he comfortable with your thoughts and friendships? Paul says this to the Corinthians:

> Or do you not know that your body is the temple of the Holy Spirit who is in you, whom you have from God, and you are not your own? For you were bought at a price. Therefore glorify God with your body.
> 1 Corinthians 6:19-20

Interpretation Question: What does Paul mean by Christ dwelling in the Ephesians' hearts "through faith"?

When Paul says that Christ will dwell in their hearts through "faith," he seems to be saying that empowerment by the Spirit creates a life of dependence upon the Lord. Christ says, "I am the vine and you are the branches, he who abides in me will produce much fruit, apart from me you can bear no fruit" (John 15:5, paraphrase).

A life empowered by the Spirit is one that is totally dependent upon God—a life of faith. This believer fears dishonoring God by any compromise or sin, knowing that it will diminish God's power in his life. He does not want to grieve the Holy Spirit. As a person matures in Christ—living more by faith than in the flesh—he is empowered by the Spirit of God in the inner being. This results in a life where Christ is at home.

Is Christ at home in your life? Or is he like an unhappy visitor—uncomfortable and constantly grieved?

Application Questions: How do you think Christ feels about your life? Consider your thoughts, words, friendships, hobbies, work, etc. How can you make him more at home?

In Order to Mature Spiritually, Believers Must Grow in Love for God and Others

so that, because you have been rooted and grounded in love
Ephesians 3:17b

In praying for the Ephesians to be "rooted and grounded in love," Paul uses terms from botany and architecture. The root is where a tree or plant gets both its nourishment and its stability. Also, the ground or foundation of a building is the most important part of a structure. If the foundation is off, one cannot continue to build.

Wiersbe's story about a building program at one of his churches is helpful:

In my second building program, we had to spend several thousand dollars taking soil tests because we were building over an old lake bed. For weeks, the men were laying out and pouring the footings. One day I complained to the architect, and he replied, "Pastor, the most important part of this building is the foundation. If you don't go deep, you can't go high." That sentence has been a sermon to me ever since.[101]

Without a root and foundation of love, a believer cannot grow spiritually, for it is the springboard for spiritual growth. With that said, although Paul does not share who the believer should love, he no doubt refers to love for both God and others (cf. Mk 12:30-31).

Our sinful nature is identified by self-love and love for the things of the world—immature believers are often still identified by these loves. Instead of serving others, they are consumed with themselves. Instead of building God's kingdom, they are consumed with building their own kingdom. However, when believers start to mature, they start being identified by love for God and others. As they continue to grow, we see more and more acts of love.

In explaining why he and the other apostles serve God, and specifically why they evangelize, Paul says, "For the love of Christ controls us, since we have concluded this, that Christ died for all; therefore all have died" (2 Cor 5:14).

What does he mean by Christ's love? He probably means that his love for Christ compelled him to witness and serve others. But he also means Christ's love working through him. Romans 5:5 says, "because the love of God has been poured out in our hearts through the Holy Spirit." God gives each believer a divine ability to love, and this love must be the foundation of our spiritual lives if we are to grow.

Application Question: How can believers build a strong foundation for their spiritual lives by growing in love?

1. Believers grow in love by acts of the will.

Paul is referring to agape love, which is not primarily an emotional love; it is an act of the will. This is why we can obey God's command to love our enemies (Matt 5:44). A believer might not feel pleasant emotions about his enemy, but he can act in love towards him because God commands it. Romans 12:20 says, "if your enemy is hungry, feed him; if he is thirsty, give him a drink." As an act of the will, we must choose to serve, forgive, and encourage all we encounter—especially believers (Gal 6:10).

Therefore, we grow in love by choosing to selflessly love those around us. Even our love for God is an act of the will. Christ says, "Anyone who loves me will obey my teachings" (John 14:23, paraphrase). He essentially makes love and obedience synonymous. We grow in love by choosing, as an act of the will, to love God and others.

2. Believers grow in love through prayer.

First Thessalonians 3:12 says, "And may the Lord cause you to increase and abound in love for one another and for all, just as we do for you." As we seek God for grace to love, he enables us by his power. If we lack love for someone, including God himself, let us earnestly pray for God's grace to love (cf. Matt 7:7-8).

Application Questions: Is there a specific person or group of people that God is calling you to show love towards? How is God calling you to grow through practicing acts of love for him and others?

In Order to Mature Spiritually, Believers Must Grow in Their Understanding of Christ's Love

> so that, because you have been rooted and grounded in love, you may be able to comprehend with all the saints what is the breadth and length and height and depth, and thus to know the love of Christ that surpasses knowledge
> Ephesians 3:17b-19

Paul's next prayer is for the Ephesians to understand the greatness of Christ's love. Understanding how much someone loves us is very powerful. For children knowing their parents' love during their formative years helps protects them from a life of fear, insecurity, and rebellion. Those whose parents aren't around because of work or other factors often struggle because they don't perceive themselves as being loved. This is why many of the young men and women in gangs, prison, and drug, alcohol, and sexual addiction come from homes missing one or both parents. Knowing and experiencing our parental love is very important, but more important than that is knowing God's love.

For this reason, Satan works very hard to make believers doubt the love of God. When Satan attacked Eve, he tempted her to believe that God was keeping the best from her. When Satan tempted Job, he tried to get Job to curse God to his face. Both temptations were essentially aimed at making one doubt the love of God. Just as not knowing one's parents' love can damage a child, doubting God's love will seriously damage a Christian. In fact, such doubting can lead to all types of sin and destruction, as it did with Eve.

Paul does not want believers to just have head knowledge of Christ's love, but also experiential knowledge. When he prays for them to know "the love of Christ" (v. 18), he is praying for them to continually know and experience this love.

However, as he prays for them to comprehend and experience it, he introduces a paradox. He says, "to know the love of Christ that surpasses knowledge" (v. 19). This love is impossible to know fully, but we must continually seek to know it nevertheless. It seems that in heaven, when we are made perfect, we will then be able to fully comprehend it. Paul says this in 1 Corinthians 13:12: "For now we see in a mirror indirectly, but then we will see face to face. Now I know in part, but then I will know fully, just as I have been fully known." When Christ comes and removes the sin from our bodies, then we will no longer know in part, but we will know him and his love fully.

Interpretation Question: How can we grow in our knowledge of Christ's love on a daily basis?

Though there are many ways, such as studying God's Word, prayer, serving, etc., Paul focuses on just one in this text. He says, "so that, because you have been rooted and grounded in love, you may be able to comprehend with all the saints what is the breadth and length and height and depth, and thus to know the love of Christ" (Eph 3:17b-18). It is only together, "with all the saints," that we can truly comprehend Christ's love.

Macdonald and Stott's comments on this provide insight:

> Before we consider the dimensions themselves, let us notice the expression, with all the saints. The subject is so great that no one believer can possibly grasp more than a small fraction of it. So there is need to study, discuss, and share with others. The Holy Spirit can use the combined meditations of a group of exercised believers to throw a flood of additional light on the Scriptures.[102]

> We shall have power to comprehend these dimensions of Christ's love, Paul adds, only with all the saints. The isolated Christian can indeed know something of the love of Jesus. But his grasp of it is bound to be limited by his limited experience. It needs the whole people of God to understand the whole love of God, all the saints together, Jews and Gentiles, men and women, young and old, black and white, with all their varied backgrounds and experiences.[103]

Interpretation Question: What is Paul referring to when he talks about the width, length, depth, and height of Christ's love for us?

Paul could just be using poetic hyperbole in referring to the vastness and completeness of Christ's love. However, if he is referring to specific aspects of Christ's love, they must come from his previous teachings in Ephesians 1 and 2. MacDonald says this:

> 1. The width is described in 2:11–18. It refers to the wideness of God's grace in saving Jews and Gentiles, and then incorporating them into the church. The mystery embraces both these segments of humanity.
> 2. The length extends from eternity to eternity. As to the past, believers were chosen in Christ before the foundation of the world (1:4). As to the future, eternity will be a perpetual unfolding of the exceeding riches of His grace in His kindness toward us through Christ Jesus (2:7).
> 3. The depth is vividly portrayed in 2:1–3. We were sunk in a pit of unspeakable sin and degradation. Christ came to this jungle of filth and corruption in order to die in our behalf.
> 4. The height is seen in 2:6, where we have not only been raised up with Christ, but enthroned in Him in the heavenlies to share His glory. These are the dimensions, then, of immensity and, indeed, infinity.[104]

We must continually endeavor to know Christ's love not just intellectually, but also experientially, and this happens through our fellowship and struggles with his people—the body of Christ. Though imperfect, they are necessary participants in our sanctification, and our ability to know Christ and his love.

Application Questions: Share a time where your awareness of Christ's love for you grew in a special way. In what ways have you experienced or come to know Christ's love for you through other believers?

In Order to Mature Spiritually, Believers Must Be Fully Controlled by God

> so that you may be filled up to all the fullness of God.
> Ephesians 3:19b

The next step in the believer's path to spiritual maturity is being filled to the measure of all the fullness of God. It seems that it is better to translate this as "unto the fullness of God." Commentator F.F. Bruce says this: "The preposition 'unto' suggests a progressive experience. The believer is to pray for God to constantly fill him, to constantly flood him with all the fullness of God."[105]

Being filled with God is to be the constant experience of believers. Now of course, this seems impossible. How can a believer be filled with the fullness of God? If the heavens cannot contain him, how can we?

Interpretation Question: What does it mean to be filled with the fullness of God?

MacDonald's book says this: "We can use illustrations to throw light on this verse, for example, the thimble dipped in the ocean is filled with water, but how little of the ocean is in the thimble!"[106]

Certainly, all of God cannot fill us, but we can nevertheless be full of him. Being full of God means:

1. The believer must be less full of himself.

If a glass is half full already, it can only be half filled with something else. This is a continual problem in our relationship with God. It is not really that we need more of him, but that we need less of ourselves. We need less pride, selfish ambition, lust, anger, etc. Paul says, "I have been crucified with Christ, I no longer live, but Christ in me" (Gal 2:20a, paraphrase). For Paul this was not just a positional experience on the cross, it was a daily practical experience. He gave up his career, religion, family, and everything else, counting them "dung" to gain Christ (cf. Phil 3:7-8).

What is keeping God from filling you completely?

2. The believer must be fully controlled by God.

MacArthur's comments on the word "full" are helpful:

> Plēroō means to make full, or fill to the full, and is used many times in the New Testament. It speaks of total dominance. A person filled with rage is totally dominated by hatred. A person filled with happiness is totally dominated by joy. To be filled up to all the fulness of God therefore means to be totally dominated by Him, with nothing left of self or any part of the old man. By definition, then, to be filled with God is to be emptied of self. It is not to have much of God and little of self, but all of God and none of self. This is a recurring theme in Ephesians. Here Paul talks about the fulness of God; in 4:13 it is "the fulness of Christ"; and in 5:18 it is the fulness of the Spirit.[107]

It should be our daily aspiration to crucify self and exalt Christ in our lives. It should be our daily endeavor to allow God to control our speech, our thoughts, our actions, and our relationships.

Certainly, we accomplish this by renouncing all sin in our lives, filling ourselves with God's Word, submitting to him, and obeying him. As we do this, God fills and controls us. Similarly, Ephesians 5:18 says, "And do not get drunk with wine, which is debauchery, but be filled by the Spirit." Like an alcoholic constantly sipping to become intoxicated and therefore controlled by wine, we must constantly drink from God's Word, prayer, worship, fellowship, and serving so God can completely fill and control us.

Are you daily seeking for God to fill and control you?

Application Questions: Why is it necessary for believers to be continually filled by God? How are you daily seeking his filling?

In Order to Mature Spiritually, Believers Must Have Faith in God

> Now to him who by the power that is working within us is able to do far beyond all that we ask or think, to him be the glory in the church and in Christ Jesus to all generations, forever and ever. Amen.
> Ephesians 3:20-21

No doubt, some might have scoffed at the idea of being totally filled and controlled by God. I often counsel young believers who feel that God's biblical standards are too high, and therefore impossible to meet. Here, Paul's doxology was meant to help the Ephesians believe that God could establish their root and foundation in love, and enable them to live lives where Christ was at home in their hearts. God could enable them to comprehend the depth, the height, the width, and the length of Christ's love for them, and ultimately, God could fill and control their lives and use them for great things. Paul wanted them to believe this.

He says, "Now to him who by the power that is working within us is able to do far beyond all that we ask or think" (v. 20). Essentially, he is saying that God is able. His power is at work in believers to do greater things than they could ever ask or imagine. When David was the least in his household, caring for sheep, he probably never imagined that God would make him king of Israel and bring the messiah through his lineage. When Joseph saw his father and brothers bowing down before him in a dream, he probably never imagined being second in command over Egypt, and saving many lives. The same power that raised Christ from the dead is working in us. However, we must have faith to access it.

In Paul's doxology, he tried to stretch the Ephesians' faith to help them believe that God could not only mature them, but also use them greatly for his kingdom. He says this in Ephesians 1:18-19a:

> since the eyes of your heart have been enlightened – so that you may know what is the hope of his calling, what is the wealth of his glorious inheritance in the saints, and what is the incomparable greatness of his power toward us who believe

This incomparably great power is working in all who believe. Certainly, it is available to every believer, but it is only applied to those who have faith. Christ says that if we have faith the size of a mustard seed, we'll be able to move mountains (Matt 17:20).

God raises mountain movers. He raises Noahs, Moseses, Pauls, and Peters to build his kingdom. And why does he do this?

He does this for his glory—that glory will go to him through the church and Christ for all generations forever and ever (Eph 3:21). God raises mountain movers for his eternal glory!

The following comment by MacArthur provides an encouraging conclusion to this discussion:

> When the Holy Spirit has empowered us, Christ has indwelt us, love has mastered us, and God has filled us with His own fullness, then He is able to do exceeding abundantly beyond all that we ask or think.

Until those conditions are met, God's working in us is limited. When they are met, His working in us is unlimited. "Truly, truly, I say to you, he who believes in Me, the works that I do shall he do also; and greater works than these shall he do; because I go to the Father. And whatever you ask in My name, that will I do, that the Father may be glorified in the Son. If you ask Me anything in My name, I will do it" (John 14:12–14). There is no situation in which the Lord cannot use us, provided we are submitted to Him.[108]

Application Questions: Why is faith so necessary for God to move in our lives? How can we grow in faith?

Conclusion

What are steps to becoming spiritually mature?

1. Believers must know their identity in Christ.
2. Believers must pray.
3. Believers must strengthen their inner being.
4. Believers must grow in love for God and others.
5. Believers must grow in their understanding of Christ's love.
6. Believers must be fully controlled by God.
7. Believers must have faith in God.

How to Live a Life Worthy of Christ's Calling

> I, therefore, the prisoner for the Lord, urge you to live worthily of the calling with which you have been called, with all humility and gentleness, with patience, bearing with one another in love, making every effort to keep the unity of the Spirit in the bond of peace. There is one body and one Spirit, just as you too were called to the one hope of your calling, one Lord, one faith, one baptism, one God and Father of all, who is over all and through all and in all.
> Ephesians 4:1-6 (NET)

How can we live a life worthy of Christ's calling?

When Jesus saved us, he didn't just save us for heaven. He saved us to live for him, to do works in his name, to rule with him, and many other things. Much of the teaching in the first half of Ephesians is about our calling. We were elected and predestined before time, redeemed, and forgiven. We were dead in our transgressions and sins, but now, we have been raised and seated with Christ in heavenly places.

How can we live in a manner worthy of all Christ did for us? In Ephesians 4:1, "live" can actually be translated "walk," as in the NASB. "Walk is frequently used in the New Testament to refer to daily conduct, day–by–day living."[109] The Teacher's Outline and Study Bible says this:

> Walking requires us to be consistent. When we were born, walking was not an immediate skill we performed. It was something that had to be learned. The same is true in the spiritual realm. Walking with God is a practical skill that takes time to learn. And once you learn to walk as a Christian, you have a lifetime to practice and keep in top form.[110]

Christians must daily strive to walk worthy of their calling. John MacArthur's comments are helpful in understanding the word "worthy."

> Axios (worthy) has the root meaning of balancing the scales—what is on one side of the scale should be equal in weight to what is on the other side. By extension, the word came to be applied to anything that

was expected to correspond to something else. A person worthy of his pay was one whose day's work corresponded to his day's wages. The believer who walks in a manner worthy of the calling with which he has been called is one whose daily living corresponds to his high position as a child of God and fellow heir with Jesus Christ. His practical living matches his spiritual position.[111]

In addition, the root of the English word "worthy" is "worth"—how much something costs or is valued. The implication of Paul's urging is that some, if not most, of the Christians in Ephesus were not living in a worthy manner. Throughout the rest of Ephesians, he addresses, in a deeper manner, how to do so. He addresses the believers' speech, relationships, marriage, work, and even spiritual warfare. The first three chapters of the book are primarily doctrinal, while the last three are practical.

In this passage, we consider the steps of a worthy Christian walk.

Big Questions: In what ways does Paul challenge the Ephesians to walk in a manner worthy of Christ's calling, and how can we apply these challenges to our lives?

Step One: We Must Continually Seek to Understand Our Calling

I, therefore, the prisoner for the Lord, urge you to live worthily of the calling with which you have been called
Ephesians 4:1

Implied in walking in a manner worthy of our calling is the fact that we must understand our calling. The NASB version translates verse 1 as, "Therefore I, the prisoner of the Lord, implore you to walk in a manner worthy of the calling with which you have been called." The word "Therefore" tells the reader that what lies ahead is based on things previously taught. As mentioned, in chapters 1-3 Paul teaches deep doctrines, including the believer's election, predestination, redemption, and spiritual resurrection. Essentially, he teaches believers about their high calling so they can live lives worthy of it.

This is what it means to be a Christian—to find out who we are in Christ, and to live out this truth daily. This is often called our "general calling"—how God calls all Christians to live. Many Christians don't live worthy of their calling because they don't know or understand it—they don't know what Christ did for them, or how he calls them to live in light of what he did.

Christ's calling for our lives is both general (as we obey the clear teachings of Scriptures) and specific. Paul was called to be an apostle.

Jeremiah was called to be a prophet. David was called to be Israel's king. In the same way, Christ has a special calling on our lives.

Application Question: How can we learn more about our general and specific callings so we can walk worthy of them?

1.   Believers must study the Word of God to understand their general calling.

A believer that does not live in the Word of God cannot live worthy of Christ's calling. Paul teaches that the Word of God "equips the man of God for all righteousness" (2 Tim 3:17 paraphrase). This includes how to be a righteous child, spouse, parent, student, teacher, employee, or employer. If it is righteous, Scripture teaches us about it. This is called the "sufficiency of Scripture." God's Word both equips us for salvation and teaches us how to live righteously— the general calling of all believers. The more we understand Scripture, as applied to various situations, the more we can fulfill our general calling.

2.   Believers must be intimate with God to know their specific calling.

Part of our calling includes specific things God has for us to complete. We are his workmanship created in Christ Jesus for good works (Eph 2:10). In order to know our specific calling, we must be intimate with God so we can hear his voice. Psalm 25:14 says, "The Lord's loyal followers receive his guidance, and he reveals his covenantal demands to them." Those who are intimate with God hear his voice and can better discern his specific call on their lives.
Are you being intimate with God? Are you living in his Word and prayer? In order to walk in a manner worthy of Christ's calling, we must know our call.

Application Questions: Why is doctrine so important to Christian living? What aspects of your calling and identity in Christ have really transformed the way you live? In what ways has God revealed aspects of your specific calling through your walk with him?

Step Two: We Must Be Willing to Suffer for Christ

> I, therefore, the prisoner for the Lord, urge you to live worthily of the calling with which you have been called
> Ephesians 4:1

No doubt when Paul mentioned his imprisonment for the Lord, he was challenging the Ephesians to walk worthy of their calling by being willing to suffer for Christ. Persecution of Christians was widespread in the early church. They were being shunned, beaten, imprisoned, and burned at the stake, and we can be sure that some fell away from the faith because of it.

As Paul writes from prison, he essentially tells them, "It is worth it!" In fact, Christ teaches that being willing to suffer is necessary for discipleship. In Matthew 10:34-38, he says,

> Do not think that I have come to bring peace to the earth. I have not come to bring peace but a sword. For I have come to set a man against his father, a daughter against her mother, and a daughter-in-law against her mother-in-law, and a man's enemies will be the members of his household. "Whoever loves father or mother more than me is not worthy of me, and whoever loves son or daughter more than me is not worthy of me. And whoever does not take up his cross and follow me is not worthy of me.

Christ says that following him separates children from parents, daughters-in-law from mothers-in-law. Sadly, many Christians have lost family members over their faith. But Christ doesn't stop there, he says that anyone who loves family more than him and does not take up their cross is not "worthy" of him. The cross in those days was a form of execution. When Christ says to take the cross, he is referring to any type of suffering that comes while walking with him, including death.

When Paul calls himself a "prisoner for the Lord," he reminds these believers that willingness to suffer for Christ is part of their calling. Anybody who is unwilling is not worthy of Christ.

This should especially challenge Christians in societies where persecution is not explicitly overt. However, we must also recognize that overt persecution is growing very quickly. If you hold biblical views, you will be considered strange, hated, discriminated against, and harmed physically. Christians must be aware of this. In Matthew 24:9, Jesus says that Christians will be hated by all nations because of him. Since Christ's death and resurrection, around 43 million Christians have died for the faith. [112] It is estimated that approximately 400 Christians die daily for the faith. [113]

Again, if we are going to walk in a manner worthy of our calling, we must willingly suffer for Christ. Christ says this in Matthew 5:10-12:

> Blessed are those who are persecuted for righteousness, for the kingdom of heaven belongs to them. "Blessed are you when people insult you and persecute you and say all kinds of evil things about you falsely on account of me. Rejoice and be glad because your reward is great in heaven, for they persecuted the prophets before you in the same way.

Suffering for righteousness is a litmus test for our salvation—it proves we are part of the kingdom of heaven. But also, if we suffer for Christ, great is our reward in heaven. Let that encourage us, as we walk worthy of our calling in the face of persecution.

Application Questions: In what ways is persecution of Christians increasing around the world? How can we walk faithfully even in the midst of persecution? In what ways have you experienced persecution for your faith?

Step Three: We Must Practice Godly Character

with all humility and gentleness, with patience, bearing with one another in love
Ephesians 4:2

Observation Question: What character traits does Paul call for the Ephesians to cultivate, and what do they look like in the life of a believer?

In order to walk in a manner worthy of our calling, we must practice godly character. Paul calls for the Ephesians to practice humility, gentleness, patience, and bearing with one another in love. We will look at each one separately.

1. Believers must practice humility.

Paul calls for the Ephesians to be completely humble. What exactly is humility? William MacDonald and John MacArthur offer helpful insights:

Lowliness—a genuine humility that comes from association with the Lord Jesus. Lowliness makes us conscious of our own nothingness and enables us to esteem others better than ourselves. It is the opposite of conceit and arrogance...[114]
Tapeinophrosunē (humility) is a compound word that literally means to think or judge with lowliness, and hence to have lowliness of mind. John Wesley observed that "neither the Romans nor the Greeks had a word for humility." The very concept was so foreign and abhorrent to their way of thinking that they had no term to describe it. Apparently this Greek term was coined by Christians, probably by Paul himself, to describe a quality for which no other word was available. ...When, during the first several centuries of Christianity, pagan writers borrowed the term tapeinophrosunē, they always used it

derogatorily—frequently of Christians—because to them humility was a pitiable weakness.[115]

The reason a believer can have lowliness of mind is because he judges himself in view of God and not men. Paul, though possibly the greatest Christian to ever live, calls himself the chief of sinners (1 Tim 1:15), the least of all God's people (Eph 3:8), and the last of all the apostles (1 Cor 15:9). This type of mindset is developed as a believer constantly lives in the presence of God, and therefore compares himself to God. This creates a lowliness of mind. He knows that he is nothing apart from God, and that he falls far short of God's glory. This leaves no room for boasting or for criticizing others. It is not that the person with lowliness of mind thinks less of himself; he just thinks less about himself. He continually thinks of God and others first.

However, the prideful person is the opposite. He refuses to live in the presence of God or to view himself in comparison to God. Rather, he compares himself to others, further cultivating the pride that is already in his heart. He is full of selfish ambition—a desire to exalt himself. But God opposes the proud and gives grace to the humble (James 4:6). In fact, God disciplines the proud so that he may become humble.

Are you completely humble? Let your words and thoughts always represent this reality, and if they do not, repent. Repent daily before God and ask for his grace so you may become completely humble, like Christ. Consider Philippians 2:6-9:

> who though he existed in the form of God did not regard equality with God as something to be grasped, but emptied himself by taking on the form of a slave, by looking like other men, and by sharing in human nature. He humbled himself, by becoming obedient to the point of death – even death on a cross! As a result God exalted him and gave him the name that is above every name,

When Christ humbled himself, he did not become something he was not. Our God has always been humble. The incarnation only fully displayed this humility. That is why it is sinful for us to be prideful. How can we be prideful when God is not? We serve a humble God who became man and died for the sins of the world.

Are you walking worthy of your calling by being completely humble in word, thought, and appearance? Scripture says that God even hates a "proud look" (Prov 6:17, KJV).

If we are going to walk worthy of our calling, we must be completely humble. Let not a trace of pride be found in our lives.

2. Believers must practice gentleness.

This is one of the harder Greek words to translate. It is often translated as "meekness", "humility," or "gentleness." Gentleness is the "attitude that submits to God's dealings without rebellion, and to man's unkindness without retaliation."[116]

Christ uses this word of himself in Matthew 11:29: "Take my yoke on you and learn from me, because I am gentle and humble in heart, and you will find rest for your souls." Our Savior is gentle.

"Meekness" or "gentleness" in contemporary English is often associated with weakness, but it-should not be. "In the Greek language, this word was used for a soothing medicine, a colt that had been broken, and a soft wind. In each case there is power, but that power is under control."[117]

As mentioned, this character trait is clearly demonstrated in our Lord. Jesus used a whip and turned over tables in the temple because the people were being cheated and God's house dishonored (John 2). However, when mocked and put on a cross, Christ was like a lamb to the slaughter. He was gentle in response to injustice done to him. But when it came to injustice done to others and God, Christ was like a lion.

The gentle person keeps his power under control. Instead of blowing up at the smallest problem, he is gentle and forgiving. This is clearly displayed in the life of David, who was a type of Christ. Very much a warrior, David killed a bear and a lion, slaughtered Goliath, and defeated armies. But when King Saul tried to kill him and David was presented with opportunities to slay his royal enemy, his response was, "I will not touch God's anointed" (1 Sam 24:6, paraphrase). When mocked by Shimei after losing the kingdom to his son Absalom, David simply said, "Let him mock. Maybe God will see his mocking and repay me with good for the cursing I received today" (2 Sam 16:11-12, paraphrase). David was gentle and meek. His power was under control so he could use it to honor God and build God's kingdom.

In contrast, Scripture says a man who cannot control his temper is like a city with broken walls (Prov 25:28). He is always open to attack, which ultimately leads to his destruction. Such is the fate of a man who does not have his power under control.

Are you meek? How do you respond when others mistreat you? How do you respond when God and others are dishonored? Lord, give us the meekness of your Son!

3.   Believers must practice patience.

The word "patience" can be translated "longsuffering" (KJV). It means the ability to suffer long under difficult circumstances or relationships. Scripture says that Christ was "a man of sorrows" (Is 53:3). He bore great pain and suffering, and those who follow him must be prepared to do the same. Trials are one of the ways that God matures us (cf. James 1:2-4). As we wait on God in our trials, we begin to see our weaknesses and learn to trust him more.

The implication of patience characterizing a worthy walk is that complaining, bitterness, anger, and self-pity are unworthy of our calling. Philippians 2:14-15 says, "Do everything without grumbling or arguing, so that you may be blameless and pure, children of God without blemish though you live in a crooked and perverse society, in which you shine as lights in the world."

When Paul says we "may be blameless and pure, children of God" because we don't complain or argue, he is not saying that this is what saves us. Rather, he is saying that displaying characteristics of God's children manifests our true identity to others.

With that said, be careful about complaining and arguing. Discipline awaits those who cultivate such character in their lives (cf. 1 Cor 10:10). It is not fitting for a child of God.

How do we develop patience? We must develop our trust in God. The reason we complain and get upset is because we don't trust God as we should. We don't trust him in our trials or when dealing with difficult people. Trust, or faith, comes by hearing and obeying the Word of God (cf. Rom 10:17) and also by continually experiencing his faithfulness. The more we trust God, the more patient we become.

4.   Believers must practice bearing with one another in love.

MacDonald's comments are helpful:

Bearing with one another in love—that is, making allowance for the faults and failures of others, or differing personalities, abilities, and temperaments. And it is not a question of maintaining a façade of courtesy while inwardly seething with resentment. It means positive love to those who irritate, disturb, or embarrass.[118]

Do you love people who irritate, disturb, or embarrass you? First Peter 4:8 says, "Above all keep your love for one another fervent, because love covers a multitude of sins."

Again, humility, gentleness, patience, and forbearance in love mark a walk that is worthy of the Lord, but pride, arrogance, impatience, and acting out of selfish anger are unworthy of Christ's calling.

Application Questions: Which character trait do you struggle with most out of the four Paul presents? How is God calling you to cultivate it so you can live in a manner worthy of Christ's calling?

Step Four: We Must Labor for Unity in the Church

> making every effort to keep the unity of the Spirit in the bond of peace.
> There is one body and one Spirit, just as you too were called to the
> one hope of your calling, one Lord, one faith, one baptism, one God
> and Father of all, who is over all and through all and in all.
> Ephesians 4:3-6

Next, Paul says to "Make every effort to keep the unity of the Spirit in the bond of peace." The fact that he calls the Ephesians "to keep" the unity of the Spirit implies that the Spirit had already given unity—they just needed to maintain it. The unity of the Spirit is not something man-made; it is something given by God. Christ prayed for this unity right before going to the (John 17:20-21):

> "I am not praying only on their behalf, but also on behalf of those who believe in me through their testimony, that they will all be one, just as you, Father, are in me and I am in you. I pray that they will be in us, so that the world will believe that you sent me.

Christ prayed for God to make the disciples one, and also that they would be "in" the Godhead. God granted Christ's prayer through the baptism of the Spirit. However, sadly, this has become a divisive doctrine in the church. Some believe it is a second work of the Spirit after salvation, where believers speak in tongues and are empowered to serve God. Those who believe this teach that all Christians should seek this experience. However, Paul teaches that every believer experiences the baptism of the Spirit at salvation, and it doesn't have to be sought. First Corinthians 12:13 says, "For in one Spirit we were all baptized into one body. Whether Jews or Greeks or slaves or free, we were all made to drink of the one Spirit."

Instead of creating two separate types of Christians—Spirit baptized and non-Spirit baptized—the baptism of the Spirit creates the complete opposite. It makes all Christians members of one body in Christ. Paul stresses this throughout Ephesians—believing Jews and Gentiles are no longer separate, but one in Christ (2:11-15, 3:6).

Many seek to create a superficial unity by imposing uniformity. They require all to worship, pray, dress, or give in a certain way. However, unity and uniformity are not necessarily the same. In fact, the metaphor of the body tells us there will be great diversity in the church. A physical body, though one, is made up of feet, eyes, a chest, and legs. Similarly, in a local church body, there will be different cultures, customs, view-points, and gifts. The Corinthian church was noted for not lacking any spiritual gifts (1 Cor 1:7) such as tongues and prophecy, but none of the other NT churches were noted for that. God made each church different, and he made each believer different. We should celebrate this diversity because it glorifies God.

Paul does not tell us to create unity, but he does challenge us to "make every effort" to keep it.

Application Question: How should we "make every effort" to keep the peace?

1. We make every effort by seeking to resolve conflict speedily.

"Make every effort" comes from a root word which means to make haste, and thus gives the idea of zealous effort and diligence."[119] Paul says this later in Ephesians 4:26, "'In your anger do not sin': Do not let the sun go down while you are still angry, and do not give the devil a foothold."

Paul says that if we are angry with somebody, we should make it right before the sun goes down. In other words, "Make haste!" The enemy wants to use that door to attack us and others, so we need to close it quickly.

2. We make every effort by doing as much as possible to resolve conflict.

"Make every effort in the Greek is emphatic. It can also be translated 'spare no effort' (NEB)."[120] Romans 12:18 says, "If possible, so far as it depends on you, live peaceably with all people." In sparing no effort, we forgive those who hurt us and reach out to those who are angry at us, but we also labor to help others reconcile. Paul says this to a member of the Philippian church in Philippians 4:3: "Yes, I say also to you, true companion, help them. They have struggled together in the gospel ministry along with me and Clement and my other coworkers, whose names are in the book of life." In sparing no effort, we must do the same.

3. We make every effort by persevering and not giving up.

"Make every effort" is a "present participle, it is a call for continuous, diligent activity."[121] In churches or families where there is deep-seated conflict, we must not cease to pray, love, forgive, and pursue reconciliation. Christ says that if somebody hurts us seventy-seven times, we must still forgive (Matt 18:22). In making every effort, we must not give up. Galatians 6:9 says, "So we must not grow weary in doing good, for in due time we will reap, if we do not give up." God will bring the harvest in his timing if we persevere.

4. We make every effort by focusing on our God-given commonalities.

Typically, when division arises, it is partially because people focus on their differences instead of their commonalities. Like one trained in modern day conflict resolution, Paul calls for the Ephesians to focus on their spiritual commonalities. In Ephesians 4:4-6, he notes seven that all believers share: "There is one body and one Spirit, just as you too were called to the one hope of your calling, one Lord, one faith, one baptism, one God and Father of all, who is over all and through all and in all." Many scholars believe this was an early church confessional hymn.[122]

Observation Question: What are the seven spiritual commonalities Paul mentions in Ephesians 4:4-6?

- Believers are one in Christ's body.

Again, this refers to how the baptism of the Spirit made all believers—Jew, Gentile, male, female, slave, and free—one man in Christ. We are one in Christ's body, so we should labor for unity.

- Believers have one Spirit.

It is God's Spirit who indwells believers (1 Cor 6:19), unifies them (1 Cor 12:13), and empowers them to perform Christ's ministry on earth (Acts 1:8). Only believers drink daily from the Spirit—this should encourage us to preserve the unity he gave us.

- Believers have one hope.

This hope refers to Christ's second coming and all that awaits the believer at his coming—the bodily resurrection, freedom from sin, ruling with Christ, and much, much more. First John 3:2-3 says,

Dear friends, we are God's children now, and what we will be has not yet been revealed. We know that whenever it is revealed we will be like him, because we will see him just as he is. And everyone who has this hope focused on him purifies himself, just as Jesus is pure).

While the world's hope is earthly, ours is heavenly—we hope in Christ and his coming. This commonality should encourage us to work for unity.

- Believers have one Lord.

This refers to Christ, our Master. First Corinthians 8:6 says, "yet for us there is one God, the Father, from whom are all things and for whom we live, and one Lord, Jesus Christ, through whom are all things and through whom we live." While those in the world follow their own desires and the desires of others, and worship false gods, we follow Christ.

Certainly, having the same Master should cause us to agree in the Lord (Phil 4:2).

- Believers have one faith.

This refers to the body of doctrine passed down to us in Scripture. Jude 1:3 says, "Dear friends, although I have been eager to write to you about our common salvation, I now feel compelled instead to write to encourage you to contend earnestly for the faith that was once for all entrusted to the saints." We must contend for the truth and faithfully pass it on. Paul says this to Timothy in 2 Timothy 1:13-14:

> Hold to the standard of sound words that you heard from me and do so with the faith and love that are in Christ Jesus. Protect that good thing entrusted to you, through the Holy Spirit who lives within us.

It is this body of doctrine that teaches our unity and calls for us to preserve it.

- Believers have one baptism.

This could mean either the baptism of the Spirit by which we become members of the body of Christ, or water baptism as a person confesses his identification with Christ's death, burial, and resurrection (cf. Rom 6:4). It is essentially the believer's wedding ceremony, as he publicly professes the name of the Father, Son, and Holy Spirit (Matt 28:19).

- Believers have one God and Father of all.

The Believer's Bible Commentary adds:

> Above all—He is the supreme Sovereign of the universe. Through all—He acts through all, using everything to accomplish His purposes. In you all—He dwells in all believers, and is present in all places at one and the same time.[123]

In considering all our commonalities as believers, let us make every effort to preserve the unity of the Spirit.

How else should we make every effort to preserve this unity, as laid out in Ephesians 4:3-6?

5. Believers make every effort by not compromising foundational truths.

An implication of Paul's focus on these seven spiritual commonalities is the need to maintain the basic foundational truths of Christianity. Paul is not promoting unity at any cost, but rather unity based on truth and righteousness. When someone teaches a different Lord other than Jesus Christ, he is not a Christian and should not be accepted as such. The apostle John says, "but every spirit that does not confess Jesus is not from God, and this is the spirit of the antichrist, which you have heard is coming, and now is already in the world" (1 John 4:3).

Similarly, in Galatians 1:9 Paul calls for anyone who teaches another gospel to be accursed. Some think we should seek unity by all means necessary. However, this is incorrect. If professed believers teach a different Lord, a different God, or a different gospel, we should not unite with them. In fact, this is not only true when a professed believer teaches heresy verbally, but also when he teaches it by ungodly living. First Corinthians 5:11-13 says,

> But now I am writing to you not to associate with anyone who calls himself a Christian who is sexually immoral, or greedy, or an idolater, or verbally abusive, or a drunkard, or a swindler. Do not even eat with such a person. For what do I have to do with judging those outside? Are you not to judge those inside? But God will judge those outside. Remove the evil person from among you.

There can be no unity where foundational doctrinal truths or the practical righteousness resulting from them are compromised. This requires wisdom and discernment. It has commonly been said, "In essentials, unity. In doubtful questions, liberty. In all things, charity."[124]

Application Questions: In what ways have you experienced disunity in the body of Christ? How is God calling you to labor for unity? When should believers separate from a local church or from individual believers?

Conclusion

How can we live a life worthy of our calling in Christ? What steps must we take?

1. Step One: We must continually seek to understand our calling.
2. Step Two: We must be willing to suffer for Christ.
3. Step Three: We must practice godly character.
4. Step Four: We must labor for unity in the Church.

God's Plan to Build the Church

But to each one of us grace was given according to the measure of the gift of Christ. Therefore it says, "When he ascended on high he captured captives; he gave gifts to men." Now what is the meaning of "he ascended," except that he also descended to the lower regions, namely, the earth? He, the very one who descended, is also the one who ascended above all the heavens, in order to fill all things. It was he who gave some as apostles, some as prophets, some as evangelists, and some as pastors and teachers, to equip the saints for the work of ministry, that is, to build up the body of Christ, until we all attain to the unity of the faith and of the knowledge of the Son of God – a mature person, attaining to the measure of Christ's full stature. So we are no longer to be children, tossed back and forth by waves and carried about by every wind of teaching by the trickery of people who craftily carry out their deceitful schemes. But practicing the truth in love, we will in all things grow up into Christ, who is the head. From him the whole body grows, fitted and held together through every supporting ligament. As each one does its part, the body grows in love. Ephesians 4:7-16 (NET)

What is God's plan to build the church?

"Church growth" is a big movement in Christianity. Some, using secular thinking, teach that you cannot grow a heterogeneous church—one with different ethnic and socio-economic groups—because people don't like to cross those boundaries. Others focus on business principles—you need a coffee shop, and a relaxing and inviting atmosphere where people's "felt needs" are met. In fact, I read one book on church growth that said in order for a church to grow the service must last no longer than an hour. The logic is that people don't want to worship for more than an hour—fix your service around what people want, and your church will grow. Clearly, most principles guiding church growth initiatives today are secular instead of spiritual.

But, what is God's plan for church growth? Christ says in Matthew 16:18, "on this rock I will build my church, and the gates of Hades will not overpower it." Christ is building his church, and we need to find out how he is building it so we can partner with him. When we build on secular principles, we get what man can build—a secular church that won't last (cf. Ps 127:1). But if we build according to Christ's principles, we get what God can build—a church that the gates of hades will not prevail against.

In Ephesians 4:7-16, Paul teaches specifics about God's plan to build his church so we can get involved and do our part—but also so that we don't build according to any lesser plan.

Big Questions: What is God's plan to build his church, as seen in Ephesians 4:7-16, and how can we apply this to our lives and to our local churches?

God Builds His Church through Gifting Believers

> But to each one of us grace was given according to the measure of the gift of Christ. Therefore it says, "When he ascended on high he captured captives; he gave gifts to men."
> Ephesians 4:7-8

When Paul says "But," it is not just a conjunction; it is meant to be adversative. It can be translated "In spite of that" or "On the other hand." He is contrasting the previous teaching of making every effort to keep the unity of the church because there is one body, one Lord, and one Spirit (v. 4-6) with what he is about to say.[125] Essentially, he says that though it is Christ's will for the church to be unified, it is also his will for it to be diverse. Each believer receives a different grace from Christ.

In this context, "grace" means "the ability to perform the task God has called us to."[126] Paul describes this grace as "gifts," saying, "'When he ascended on high he captured captives; he gave gifts to men.'" He pictures Christ as a conquering king, distributing booty to his followers. This is similar to what Paul teaches in Romans 12:6-8:

> And we have different gifts according to the grace given to us. If the gift is prophecy, that individual must use it in proportion to his faith. If it is service, he must serve; if it is teaching, he must teach; if it is exhortation, he must exhort; if it is contributing, he must do so with sincerity; if it is leadership, he must do so with diligence; if it is showing mercy, he must do so with cheerfulness.

When Christ ascended to heaven—conquering death, sin, and Satan in his resurrection—he distributed gifts of grace to his people. Now, it must be understood that spiritual gifts are not the same as talents. Talents are natural gifts received at birth. However, spiritual gifts are received at spiritual birth or sometime later, as Christ through the Spirit distributes them (cf. 1 Cor 12:7).

There is some controversy over this, as some believe people only receive spiritual gifts at salvation. However, several passages seem to indicate otherwise. In 1 Corinthians 12:31, Paul calls believers to "be eager for the greater gifts." This statement wouldn't make sense if there were no opportunity to receive greater gifts. Also, Paul exhorts Timothy to "rekindle God's gift that you possess through the laying on of my hands" (2 Timothy 1:6). It seems clear that Timothy received another spiritual gift after salvation. Therefore, I believe it is good to both desire and pray for spiritual gifts.

God gifts believers to serve and build up the church. First Corinthians 12:7 says, "To each person the manifestation of the Spirit is given for the benefit of all." In Ephesians 4:16, Paul adds, "From him the whole body grows, fitted and held together through every supporting ligament. As each one does its part, the body grows in love." As each person uses his specific gifts, the church grows.

Interpretation Question: What are these spiritual gifts?

The five lists of spiritual gifts in the Bible, 1 Corinthians 12:8-10, 1 Corinthians 12:28-30, Romans 12:6-8, 1 Peter 4:10-11, and Ephesians 4:11 contain around 20 gifts, depending on how you interpret and count them. They include teaching, administration, mercy, exhortation, helps, tongues, faith, miracles, and giving, among others. However, it is clear that the authors do not mean these lists to be exhaustive. In fact, we see other gifts mentioned in the Bible. In 1 Corinthians 7, Paul talks about the gifts of singleness and marriage. In Exodus 31, Bezalel was gifted by God with craftsmanship in order to build the tabernacle. For this reason, many believe there could be numerous gifts not mentioned specifically in the Bible such as intercession, casting out demons, and leading worship. As we find our gifts and use them to build the body of Christ, the church grows. God empowers us with grace—unmerited favor—to build his church. This is his plan.

Application Question: How do we find our spiritual gifts?

Because spiritual gifts are given to build the body of Christ, we find them by getting involved and serving. As we serve, it becomes clear what our gifts are. Here are two tests to determine them. First Corinthians 14:4 says, "The one who speaks in a tongue builds himself up, but the one who prophesies builds up the church." I think we discern two characteristics of spiritual gifts from this verse. (1) They typically edify the person using them, even as a person speaking in tongues edifies himself. As one uses his gift of teaching, he will grow in faith and come to know God better. As he uses his gift of mercy—listening and ministering to the hurting—he himself will be built up. (2) And of course, using these gifts will build others up, as prophecy was said to edify the church.

Therefore, if you think you have the gift of teaching and as you teach you feel edified, good! But if nobody else is edified or encouraged by your teaching, it may not be your gift. Typically, spiritual gifts edify both the user and the receiver. One exception might be the gift of tongues. When a person uses this gift, it only builds him up unless it is interpreted. That is why Paul places tongues last in the list in 1 Corinthians 12:28. He implies that it is the least important gift.

So how do you find your gifts? Find a way to serve the church. While serving, you will find out what edifies you and others and what doesn't. You will find out which gifts you have and which ones you don't have. And as you continue to use your gifts, they will get stronger. Paul tells Timothy not to neglect his gift, but rather to stir it into flame (cf. 1 Tim 4:14, 2 Tim 1:6). We are all responsible for developing our gifts-to their fullest potential for the kingdom of God.

Application Questions: What are your spiritual gifts? In what ways has God called you to develop and use them?

God Builds His Church through the Ascended Christ's Authority and Rule

> Therefore it says, "When he ascended on high he captured captives; he gave gifts to men." Now what is the meaning of "he ascended," except that he also descended to the lower regions, namely, the earth? He, the very one who descended, is also the one who ascended above all the heavens, in order to fill all things
> Ephesians 4:8-10

When Paul refers to Christ ascending on high, this is not just a change of location, but also a change of position. Ascending on high represents Christ's authority in heaven at the right of hand of God, which Paul previously referred to in Ephesians 1:19-21:

> and what is the incomparable greatness of his power toward us who believe, as displayed in the exercise of his immense strength. This power he exercised in Christ when he raised him from the dead and seated him at his right hand in the heavenly realms far above every rule and authority and power and dominion and every name that is named, not only in this age but also in the one to come.

Since Christ's ascension, he rules the universe as king, far above all rule, authority, power, and dominion. And one day, he will rule it not only positionally, but actually—at his second coming. And this current rule and authority play a part in God's plan to build his church. In fact, Christ said this before his ascension-in Matthew 28:18-20:

> Then Jesus came up and said to them, "All authority in heaven and on earth has been given to me. Therefore go and make disciples of all nations, baptizing them in the name of the Father and the Son and the Holy Spirit, teaching them to obey everything I have commanded you. And remember, I am with you always, to the end of the age.

When believers evangelize, serve, and build God's church, they are working through the authority of the ascended Christ. God has given us the power and authority of Christ, which is why Paul teaches that we are seated in heavenly places with Christ (Eph 2:6). He is referring to Christ's authority, and our authority in him. And one day we will, along with Christ, even judge angels at the second coming (1 Cor 6:3).

In Ephesians 4:8-10, Paul describes how this authority to rule and distribute gifts was secured by Christ. As mentioned, in the passage about Christ ascending on high, leading captives in his train and giving gifts to men, he pictures Christ as a conquering king parading through the city and distributing booty. Paul quotes Psalm 68:18. In this psalm, David depicts God "as marching in triumph before all Israel after the Exodus."[127] God not only conquered Egypt for Israel, but also the nations who attacked them in the wilderness.

However, as we compare the Old Testament passage with Paul's quotation, there is a slight difference. Psalm 68:18 says that God "received" gifts from men instead of giving them—this may refer to Egypt giving gifts to Israel as they left for the wilderness. Therefore, Psalm 68 is not a prophecy about Christ. Rather, Paul is making a "general allusion to the passage for the sake of analogy."[128] He is showing Christ as the victorious one through his death, resurrection, and ascension, even as God was victorious over Egypt and other nations. Christ conquered sin, death, and Satan in his ascension, and he distributed spiritual gifts to his people, even as God conquered nations and gave gifts to Israel.

Interpretation Question: Who were the slaves in Christ's victory parade?

1. Conquering kings (or generals) commonly brought back captured enemies as slaves, which might picture Christ making a public spectacle of Satan and his demons. Colossians 2:15 says, "Disarming

the rulers and authorities, he has made a public disgrace of them, triumphing over them by the cross."

2.   Conquering kings also commonly recaptured their own soldiers who were previously prisoners and brought them back to their cities in victory parades. [129] The captives in Christ's victory parade also probably picture believers who were previously slaves to Satan, but now are free in Christ.

Interpretation Question: What is Paul referring to when he says Christ descended to "the lower, earthly regions"?

There are at least three different views on this.

1.   The reformers believed it referred to the incarnation.[130] When Christ descended, he left heaven and came to earth as a man to die for the sins of the world. But, at his resurrection, he ascended to heaven to rule. Support for this may be found in John 3:13, which says, "No one has ascended into heaven except he who descended from heaven, the Son of Man" (ESV).

2.   The early church fathers believed it referred to Christ going to hades during his three days in the grave.[131] Support for this is found in 1 Peter 3:18-19, a controversial passage:

For Christ died for sins once for all, the righteous for the unrighteous, to bring you to God. He was put to death in the body but made alive by the Spirit, through whom also he went and preached to the spirits in prison

They believed that during Christ's time in the grave, he went to hades—the abode of the dead—and proclaimed his victory over the devil (cf. Col 2:15). Support for this is found in Christ saying he would spend three days in the "heart of the earth" (Matthew 12:40), as the heart of something typically refers to the center. Further support is seen in Christ telling the thief on the cross that on that same day he would be with him in paradise (Luke 23:43).

Hades, or sheol, had two compartments. One was paradise (i.e. Abraham's Bosom), where the righteous dwelled, and across from it was a place of torment. In the Old Testament, the righteous did not dwell in heaven but in paradise—across from the damned. In fact, communication took place between the two places, as seen by the rich man communicating with Abraham about Lazarus in Christ's story in Luke 16:19-31. Some scholars believe this was a parable—meant to share a specific point—and that one can't accept all the details (such as the righteous dwelling in sheol). However, this story doesn't read like a parable. Typically, the people in parables aren't named; Lazarus was most likely a real person, just like Abraham.

In the New Testament, it is clear that believers now live in heaven. In 2 Corinthians 12:2 and 4, Paul equates paradise with the third heaven. He also teaches that to be absent from the body is to be present with the Lord (2 Cor 5:8), who is in heaven. The question then becomes, "When did paradise, and therefore the righteous, move to heaven?"

Many believe Paul is alluding to this in his conquering king illustration. They say that when Christ descended to the lower part of the earth—hades—to declare victory over the enemy, he took paradise and its inhabitants, the Old Testament faithful, back to heaven to be with him.

John MacArthur says this about the early church's understanding of this doctrine:

> Early church dogma taught that the righteous dead of the Old Testament could not be taken into the fullness of God's presence until Christ had purchased their redemption on the cross, and that they had waited in this place for His victory on that day. Figuratively speaking, the early church Fathers said that, after announcing His triumph over demons in one part of Sheol, He then opened the doors of another part of Sheol to release those godly captives. Like the victorious kings of old, He recaptured the captives and liberated them, and henceforth they would live in heaven as eternally free sons of God.[132]

3. Others believe it refers generally to Christ's ultimate humiliation in his death.[133]

They say that Paul is simply referring to Christ's ultimate humiliation on the cross, as taught in Philippians 2:6-11:

who though he existed in the form of God did not regard equality with God as something to be grasped, but emptied himself by taking on the form of a slave, by looking like other men, and by sharing in human nature. He humbled himself, by becoming obedient to the point of death – even death on a cross! As a result God exalted him and gave him the name that is above every name, so that at the name of Jesus every knee will bow – in heaven and on earth and under the earth – and every tongue confess that Jesus Christ is Lord to the glory of God the Father.

Christ descended to the depths of the earth in his death. Humbling himself and becoming obedient to death—even death on a cross—was the ultimate descent of Christ. There he bore hell itself, enduring God's wrath for our sins. And because of this humiliation, God exalted him and gave him a name higher than any other name, that at the name of Jesus every knee would bow in heaven and on earth. And all will call him "Lord."

Whatever view (or compilation of views) we take, Paul's point is that Christ's descent led to his victory. God exalted his victorious Son above every power and principality in heaven and on earth, and this enables him, as the conquering King, to give gifts to believers.

Application Question: How should believers apply the reality of Christ's authority over the universe and his ultimate rule?

1. Believers must remember that they minister with Christ's authority.

Believers have been raised with Christ, and his authority goes with them as they minister. Christ says, "All authority in heaven and on earth has been given to me. Therefore go and make disciples of all nations" (Matt 28:18-19). We should not feel insecure, fearful, or incompetent as we minister, for Christ gives us his very own power and authority to build his church. Indeed, Christ has given us his Spirit—a Spirit of power, love, and self-discipline to do his work (2 Tim 1:7).

2. Believers must remember the authority of Christ when engaged in spiritual warfare.

The devil was defeated in Christ's resurrection and ascension (Col 2:15), and believers are seated in heavenly places with Christ. Therefore, Christ's authority ministers through us when we confront the devil's works. Jesus says the gates of Hades will not prevail against his church (Matt 16:18). We must remember this when the lion roars and tries to instill fear, doubt, or worry. We walk in our ascended Lord's authority to minister to those oppressed by demons and blinded by the enemy. Christ has anointed us to preach the good news, to proclaim freedom to prisoners, and to set the oppressed free (cf. Luke 4:18). Thank you, Lord, for your victory!

3. Believers should continually pray for Christ's full reign on this earth.

When Paul says that Christ's descent and ascension were "in order to fill all things" (Eph 4:10), he refers to Christ's ultimate rule in heaven and on earth. Believers should desire this and pray for it. Christ himself teaches that we should pray, "Thy kingdom come, thy will be done" (Matt 6:10, KJV) and this must be our hearts' desire. We are Christ's ambassadors on earth: awaiting his return and building his church until he comes. Lord, come. Lord, come! Amen.

4.   Believers should remember that humility leads to exaltation.

This is true not only for Christ but for us as well. The first will be last and the last will be first (Matt 20:16). Whoever wants to be first must be last—the slave of all (Mark 9:35). We live in a world system where everybody wants to be served, and nobody wants to serve others. However, it is the humble—the ones who serve—that God exalts. "'God opposes the proud, but he gives grace to the humble'" (James 4:6).

Application Questions: Why is understanding Christ's authority so important to building the church? How can we apply this truth in our daily lives and ministries?

God Builds His Church through the Ministry of Gifted Leaders

It was he who gave some as apostles, some as prophets, some as evangelists, and some as pastors and teachers, to equip the saints for the work of ministry, that is, to build up the body of Christ, until we all attain to the unity of the faith and of the knowledge of the Son of God – a mature person, attaining to the measure of Christ's full stature. So we are no longer to be children, tossed back and forth by waves and carried about by every wind of teaching by the trickery of people who craftily carry out their deceitful schemes.
Ephesians 4:11-14

Observation Questions: What ministry leaders does Paul list in Ephesians 4:11, and what are their ministries?

Next, Paul describes the gifts that the ascended Christ distributes. To our surprise, they are not really "gifts" at all—they are gifted leaders. Certainly, each believer receives a gift(s), but here Paul focuses on gifted leaders—apostles, prophets, evangelists, pastors, and teachers.

The apostles were the original twelve disciples (minus Judas), Paul, James the brother of Jesus, Matthias, and a few others. They had to have seen the risen Christ so they could bear witness of him (Acts 1:22). God authenticated their ministry through miracles (Heb 2:1-4, 2 Cor 12:12).

Along with the prophets, they built the foundation of the church (Eph 2:20) by writing the New Testament and teaching its doctrines. Since the foundation of the church is already built, there are no apostles in that sense today. However, there may be apostles in a secondary sense. The Greek word "apostolos" simply means "sent one." It was also used of those officially sent out from churches. If there are apostles today, they would be missionaries, church planters, ministry leaders, etc.

The next leaders Christ gave the church were prophets. They gave messages that were directly from God, and, like the apostles, built the foundation of the church by writing the New Testament and teaching its doctrines. There are, of course, no modern-day prophets in this sense of the word. However, there are prophets in a secondary sense. Paul describes them in 1 Corinthians 14:3 as speaking to people "for their strengthening, encouragement and consolation." They may at times be identified by addressing social sins and failures of God's people, even as the Old Testament prophets did. God often gives them insight into an individual's life, a church, or even a nation in order to strengthen and encourage people.

The next gift Christ gave the church was evangelists. Evangelists are gifted in sharing the gospel with people either one-on-one or corporately through evangelistic preaching. They typically feel very comfortable around unbelievers, and are often gifted at answering questions that are hindering these people from coming to the Lord. God uses the evangelist to bring people to Christ, and he uses the church to disciple these new believers.

Finally, he gave pastors and teachers. Because "teachers" lacks the article in the Greek, some believe this is one gift, pastor-teachers. The main responsibility of a pastor is to feed the church through teaching. However, it is possible for a person to be gifted in teaching but not in pastoring. Paul mentions the gift of teaching individually in 1 Corinthians 12, so he is probably referring to two separate gifts in Ephesians 4:11. Pastors, or "shepherds," care for people, while teachers have a special gifting to understand the Word of God and to help others understand it.

Application Question: How should we respond to the fact that Paul calls these leaders "gifts" to the church?

1. The fact that Paul calls these leaders "gifts" reminds us to be thankful for them.

Our leaders are subject to many attacks, and they are prone to discouragement and burnout. In the US, more than 1,700 pastors leave the ministry every month.[134] If Satan had only one bullet, he would aim it at our spiritual leaders. And since they are our gifts, we must always be thankful for them instead of criticizing and neglecting them.

2. The fact that Paul calls these leaders "gifts" reminds us to take care of them.

As with any other gift, we should be good stewards. Galatians 6:6 says, "Now the one who receives instruction in the word must share all good things with the one who teaches it." Of course, we should make sure that their financial needs are met, for Jesus says, "the worker deserves his provisions" (Matt 10:10, cf. 1 Tim 5:18). But sharing "all good things" also refers to giving our leaders protection, encouragement, and love, among other things.

3. The fact that Paul calls these leaders "gifts" reminds us to not overly exalt them.

Paul rebuked the church in Corinth for overly exalting their spiritual leaders and separating into rival factions over them. Some were saying, "I am of Paul," and others, "I am of Apollos." Paul responded, "What, after all, is Apollos? And what is Paul? Only men" (1 Cor 3:5). In 1 Corinthians 3:21-23, he added,

> So then, no more boasting about mere mortals! For everything belongs to you, whether Paul or Apollos or Cephas or the world or life or death or the present or the future. Everything belongs to you, and you belong to Christ, and Christ belongs to God.

Paul reminded the Corinthians that all things were theirs—meaning that these men were given by God to aid them. We should definitely honor and obey our spiritual leaders (Heb 13:17), but we must make sure not to idolize them.

Interpretation Question: How do these leaders help the church grow?

Paul says these leaders are given:

> to equip the saints for the work of ministry, that is, to build up the body of Christ, until we all attain to the unity of the faith and of the knowledge of the Son of God – a mature person, attaining to the measure of Christ's full stature.
> Ephesians 4:12-13

1. Gifted leaders help the church by preparing God's people for works of ministry.

Scripture does not endorse a model where pastors and teachers are paid professionals who do all the work while the congregation does nothing. In a very real sense, good pastors try to work themselves out of a job. They train the church to evangelize, baptize, disciple, and serve in various other ways.

The establishment of clergy and laymen has greatly hurt the church. John Stott shares a helpful story about a congregation he visited in the US.

On the front cover of their Sunday bulletin I read the name of the Rector, the Reverend Everett Fullam, then the names of the Associate Rector and of the Assistant to the Rector. Next came the following line: 'Ministers: the entire congregation'. It was startling, but undeniably biblical.[135]

This is a biblical model of church ministry. The whole church ministers to its members and to the world. As it does this, it is "built up."

2.   Gifted leaders help the church come to a unity of the faith.

They do so by teaching sound doctrine, faithfully feeding the church the Word of God. Paul says that God gave gifted leaders, "that is, to build up the body of Christ ... to the unity of the faith" (v. 12).

The church in general is full of doctrinal disunity, but God has provided godly leaders to help us know and become united in the truth. For this reason, pastors should not avoid difficult texts or controversial doctrines—it is their job to help the church to come to a unity of the faith.

Regarding selecting an elder, Paul says, "He must hold firmly to the faithful message as it has been taught, so that he will be able to give exhortation in such healthy teaching and correct those who speak against it" (Titus 1:9). Godly leaders help the church come to a unity of faith by opposing wrong doctrine. Just as much of Paul's teaching addressed false doctrine in the church, good leaders uphold sound doctrine today.

3.   Gifted leaders help the church come to know Christ.

They help the church come to "the knowledge of the Son of God" (Eph 4:13), a knowledge that is not only mental, but is primarily experiential. We certainly see this in Paul's pastoral prayer for the Ephesians: "I pray that the God of our Lord Jesus Christ, the Father of glory, may give you spiritual wisdom and revelation in your growing knowledge of him" (Eph 1:17). His hope was for the Ephesian congregations to know God more. And this was his desire for himself as well. In Philippians 3:8-11, he said:

More than that, I now regard all things as liabilities compared to the far greater value of knowing Christ Jesus my Lord, for whom I have suffered the loss of all things – indeed, I regard them as dung! – that I may gain Christ, and be found in him, not because I have my own righteousness derived from the law, but because I have the righteousness that comes by way of Christ's faithfulness – a righteousness from God that is in fact based on Christ's faithfulness. My aim is to know him, to experience the power of his resurrection, to share in his sufferings, and to be like him in his death, and so, somehow, to attain to the resurrection from the dead.

Paul wanted to know Christ and to help others know him as well. Lord, help your church know you!

4.   Gifted leaders help the church to become more like Christ.

Ephesians 4:13 says, "attaining to the measure of Christ's full stature." Romans 8:29 says, "because those whom he foreknew he also predestined to be conformed to the image of his Son, that his Son would be the firstborn among many brothers and sisters." God saved the church to conform it to the likeness of his Son, and he predestined believers for this purpose, even before time. As gifted leaders teach the Word, pray, and serve, the church comes to look more like Christ.

As the church matures, believers are no longer tossed to and fro by various false doctrines (Eph 4:14). Paul describes the spiritually immature as infants, and like physical infants, they lack knowledge and discernment—making them vulnerable. This is why cults and false teachers prey on spiritual infants, and why gifted leaders must protect them by helping them mature and grow strong in Christ.

Application Questions: Why are spiritual leaders so prone to discouragement and burnout? How is God calling you to better care for your spiritual leaders? Why are spiritual infants so prone to strongholds and false teaching? How can churches better care for spiritual infants?

God Builds His Church through the Ministry of Gifted Members

But practicing the truth in love, we will in all things grow up into Christ, who is the head. From him the whole body grows, fitted and held together through every supporting ligament. As each one does its part, the body grows in love.
Ephesians 4:15-16

God's plan is not just to build the church through the ministry of gifted leaders, but also through the ministry of every member. As mentioned, he provides these leaders to equip the church for ministry, and as each person serves the church, it grows. In Ephesians 4:15-16, Paul focuses on the members' role in building the church.

Interpretation Question: How do church members help the body of Christ to grow?

1.   Members help the body of Christ grow by living out the truth.

The text "practicing the truth in love" is very hard to translate into English. Some translate it "truthing in love."[136] The Greek verb "alētheuō" literally means "to speak, deal, or act truthfully."[137] It refers not just to speaking, but also to acting in accord with the truth. When believers live out God's truth in speech and action, the church grows.

However, when the church is not living out the truth, it hinders growth, pushing people away from God and one another. First Corinthians 5:6 says, "a little yeast affects the whole batch of dough." Sin and compromise spread and affect everybody—destroying the spiritual atmosphere of the church. In addition, Christ says we either gather with him or scatter (Matt 12:30). There is no in between. When believers live out the truth, the church grows—and when they don't, it dies.

2.   Members help the body of Christ grow by loving one another.

Truth without love leads to pride and division. First Corinthians 8:1 says, "knowledge puffs up, but love builds up." Speaking the truth without love only pushes people away. Christ taught the truth, but he also ate and drank with sinners, and he forgave the prostitute. We must speak and practice the truth in a loving manner, which includes forgiving and being patient with others. Love is the ground in which the seed of truth grows. If there is no love, people are pushed away. However, if we only have love and not truth, then we have liberalism—a gross acceptance of sin.

3.   Members help the body of Christ grow by being connected.

Paul describes the growing church as being "fitted and held together through every supporting ligament" (Eph 4:16). It does not grow when the members are separated. When we live in isolation from one another, just attending church but not getting involved, the entire church suffers. The parts of Christ's body need each other, just as the eye needs the hand and the hand needs the eye.

Therefore, we must make effort to be connected and also to keep the unity of the body of Christ (Eph 4:3). We must work to heal any division that tries to destroy the body or keep it from growing.

4.   Members help the body of Christ grow by serving.

As mentioned, Paul says the body grows "as each one does its part" (Eph 4:16). Each member of the body has a role, even the little toe. Without it, the body is unstable. This is how most churches function: they are unstable and not functioning properly because people aren't fulfilling their roles.

What is your role in the church? How is God calling you to fulfill it? God builds his church through the service of gifted members.

Application Questions: Using the body as a metaphor, what part(s) of the body would you be and why? In what ways can you better encourage the participation and unity of other members in your local church or ministry?

Conclusion

Christ says, "On this rock, I will build my church." God is building his church today. What is his plan? How is he building the church, and how can we get involved?

1.   God builds his church through gifting believers.
2.   God builds his church through the ascended Christ's authority and rule.
3.   God builds his church through the ministry of gifted leaders.
4.   God builds his church through the ministry of gifted members.

Be Different from the World

So I say this, and insist in the Lord, that you no longer live as the Gentiles do, in the futility of their thinking. They are darkened in their understanding, being alienated from the life of God because of the ignorance that is in them due to the hardness of their hearts. Because they are callous, they have given themselves over to indecency for the practice of every kind of impurity with greediness. But you did not learn about Christ like this, if indeed you heard about him and were taught in him, just as the truth is in Jesus. You were taught with reference to your former way of life to lay aside the old man who is being corrupted in accordance with deceitful desires, to be renewed in the spirit of your mind, and to put on the new man who has been created in God's image – in righteousness and holiness that comes from truth.
Ephesians 4:17-24 (NET)

Why should believers be different from the world?

Often Christians are no different from the world in the way they think, talk, dress, and entertain themselves. Clearly, this was a problem with the Ephesian Christians, as well. Paul writes to them and says that they must no longer live as the Gentiles.

This exhortation to them to be different from the world was particularly important, considering the ungodly culture of Ephesus. John MacArthur shares some very telling insights:

> Ephesus was a leading commercial and cultural city of the Roman empire... But it was also a leading city in debauchery and sexual immorality. Some historians rank it as the most lascivious city of Asia Minor... The fifth–century B.C. Greek philosopher Heraclitus, himself a pagan, referred to Ephesus as "the darkness of vileness. The morals were lower than animals and the inhabitants of Ephesus were fit only to be drowned." There is no reason to believe that the situation had changed much by Paul's day. If anything, it may have been worse.[138]

The temple of Artemis (or Diana) was located in the city, along with hundreds of temple prostitutes who promoted her worship. Many in the church at Ephesus previously worshiped Diana and indulged in her immorality. This small, despised community of believers was constantly tempted to compromise and imitate the rest of the pagan world.

Here, Paul teaches them why they must be different. In this study, we will consider four reasons for believers to be different from the world.

Big Question: Why must believers be different from the world according to Paul in Ephesians 4:17-24?

Believers Must Be Different Because God Commands It

> So I say this, and insist in the Lord, that you no longer live as the Gentiles do, in the futility of their thinking.
> Ephesians 4:17

When Paul says, "So I say this, and insist in the Lord," he is saying the following instruction is God's command and not his own.

God called believers to be different from the world throughout biblical history. When he called Israel to be his people out of all the nations, he said this to them through Moses:

> "Speak to the Israelites and tell them, 'I am the Lord your God! You must not do as they do in the land of Egypt where you have been living, and you must not do as they do in the land of Canaan into which I am about to bring you; you must not walk in their statutes. You must observe my regulations and you must be sure to walk in my statutes. I am the Lord your God.
> Leviticus 18:2-4

Later, in Leviticus 19:2, he said, "You must be holy because I, the Lord your God, am holy." Essentially, while the pagan nations worshipped many gods, and were known for promiscuity, dishonest business practices, etc., Israel was called to be different.

In fact, he gave the Israelites over 600 laws to distinguish them from the pagan nations, and also to teach them how to worship him. This applies to us as well. We live in a society that is perverse, ungodly, and full of sin, and we must be different because God commands it. He commands us to be like himself—separate, holy, and righteous.

When Paul calls unbelievers "Gentiles," he is not referring to their race. Jews used this word in two ways: "first to distinguish all other people from Jews and second to distinguish all religions from Judaism... Gentiles here represent all ungodly, unregenerate, pagan persons." [139] The Ephesian Christians previously lived like pagans, but God called them to turn away from that lifestyle.

Similarly, Peter said this to scattered Christians throughout the Roman Empire:

> For the time that has passed was sufficient for you to do what the non-Christians desire. You lived then in debauchery, evil desires, drunkenness, carousing, drinking bouts, and wanton idolatries. So they are astonished when you do not rush with them into the same flood of wickedness, and they vilify you.
> 1 Peter 4:3-4

And Paul said this to the Corinthians:

> Do you not know that the unrighteous will not inherit the kingdom of God? Do not be deceived! The sexually immoral, idolaters, adulterers, passive homosexual partners, practicing homosexuals, thieves, the greedy, drunkards, the verbally abusive, and swindlers will not inherit the kingdom of God. Some of you once lived this way. But you were washed, you were sanctified, you were justified in the name of the Lord Jesus Christ and by the Spirit of our God.
> 1 Corinthians 6:9-11

The Ephesians, Romans, and Corinthians were saved out of a sinful lifestyle to worship the living God, and God called them to not go back. Similarly, many of us were saved out of all kinds of sin: drunkenness, sexual immorality, deceit, pride, rebellion, and selfishness—and we are called to not return.

Is your life different from the world? If not, remember that God delivered you from worldliness so you could know him and live for him.

Application Questions: In what ways has God delivered you from worldliness? How do you guard yourself from falling back into it?

Believers Must Be Different Because the World Rebels against God

> So I say this, and insist in the Lord, that you no longer live as the Gentiles do, in the futility of their thinking. They are darkened in their understanding, being alienated from the life of God because of the ignorance that is in them due to the hardness of their hearts. Because they are callous, they have given themselves over to indecency for the practice of every kind of impurity with greediness.

Ephesians 4:17-19

Ephesians 4:17-19 is very similar to Romans 1:18-32, where Paul describes the consequences of the pagan world denying God. They suppress the knowledge of God because of sin (Rom 1:18) and therefore live in sexual immorality, homosexuality, idolatry, and all kinds of wickedness (18-32).

This was true of Ephesus. They rebelled against God, and the consequence was a lifestyle of depravity.

Observation Questions: In what ways does Paul describe the world's rebellion against God, and what do these descriptions represent?

1. The world is futile in their thinking.

Paul says that people of the world live in the "futility of their thinking" (v. 17). The word "futility" means "waste", "emptiness" or "vanity." The problem with the world is wrong thinking—wrong thinking about God, which ultimately affects everything else. It affects how people view life, death, success, parenting, marriage, money, etc.

The Greek word for "futility" is translated "vanity" thirty-six times in the Septuagint version of Ecclesiastes.[140] Throughout the book, Solomon describes how he tried money, knowledge, women, pleasure, etc., and how everything was "vanity of vanities" (KJV)—a grasping of the air. This was the version of the Old Testament Paul commonly quoted in his epistles, so he probably chose this word intentionally to describe the vain thinking and pursuits of the world.

Isn't this a true description of the world? The world tries to find success and happiness through money, education, sex, entertainment, and pleasure, and yet continually find themselves empty. When Solomon described his journey in Ecclesiastes, he called it life under the sun (2:17 KJV)—essentially, life without God.

As believers, our thinking should be different from that of the world—we need to consider what is above the sun. We must consider God when it comes to education, marriage, success, and purpose. The world's thought process is vanity—just a grasping of the air—but the believer's thought process must be saturated with God.

2. The world is darkened in their understanding.

Paul also says that people of the world are "darkened in their understanding" (Eph 4:18). In what ways is the world's understanding darkened? Paul is primarily referring to the knowledge of God and the things of God. We see this taught throughout Scripture. First Corinthians 2:14 says, "The unbeliever does not receive the things of the Spirit of God, for they are foolishness to him. And he cannot understand them, because they are spiritually discerned."

To the man without God's Spirit, a world created by God in seven days is laughable. A life defined and guided by the Word of God is simply a crutch. A God who becomes a man and dies for the sins of the world is utter foolishness. Indeed, the world is darkened in their understanding.

Romans 1:22 says, "claimed to be wise, they became fools." They worship created things instead of the Creator (v. 25). They exchange natural relationships between men and women for perverse relationships between men and men, and women and women (v. 26-27). They call this wise and progressive, and the biblical view ignorant and archaic. That is the darkness of the pagan world—without God and lacking true understanding.

Now, the pagan world has much knowledge. In fact, the Greek world Paul wrote to in Ephesus was known for their advanced knowledge in philosophy, art, politics, and science. Greek slaves were highly sought after by Romans and other nations as tutors for their children.[141] The Greeks were academics, and yet Paul calls them "darkened in their understanding." It is no different today. We obtain degree after degree and have access to unlimited information on the Internet, but our world is still without true understanding because it rejects God.

3.   The world is separated from God.

Paul says the world is "alienated" or "separated" from "the life of God" (Eph 4:18). In Ephesians 2:1, Paul describes the Ephesians as "dead" in transgressions and sins. Death really means separation. In the same way that physical death means separation of the body from the spirit, spiritual death means separation from God because of sin.

This is the problem with the world. Because God is holy and perfect, we cannot commune with him because of our sin (cf. Heb 12:14). Instead, we are under his wrath (cf. John 3:36, Rom 6:23). It is for this reason that Christ died on the cross for our sins—to pay our just penalty and to reconcile us to God (Rom 6:23).

Because of sin, the world is separated from God and dead to spiritual stimuli.

4.   The world is "ignorant."

The word "ignorant" in the Greek means "without knowledge" (Eph 4:18). It comes from the Greek word from which we get the English word "agnostic."[142] The world is alienated from God because they are ignorant of him.

Why is the world ignorant—without knowledge—of God? It is because people reject his revelation. Consider again Romans 1:18-21:

For the wrath of God is revealed from heaven against all ungodliness and unrighteousness of people who suppress the truth by their unrighteousness, because what can be known about God is plain to them, because God has made it plain to them. For since the creation of the world his invisible attributes – his eternal power and divine nature – have been clearly seen, because they are understood through what has been made. So people are without excuse. For although they knew God, they did not glorify him as God or give him thanks, but they became futile in their thoughts and their senseless hearts were darkened.

Paul describes two ways God reveals himself to man. He makes himself known through creation. The sun, moon, stars, earth, plants, animals, and humanity all boast of a Creator (cf. Psalm 19:1). They tell us that the Creator is powerful and divine (Romans 1:19). When man worships animals or claims to be God himself, he denies general revelation (revelation given to everyone). If God created the earth, then he must be greater than any created thing. He cannot be a cat, a dog, a cow, or a human. He is divine. That's what general revelation tells us.

But God also reveals himself to man through the conscience. Romans 1:19 (NASB) says, "because that which is known about God is evident within them; for God made it evident to them." Many scholars believe this evidence "within" man refers to the conscience. God has given man an innate knowledge of him, and of right and wrong. In Romans 2:14-16, Paul says that the Gentiles, who never received the Old Testament law, will be judged based on their conscience.

God has revealed himself to all, but the world has chosen to reject his revelation. People reject general revelation through creation and the conscience, and also special revelation (revelation given only to specific people) through Scripture and the historical person of Christ. Therefore, the world is "ignorant" by choice. They don't want to know or obey God. They willfully reject his revelation.

Why do they do this? The apostle John says,

Now this is the basis for judging: that the light has come into the world and people loved the darkness rather than the light, because their deeds were evil. For everyone who does evil deeds hates the light and does not come to the light, so that their deeds will not be exposed.
John 3:19-20

People reject the light of God that shines through creation, their conscience, Christ, his Word, etc.—because they love sin. That is a description of the world—willfully ignorant of God.

5.   The world is hardened and calloused to sin.

Ephesians 4:18-19a says: "They are darkened in their understanding, being alienated from the life of God because of the ignorance that is in them due to the hardness of their hearts. Because they are callous, they have given themselves over to indecency."

Paul describes the hearts of unbelievers as hardened and having lost all sensitivity. Kent Hughes says this about the word "hardened": "The Greek word for 'hardening' is porosis, which comes from the word poros, which originally meant 'a stone harder than marble.' In our own terms we might call this 'a heart of stone.'"[143]

"Calloused" can be translated "having lost all sensitivity." It literally means to be "past feeling" or "having arrived at a condition of freedom from pain."[144] This again refers to a man's conscience. It bothers him for a time when he rejects God's law and practices sin, but as he continues to do so his conscience hardens like a rock and he no longer feels convicted. This happens to all of us to some extent when we rebel against God. Eventually, our conscience stops working.

First Timothy 4:1-2 gives an example of this in false teachers. It says,

Now the Spirit explicitly says that in the later times some will desert the faith and occupy themselves with deceiving spirits and demonic teachings, influenced by the hypocrisy of liars whose consciences are seared

False teachers live hypocritical lives. As they reject God's ways, their consciences become seared and hardened, and this opens the door to deception by demons and demonic doctrines.

This is what happens to people in the world. Their conscience becomes hard by accepting sin in their entertainment, education, relationships, and other aspects of their lives. They curse, fornicate, lie, steal, and sometimes kill, and yet feel no conviction or pain. And without the protection of a conscience, they are totally susceptible to deception.

Because of this, there are no concrete ethics or absolute truths in the world. What used to be right is now considered wrong and what was wrong is now considered right. The prophet Isaiah says, "Those who call evil good and good evil are as good as dead, who turn darkness into light and light into darkness, who turn bitter into sweet and sweet into bitter" (Isaiah 5:20).

To be honest, I hate watching movies where the bad guy wins because it's really a picture of the direction our world is heading. Bad is good and good is bad. This is also seen in how gangster rappers, who make music about their crimes—selling drugs and killing people—become multi-millionaires because everybody, including Christians, buys their records. Our world is backwards because it has hardened hearts and seared consciences.

6. The world is consumed with indecency or sensuality.

As Paul says in Ephesians 4:19, "Because they are callous, they have given themselves over to indecency for the practice of every kind of impurity." "Aselgeia (sensuality) refers to total licentiousness, the absence of all moral restraint, especially in the area of sexual sins."[145] It is the "vice that throws off all restraint and flaunts itself."[146]

Again, this is a picture of the pagan world described in Romans 1:24-27:

> Therefore God gave them over in the desires of their hearts to impurity, to dishonor their bodies among themselves. They exchanged the truth of God for a lie and worshiped and served the creation rather than the Creator, who is blessed forever! Amen. For this reason God gave them over to dishonorable passions. For their women exchanged the natural sexual relations for unnatural ones, and likewise the men also abandoned natural relations with women and were inflamed in their passions for one another. Men committed shameless acts with men and received in themselves the due penalty for their error.

A disregard for God led to the sexual revolution, as the hearts of men and women were given to sexual impurity—degrading their bodies with one another. It also led to what Scripture calls "shameful lusts," referring to homosexuality—men burning in passion for one another, and women for women. Paul describes the world culture as sexually crazed.

In the Roman Empire homosexuality and bi-sexuality were normal. In fact, I read one historical article that said it was considered strange for a man to prefer one sex over the other. This was normative for the pagan world, as rejection of God leads to sexual immorality and shameful lusts.

7. The world is greedy for sin, and therefore makes an occupation of it.

Ephesians 4:19 says, "Because they are callous, they have given themselves over to indecency for the practice of every kind of impurity with greediness." The world is "greedy" for sin (the NIV translates this word as "indulge")—it has an uncontrollable lust for more. This uncontrollable lust leads people to make an occupation of sin.

"Ergasia (practice) can refer to a business enterprise, and that idea could apply here."[147] When a person starts a law firm, it is called a practice—a business. This also describes our contemporary culture and how it makes a profit from sin. I read that pornography makes more money than the NFL, NBA, and MLB combined in the US.[148] It is one of the biggest businesses, if not the biggest, and it's the same with trafficking, drugs, etc., in many nations. The world practices sin as a business.

Paul essentially says, "Believers, you must live differently than the world because God commands it, and also because the world is in rebellion against God. Don't live like the world!"

Application Question: What specific characteristic(s) of the world, as described by Paul, jumped out to you and why?

Believers Must Be Different Because They Know Christ

> But you did not learn about Christ like this, if indeed you heard about him and were taught in him, just as the truth is in Jesus.
> Ephesians 4:20-21

Observation Question: What teaching terms does Paul use in reference to Christ in Ephesians 4:20-21 and what do they represent?

The next reason Paul gives for being different from the world is the believers' relationship to Christ. He says, "you did not learn about Christ like this." It can be translated literally as, "You did not learn Christ." This is very unique terminology. James Boice says,

> The reason this is "extraordinary" is that the idea of learning a person, rather than a mere fact or doctrine, is found nowhere else in the Greek Bible. Nor has it been found in any other pre-biblical document.[149]

Paul could say that they learned "about" Christ, but he doesn't. Why not? Because Christianity is a relationship with Christ. This is very similar to Christ's teaching about salvation in John 17:3: "Now this is eternal life – that they know you, the only true God, and Jesus Christ, whom you sent." Salvation is knowing God the Father and God the Son.

Paul uses pedagogical (teaching) terms. The phrase "you heard about him" should actually be translated as "you heard him"—"about" isn't in the original language. This is special. As the majority of these Asian believers had never heard Christ teach in person, Paul is saying that any time they heard Scripture, Christ spoke to them. This is very similar to Ephesians 5:25-27:

> Husbands, love your wives just as Christ loved the church and gave himself for her to sanctify her by cleansing her with the washing of the water by the word, so that he may present the church to himself as glorious – not having a stain or wrinkle, or any such blemish, but holy and blameless.

Paul describes Christ washing the church with the Word of God to make it a pure and blameless bride. When does this happen? It happens every time we hear the preaching of the Word of God. It happens when we study and meditate on the Word. Christ is involved in every biblical transmission of Scripture to his people. He is present to give us understanding and to help us apply it.

But this is not all. Christ is the subject, the teacher, and the classroom. We were taught "in him" (Eph 4:21). This refers to our union with Christ, which happens at salvation. First Corinthians 12:13 says that we were all baptized by one Spirit into one body. As believers, we are the body of Christ—forever connected to him. Throughout Ephesians, Paul mentions this reality many times. Believers are the faithful "in Christ" (1:1). We have every spiritual blessing "in Christ" (1:3). We were chosen "in him" before the foundation of the world (1:4). God has given us his grace "in the One" he loves (1:6). "In him" we have redemption through his blood and the forgiveness of sins (1:7). In Christ we have so many wonderful blessings, and it is in this dynamic union that he teaches and changes us day by day.

Finally, Christ is not only the subject, the teacher, and the classroom, but also the truth. Paul says, "if indeed you heard about him and were taught in him, just as the truth is in Jesus" (Eph 4:21). Jesus is the way, the truth, and the life; no one comes to the Father but by him (John 14:6). When speaking to Pilate before his death, Christ said he came to "bear witness" to the truth (John 18:37, KJV). There are many ways claiming to be true and the way to God; however, Christ is the truth and the only way to a relationship with God.

Essentially, Christians should be different because they are in the school of Christ. At some point, they became disciples of Christ, and now they daily sit at his feet—listening to his voice and conforming to his image. James Boice adds this about Paul's reason for focusing on Christ's training of believers:

> It is because in the previous verse he has described the condition of the secular or gentile world as due chiefly to ignorance. He was pointing out that the depravity of the gentile world was due to its willful ignorance of God. The world has hardened its heart against God and

so is alienated from him intellectually and in every other way. It follows, then, that when Paul speaks of the difference Jesus makes he does so in exactly parallel terms. The world is ignorant of God, but Christians have come to know him. The secular mind is hostile to Christ's teaching, but the believer joyfully enrolls in and continually makes progress in Christ's school.[150]

Application Question: How should we apply the reality of the teaching we receive from Christ?

1.   We must be eager learners.

Our Savior wants to teach us, and therefore, we must wake up every morning ready to learn. When young Samuel heard God speak to him, Eli, the high priest, told him to say, "Speak, LORD, for your servant is listening" (1 Sam 3:9). We would do well to say the same thing to our Lord every day. Speak, LORD, your servants are listening.
Are you an eager leaner?

2.   We must be obedient learners.

James said, "But be sure you live out the message and do not merely listen to it and so deceive yourselves" (1:22). What are they deceived about? They are deceived about their faith. They are not truly Christ's disciples. Only those who hear and obey God's Word are truly born again. Christ says, "Not everyone who says to me, 'Lord, Lord,' will enter into the kingdom of heaven – only the one who does the will of my Father in heaven" (Matt 7:21). Only those who do the Father's will enter the kingdom of heaven.
Are you an obedient learner?

Application Questions: What have you been learning recently in the school of Christ? Is Christ calling you to make any changes to be a better student?

Believers Must Be Different Because They Are New in Christ

You were taught with reference to your former way of life to lay aside the old man who is being corrupted in accordance with deceitful desires, to be renewed in the spirit of your mind, and to put on the new man who has been created in God's image – in righteousness and holiness that comes from truth.
Ephesians 4:22-24

Paul explains some lessons every believer learns in the school of Christ. He says,

> You were taught with reference to your former way of life to lay aside the old man who is being corrupted in accordance with deceitful desires, to be renewed in the spirit of your mind, and to put on the new man who has been created in God's image – in righteousness and holiness that comes from truth.

When Paul uses the phrases "lay aside" and "put on," these were commonly used of taking off or putting on clothing (cf. Acts 7:58). There is some controversy about the interpretation of this passage. Some believe these phrases should be interpreted as commands (as in the NIV), and others believe they should be in the past tense. In my study, I've found that most commentators, including John Stott, Martin Lloyd-Jones, and John MacArthur, believe they should be translated as past tense since the verbs are in the "aorist middle." Because of this, the Holman Christian Standard Bible translates the passage like this:

> You took off your former way of life, the old self that is corrupted by deceitful desires; you are being renewed in the spirit of your minds; you put on the new self, the one created according to God's likeness in righteousness and purity of the truth.
> Ephesians 4:22-24 (HCSB)

If this is true, Paul is describing the new identity of believers. When Christ saves us, we become new creations in him—old things pass away, and all things become new (2 Cor 5:17). We are born again through the Spirit of God.

Observation Question: How does Paul describe the changes in believers?

1. Believers have laid aside the old self.

The "old self" refers to what believers were before salvation. It refers to the sinful life we lived before following Christ. When born again, our old self (in the sense of its power over us) dies. Romans 6:6-7 says, "We know that our old man was crucified with him so that the body of sin would no longer dominate us, so that we would no longer be enslaved to sin. (For someone who has died has been freed from sin)." On the cross, Christ crucified our old self so that it might be done away with.

Well, why do we still struggle with sinful urges, some might ask. The answer is that we still have a sin nature; however, its power over us has been broken. Before, we sinned and lived like the world because we had to—we were slaves to our urges. But now we are not slaves of sin, but of Christ and righteousness (cf. Rom 6:13, 18).

This is important to understand when one feels bound to some habitual sin, addiction, or stronghold. Christ is our abolitionist. He has set us free. John 8:34 and 36 says, "Everyone who practices sin is a slave of sin… So if the Son sets you free, you will be really free."

Paul wants believers to understand their freedom. Since they previously were slaves of sexual lusts, lying, selfishness, and discord as unbelievers, why would they run back to their slave master after being set free? We should enjoy our freedom in following Christ, and not run back to slavery to sin, the world, and the devil.

2. Believers received a new mind.

Paul says, "to be made new in the attitude of your minds." "The word new (kainos) does not mean renovated but entirely new—new in species or character."[151] First Corinthians 2:16 says, "But we have the mind of Christ." In salvation, we repent of our former ways and choose to follow Christ. "Repentance" really means "a change of mind." God gives us the mind of Christ—a desire to follow and obey God.

However, this does not remove the need to continually renew our minds. Romans 12:2 says: "Do not be conformed to this present world, but be transformed by the renewing of your mind, so that you may test and approve what is the will of God – what is good and well-pleasing and perfect." John Stott says this about the renewal of the mind: "If heathen degradation is due to the futility of their minds, then Christian righteousness depends on the constant renewing of our minds."[152]

Application Question: How do we renew our minds?

Philippians 4:8 says, "Finally, brothers and sisters, whatever is true, whatever is worthy of respect, whatever is just, whatever is pure, whatever is lovely, whatever is commendable, if something is excellent or praiseworthy, think about these things."

In order to think on what is good and thereby renew our minds, we must do two things:

- We must reject the ungodly.

This is where many Christians fail. It is not that they don't think on what is good; it's that they still think on and enjoy the bad. This includes ungodly music, books, TV, and conversation. We renew our minds by rejecting what is ungodly.

- We must think on the godly.

Whatever we think on, we will eventually do. The world lives in an ungodly manner because of the "futility of their thinking" (Eph 4:17). However, believers live godly lives by redeeming their minds from the foolishness of the world. They develop a biblical worldview by meditating on and obeying God's Word.

3. Believers put on the new self.

Peter says believers participate in the Divine nature (2 Peter 1:4). God not only gives us a new mind at salvation, but also his very nature, including new affections and desires. Jonathan Edwards calls these "religious affections."

True believers desire the Word of God, and God's righteousness. Jesus says, "Man does not live by bread alone, but by every word that comes from the mouth of God" (Matt 4:4). We desire God's Word and the righteousness that comes from obeying it. Christ says, "Blessed are those who hunger and thirst for righteousness, for they will be satisfied" (Matt 5:6). True believers desire to see people saved, discipled, and daily conforming to God's image. They have a new self—a new nature from God.

Paul says, "But the fruit of the Spirit is love, joy, peace, patience, kindness, goodness, faithfulness, gentleness, and self-control" (Gal 5:22-23). These will be in our lives to some extent if God's Spirit lives in us.

However, with all this said—believers having put off the old self and put on the new self, and also having a new mind—we still need to apply these realities daily. Colossians 3:9-10, a parallel passage, says: "Do not lie to one another since you have put off the old man with its practices and have been clothed with the new man that is being renewed in knowledge according to the image of the one who created it."

Paul emphasizes this in the following verses and throughout the rest of Ephesians. In 4:24, he says we were "created in God's image – in righteousness and holiness that comes from truth." Every day we must make it our aim to fulfill God's original purpose in saving us—to be like him. We must get rid of sin, renew our minds, and practice righteousness.

Do you know your new identity? We must be different from the world because of how Christ changed us. We are new—created for righteousness (Eph 2:10).

Application Questions: Why is knowing our new identity in Christ so important? How is God calling you to apply your new identity today?

Conclusion

Why should believers be different from the world?

1. Believers must be different because God commands it.
2. Believers must be different because the world rebels against God.
3. Believers must be different because they know Christ.
4. Believers must be different because they are new in Christ.

The Divine Wardrobe of Believers

> Therefore, having laid aside falsehood, each one of you speak the truth with his neighbor, for we are members of one another. Be angry and do not sin; do not let the sun go down on the cause of your anger. Do not give the devil an opportunity. The one who steals must steal no longer; rather he must labor, doing good with his own hands, so that he may have something to share with the one who has need. You must let no unwholesome word come out of your mouth, but only what is beneficial for the building up of the one in need, that it may give grace to those who hear. And do not grieve the Holy Spirit of God, by whom you were sealed for the day of redemption. You must put away every kind of bitterness, anger, wrath, quarreling, and evil, slanderous talk. Instead, be kind to one another, compassionate, forgiving one another, just as God in Christ also forgave you.
> Ephesians 4:25-32 (NET)

What type of clothing should believers wear and not wear?

In Ephesians 4:22-24, Paul describes what happens at conversion. He says,

> You were taught with reference to your former way of life to lay aside the old man who is being corrupted in accordance with deceitful desires, to be renewed in the spirit of your mind, and to put on the new man who has been created in God's image – in righteousness and holiness that comes from truth.

Most commentators believe that "put off your old self" and "put on the new self" should not be translated as a command, but in the past tense. One of the things that happens at salvation is that our old self—who we were before Christ—dies, and God gives us a new self—a new nature that loves God and wants to obey his Word. Second Corinthians 5:17 says, "So then, if anyone is in Christ, he is a new creation; what is old has passed away – look, what is new has come!" Just as there is a specific uniform expected of a police officer, a soldier, and others in specific professions, Christians have appropriate "clothes" as well—referring to attitudes and actions.

In Ephesians 4:25-32, Paul leaves the believer's position in Christ to focus on his practice. Our old nature died and we received a new nature in Christ. "Therefore" (Ephesians 4:25), we must daily take off old clothes—

attitudes and actions—that no longer fit our position, and put on our new clothes.

Are you wearing the right clothes? Or, are you still wearing the clothes from your old self? In this study, we will consider the contrasting clothes of the old self and the new self. This will help us strive daily to look more like Christ and less like the world.

Big Question: How should believers respond to their new position in Christ according to Ephesians 4:25-32?

Because of Our New Position in Christ, We Must Stop Lying and Tell the Truth

> Therefore, having laid aside falsehood, each one of you speak the truth with his neighbor, for we are members of one another.
> Ephesians 4:25

First, Paul says that we must put off falsehood and speak truthfully to our neighbors. Falsehood "includes every form of dishonesty, whether it is shading of the truth, exaggeration, cheating, failure to keep promises, betrayal of confidence, flattery, or fudging on income taxes."[153]

Interpretation Question: Why do believers (and people in general) practice lying, even though it is harmful?

- We lie in order to make ourselves look better (a little exaggeration makes a story better).
- We lie to protect ourselves from consequences (often to cover up a failure).
- We lie to gain something we want (like a good grade, a promotion, or tax benefits).

These are old and filthy clothes—not appropriate for believers to wear.

Scripture says that Satan is "a liar and the father of lies" (John 8:44). When we lie, cheat, or exaggerate, we mimic our old father, Satan. It was his lie in the Garden that led to the fall. In fact, as ruler of this world, he built the entire world system on lies. Success is this, beauty is that, marriage is this, etc. The world is built on lies. The enemy lies to pull people further away from God, and further away from God's plans for their lives. This is exactly what Satan did in the Garden to lead Adam and Eve away from God, and he does the same to people today.

When Christians lie, they not only mar the image of God, but also push themselves and others farther away from God. The world says, "If this person is a Christian, then I want nothing to do with Christ." When we lie, cheat, and deceive, we open the door for the devil to work in and through us.

In addition, Revelation 22:15 says, "Outside are the dogs and the sorcerers and the sexually immoral, and the murderers, and the idolaters and everyone who loves and practices falsehood!" This doesn't mean that we are saved by our works, but our works do prove if we are saved. Those who practice a lifestyle of lying are not saved. Yes, a believer may stumble in this area, and if he does, he must confess and repent. But if this is his continual practice, then he may not be born again.

Paul says something similar in 1 Corinthians 6:9-10:

> Do you not know that the unrighteous will not inherit the kingdom of God? Do not be deceived! The sexually immoral, idolaters, adulterers, passive homosexual partners, practicing homosexuals, thieves, the greedy, drunkards, the verbally abusive, and swindlers will not inherit the kingdom of God.

A swindler is a person that lies and deceives people. Paul says such people will not inherit the kingdom of God.

Has God changed your relationship with lying and deception?

Application Question: How should believers speak the truth to their neighbor?

When Paul refers to speaking truthfully, he does not just mean to stop telling lies, he means many other things as well:

1. Believers speak the truth by speaking God's Word.

In John 17:17, Jesus prays, "Set them apart in the truth; your word is truth." As believers, we must speak the Word of God to one another. When God called Joshua to lead Israel into the promised land, he told him never to let the Word depart from his mouth, but to meditate on it day and night (Josh 1:8). Joshua was called to always speak the Word of God to others, and we must do likewise.

2. Believers speak the truth by exposing lies.

Many times, by standing quietly while others lie or believe lies, we implicitly take part in the deception. No! Speaking the truth includes exposing lies, as Paul later clarifies in Ephesians 5:11: "Do not participate in the unfruitful deeds of darkness, but rather expose them."

Sometimes the need arises to expose falsehood in an interpersonal or business relationship. When Christ went into the temple (John 2), he exposed cheating by speaking the truth. In the majority of Paul's letters, he combats lies by teaching truth. We must do the same in our personal, church, and work relationships. We do this because it protects people, and because it honors God.

3. Believers speak the truth by challenging people in sin.

A common lie propagated in the world is that it's polite, and therefore preferable, to be untruthful if the truth would upset somebody or make them angry. Scripture teaches the opposite. Proverbs 27:6 says, "Faithful are the wounds of a friend, but the kisses of an enemy are excessive." One of the ways that we speak truthfully is by lovingly challenging people in sin or who are falling away from God. This is what a true friend or neighbor does. Paul tells us how the church grows in Ephesians 4:15: "But practicing the truth in love, we will in all things grow up into Christ, who is the head." When we lovingly speak the truth to one another, especially when one member is sinning, the body grows.

Interpretation Question: Who is Paul referring to when he says "neighbor" in Ephesians 4:25?

Now, honesty is a duty that believers owe everybody; however, in this passage, Paul specifically refers to our Christian neighbors—the church. This is clear from the rest of the verse, "speak the truth with his neighbor, for we are members of one another." Paul's argument is that lying to a member of the church is as foolish as the eye lying to the brain. It is like lying to ourself. It is both illogical and dangerous.

However, let us also consider that Paul probably says this to the Ephesians because they were still lying to each other. They were still wearing the old clothes of deception, and we often are as well.

Application Questions: In what situations are you most tempted to lie or embellish the truth? What type of lies are you most prone to? How is God working in that area of your life?

Because of Our New Position in Christ, We Must Control Our Anger

Be angry and do not sin; do not let the sun go down on the cause of your anger.
Ephesians 4:26

The next clothing believers must take off is unrighteous anger. Paul quotes Psalm 4:4a, "In your anger do not sin" (NIV). Most versions translate this as, "Be angry and do not sin." It reminds us that there is a righteous anger every believer should have. Sometimes, it is even sinful for us not to be angry. Psalm 7:11 says, "God is a just judge; he is angry throughout the day." God expresses his wrath at sin every day, and we should as well.

There should be a righteous anger in the lives of believers. Anger, as part of the image of God, is meant to motivate us to correct what is wrong. Holy anger leads believers to get rid of sin, including their own. Matthew 5:29-30 says,

> If your right eye causes you to sin, tear it out and throw it away! It is better to lose one of your members than to have your whole body thrown into hell. If your right hand causes you to sin, cut it off and throw it away! It is better to lose one of your members than to have your whole body go into hell.

Many times, habitual sin lingers in the lives of believers because they are not righteously angry about it. In that case, they should hear the words, "Be angry." They should also consider Christ's admonition to be so angry that we will cut off things dear to us in order to be holy and not fall again.

Righteous anger in a believer should not only be about his own sins, but also the sins of others. No doubt, we see this anger in Christ. Again, when he saw people stealing and cheating in the temple, he used a whip and turned over tables, declaring, "'My house will be a house of prayer,' but you have turned it into a den of robbers" (Luke 19:46). When God was dishonored and others were hurt, Christ became angry.

Through Christ's example, we can learn a great deal about unrighteous and righteous anger. Unrighteous anger is typically selfish and vengeful. John MacArthur says, "Anger that is sin, on the other hand, is anger that is self–defensive and self–serving, that is resentful of what is done against oneself. It is the anger that leads to murder and to God's judgment (Matt. 5:21–22)."[154] Righteous anger, on the other hand, is primarily concerned with offenses against God and others.

Application Question: How can we be angry and not sin?

1. When angry, we must evaluate the reason for the anger.

Is this anger selfish—rooted in pride, and a response to personal injustice? Or is it about sin against God and others? If our anger is rooted in pride and a response to personal injustice, we must confess our sin to God (and others if we sinned against them) and repent.

2.   When angry, we should probably take time before responding.

It is possible to be righteously angry and still sin in response. In fact, righteous anger can lead to cursing, physical violence, and many other sins. Nehemiah provides a good example of taking time before responding to a report of gross injustice:

> I was very angry when I heard their outcry and these complaints. I considered these things carefully and then registered a complaint with the wealthy and the officials. I said to them, "Each one of you is seizing the collateral from your own countrymen!" Because of them I called for a great public assembly.
> Nehemiah 5:6-7

After hearing of the charges, Nehemiah didn't respond immediately—he "considered these things carefully." This can be translated literally as he, "took counsel with myself." Similarly, one of the ways that we keep ourselves from sinning in anger is by taking time to reflect, pray, and get counsel before responding.

3.   When angry, we must seek to resolve it as soon as possible.

When Paul says, "Be angry and do not sin; do not let the sun go down on the cause of your anger," he probably just means to resolve the situation as soon as possible.

Application Question: How should we seek to resolve our anger quickly?

- To quickly resolve anger, we should always forgive the offender.

Christ says we should forgive seventy-seven times (Matt 18:22). Whether the person repents or not, our duty is to forgive as Christ forgave us. This is the first way to resolve our anger.

- To quickly resolve anger, sometimes when a person sins against us or others, we should biblically confront them. Matthew 18:15-17 says,

> "If your brother sins, go and show him his fault when the two of you are alone. If he listens to you, you have regained your brother. But if he does not listen, take one or two others with you, so that at the

testimony of two or three witnesses every matter may be established. If he refuses to listen to them, tell it to the church. If he refuses to listen to the church, treat him like a Gentile or a tax collector.

(1) Without talking to others first (gossiping), approach the offender one on one. When doing this, speak gently to not offend. Proverbs 15:1 says, "A gentle response turns away anger." This one on one meeting is important because the problem may be a simple misunderstanding. Or, if the offender has sinned, the private confrontation might lead to repentance. (2) If he doesn't respond, take another person to help challenge him, and also for a witness. (3) If he still doesn't respond, bring the matter before the church. (4) Then if he still doesn't respond, the church should discipline him with the hope of his eventual repentance.

This is not often practiced in the church, and for that reason, many continue in sin. This method applies to a person stealing, committing sexual immorality, being abusive to his or her spouse, gossiping, etc. It is especially important for struggling married couples to consider. God's method of reconciliation for divided homes is through the church—his body. It is not, "Let's keep our struggles a secret." We should handle righteous anger when it involves the sin of others by seeking restoration through biblical confrontation.

- To quickly resolve anger, sometimes, instead of confronting the person, we should cover their failure, especially if it is not a moral issue or if it resulted from ignorance.

First Peter 4:8 says, "Above all keep your love for one another fervent, because love covers a multitude of sins." This is probably how God would have us respond to most situations. We should forgive and let go of small and big injuries. Love covers sin and doesn't hold a record of wrongs (1 Cor 13:5).

How else can we be angry and not sin?

4. When angry, we must remember the demonic consequences of unbridled anger.

Finally, Paul says, "Be angry and do not sin; do not let the sun go down on the cause of your anger. Do not give the devil an opportunity" (Eph 4:26).

When we handle anger inappropriately, we open the door for Satan to attack us and others. Christ says that anger is the root of murder (Matt 5:21-22), and that Satan was a murderer from the beginning (John 8:44). Satan's only desire is to steal, kill, and destroy (John 10:10). When unrighteous anger is found in a Christian, Satan fans it into flame. He cultivates the burning embers of anger in an upset person in order to destroy his relationships—both with God and others. Satan fans anger and unforgiveness in church members to cause splits. In many churches, grudges and feuds linger for years, opening doors for the enemy to wreak havoc.

Christ gives the disciples a stern warning against unforgiveness, which is often rooted in anger: God will hand them over to torturers if they don't forgive others from the heart (Matt 18:34-35). Who are these torturers? I believe they are demons (cf. 1 Cor 5:5). The unforgiveness and anger that people choose to cultivate allow the devil to torment and tempt them. They often struggle with anxiety, depression, irrational thoughts, and sometimes sickness all because they opened the door to the devil many years ago by not forgiving somebody. Therefore, Satan launches all-out assaults against them and others from the beachhead of their unforgiveness.

One of the reasons we must rid ourselves of anger is because of the demonic consequences associated with cultivating it. Satan works through anger to steal, kill, and destroy.

Application Questions: In what ways do you still struggle with the old clothing of anger? How has God called you to work on taking it off?

Because of Our New Position in Christ, We Must Stop Stealing, and Work to Help Those in Need

> The one who steals must steal no longer; rather he must labor, doing good with his own hands, so that he may have something to share with the one who has need.
> Ephesians 4:28

Believers must take off the clothing of stealing and instead work to help others in need. It might seem strange to say this to Christians, but no doubt, the Ephesians committed theft, as Christians often do today. The early church membership included a large population of slaves. This is clearly seen by all the admonitions to slaves in the New Testament (cf. Ephesians 6:5, Colossians 3:22, Titus 2:9). Warren Wiersbe says this about slaves in the ancient world:

> Stealing was particularly a sin of the slaves in Paul's day. Usually they were not well cared for and were always in need, and the law gave them almost no protection. When he wrote to Titus, Paul urged him to admonish the slaves not to "purloin" but to be faithful to their masters (Titus 2:10).

However, in this text Paul is not referring to slaves in particular, but to the church in general. Stealing could mean grand larceny, nonpayment of debts, using false measurements, etc. No doubt, there were acceptable forms of stealing in the ancient world, just as there are today. Illegal downloading, watching bootleg movies, stealing supplies from employers, and wasting the employer's time are considered normal by many in our society, and many Christians are guilty of them.

But, Paul says these old clothes must not be part of the Christian's wardrobe—for we have put off our old nature and put on the divine nature of Christ. Therefore, we must seek to dress like Christ, our Savior.

Paul tells the Ephesians not only to stop stealing, but also to work. It must be remembered that work is not part of the curse. God gave Adam and Eve the Garden to tend before sin came into the world (Gen 2:15). It was always his plan for people to work, and to glorify him through the work. Colossians 3:23 says, "Whatever you are doing, work at it with enthusiasm, as to the Lord and not for people."

It is interesting to consider that many of those God used greatly in biblical history were working when he called them. "Moses was caring for sheep; Gideon was threshing wheat; David was minding his father's flock; and the first four disciples were either casting nets or mending them. Jesus Himself was a carpenter."[155]

Good (Useful) Work

It is God's will for us to work and to glorify him through it. But Paul does not just command the Ephesians to work, he commands them to do "useful" work (Eph 4:28). The word "useful" can also be translated "good." The implication is that some jobs are unuseful and immoral, and therefore unfit for Christians. If an occupation requires dishonesty, tempts people to sin, or dishonors God, a Christian should not participate in it. Everything believers do should honor God and build his kingdom—including our occupation.

And since work is one of the primary time commitments people have (typically at least forty hours a week), Christians should pray hard and long about the type of work they commit to. Work should not be their god, keeping them away from church and caring for family. Some companies essentially demand disobedience to God—as people are expected to neglect their faith and their families. Sometimes Christians may need to accept a lesser job or career in order to be faithful to God. Paul could be alluding to this by commanding the Ephesians to do useful work with their "hands." "Greeks despised manual labour; they saw it as an occupation fit for slaves."[156] Christians, however, must make sure their career is useful and honoring to God, even if it is despised by the world.

Help Those in Need

Observation Question: Why does Paul tell Christians to work to support those in need?

In addition, one must notice the reason Paul tells the Ephesians to work. It is not just to meet their needs and to provide a stable living for themselves. He says that a Christian "must work, doing something useful with his own hands, that he may have something to share with those in need."

This is radical. Typically, people work to make more money, and with that money, they get a bigger house, a better car, a better entertainment system, and a better phone. However, one of the reasons Christians should work is to meet other people's needs. This means they save not just to give their tithes and offerings, but also to help someone struggling financially, to support missionaries, to fund seminary students, etc. This is the clothing of a Christian.

While I was attending seminary, I was told how many of my professors used the same accountant. This accountant really struggled with how they used their money: It wasn't all about their portfolio and saving for a comfortable retirement. These seminary professors put so much money into missions and other charitable ministries that the accountant was really challenged, and eventually gave his life to Christ. He must have reasoned, "Their lives are too different. There must be something to Christianity."

In Luke 16:9, Christ says, "And I tell you, make friends for yourselves by how you use worldly wealth, so that when it runs out you will be welcomed into the eternal homes." He teaches his followers to use their money to make friends in heaven—meaning to use their money to lead people to Christ by supporting missions and helping those in need. Then, when they enter heaven, many will welcome them because of their financial ministry.

Every Christian should ask himself, "Do I have a financial ministry?" "Am I using my money to see people saved and to build God's kingdom?" This is the clothing of Christians—our divine wardrobe. The clothing of greed, selfishness, and stealing often demonstrated in the world is not fitting for Christians. Believers follow a Savior that gave up everything so others might become rich (2 Cor 8:9), and therefore, their lives should be full of sacrificial giving.

Application Questions: In what ways do Christians commonly practice stealing? How has God challenged you to develop a financial ministry?

Because of Our New Position in Christ, We Must Rid Ourselves of Ungodly Talk and Speak God's Words Instead

> You must let no unwholesome word come out of your mouth, but only what is beneficial for the building up of the one in need, that it may give grace to those who hear.
> Ephesians 4:29

The next clothing believers must take off is ungodly speech. Paul says, "You must let no unwholesome word come out of your mouth." The word "unwholesome" is used in Matthew 7:17-18 to refer to "bad fruit" or "rotten fruit." It refers to "that which is worthless, bad, or rotten."[157] MacArthur's words on this are instructive:

> Corrupt speech generally means conversation that is filthy and suggestive; this would include off-color jokes, profanity, and dirty stories. But here it probably has the wider sense of any form of conversation that is frivolous, empty, idle, and worthless. Paul deals with obscene and vile language in 5:4; here he is telling us to abandon profitless speech and substitute constructive conversation.[158]

A believer's speech should not only be void of filthy or suggestive language, but also idle words. Christ says that we will be judged for every idle word we speak (Matt 12:36). Man is made in the image of God, and God created the earth with his speech. Therefore, our speech is also powerful. Proverbs says that the power of life and death is in the tongue (Prov 18:21). If our speech is this powerful, then it is not to be used in an idle or worthless way.

Paul then describes how Christians should speak.

Observation Question: How does Paul positively describe the believer's speech?

1.   The believer's speech should be "beneficial for the building up" or "edifying" (KJV).

This means that the believer's speech should encourage and instruct. Proverbs 12:18 says, "speaking recklessly is like the thrusts of a sword, but the words of the wise bring healing." The mouth of a believer should be used for healing, not destruction.

With that said, helpful speech also includes rebuke. Proverbs 25:12 says, "Like an earring of gold and an ornament of fine gold, so is a wise reprover to the ear of the one who listens." Proverbs 27:6 (KJV) says, "Faithful are the wounds of a friend." Good friends edify one another, and sometimes that includes causing injury so that the other can become truly healthy.

2. The believer's speech should be "according to their needs" (NIV), or "as fits the occasion" (ESV).

Knowing the right words to say is important, but knowing the right words to say at the right time is more important. Proverbs 15:23 says, "A person has joy in giving an appropriate answer, and a word at the right time – how good it is!" Not only does the hearer have tremendous joy in receiving the right word at the right time, but so does the giver.

How can we say the right words at the right time?

Proverbs 17:27 says, "The truly wise person restrains his words." Many times in counseling a person, I know exactly what to say, but I can also discern they are not yet ready to receive it. And, often there is too much to try to fix at once. It is better to just listen and pick the most important battle. We must wisely discern the occasion in order to best use our words.

3. The believer's speech should "give grace to those who hear."

"Grace" means "unmerited favor." This means that it doesn't matter how mean or undeserving a person is; our words should bless him. Christ teaches that even our enemies should be blessed by our speech. In fact, we are called to bless those who curse us and pray for them (Luke 6:28).

Is your speech gracious? Colossians 4:6 says, "Let your conversation be always full of grace, seasoned with salt, so that you may know how to answer everyone." Gracious speech is like salt—it preserves and cleanses people from what is sinful and distasteful.

Application Question: How can a believer be more effective at speaking godly words instead of ungodly words?

1. Our words must be both filled with and guided by Scripture.

Scripture is useful for teaching, rebuking, correcting, and training in righteousness so the man of God may be thoroughly equipped for every good work (2 Tim 3:16-17). If our speech is going to be helpful, we must know and use Scripture.

2. Our words must be guided by the Holy Spirit.

We should pray over our words. We should ask the Lord what to say, when to say it, and how to say it. In Ephesians 6:19, Paul said, "Pray for me also, that I may be given the message when I begin to speak – that I may confidently make known the mystery of the gospel." Lord, give us the words that will honor you and bless your people.

Application Questions: What are the primary ways you struggle with unwholesome speech? In what ways is God challenging you to grow in this area?

Because of Our New Position in Christ, We Must Put Off All Acts that Grieve the Spirit, and Produce the Fruit of the Spirit Instead

> And do not grieve the Holy Spirit of God, by whom you were sealed for the day of redemption. You must put away every kind of bitterness, anger, wrath, quarreling, and evil, slanderous talk. Instead, be kind to one another, compassionate, forgiving one another, just as God in Christ also forgave you.
> Ephesians 4:30-32

These verses seem to be a summary statement of the previous exhortations. Sin in the life of a believer grieves the Holy Spirit. We are called to put off all sinful acts, and to produce the fruit of the Spirit instead.

Interpretation Question: What does Paul's admonition to "not grieve the Holy Spirit" tell us about the Holy Spirit?

1. The Holy Spirit is a person, not a force. Only a person can be grieved.
2. The Holy Spirit loves us. Only a person who cares about others can be grieved by them.
3. The Holy Spirit's role is to make us holy, and that is why sin grieves him.
4. The Holy Spirit sealed believers till the day of redemption.

Interpretation Question: What does it mean to be sealed by the Holy Spirit?

1. The seal of the Holy Spirit speaks of ownership and authenticity.

In ancient times, owners put their personal seal on their property, including slaves and animals. God does the same with us through his Spirit. Romans 8:9 says, "You, however, are not in the flesh but in the Spirit, if indeed the Spirit of God lives in you. Now if anyone does not have the Spirit of Christ, this person does not belong to him."

The Spirit of God is a sign that proves to us and others that we belong to God. Romans 8:16 says, "the Spirit himself bears witness to our spirit that we are God's children." The way he testifies to our spirit is by changing us and giving us new desires—holy affections for God. Romans 8:15 says that by the Holy Spirit we cry, "Abba, Father." He works in us to pray, to read the Word, to serve, to worship, and to obey—in short, he makes us holy. If we do not have the Holy Spirit and his work in our lives, we are not his.

But, he does not just testify to us that we are God's, but also to others. Jesus says, "Everyone will know by this that you are my disciples – if you have love for one another" (John 13:35). This love is a supernatural work of the Holy Spirit. Romans 5:5 says the love of God was shed abroad in our hearts by the Holy Spirit. The Spirit of God is our mark, our seal. He proves to us and others that we belong to God.

Is there proof in your life that you belong to God? Is the Holy Spirit making you holy—changing your life? This work is so important that when Paul met some Christians in Acts 19:2, he asked them, "Did you receive the Holy Spirit when you believed?" They responded, "No, we have not even heard that there is a Holy Spirit" (paraphrase). Paul believed that the work of the Holy Spirit was unmistakable. If the Spirit is changing us, we will notice and so will others.

2. The seal of the Holy Spirit speaks of preservation.

Again, Paul says, "And do not grieve the Holy Spirit of God, by whom you were sealed for the day of redemption" (Ephesians 4:30). One of the uses of a seal was to keep and protect something. When Christ was buried, the guards sealed the tomb to make sure his body couldn't be taken out (Matt 27:66). A contemporary example is that of sealing food to preserve it. When we buy food or drink and the seal is broken, we know something is wrong with it. Similarly, God seals every true believer till the day of redemption—the redemption of their bodies.

Jesus says that he puts believers in his own hand and in his Father's hand, and that "no one can snatch them from my Father's hand" (John 10:28-29). God seals believers till the day of redemption.

Interestingly, Paul uses the eternal security of a believer as an encouragement not to sin. Those who believe one can lose their salvation often teach the very opposite. They say, "Don't sin because you will lose your salvation!" Paul says, "Don't sin, because God eternally saved you." Out of thanksgiving to God for his great eternal salvation, a believer should not grieve the Holy Spirit.

Vices to Put Off

Observation Question: What vices does Paul call for believers to get rid of in this passage?

Next, Paul shares some vices that grieve the Holy Spirit. "Though it is not possible to distinguish each one precisely, the overall meaning is clear:

- Bitterness—Smoldering resentment, unwillingness to forgive, harsh feeling.
- Wrath—Bursts of rage, violent passion, temper tantrums.
- Anger—Grouchiness, animosity, hostility.
- Clamor—Loud outcries of anger, brawling, angry bickering, shouting down of opponents.
- Evil speaking—Insulting language, slander, abusive speech.
- Malice—Wishing evil on others, spite, meanness."[159]

Paul seems to be describing a pathway of evil. First a person is bitter, leading to outbursts of wrath. Wrath leads to a settled anger. Anger leads to brawling or clamor—loud yelling and potentially a fist fight. Brawling leads to slander—evil speaking. Finally, slander leads to malice—a desire to injure or inflict harm. These clothes are not fitting for believers. Obviously, if we are going to stop from going down the path to brawling and malice, we must stop it at the heart level. We must repent of bitterness—feelings of resentment that lead to wrath and anger. Again, Christ taught that anger is the seed that leads to murder (cf. Matt 5:21-22).

Are you bitter or angry? Repent before God and ask him to give you a right heart—one that loves him and people.

Virtues to Put On

Observation Question: What virtues does Paul call for believers to put on, and what do they mean?

Next, Paul describes virtues a believer must put on. Ephesians 4:32 says, "Instead, be kind to one another, compassionate, forgiving one another, just as God in Christ also forgave you."

- "Kindness—An unselfish concern for the welfare of others, and a desire to be helpful even at great personal sacrifice.
- Tenderheartedness [compassionate]—A sympathetic, affectionate, and compassionate interest in others, and a willingness to bear their burden.
- Forgiveness—A readiness to pardon offenses, to overlook personal wrongs against oneself, and to harbor no desire for retaliation."[160]

"Forgiving one another" can be translated literally as, "acting in grace."[161] In the same way that God extended grace to us in dying for us and forgiving us, we must extend grace towards others. We must forgive as Christ forgives—not holding failures against others but extending unmerited favor towards them.

Are you still harboring bitterness, grudges, and unforgiveness towards others? Those are old clothes that Christ put to death on the cross and buried in the grave (cf. Rom 6:1-11). Therefore, put on the new clothes of the resurrected life—kindness, compassion, and forgiveness. Instead of grieving the Holy Spirit, allow him to bear his supernatural fruit in your life (Gal 5:22-23).

Application Questions: Who is the Holy Spirit? Why should the Holy Spirit's ministry of sealing encourage us to put off ungodly vices and put on godly virtues?

Conclusion

At salvation, Christ put to death our old nature and gave us a new one. Therefore, each day we must put off old attitudes and actions, and put on godly ones which fit our new nature.

1. Because of our new position in Christ, we must stop lying and tell the truth.
2. Because of our new position in Christ, we must control our anger.
3. Because of our new position in Christ, we must stop stealing, and work to help those in need.
4. Because of our new position in Christ, we must rid ourselves of ungodly talk and speak God's words instead.
5. Because of our new position in Christ, we must put off all acts that grieve the Spirit, and produce the fruit of the Spirit instead.

Are you wearing your divine wardrobe?

Imitating God

Therefore, be imitators of God as dearly loved children and live in love, just as Christ also loved us and gave himself for us, a sacrificial and fragrant offering to God. But among you there must not be either sexual immorality, impurity of any kind, or greed, as these are not fitting for the saints. Neither should there be vulgar speech, foolish talk, or coarse jesting – all of which are out of character – but rather thanksgiving. For you can be confident of this one thing: that no person who is immoral, impure, or greedy (such a person is an idolater) has any inheritance in the kingdom of Christ and God. Let nobody deceive you with empty words, for because of these things God's wrath comes on the sons of disobedience. Therefore do not be partakers with them.
Ephesians 5:1-7 (NET)

How can we imitate God?

Paul has been calling for the Ephesians to put off the clothing of anger, dishonesty, unwholesome words, etc., and to put on godly characteristics like truthfulness, kindness and forgiveness. These are clothes fitting for believers. In this passage, he calls believers to "be imitators of God" (Eph 5:1). Mimētēs ("imitator") is the word from which we get "mimic"— someone who copies specific characteristics of another person. We must mimic God—seeking to be just like him.

It is an impossible challenge to be like God. However, Scripture commands it. Jesus says, "be perfect, as your heavenly Father is perfect" (Matt 5:48). Peter says, "but, like the Holy One who called you, become holy yourselves in all of your conduct, for it is written, 'You shall be holy, because I am holy'" (1 Peter 1:15-16). God calls us to be just like himself.

This is how God created humanity—in his own image. However, at the fall, that image was marred, though not destroyed (cf. Gen 9:6). At conversion, God begins to transform us back into his image. Colossians 3:10 says, "and have been clothed with the new man that is being renewed in knowledge according to the image of the one who created it." God is daily renewing believers back into his perfect image (cf. Rom 8:29).

We also have a role to play in this transformation (cf. Phil 2:12-13). How should we imitate God? How can we live like God while residing among the ungodly? Ephesus was a place of tremendous immorality, where orgies were held in the temple of Diana. It was difficult for the Ephesians to imitate God while living among pagans, and it is hard for us as well. In this study, we will consider six principles needed for us to imitate God.

Big Question: How should believers imitate God according to Ephesians 5:1-7?

Believers Imitate God by Recognizing that They Are His Children

> Therefore, be imitators of God as dearly loved children
> Ephesians 5:1

Here Paul uses terminology every person can relate to—that of being a child. There are many things we can learn about imitating God from the fact that he calls believers "dearly loved children."

Interpretation Question: How should we, as dearly loved children, imitate God?

1. As dearly loved children, we must recognize that God's nature is in us in order to imitate him.

It's natural to believe that being like God is impossible. However, it is not. Because we are his children, we have the DNA of our Father. At conversion, he gave us his nature. Second Peter 1:3-4 says,

> I can pray this because his divine power has bestowed on us everything necessary for life and godliness through the rich knowledge of the one who called us by his own glory and excellence. Through these things he has bestowed on us his precious and most magnificent promises, so that by means of what was promised you may become partakers of the divine nature, after escaping the worldly corruption that is produced by evil desire.

God gives us everything we need to be like him—we each participate in his divine nature. Second Corinthians 5:17 says, "He who is in Christ is a new creation, old things are passed away, behold all things are become new" (KJV). Therefore, God's command to be like him is a recognition of who we are as his children. Because we are his children, God gave us his Spirit to empower and change us into his image. By his Spirit, we put sin to death in our lives, and by his Spirit we cry out to God, calling him, "Abba Father" (Rom 8:13, 15). As God's children we possess his nature, and this enables us to conform to his very image.

2.   As dearly loved children, we must know that God loves us in order to imitate him.

Another implication from Paul's exhortation is that we must know that God loves us in order to imitate him. He calls believers "dearly loved" children. If a child thinks that his parents don't love him, he will not try to imitate them. In fact, the world is full of children who are angry at their parents and want nothing to do with them. This is also true of us. If we don't know how much God loves us, we won't want to imitate him.

No doubt, this is why Satan works so hard to tempt believers to doubt God's love for them. This is what he did with Eve. He deceived her about the character of God, tempting her to think that God was the ultimate killjoy. He wanted her to think that she could not eat from "all" the trees in the Garden. He tempted her to think that God was both untruthful and unkind, keeping the best from her. Similarly, with Job, Satan tempted him to curse God to his face (Job 1:11). That was his purpose in Job's trials. Satan works overtime to make believers doubt God's love because he understands that if we comprehend God's love it will change us.

In Ephesians 3:17-19, Paul prays,

"that Christ may dwell in your hearts through faith, so that, because you have been rooted and grounded in love, you may be able to comprehend with all the saints what is the breadth and length and height and depth, and thus to know the love of Christ that surpasses knowledge, so that you may be filled up to all the fullness of God.

Paul prays for the Ephesians to grasp the greatness of Christ's love for them so that they might be "filled to the measure of the fullness of God." To be filled means to be influenced and controlled by (cf. Eph 5:18). Paul realized that they would look more like God when they knew the greatness of his love for them.

We must pray this prayer often for ourselves and others. We must know how much God loves us if we are going to imitate him.

3.   As dearly loved children, we must constantly watch God in order to imitate him.

A child watches his father walk and talk in order to imitate him. As a child, I remember standing in awe of my father. He was big and strong, and I wanted to imitate him and receive his approval. Therefore, I studied him often.

In the same way a child studies his father, we must study God. Hebrews 12:2-3 says,

> [Keep] our eyes fixed on Jesus, the pioneer and perfecter of our faith. For the joy set out for him he endured the cross, disregarding its shame, and has taken his seat at the right hand of the throne of God. Think of him who endured such opposition against himself by sinners, so that you may not grow weary in your souls and give up.

These Christians were being persecuted for their faith, and Scripture encourages them to consider Christ and his sufferings in order to endure suffering well. In the same way, we must study God through his Word to imitate him.

4.   As dearly loved children, we must constantly abide in God in order to imitate him.

When we hang around a person often, his character starts to rub off on us. It's the same with God. We must be in constant prayer—enjoying his presence. We must often fellowship with his people—where he is present (Matt 18:20). We must worship him constantly, as God inhabits the praises of his people (Ps 22:3, KJV, paraphrase). As we spend time with God, he changes us into his image, from "glory to glory" (2 Cor 3:18, KJV). Let this be true of us so we can continue to grow into his image.
Are you imitating God as his dearly loved child?

Application Questions: Name a few characteristics of God. Which communicable characteristic (one such as love, which humans can imitate, as opposed to one like omnipresence, which cannot be imitated) would you like to grow in most, and why?

Believers Imitate God by Loving Others

> and live in love, just as Christ also loved us and gave himself for us, a sacrificial and fragrant offering to God.
> Ephesians 5:2

Observation Question: How does Paul describe God's love in order for believers to imitate it?

Another way that believers imitate God is by living a life of love. First John 4:8 says, "God is love"—love is a definitive characteristic of God. Before God created man, he lived in a perfect loving relationship with God the Son and God the Holy Spirit. Believers are called to imitate this perfect love.

The word "live" can also be translated "walk." This pictures believers making daily choices to love as God loves. However, we must understand that this love is not primarily emotional—it is an act of the will. Paul gives Christ's loving sacrifice for the sins of the world as an example to model. His sacrifice was both an act of love for humanity and an act of love for God, a "fragrant offering" (Eph 5:2). John 3:16 says, "For this is the way God loved the world: He gave his one and only Son, so that everyone who believes in him will not perish but have eternal life."

Love is not only commanded by Paul, but by Christ as well. In John 13:34-35, Christ tells his disciples, "I give you a new commandment – to love one another. Just as I have loved you, you also are to love one another. Everyone will know by this that you are my disciples – if you have love for one another." Love is a fruit in every true believer—a fruit of being born again. Others will identify us by this love, and it should assure our hearts that we are truly born again.

First John 3:14-15 supports this: "We know that we have crossed over from death to life because we love our fellow Christians. The one who does not love remains in death. Everyone who hates his fellow Christian is a murderer, and you know that no murderer has eternal life residing in him." Love for the brothers will identify every true believer.

The question we must then ask is, "What does this divine love look like in a believer's daily walk?" We can discern the answer by considering Christ's loving, sacrificial death for the world.

Interpretation Question: What does Christ's sacrificial death demonstrate to us about how to love others?

- Christ's sacrificial death demonstrates God's forgiveness for our sins.

First Corinthians 13:5 (NIV) says that love "keeps no record of wrongs." Are you keeping a record of the failures of others? Or, in imitation of God, are you forgiving others for their failures? In the words of the English poet Alexander Pope, "To err is human; to forgive, divine."

- Christ's sacrificial death demonstrates meeting the needs of others.

Man could not save himself—he was helpless. Christ had to die for our sins. In the same way, believers must help the hurting, the poor, the despised, and even the unborn—those who have no advocate. Paul previously called for believers to stop stealing and to save in order to help those in need (Eph 4:28).

This is divine love. Selfish love only cares about its own needs, but divine love cares about the needs of others.

- Christ's sacrificial death demonstrates the opportunity for salvation.

We must love people enough to preach the gospel to them. Yes, it will offend and push some away, but it is the most loving thing that we can do. The reason we don't evangelize is because we don't love others as we should.

- Christ's sacrificial death demonstrates the great cost suffered by God and Christ for us.

In the same way, believers must love God enough to sacrifice everything for him—we must be willing to leave family, home, and career if needed. We must also love others enough to sacrifice for them. The believers in the early church sold all they owned to help other Christians in need (Acts 2:45). We must love one another in the same way, and by this, all men will know we are Christ's disciples (John 13:34-35).

Application Question: How is God calling you to grow in sacrificial love for God and others?

Believers Imitate God by Abstaining from Sexual Immorality

> But among you there must not be either sexual immorality, impurity of any kind, or greed, as these are not fitting for the saints.
> Ephesians 5:3

Next, Paul commands believers to abstain from sexual immorality. This is important since one of the results of rebelling against God is a sexually immoral lifestyle. Paul describes this in Romans 1:21-27:

> For although they knew God, they did not glorify him as God or give him thanks, but they became futile in their thoughts and their senseless hearts were darkened... [24] Therefore God gave them over in the desires of their hearts to impurity, to dishonor their bodies among themselves... [26] For this reason God gave them over to dishonorable passions. For their women exchanged the natural sexual relations for unnatural ones, and likewise the men also abandoned natural relations with women and were inflamed in their passions for one another. Men

committed shameless acts with men and received in themselves the due penalty for their error.
Romans 1:21-27

Rejection of God led to sexual immorality and shameful lusts—including homosexuality. Historically, the Roman Empire was known for loose sexual ethics. It was normal for a man to prefer both genders, and it was considered strange for him to prefer only one. A world that rejects God is a world handed over not only to idolatry but to a sexual revolution. This is what we are experiencing in much of the world today.

Observation Question: What words does Paul use to describe the sexual behavior that the Ephesians should not participate in?

1. Sexual immorality

"Sexual immorality" (Eph 5:3) comes from the Greek word porneia, from which we get the English word "pornography." It refers to all types of sexual immorality.

2. Impurity

"Impurity" is a more general term than "sexual immorality" in that it refers to anything that is unclean and filthy. John MacArthur says this about the term:

> Jesus used the word to describe the rottenness of decaying bodies in a tomb (Matt. 23:27). The other ten times the word is used in the New Testament it is associated with sexual sin. It refers to immoral thoughts, passions, ideas, fantasies, and every other form of sexual corruption.[162]

3. Greed

The word "greed" can also be translated "covetousness." In the context, it is not referring to money or wealth but to "someone else's body."[163] Covet was also used this way in the Ten Commandments about not coveting one's neighbor's wife. We must keep ourselves from lusting after others. Instead, we must be content.

Sexual immorality, impurity, and greed are improper for God's holy people. The word "holy" has to do with being "set apart" (Eph 5:3). God set us apart from the sexual promiscuity of the world. In 1 Thessalonians 4:4-5, Paul says that each believer must "know how to possess his own body in holiness and honor, not in lustful passion like the Gentiles who do not know God."

Interpretation Question: What must a believer learn to keep his body pure in a sexually charged world?

As translated in the NIV, Paul says there should not even be a "hint" of sexual immorality (Eph 5:3). This is where most believers fail. They don't understand how dangerous sexual immorality is, and therefore open the door to sexually charged music, movies, TV shows, and Internet sites. They reason that "only a little won't hurt," and the enemy catches and binds them in sexual addictions. Lust is like a small flame, which has the ability to burn down an entire forest.

Not only do believers allow hints of sexual immorality in their hearts through the media, but also through relationships. They practice the world's model in their dating relationships—opening the door to the enemy. They reason that a little holding hands won't hurt, a little kissing is harmless, and a little intimate touching is normal. By doing this, the fan the fire of lust. Paul said, "Don't even allow a hint of sexual immorality in your life."

Here is the model Scripture gives for one's dating/courtship relationships. First Timothy 5:1b-2 says, "Speak to younger men as brothers, older women as mothers, and younger women as sisters – with complete purity." Believers should treat members of the opposite sex as natural family members with all purity. There should be no hint of sexual immorality in these relationships.

Personally, because of the temptation to sexual immorality, I often recommend that unmarried couples implement a firm "no touch" policy. I think that's in line with Paul's exhortation of "no hint" of sexual immorality between Christian brothers and sisters. Believers should close every potential door to sexual immorality (cf. Matt 5:27-30).

Application Question: What are some other strategies for believers (married and unmarried) to practice in order to help them remain pure?

Believers Imitate God by Keeping Their Mouths Clean

Neither should there be vulgar speech, foolish talk, or coarse jesting – all of which are out of character – but rather thanksgiving.
Ephesians 5:4

Observation Question: How does Paul describe inappropriate language for a believer?

Next, in imitating God, Paul describes the believer's words. While Jesus was on earth, the Roman guards said of him, "No one ever spoke like this man" (John 7:46). In addition, the people from his hometown were amazed at his "gracious words" (Luke 4:22). Our Savior's words were always godly and gracious, and since he is our Lord, it is inappropriate for our words to be otherwise.

Paul uses several terms to describe inappropriate language:

1. Vulgar speech

This refers to any talk that is degrading and disgraceful, including cursing and saying the Lord's Name in vain.

2. Foolish talk

The word used for "foolish talk" is morologia. Moro means "fool," or "stupid." It is where we get the English word "moron." Therefore, moronic talk is not fitting for a believer. "Empty, wasteful, idiotic talk is sub-Christian."[164] Christ even says that we will be judged for every idle word (Matt 12:36).

One reason for not talking foolishly is that it leads to more sin. Proverbs 10:19 says, "When words abound, transgression is inevitable, but the one who restrains his words is wise." Too many words lead to sin—to saying or joking about something inappropriate. People seem to be more prone to moronic talk when staying up late at night or wasting time. Their inhibitions are down, and their tongues gush foolishness and sin. Paul says to beware of this.

Now it must also be said that Paul is not condemning laughing and joking. Proverbs 17:22 says a cheerful heart is like good medicine, and Ecclesiastes says there is a "time to laugh" (Ecc 3:4). There is nothing wrong with good fun, but we must be careful of ungodly fun, which often begins with an unrestrained tongue.

3. Coarse jesting

Coarse jesting comes from a word that means "'able to turn easily.' This suggests a certain kind of conversationalist who can turn any statement into a coarse jest."[165] This type of wit is common for a late-night TV show host. They are paid to turn news events, articles, and statements—no matter how innocent—into something crude and perverse.

Though all of these terms refer to negative speech in general, in this context they probably refer specifically to sexual speech. Sadly, believers who practice sexual abstinence often find it acceptable to talk loosely about sex. They reason, "Well, I'm not having sex like everybody else, so I can at least joke about it." However, one of the problems with this is that words reveal what is really in the heart. Listen to what Christ says about words in Matthew 15:18-19:

> But the things that come out of the mouth come from the heart, and these things defile a person. For out of the heart come evil ideas, murder, adultery, sexual immorality, theft, false testimony, slander. These are the things that defile a person; it is not eating with unwashed hands that defiles a person.

When Christ says a man is "unclean," he means unclean before God. This person might not be committing the physical act of adultery, but to God he is an adulterer. It is in his heart, as revealed by his mouth. Christ teaches that lusting after a woman is equivalent to committing adultery in one's heart (Matt 5:28). Our hearts condemn or approve us before God.

What do your words say about your heart? Are you imitating your Father by only speaking gracious words?

Observation Question: How does Paul describe appropriate speech for a believer?

Paul says it should be marked by "thanksgiving." In Romans 1:21, Paul described the unbelieving world as not glorifying God or giving thanks to him. It says, "For although they knew God, they did not glorify him as God or give him thanks." People who deny God are prone to selfishness and pride, expecting the world to revolve around them and becoming angry and bitter when it does not. However, believers should recognize God as loving, wise, and working all things out for their good (Romans 8:28) and, therefore they should constantly practice speech marked by thanksgiving rather than bitterness and ungodliness. First Thessalonians 5:18 says to "in everything give thanks. For this is God's will for you in Christ Jesus."

As mentioned, the negative terms describing speech are probably referring to perverse sexual talk; therefore, thanksgiving in this context might specifically refer to a believer's view of sex. John Stott says,

> But the reason why Christians should dislike and avoid vulgarity is not because we have a warped view of sex, and are either ashamed or afraid of it, but because we have a high and holy view of it as being in its right place God's good gift, which we do not want to see cheapened. All God's gifts, including sex, are subjects for thanksgiving, rather than for joking. To joke about them is bound to degrade them; to thank God for them is the way to preserve their worth as the blessings of a loving Creator.[166]

Application Questions: Why is it so common for believers to practice debased speech instead of speech that glorifies God? How is God challenging you to grow in your speech—especially in the area of thanksgiving? Why should believers possess a thankful attitude (or a holy attitude) instead of a debased one in regards to sex?

Believers Imitate God by Remembering His Judgment

> For you can be confident of this one thing: that no person who is immoral, impure, or greedy (such a person is an idolater) has any inheritance in the kingdom of Christ and God. Let nobody deceive you with empty words, for because of these things God's wrath comes on the sons of disobedience.
> Ephesians 5:5-6

Interpretation Questions: What does Paul mean by teaching that those who practice sin have no inheritance in the kingdom? Is he saying that people are saved or condemned by their works?

The next reason given for imitating God is a warning of God's judgment. Paul reminds believers that "no immoral, impure or greedy person—such a man is an idolater—has any inheritance in the kingdom." He is referring to someone practicing the sexual characteristics that he previously addressed. He calls this person an idolater because sex has taken the place of God in his life. He constantly thinks about sex, talks about it, and practices it. This is essentially worship. Paul is clear—those practicing sexual immorality are not saved. Christ says the same thing in Matthew 5:27-30:

> "You have heard that it was said, 'Do not commit adultery.' But I say to you that whoever looks at a woman to desire her has already committed adultery with her in his heart. If your right eye causes you to sin, tear it out and throw it away! It is better to lose one of your members than to have your whole body thrown into hell. If your right hand causes you to sin, cut it off and throw it away! It is better to lose one of your members than to have your whole body go into hell.

> The judgment for the sexually immoral is hell—eternal separation from God's blessings. Now, Christ and Paul are not saying that a person goes to heaven or hell based on works (cf. Eph 2:8-9). However, they are teaching that a person's works prove if he is truly saved or not. True salvation changes the direction and pattern of a person's life. Therefore, if a person continually practices sexual immorality, impurity, and covetousness—he is not saved.

There is no new life in him. He is spiritually dead in his trespasses and sins (Eph 2:1).

True believers stumble in these areas, but when they do, they hate their sin and repent of it. Unbelievers practice these things as a lifestyle because that is their nature. There are similar warnings to this throughout the New Testament. First Corinthians 6:9-10 says,

> Do you not know that the unrighteous will not inherit the kingdom of God? Do not be deceived! The sexually immoral, idolaters, adulterers, passive homosexual partners, practicing homosexuals, thieves, the greedy, drunkards, the verbally abusive, and swindlers will not inherit the kingdom of God.

Those who practice unrepentant sin as a lifestyle will not enter the kingdom of God. It must be noticed that Paul includes homosexuality. There are a great number of Christians today declaring that homosexuality is all right with God. Here again, we must note Paul's warning, "Do not be deceived." Homosexuality is not all right, and neither is any sex outside of a married man and woman.

Interpretation Question: Why does Paul teach believers to not be deceived? What types of deceptions were happening in the early church? How are we experiencing them today?

When Paul says, "Let nobody deceive you with empty words" (Eph 5:6), the implication is that some in the church were teaching a permissive view of morality and God's judgment. One of the things we know about the early church is that Gnosticism was rampant. Gnosticism came from a Greek philosophy which taught that the body was evil and the spirit was good. Therefore, Gnostics believed that whatever one did with the body didn't matter because God only cared about the spirit. This meant that believers could live in sexual immorality, stealing, lying, etc., and God would still accept them. However, this is not true. God cares about every part of us—body, mind, and spirit. One day he will resurrect our bodies to be with him eternally—he doesn't just care about our spirits.

Today, we have a false belief system called "universalism" that teaches that all people will be saved. However, Ephesians 5:5 denies this reality—along with a plethora of other Scriptures that teach God's judgment (cf. Matt 13:41-42, 25:46). Sadly, many professing Christians believe this false doctrine. Obviously, these Christians do not read their Bibles, or simply don't believe them. God wiped out the entire earth with a flood because of sin. He judged the nations in Canaan, commanding the Israelites to wipe them out.

When the people of Israel sinned, he judged them. In the early church, God killed Ananias and Sapphira for lying.

God is currently judging people, and there will be a future judgment as well. God will not let the world continue to dishonor him. Peter also warns of false teachers who deny Christ's second coming and a future judgment. Consider what he says:

> Above all, understand this: In the last days blatant scoffers will come, being propelled by their own evil urges and saying, "Where is his promised return? For ever since our ancestors died, all things have continued as they were from the beginning of creation." For they deliberately suppress this fact, that by the word of God heavens existed long ago and an earth was formed out of water and by means of water. Through these things the world existing at that time was destroyed when it was deluged with water. But by the same word the present heavens and earth have been reserved for fire, by being kept for the day of judgment and destruction of the ungodly. Now, dear friends, do not let this one thing escape your notice, that a single day is like a thousand years with the Lord and a thousand years are like a single day. The Lord is not slow concerning his promise, as some regard slowness, but is being patient toward you, because he does not wish for any to perish but for all to come to repentance. But the day of the Lord will come like a thief; when it comes, the heavens will disappear with a horrific noise, and the celestial bodies will melt away in a blaze, and the earth and every deed done on it will be laid bare. Since all these things are to melt away in this manner, what sort of people must we be, conducting our lives in holiness and godliness
> 2 Peter 3:3-11

Why should we imitate God and be holy? We should imitate him because he is a holy God who judges sin. The Lord is coming soon. Are you following him?

Application Questions: In what ways do you see this deception—a denial of God's judgment—in the church? Why is it so prevalent?

Believers Imitate God by Separating from Those Living in Sin

> Therefore do not be partakers with them
> Ephesians 5:7

Interpretation Question: Who is Paul referring to when he says "do not be partners with them"?

Finally, Paul says that if we are going to imitate God, we must separate from those living in sin or teaching deception—we must not partner with them. First Corinthians 15:33 says, "Do not be deceived: 'Bad company corrupts good morals.'" Proverbs 13:20 says, "The one who associates with the wise grows wise, but a companion of fools suffers harm."

Our relationships will either help us to know God better or pull us away from him. In Proverbs, wisdom and foolishness do not refer to a person's intellect, but to his relationship with God and obedience to him. That is why Psalm 14:1 says, "Fools say to themselves, 'There is no God.'" Proverbs 13:20 says that if we walk with those who obey and love God, we will grow in obedience and love for him. But, if we walk with those who rebel against God, we will also rebel against him.

This is why Paul says we must not partner with people practicing sin or denying God's judgment. Second Corinthians 6:14 says, "Do not become partners with those who do not believe, for what partnership is there between righteousness and lawlessness, or what fellowship does light have with darkness?"

Certainly, believers must be light to the world, and they must share the gospel with those who don't know Christ. But we should not be in yoking relationships where we are pulled away from God—even with those who profess Christianity.

Are you partnering with those who deny God by their lifestyle or teaching? Paul says, "Don't do it!"

Application Questions: How do we balance being in the world but not of the world? How can we reach the world without being contaminated by it? Also, how should we treat those who profess Christ, but practice immorality or deny God's judgment?

Conclusion

How can believers imitate God?

1. Believers imitate God by recognizing that they are his children.
2. Believers imitate God by loving others.
3. Believers imitate God by abstaining from sexual immorality.
4. Believers imitate God by keeping their mouths clean.
5. Believers imitate God by remembering his judgment.
6. Believers imitate God by separating from those living in sin.

Living in the Light While Residing in a Dark World

For you were at one time darkness, but now you are light in the Lord. Walk as children of the light— for the fruit of the light consists in all goodness, righteousness, and truth— trying to learn what is pleasing to the Lord. Do not participate in the unfruitful deeds of darkness, but rather expose them. For the things they do in secret are shameful even to mention. But all things being exposed by the light are made evident. For everything made evident is light, and for this reason it says: "Awake, O sleeper! Rise from the dead, and Christ will shine on you!" Ephesians 5:8-14 (NET)

How can we live in the light while residing in a dark world?

Paul is continuing his exhortation to imitate God that began in Ephesians 5:1-7. He called the believers to imitate God by living a life of love, and by getting rid of sexual immorality of every sort, including activities, thoughts, and words. Here the believers are called to imitate God by walking as children of light.

John MacArthur says this about the figurative use of the word "light":

In Scripture the figurative use of light has two aspects, the intellectual and the moral. Intellectually it represents truth, whereas morally it represents holiness. To live in light therefore means to live in truth and in holiness. The figure of darkness has the same two aspects. Intellectually it represents ignorance and falsehood, whereas morally it connotes evil.[167]

We see this in many places. Psalm 119:105 says, "Your word is a lamp to walk by, and a light to illumine my path." In this reference, "light" refers to intellectual truth as found in God's Word. In Romans 13:12-14, "light" refers to moral deeds and "darkness" to immoral deeds.

The night has advanced toward dawn; the day is near. So then we must lay aside the works of darkness, and put on the weapons of light. Let us live decently as in the daytime, not in carousing and drunkenness, not in sexual immorality and sensuality, not in discord and jealousy. Instead, put on the Lord Jesus Christ, and make no provision for the flesh to arouse its desires.

In Isaiah 5:20, these words refer to both the intellectual and the moral. It says, "Those who call evil good and good evil are as good as dead, who turn darkness into light and light into darkness, who turn bitter into sweet and sweet into bitter."

Believers are in the light because they have been changed intellectually and morally. How can believers continually imitate God by living in the light? In this study, we will consider six truths about living in the light.

Big Question: How can believers live in the light, as commanded in Ephesians 5:8-14?

To Live in the Light, Believers Must Remember that Light, Not Darkness, Is Their Nature

> For you were at one time darkness, but now you are light in the Lord. Walk as children of the light
> Ephesians 5:8

Here, Paul reminds believers that they were once darkness, but are now light in the Lord. It is interesting to consider that he does not say believers were "in" darkness, but they "were" darkness. That is the character of every believer before coming to Christ. There has been a definite character change in the life of every true believer. By using the term "children of light," Paul reminds us that we have our Father's nature (cf. 2 Peter 1:4).

In John 8:12, Jesus says, "I am the light of the world. The one who follows me will never walk in darkness, but will have the light of life." In Psalm 27:1 (ESV), God is called "light" and "salvation." This is the character and nature of God our Father, and we have his nature.

Interpretation Question: In what ways is the believer light and the world darkness?

1. The believer is light because he knows God.

Romans 1:21-23 describes the world as intellectually darkened in reference to knowing God the Creator. It says,

For although they knew God, they did not glorify him as God or give him thanks, but they became futile in their thoughts and their senseless hearts were darkened. Although they claimed to be wise, they became fools and exchanged the glory of the immortal God for an image resembling mortal human beings or birds or four-footed animals or reptiles.

People of the world have darkened minds. They profess to be wise when they are really fools. They deny the living God by worshiping false gods or denying his existence. Psalm 14:1 says the fool says in his heart there is no God. The world is dark because people do not know or even acknowledge God. But believers are light because they know the light—they know God.

2. The believer is light because he knows the gospel and Scripture in general.

Second Corinthians 4:4 says, "among whom the god of this age has blinded the minds of those who do not believe so they would not see the light of the glorious gospel of Christ, who is the image of God." The world is blinded to the light of the gospel. First Corinthians 1:18 says, "For the message about the cross is foolishness to those who are perishing, but to us who are being saved it is the power of God." Though the world rejects the gospel, to the believer, it is the power and wisdom of God.

Not only are unbelievers blinded to the gospel, they are also blinded to Scripture in general. First Corinthians 2:14-says, "The unbeliever does not receive the things of the Spirit of God, for they are foolishness to him. And he cannot understand them, because they are spiritually discerned." While the world rejects Scripture and cannot understand it, it is the believer's daily bread (Matt 4:4), constant meditation (Psalm 1:2), and joy (Psalm 119:24).

3. The believer is light because he practices the character of righteousness.

Romans 13:12-14 says,

The night has advanced toward dawn; the day is near. So then we must lay aside the works of darkness, and put on the weapons of light. Let us live decently as in the daytime, not in carousing and drunkenness, not in sexual immorality and sensuality, not in discord and jealousy. Instead, put on the Lord Jesus Christ, and make no provision for the flesh to arouse its desires.

As believers, we called to put aside the deeds of darkness and clothe ourselves with Christ.

Similarly, 1 John 3:10 says, "By this the children of God and the children of the devil are revealed: Everyone who does not practice righteousness—the one who does not love his fellow Christian—is not of God." Children of God are identified by their obedience to God, and unbelievers are identified by their disobedience.

Essentially, to be in darkness is to be ignorant of God and his Word and to practice rebellion in regards to those things. The world is darkness, but the believer is light. He knows the truth about creation, the gospel, and God, and he lives in view of these realities that the world rejects.

Application Question: What applications can we take from believers being children of light?

1. Believer must shine their light by placing it in the most strategic places.

    Christ says this in Matthew 5:14-16:

    "You are the light of the world. A city located on a hill cannot be hidden. People do not light a lamp and put it under a basket but on a lampstand, and it gives light to all in the house. In the same way, let your light shine before people, so that they can see your good deeds and give honor to your Father in heaven."

    Christians must put their light on a stand (Matt 5:15). When placing a lamp in a house, people put it in the most advantageous position. We must do the same with our lives. We must consider this when deciding where we will work, live, and go to church. How can we most effectively spread our light?

    Also, we must remove anything that might dim our light or make it ineffective. There are certain environments that could hinder the effectiveness of our light by either causing us to hide it or by blowing it out as we succumb to temptation. Believers must place their light on a stand for all to see.

    Placing our light in the most strategic places also includes helping it get stronger and shine the brightest. For example, this might include things like being involved in a good church, seeking godly mentors, and reading the right books.

2. Believers must avoid the temptation to hide their light.

    In Mark 4:21, Christ asks, "He also said to them, 'A lamp isn't brought to be put under a basket or under a bed, is it? Isn't it to be placed on a lampstand?'" Many commentators believe the bowl and the bed represent common reasons that people hide their light. Some hide it because of work. The bowl which Christ refers to is probably a bushel for collecting grain. Many believers get so busy at work that they hide the light of Christ, or they hide it so as to not hinder their chances of promotion. However, our light should not be hidden under the bushel of work. Secondly, Christians tend to hide their light simply because of laziness, as symbolized by a bed. They are too lazy to go to church, read their Bibles, serve on missions, or share the gospel.

No wise person puts a lamp under a bowl or a bed—and neither should believers. Our light is more important than any lamp in a house. We must strategically place our lamps in places that will maximize their output and effectiveness for the kingdom of God.

Application Questions: In what ways are you tempted to hide your light? In what ways do you believe God is calling you to place your light in the most effective location?

To Live in the Light, Believers Must Produce the Fruit of Light

> for the fruit of the light consists in all goodness, righteousness, and truth
> Ephesians 5:9

Observation Question: With what terms does Paul describe the fruit of the light?

The next thing believers must do to live in the light is to produce fruit consistent with light. Paul uses several terms in describing the fruit of the light. We can understand these terms better by comparing them with their opposites.

1. Goodness.

Goodness refers to anything that is morally excellent, including generosity.[168] One commentator calls it "love in action."[169] It probably focuses on our relationship to others, including meeting the needs of those around us, serving them, and caring for them. Galatians 6:10 says, "So then, whenever we have an opportunity, let us do good to all people, and especially to those who belong to the family of faith."

It is the opposite of selfishness and apathy towards the needs of others. Like Christ, who is the light, we must go out of our way to serve and minister to the needs of the world, and especially to-believers.

Are you bearing the fruit of goodness? Or are you cultivating apathy and selfishness?

2.   Righteousness.

There are two aspects to this fruit. First, it has to do with our relationship with God. Romans 4:5 says, "But to the one who does not work, but believes in the one who declares the ungodly righteous, his faith is credited as righteousness." In salvation, God gives us his Son's righteousness to make us acceptable in his eyes.

Secondly, it has to do with how we live. As those justified and made righteous by God, we must daily practice righteousness. James 2:17 says, "So also faith, if it does not have works, is dead being by itself." First John 2:29 says, "If you know that he is righteous, you also know that everyone who practices righteousness has been fathered by him." True believers practice a lifestyle of righteousness. These fruits should be continually borne in our lives, instead of the fruits of evil and sin.

3.   Truth.

"The third fruit of the light is truth. Truth has to do with honesty, reliability, trustworthiness, and integrity—in contrast to the hypocritical, deceptive, and false ways of the old life of darkness."[170] It is conformity to the Word of God in thought and action. Is the fruit of truth growing in your life? Or is hypocrisy and deception?

Many have noted how goodness seems to focus primarily on how we relate to others, righteousness on how we relate to God, and truth on how we relate to ourselves.

Application Question: How can we produce the fruit of light?

As with any fruit, it is produced in the right environment. What is the right environment? Essentially, it is our relationship with Christ. John 15:5 says, "'I am the vine; you are the branches. The one who remains in me— and I in him—bears much fruit, because apart from me you can accomplish nothing."

We must make our home in Christ through prayer, his Word, fellowship with the saints, worship, and service. As we do this, the fruits of goodness, righteousness, and truth are produced in our lives.

Are you bearing the fruit of light in your life or the fruit of darkness?

Application Question: What fruit do you most desire to produce in your spiritual life and why?

To Live in the Light, Believers Must Continually Discern What Pleases God

> trying to learn what is pleasing to the Lord.
> Ephesians 5:10

Not only must believers produce the fruit of light, but they also must continually find out what pleases the Lord. "Trying to learn" can also be translated "to test, discern, and approve."[171] It was used of testing a metal to see if it was genuine.[172]

William MacDonald says this about "finding out what pleases the Lord":

> Those who walk in the light not only produce the type of fruit listed in the preceding verse, but also find out what is acceptable to the Lord. They put every thought, word, and action to the test. What does the Lord think about this? How does it appear in His presence? Every area of life comes under the searchlight—conversation, standard of living, clothes, books, business, pleasures, entertainments, furniture, friendships, vacations, cars, and sports.[173]

Certainly, finding out what pleases the Lord also applies to knowing God's will in specific circumstances.

Interpretation Question: How can believers test and discern if something is pleasing to God or if it is his specific will for our lives?

1. Believers test and discern God's will by using God's Word.

God's Word either tells us what to do, or gives us principles to apply to discern God's will. In applying Scripture, we should ask questions like, "Is it moral?" "Is it helpful to others?" and "Is it honoring to God?"
God's will never conflicts with his Word. God's Word is the revelation of his character and being, and it trains the man of God for all righteousness (2 Tim 3:17).

2. Believers test and discern God's will by putting God first in their lives.

Proverbs 3:6 says, "Acknowledge him in all your ways, and he will make your paths straight." The more we put God first in our daily lives—through family, work, entertainment, etc., the more God will make his will clear to us. If we neglect God or de-prioritize him, we will not be able to discern his good and pleasing will.

3. Believers test and discern God's will by not conforming to the pattern of the world.

Romans 12:2 says, "Do not be conformed to this present world, but be transformed by the renewing of your mind, so that you may test and approve what is the will of God—what is good and well-pleasing and perfect." If a believer is conforming to the world in thought or action, it will inhibit his ability to hear and discern God's guidance.

4. Believers test and discern God's will by considering both their heart desires and whether they have peace in their hearts.

Philippians 2:13 says he works in us "for the one bringing forth in you both the desire and the effort—for the sake of his good pleasure—is God." This means that God is always working in our hearts to help us discern and do his will. Psalm 37:4 says, "Then you will take delight in the Lord, and he will answer your prayers." When I am walking with God—abiding in his Word, prayer, and the fellowship of the saints—many times the desires in my heart are of the Lord. In discerning what is pleasing to God, we must discern what God is doing in our hearts.

But also, in considering our hearts, we must consider whether or not we have peace, as this often is an indicator of God's leading. Consider what Paul says in 2 Corinthians 2:12-13:

> Now when I arrived in Troas to proclaim the gospel of Christ, even though the Lord had opened a door of opportunity for me, I had no relief in my spirit, because I did not find my brother Titus there. So I said goodbye to them and set out for Macedonia.

Paul lived for open doors to preach the gospel; however, he left Troas because he had no peace of mind. Many times, God leads us through peace or lack of it. Colossians 3:15 says, "Let the peace of Christ be in control in your heart." "Be in control," or it can be translated "rule," was used of an umpire at an athletic game. The umpire calls, "Safe!" "Out!" or "Winner!" This text can also be translated as, "Let the peace of Christ decide."

Sadly, instead of being led by God's peace, many are led by fear of the future, fear of what people think, or fear of failure. God works in our hearts to will and do of his good pleasure. He guides us by his peace, not by fear and anxiety.

5. Believers test and discern God's will by considering the counsel of other believers.

Proverbs 11:14 says there is safety and victory in the multitude of counselors. Scripture records that when God called somebody to do something, he often confirmed it through a prophet or another believer. God does the same with us. We should seek the counsel of other believers, especially in major decisions like who to marry, what school to go to, what job to take, etc. God often guides us through the counsel of wise believers. Proverbs 15:22 says, "Plans fail when there is no counsel, but with abundant advisers they are established."

6. Believers test and discern God's will by considering open and closed doors.

God is sovereign over all things. Many times, he makes his will clear by closing or opening doors.

If we are going to walk in the light, we must find out what is pleasing to God. We do this by bringing every thought and decision before the Lord so he can shine his light on it. He clarifies his will through his Word, other believers, our hearts, and his sovereignty, among other things.

Application Questions: In what other ways can believers discern what is pleasing to the Lord? Describe a time when God clearly guided you.

To Live in the Light, Believers Must Not Partake in Darkness, but Expose It

> Do not participate in the unfruitful deeds of darkness, but rather expose them. For the things they do in secret are shameful even to mention. Ephesians 5:11-12

The next thing believers must do to live in the light is to not partake in darkness, but to expose it instead. "The verb translated here as 'expose' (from elegchō) can also carry the idea of reproof, correction, punishment, or discipline."[174]

Interpretation Question: How should believers expose the deeds of darkness?

1. Believers expose darkness indirectly by living holy lives.

Many times it will simply be the fact that believers do not curse, cheat, get drunk, have sex outside marriage, or lie that exposes the sin in others' lives. A life of light exposes the sin of those around it. The rebuke of the light typically invokes either desire to change or anger. First Peter 4:3-4 says:

For the time that has passed was sufficient for you to do what the non-Christians desire. You lived then in debauchery, evil desires, drunkenness, carousing, drinking bouts, and wanton idolatries. So they are astonished when you do not rush with them into the same flood of wickedness, and they vilify you.

In a world that loves darkness and hates light, believers will constantly be mocked, thought strange, and sometimes persecuted for living a lifestyle of holiness. John 3:19-20 says:

Now this is the basis for judging: that the light has come into the world and people loved the darkness rather than the light, because their deeds were evil. For everyone who does evil deeds hates the light and does not come to the light, so that their deeds will not be exposed.

One must realize that living a holy life is both rare and strange in this world. Shadrach, Meshach and Abednego were thrown into the fire for not bowing down to Nebuchadnezzar (Daniel 3). Daniel was cast into the lions' den simply because he prayed three times a day to the true God instead of false gods (Dan 6). Jesus was crucified. We must welcome the cross our own Savior bore. He was the Light and the world hated him; we will often receive that same displeasure.

Are you willing to be different even if it means being considered strange or hated?

2. Believers expose darkness directly by words of correction.

Our exposure of darkness is not just indirect; it is also direct. We must call lying "sin," cheating "sin," adultery "sin," and fornication and homosexuality "sin"—again, often incurring the wrath of the world for doing so.

Kent Hughes says:

We need to be ethical light when we are in the office, in the classroom, in the shop, and in the Church. We must be willing to risk being called "negative," "narrow," "judgmental," "puritanical," or "bigoted." If God's Spirit is calling us to stand up against wrong, it is up to us to be faithful.[175]

But we must not only expose the darkness by calling it darkness, we must also expose the darkness with the gospel. One cannot preach the gospel without exposing sin. Sadly, this is often neglected in gospel presentations. The gospel says that all men are sinners under the judgment of a holy God (Rom

3:23, 6:23). It calls men to repent of their lifestyles of sin and turn to Jesus to save them. Yes, we must expose the darkness by teaching the gospel to a world under God's wrath.

Are you willing to expose sin through correction and sharing the gospel with others?

3. Believers expose darkness by not even talking about things that happen in the dark.

Believers must wisely not discuss many of the details of events that happen in the darkness. By discussing these, they give life to them and contaminate others with filth.

John MacArthur sheds light on Paul's comment:

Some things are so vile that they should be discussed in as little detail as possible, because even describing them is morally and spiritually dangerous.

Some diseases, chemicals, and nuclear by-products are so extremely deadly that even the most highly trained and best-protected technicians and scientists who work with them are in constant danger. No sensible person would work around such things carelessly or haphazardly.

In the same way, some things are so spiritually disgraceful and dangerous that they should be sealed off not only from direct contact but even from conversation. They should be exposed only to the extent necessary to be rid of them.

Some books and articles written by Christians on various moral issues are so explicit that they almost do as much to spread as to cure the problem. We can give God's diagnosis and solution for sins without portraying every sordid detail.[176]

By choosing to refrain from certain conversations and jokes, it again shows how perverse the world is. Believers must use wisdom in their conversations and interactions. Every word must be "gracious" and "seasoned with salt" (Col 4:6).

Application Questions: What makes exposing the darkness in a company, a church, or a relationship difficult? How can we do this wisely? Share a time when God called you to expose darkness. How did it turn out?

In Order to Live in the Light, Believers Must Convert Darkness into Light

But all things being exposed by the light are made evident.
Ephesians 5:13

Interpretation Question: What does Paul mean by "all things being exposed by light are made evident"?

Next, in order to live in the light, believers must convert darkness into light. "All things being exposed by light are made evident" can also be translated "for everything that becomes visible is light" (NASB). "When light touches something, it becomes light. It is lit up; and, to some degree, the object gives off light itself. It is converted and changed."[177]

In the same way, the light of a believer's life often changes a work environment as sin is exposed and righteousness replaces it. It changes people's lives as they repent and give their lives to Christ. Light is by nature more powerful than darkness. It changes environments and lives.

First Peter 2:12 says, "and maintain good conduct among the non-Christians, so that though they now malign you as wrongdoers, they may see your good deeds and glorify God when he appears." Though believers are persecuted and mocked by the world, their conduct often leads to change in those around them, even if only slowly. When Christ comes, many will glorify God for the chaste life of a Christian co-worker, friend or family member who led them to Christ.

Peter also says this to believing wives of unbelieving husbands (1 Peter 3:1-2):

In the same way, wives, be subject to your own husbands. Then, even if some are disobedient to the word, they will be won over without a word by the way you live, when they see your pure and reverent conduct.

The pure and holy life of a godly wife often changes an unbelieving husband, even without words.

Application Question: How have you seen or experienced light converting darkness in your life or the lives of others?

To Live in the Light, Believers Must Preach to the Sleeping

For everything made evident is light, and for this reason it says: "Awake, O sleeper! Rise from the dead, and Christ will shine on you!"
Ephesians 5:14

Interpretation Question: Where is Paul quoting from in Ephesians 5:14?

Commentators are not sure where this quote comes from. Some believe he is drawing from Isaiah 60:1: "Arise! Shine! For your light arrives! The splendor of the Lord shines on you!" Others believe he is drawing from an Easter hymn sung by the early church. It was probably used as an invitation to unbelievers visiting congregations.[178]

Either way, Paul clearly calls for Christians to preach to those who are asleep. The actions and words of Christians should speak to unbelievers—encouraging them to repent and follow Christ. But, they also speak to believers, as is probably the focus in this context. There are many believers living a lifestyle of darkness who need to repent.

In Romans 13:11-13, Paul uses the same terminology with reference to believers. He says,

> And do this because we know the time, that it is already the hour for us to awake from sleep, for our salvation is now nearer than when we became believers. The night has advanced toward dawn; the day is near. So then we must lay aside the works of darkness, and put on the weapons of light. Let us live decently as in the daytime, not in carousing and drunkenness, not in sexual immorality and sensuality, not in discord and jealousy.

Yes, many believers are slumbering in their spiritual lives. They are lukewarm—not on fire for God. By practicing the deeds of darkness—sexual immorality, drunkenness, dissension and jealousy—they live as though our Master is not returning soon. Believers must continually challenge them to wake up—to turn away from the darkness and to put on the light!

If we are going to walk in the light, we must not only seek the salvation of unbelievers, but also that of the church—for not all who profess Christ are living for him, or even saved (cf. Matt 7:21-23). There are many foolish virgins without oil who will be shut out of the wedding banquet—they have a form of godliness but not the inward reality (cf. Matt 25:1-13, 2 Tim 3:5). They must be warned in love (Eph 4:15).

Application Questions: How should we respond to believers who are asleep and living in the darkness? Why are so many believers spiritually lethargic?

Conclusion

How can believers live in the light while residing in a dark world?

1. To live in the light, believers must remember that light, not darkness, is their nature.
2. To live in the light, believers must produce the fruit of light.
3. To live in the light, believers must continually discern what pleases God.
4. To live in the light, believers must not partake in darkness, but expose it.
5. To live in the light, believers must convert darkness into light.
6. To live in the light, believers must preach to the sleeping.

Living a Life of Wisdom Instead of Foolishness

Therefore be very careful how you live—not as unwise but as wise, taking advantage of every opportunity, because the days are evil. For this reason do not be foolish, but be wise by understanding what the Lord's will is. And do not get drunk with wine, which is debauchery, but be filled by the Spirit, speaking to one another in psalms, hymns, and spiritual songs, singing and making music in your hearts to the Lord, always giving thanks to God the Father for each other in the name of our Lord Jesus Christ, and submitting to one another out of reverence for Christ.
Ephesians 5:15-21 (NET)

How can we live a wise life?

Paul calls believers to imitate God (cf. Ephesians 5:1). We imitate God by living a life of love (Eph 5:1), by living as light (v. 8), and finally, by living wise lives (v. 15).

In Scripture, foolishness and wisdom are not intellectual issues; they are moral issues. According to Psalm 14:1, "Fools say to themselves, 'There is no God.' They sin and commit evil deeds; none of them does what is right." The fool does not recognize God, and lives a life of evil. However, the wise man knows God and obeys him. Proverbs 9:10 says, "The beginning of wisdom is to fear the Lord, and acknowledging the Holy One is understanding." If we are going to live wise lives, we must worship and obey God.

In this section, we will consider four characteristics of a wise life.

Big Question: How can we live a life of wisdom according to Ephesians 5:15-21?

Believers Live a Life of Wisdom by Making the Most of Their Time

Therefore be very careful how you live—not as unwise but as wise, taking advantage of every opportunity, because the days are evil.

Ephesians 5:15-16

One characteristic of wise people is that they make the most of their time in knowing and doing God's will, whereas the fool wastes spiritual opportunities. Each day opportunities are lost to know God better, serve him, and build up his people.

"Taking advantage of every opportunity," can be translated "redeeming the time." It "has the basic meaning of buying, especially of buying back or buying out. It was used of buying a slave in order to set him free."[179]

History is full of great examples of wise, godly people who redeemed their time to the maximum potential. For example, "Jonathan Edwards, the philosopher-theologian who became God's instrument in the 'Great Awakening' in America in 1734–5, wrote in the seventieth of his famous Resolutions just before his twentieth birthday: 'Resolved: Never to lose one moment of time, but to improve it in the most profitable way I possibly can.'"[180] Similarly, "the great sixteenth–century reformer Philipp Melanchthon kept a record of every wasted moment and took his list to God in confession at the end of each day. It is small wonder that God used him in such great ways."[181]

In contrast, "Judas, the most tragic example of wasted opportunity, spent three years in the very presence of the Son of God, as one of the inner circle of disciples, yet he betrayed His Lord and forfeited his soul for thirty pieces of silver."[182]

As we consider these examples, we must ask ourselves, "How can we make the most of our opportunities to serve God and honor him?"

Application Question: How can we make the most of our time?

1. We must recognize how short our time is.

Moses says in Psalm 90:12 (NIV), "Teach us to number our days aright, that we may gain a heart of wisdom." The NLT translates this as, "Teach us to realize the brevity of life, so that we may grow in wisdom." If we do not realize how short our time is, we will not make the most of it. Our time is short because death awaits us. It is short because certain opportunities currently before us will not always be there. These opportunities include such things as the ability to cultivate relationships, serve in ministry, and pursue education. Finally, our time is short because Christ could come at any moment.

Some, in the foolishness of youth, live like they will be young forever. "Let's eat, drink, and have as much fun as possible," they say, not realizing that today could be their last. But we should pray as Moses did: "Lord, help us to know the brevity of life so we can make the most of it for your kingdom and purposes."

What else must we do to make the most of our time?

2. We must plan prayerfully.

Proverbs 21:5 says, "The plans of the diligent lead only to plenty, but everyone who is hasty comes only to poverty." Believers should prayerfully make long term plans: one-year, five-year and ten-year plans that include spiritual, vocational, family, and educational goals. They should also make daily plans. In fact, while taking a leadership class in seminary, I was taught to map out every hour of the day so I could best use it for God. Unaccounted hours are typically wasted hours.

It has often been said, "He who fails to plan, plans to fail." Spiritual progress doesn't happen by accident. It goes to the diligent who prayerfully seek God for the best and wisest ways to live.

Wise people are planners—they are not drifting through life. We must plan prayerfully even with our limited knowledge, while trusting God's ultimate plan and his sovereignty over everything.

3. We must be willing to pay the price.

As mentioned, "taking advantage" can be translated "redeeming," or "buying." There is a cost to making the most of our time. It means giving up other things we could do in order to best use our time. Be very careful of time wasters such as TV, social media, and video games. Yes, rest and recreation are important, but they must be limited. Doing so may well be part of the cost of living a wise life.

In addition, sometimes we may need to let go of relationships and other "good" things in order to make the most of our time for God. In business, these "good things" are called "opportunity costs"—things we must give up to take the best opportunities. Wise people are often brutal in cutting things out of their life that make them unproductive.

4. We must stay away from evil.

Finally, if we are to redeem our time, we must stay away from the foolishness of sin. Sin is the biggest waste of time. Paul implies this when he says to make "the most of every opportunity, because the days are evil." We live in a world full of evil and temptation. If we are not making the most of our time for God, then we will fall into the evil of the day.

As far as church is concerned, it is often the people who are not involved who tend to get trapped in evil—drunkenness, dishonest practices, ungodly relationships, addictions, etc. Instead of living wisely, they live as fools. If you don't use your time for God, Satan will use it for his purposes. There are really only two options.

Application Questions: In what other ways can we make the most of our time? In what other ways do people tend to waste time and opportunities?

Believers Live a Life of Wisdom by Understanding God's Will

> For this reason do not be foolish, but be wise by understanding what the Lord's will is.
> Ephesians 5:17

The next way to live a wise life is to know and understand God's will. No doubt, we see this in Christ—the wisest man ever to live on the earth. Before going to the cross, he prayed, "Not my will but your will be done." In fact, he taught us to pray, "Thy kingdom come, thy will be done on earth as it is in heaven." If we are going to live wise lives, we must be consumed with knowing and doing God's will. We considered this in our discussion of Ephesians 5:10—"trying to learn what is pleasing to the Lord." Therefore, we will cover it only briefly here.

Application Question: How can we know and understand God's will?

1. To understand God's will, we must know the Word of God.

   Second Timothy 3:16-17 says that the Word of God equips the man of God for all righteousness. If it is righteous, God wants to equip us for it through his Word. David said, "Your word is a lamp to walk by, and a light to illumine my path" (Psalm 119:105). If we are going to know God's will in a dark world, we must walk in the light of God's Word.
   Through his Word, God tells us exactly what to do in situations where there is a moral choice, and gives us principles to apply in other situations. We must know God's Word in order to understand God's will.

2. To understand God's will, we must pray.

   James 1:5 says, "But if anyone is deficient in wisdom, he should ask God, who gives to all generously and without reprimand, and it will be given to him." God wants to give us wisdom so we can make wise decisions that honor him. To know God's will, we must be people of prayer.

3. To understand God's will, we must rely on the body of Christ.

God often gives direction through the body of Christ. First Corinthians 12:21 says, "The eye cannot say to the hand, 'I do not need you," nor in turn can the head say to the foot, 'I do not need you.'" As we rely on the body, God gives insight and direction through its members. To not rely on the body is to spiritually impoverish ourselves, and often to miss God's best.

Application Questions: What are some other ways that God guides us into his perfect will? Is there something specific for which you are currently seeking the Lord about?

Believers Live a Life of Wisdom by Staying Sober

> And do not get drunk with wine, which is debauchery
> Ephesians 5:18a

Interpretation Question: In what ways does Scripture condemn the abuse of alcohol?

Another way believers live wisely is by being sober. Drunkenness was a common pastime in the ancient world, as it is today. Some people live to get drunk in their free time and on the weekends. Sadly, it is often seen as the only way to have fun. Living to get drunk is a wasted life, and Scripture condemns it. Isaiah 5:22 says, "Those who are champions at drinking wine are as good as dead, who display great courage when mixing strong drinks." MacDonald's comments are helpful in understanding Scripture's teaching on alcohol.

> The Scriptures do not condemn the use of wine, but they do condemn its abuse. The use of wine as a medicine is recommended (Prov. 31:6; 1 Tim. 5:23). The Lord Jesus made wine for use as a beverage at the wedding in Cana of Galilee (John 2:1–11). But the use of wine becomes abuse under the following circumstances and is then forbidden:
>
> 1. When it leads to excess (Prov. 23:29–35).
> 2. When it becomes habit-forming (1 Cor. 6:12b).
> 3. When it offends the weak conscience of another believer (Rom. 14:13; 1 Cor. 8:9).
> 4. When it hurts a Christian's testimony in the community and is therefore not to the glory of God (1 Cor. 10:31).
> 5. When there is any doubt in the Christian's mind about it (Rom. 14:23).[183]

With all that said, abusing wine leads to debauchery. Debauchery, according to Webster's online dictionary, refers to "bad or immoral behavior that involves sex, drugs, alcohol, etc."[184]

However, when Paul commands Christians not to get drunk, he is probably not only addressing a social issue, but also a theological issue. In the ancient world, worshipers commonly sought communion with their gods through various forms of ecstasy. This was achieved in part through taking drugs, heavy drinking, dancing, singing, and sexual orgies. In fact, witchcraft, or sorcery, in Scripture is the Greek word pharmakeia, from which we get our English word "pharmacy"—a place to buy medicine.

Paul might have had in mind the worship of the Greek God, Dionysius (Bacchus in Rome)—the wine God.[185] Festivals to Dionysius included drunken orgies and happened as often as five times a month.[186] Paul may be referring to this as he calls the Ephesians to instead be "filled with the Spirit." The Ephesians were not to worship the living God in the same way that pagans worshiped false gods, and neither should we.

With that said, believers should not just stay away from drunkenness and experimenting with drugs because they are morally wrong, but also because they open the doors to evil spirits—as experienced by those in cult religions. Scripture seems to affirm this in 1 Peter 5:8 (KJV). It says, "Be sober, be vigilant; because your adversary the devil, as a roaring lion, walketh about, seeking whom he may devour." To "be sober" means to be free of intoxicants. Believers should be free of intoxicants because these substances open doors to the devil.

When a person becomes intoxicated, he submits control of his mind and body to a drug. No doubt this lack of control opens doors for evil spirits. We should not be surprised that in the majority of rapes, robberies, and murders, the perpetrator is under the influence of drugs.

If a Christian is going to live a life of wisdom, he must not abuse alcohol or drugs.

Application Questions: What do you think about the belief that abusing drugs and alcohol opens doors for demons? What is your personal practice with the freedom of drinking? How can Christians wisely handle this freedom?

Believers Live a Life of Wisdom by Being Filled with the Spirit

But be filled by the Spirit, speaking to one another in psalms, hymns, and spiritual songs, singing and making music in your hearts to the Lord, always giving thanks to God the Father for each other in the

name of our Lord Jesus Christ, and submitting to one another out of reverence for Christ.
Ephesians 5:18b-21

Finally, if we are going to live wisely, we must be filled with the Spirit. The filling of the Spirit is a commonly misunderstood teaching; therefore, it might be helpful to first state what it is not.

Common Misunderstandings

Interpretation Question: What are some common misunderstandings of the filling of the Spirit?

1. To be filled with the Spirit is not a crazy, ecstatic experience that involves falling on the floor, shaking uncontrollably, or barking like a dog.

Scripture says one of the fruits of the Spirit is "self-control" (Galatians 5:23), and that the spirit of the prophets is subject to the prophets (1 Cor 14:32, KJV). This means when the Spirit of God moves in a person's life, the person has self-control—not a lack of control. The Spirit-filled person is able to control his lust, language, and emotions.

In 1 Corinthians 12:3, Paul says that "no one speaking by the Spirit of God says, 'Jesus is cursed,' and no one can say, 'Jesus is Lord,' except by the Holy Spirit." This needed to be said because the Corinthians were accepting many counterfeits in the church. They were probably so excited about power and charismatic gifts that they accepted everything without question. Paul says, "No, the Spirit of God won't say Jesus is cursed." In the same way, many churches today are so excited about the things of the Spirit that they lack discernment.

One of the tricks of the Anti-Christ in the end times will be "miracles and signs and false wonders" (2 Thess 2:9). The enemy deceives people with these types of wonders even today. People in churches are barking like dogs, roaring like lions, falling down, shaking, and everything else. John commands believers to test the spirits to see if they are of God (1 John 4:1). We do this by the spirit's fruit. One question we must ask is, "Does this 'spirit' produce self-control or lack of control?"

2. To be filled with the Spirit is not the same as the baptism of the Spirit.

Another common misunderstanding of the filling of the Spirit is confusing it with the baptism of the Spirit. When a person accepts Christ, the Spirit baptizes him into the body of Christ. First Corinthians 12:13 says that we have all been baptized by one Spirit into one body. It is a one-time experience whereby we become part of Christ's body. Some believe the baptism is a second experience that believers must seek, and that it is commonly associated with speaking in tongues. However, again, 1 Corinthians 12:13 say that we have all been baptized by the Spirit, and verses 28-31 of the same chapter indicate that not everybody has the gift of tongues. Further evidence that we have all been baptized by the Spirit is the fact that Scripture never commands us to seek the baptism. If it were an important experience for all believers to pursue, wouldn't there be at least one command for us to seek it? But, there isn't.

Sadly, because the filling of the Spirit is commonly associated with the baptism of the Spirit in some circles, it has created two tiers of Christians—"Spirit-filled" and "unSpirit-filled." In some churches, Christians who don't speak in tongues are looked at as second-class citizens. This is the opposite of what the baptism of the Spirit is meant to do. The baptism makes us one body—not two, and this incorrect theology divides what God unified.

Well then, we must ask, "What is the filling of the Spirit?"

Interpretation Question: What does it mean to be filled by the Spirit?

Whereas in the baptism of the Spirit we become part of the body of Christ, in the filling of the Spirit we offer our bodies to God. While the baptism of the Spirit is a one-time experience, the filling of the Spirit is to be a continual experience for believers. There is one baptism and multiple fillings. This is seen in the Greek tense of the word. It is a present imperative that can actually be translated "keep on being filled." This verb is also passive—meaning "we do not fill ourselves but permit the Spirit to fill us."[187]

Wiersbe's comments on the word "filled" are helpful:

In the Bible, filled means "controlled by." "They … were filled with wrath" (Luke 4:28) means "they were controlled by wrath" and for that reason tried to kill Jesus. "The Jews were filled with envy" (Acts 13:45) means that the Jews were controlled by envy and opposed the ministry of Paul and Barnabas. To be "filled with the Spirit" means to be constantly controlled by the Spirit in our mind, emotions, and will.[188]

The filling of the Spirit brings power in the Christian life to be holy, to witness, and to accomplish all God calls us to do. It should be the continual experience and endeavor of every believer. Believers should constantly seek this experience in their lives. If they don't, they will produce little fruit for God's kingdom.

How to Be Filled

Interpretation Question: How should believers seek the filling of the Spirit?

1.   Believers are filled through yielding to the Spirit's control.

Again, the word "fill" is passive, meaning that the Holy Spirit fills us. Therefore, in order for the Spirit to control us, we must yield to his will in our lives. We do this by obeying the commands in Scripture, heeding his promptings, and not grieving him through sin. If we commit sin, we must turn to God and confess it.

We must offer our bodies as living sacrifices unto God, as Romans 12:1 says. This is where many Christians fail. They continually hold back their best from God—not wanting to fully submit to him for fear of what he might say or where he might lead. As long as believers hold back from full obedience to God, they cannot be filled as they should be.

Are you yielding to the Spirit? Or are you holding back from full obedience?

2.   Believers are filled through dwelling in the Word of God.

Consider what Colossians 3:16-18 says,

Let the word of Christ dwell in you richly, teaching and exhorting one another with all wisdom, singing psalms, hymns, and spiritual songs, all with grace in your hearts to God. And whatever you do in word or deed, do it all in the name of the Lord Jesus, giving thanks to God the Father through him.

It is hard not to notice the similarities with Ephesians 5:18-21. The results of being filled with the Spirit and letting the Word of Christ dwell in us richly are almost synonymous; they are worship, thanksgiving, and submitting to others.

Since the Spirit is the author of Scripture, to be filled by him means to dwell in the Word of God. The word "dwell" actually means "to be at home." Many Christians can't be filled and empowered by the Spirit because the Word of God is not "at home" in their lives. It is more like a visitor than a resident. They visit the Word of God on occasion. They say, "Maybe I'll read the Bible today or maybe I won't." Therefore, they don't have power in their lives, and they struggle with self-control, which is a fruit of the Spirit.

If we are going to be filled with the Spirit, we must dwell daily in the Word of God (Psalm 1:2-3). There the Spirit instructs and equips us for all righteousness (2 Tim 3:16-17).

3.   Believers are filled through prayer.

In Acts 4:29-31, the church gathered to pray because of the persecution they experienced for preaching the gospel. The text shows their prayer and the result:

> "And now, Lord, pay attention to their threats, and grant to your servants to speak your message with great courage, while you extend your hand to heal, and to bring about miraculous signs and wonders through the name of your holy servant Jesus." When they had prayed, the place where they were assembled together was shaken, and they were all filled with the Holy Spirit and began to speak the word of God courageously.

When they finished praying the place was shaken, and they were empowered by the Holy Spirit to speak the Word of God boldly. Instead of fearing the threats of men, they had spiritual power to continue God's ministry.

How do we get filled and empowered by the Spirit of God? We get filled and empowered by having a thriving prayer life. Your ability to serve God, be holy, and have joy will often be proportionate to your time in prayer. One of the ways the Spirit fills us is through our prayers.

As we consider Acts 4, we must also see the importance of corporate prayer. Even Jesus, when confronted with the cross, threw a prayer meeting to get ready for it (Mark 14:34-42). We should do the same when encountering trials and temptations in our lives. It is one of the ways that God fills and empowers us.

4.   Believers are filled through worship.

In 2 Kings 3:12-15, Elisha is approached by Jehoshaphat and Ahab, who were seeking God's wisdom about going to war. Elisha responds, "'But now, get me a musician.' When the musician played, the Lord energized him," Elisha is filled by God's Spirit and empowered as he worships. It's the same with us—God empowers us through worship. In another story, God routs the enemy while Jehoshaphat and his army worship (2 Chr 20).

The Bible says God inhabits the praises of his people (Psalm 22:3 paraphrase). Wherever there is true worship, God manifests his presence and empowers his people.

5.   Believers are filled through faithfully enduring trials.

We get a picture of this with Christ in the wilderness. Matthew 4:1 says he was led by the Spirit into the wilderness to be tempted by the devil. But Luke 4:13-14 says this about his leaving: "So when the devil had completed every temptation, he departed from him until a more opportune time. Then Jesus, in the power of the Spirit, returned to Galilee, and news about him spread throughout the surrounding countryside." When Christ left the wilderness after faithfully enduring temptation, he was empowered by the Spirit of God.

It is no surprise that the believers God used greatly in Scripture, he often sent first into the wilderness—trials—to be filled and empowered. Trials empty us of our self-reliance so we can fully rely on God's strength. God said this to Paul about his thorn in the flesh in 2 Corinthians 12:9, "My grace is enough for you, for my power is made perfect in weakness."

God uses trials to weaken us so the power of his Spirit may be made perfect in us. With that said, some believers allow their trials to turn them away from God. Instead of running to him for strength and comfort, they run to something else like alcohol or other addictions. These people forfeit God's power and give something or someone else control of their lives.

Are you drawing near God in your trial, or are you looking elsewhere for help? Your trial is strategic. It is there for God to empower and equip you for service.

Results

Observation Question: What are the results of being filled by the Spirit, according to Ephesians 5:19-21?

In conclusion, Paul shares the results of being filled with the Spirit. We would naturally think of being bold witnesses, miracles, prayer that moves mountains, healings, etc., but those manifestations aren't listed in this passage. Instead, he says,

> Speaking to one another in psalms, hymns, and spiritual songs, singing and making music in your hearts to the Lord, always giving thanks to God the Father for each other in the name of our Lord Jesus Christ, and submitting to one another out of reverence for Christ. Ephesians 5:19-21

1. A result of being filled is corporate worship.

Paul said speak to one another with psalms, hymns, and spiritual songs. MacDonald's comments are helpful here:

> While some see all three categories as parts of the Book of Psalms, we understand only psalms to mean the inspired writings of David, Asaph, and others. Hymns are noninspired songs which ascribe worship and praise directly to God. Spiritual songs are any other lyrical

compositions dealing with spiritual themes, even though not addressed directly to God.[189]

It must be noted that Paul says, "speaking to one another." Corporate worship is focused on God, but it also involves speaking to and edifying one another. We commonly see this in the Psalms. Psalm 95:1-3 says:

Come! Let's sing for joy to the Lord! Let's shout out praises to our protector who delivers us! Let's enter his presence with thanksgiving! Let's shout out to him in celebration! For the Lord is a great God, a great king who is superior to all gods.

This reminds us that when we sing to God, it not only blesses him, but it also blesses others. As we raise our voices in worship, we speak to others about the greatness of God, and we edify them. Therefore, when we don't sing, we rob others of this blessing. Some are certainly more gifted at singing than others, but Spirit-filled singing has nothing to do with being in tune or sounding good. It is with the heart that we honor God and edify others.

2. A result of being filled is individual worship.

Paul says to be "making music in your hearts to the Lord." When filled with the Spirit, we find ourselves continually praising God—humming songs in our heart throughout the day. This is because the Spirit's job is to glorify Christ and God (cf. John 16:14-15).

3. A result of being filled is thankfulness.

When a person is critical and complaining, they are not filled with the Spirit, but with the flesh (cf. Gal 5:19-21, Phil 2:14). When the Spirit fills us we give thanks in all circumstances, for this is God's will for our lives (1 Thess 5:18).

4. A result of being filled is submission.

Instead of constantly seeking our own rights and our glory, we lay our rights down to serve and honor others as Christ did. Philippians 2:3 says, "Instead of being motivated by selfish ambition or vanity, each of you should, in humility, be moved to treat one another as more important than yourself." This includes both submitting to those in authority over us, and also to those under our authority. When Christ washed the feet of his disciples, he essentially submitted to them as a servant. That is why the disciples were so shocked and Peter at first refused this ministry (John 13). Like Christ, we must humbly submit to others, even those who submit to us.

Finally, in considering these results, we must understand that some commentators believe they are not just results, but also means of being filled with the Spirit.[190] Certainly, they are both. When we worship individually and corporately, we are filled with God's Spirit, even as Elisha was empowered as the harpist played worship music. When we are thankful, we are filled with the Spirit. But when we complain, we "extinguish the Spirit" (1 Thess 5:18-19). When we submit to one another God fills us, but when we are selfish and prideful, we lose his filling.

As believers, we must constantly be aware of the Spirit's filling, for we need it to worship, to be thankful, to submit to God and others, and ultimately to accomplish everything God commands of us.

Application Questions: How have you experienced the filling of the Spirit? Are believers conscious of this experience or not conscious of it? How is God calling you to continually seek it?

Conclusion

How can believers live a life of wisdom that honors God, instead of a foolish life that dishonors him?

1. Believers live a life of wisdom by making the most of their time.
2. Believers live a life of wisdom by understanding God's will.
3. Believers live a life of wisdom by staying sober.
4. Believers live a life of wisdom by being filled with the Spirit.

Characteristics of a Spirit-filled Marriage

> Wives, submit to your husbands as to the Lord, because the husband is the head of the wife as also Christ is the head of the church—he himself being the savior of the body. But as the church submits to Christ, so also wives should submit to their husbands in everything. Husbands, love your wives just as Christ loved the church and gave himself for her to sanctify her by cleansing her with the washing of the water by the word, so that he may present the church to himself as glorious—not having a stain or wrinkle, or any such blemish, but holy and blameless. In the same way husbands ought to love their wives as their own bodies. He who loves his wife loves himself. For no one has ever hated his own body but he feeds it and takes care of it, just as Christ also does the church, for we are members of his body. For this reason a man will leave his father and mother and will be joined to his wife, and the two will become one flesh. This mystery is great—but I am actually speaking with reference to Christ and the church. Nevertheless, each one of you must also love his own wife as he loves himself, and the wife must respect her husband.
> Ephesians 5:22-33 (NET)

What are characteristics of a Spirit-filled marriage?

In Ephesians 5:18, Paul commands the Ephesians to be filled with the Spirit. This means to be controlled and empowered by the Spirit of God. This is a command for all believers of all ages. What God has called us to, he equips us for by his Spirit. This happens as we yield in obedience to God, as we abide in his Word (Col 3:16), and as we worship.

Then in Ephesians 5:19-21, he gives both results and means of being filled. We are filled as we worship singing Psalms, hymns, and spiritual songs to the Lord. We are filled as we give thanks to God in everything. And finally, we are filled as we submit to one another. Submission "(hupotassō) 'means to relinquish one's rights'... submission is to be a voluntary response to God's will in giving up one's independent rights to other believers in general and to ordained authority in particular—in this case the wife's own husband."[191] We will see this Spirit-filled submission in several ways throughout the rest of the book. Wives are called to submit to their husbands, children to their parents, and slaves to their masters. Worship, gratitude, and submission lead to being filled with the Spirit and are at the same time results of this filling.

Therefore, in this text, we are introduced to characteristics of a Spirit-filled marriage. When couples are walking in the Spirit and being controlled by him, they will see wonderful fruits in marriage. With that said, we should understand how radical this message was to the Ephesians. Pagan marriages and families in general were in shambles. Kent Hughes shares this about marriage in the pagan world:

> Demosthenes [a prominent Greek statesman and orator] said, "We have courtesans [prostitutes] for the sake of pleasure; we have concubines for the sake of daily cohabitation; we have wives for the purpose of having children legitimately, and of having a faithful guardian for all our household affairs." Xenophon [a Greek historian] said it was the husband's aim that a wife "might see as little as possible, hear as little as possible and ask as little as possible." Similarly Socrates said, "Is there anyone to whom you entrust more serious matters than to your wife — and is there anyone to whom you talk less?" The ancient pagan man breathed adultery. The marriage bond was virtually meaningless. It was better with the Jews, of course, except that the ultra-liberal and very popular school of Hillel allowed a man to divorce his wife for virtually anything — like putting too much salt in his food or becoming less attractive in his eyes.[192]

Marriage was broken in the pagan world, and Paul calls for the Ephesians to restore it by returning to God's original design for marriage.

It is not much better in our society, where around fifty percent of marriages end in divorce. In fact, this institution is so pitiful in our society that many couples refuse to marry, choosing to simply live together. Others prefer open relationships without any promise of commitment.

How can we have the kind of marriages God originally planned for mankind? In order to fix what is broken, God gave us his Spirit, and when we are being filled with the Spirit, we will see much fruit in marriage. In this study, we will consider three characteristics of a Spirit-filled marriage.

Big Questions: What does a Spirit-filled marriage look like? How does the Spirit's filling affect the wife and the husband, according to Ephesians 5:22-33?

In a Spirit-filled Marriage, the Wife Submits to Her Husband

> Wives, submit to your husbands as to the Lord, because the husband is the head of the wife as also Christ is the head of the church—he himself being the savior of the body. But as the church submits to Christ, so also wives should submit to their husbands in everything.
> Ephesians 5:22-24

Paul says, "Wives, submit to your husbands as to the Lord." Unfortunately, "submission" carries a nasty connotation in our society, but it must be noted that this word does not mean "inferiority." "Submit" is actually a military word that means "to arrange under rank"[193] and to "come up under." A sergeant is not inferior to a captain. They are equal. However, authority is necessary to maintain order in the military. Otherwise, there will be chaos. In the same way, God made the husband and wife relationship with order and authority so that it would function properly.

What's interesting in this passage is that Paul gives the wife reasons to submit. Since God is our sovereign he does not have to give reasons, but here in this text, he does.

Observation Questions: What reasons does Paul give for the wife submitting to her husband? How is this reflected in the rest of Scripture?

1. The wife must submit to her husband because it is her duty to Christ.

The command, "Wives submit to your husbands as to the Lord," means that this is part of the Christian wife's duty to Christ. When she submits to her husband, she is submitting to Christ.

Submission is really an obedience issue to God. It has nothing to do with the husband's ability to lead, or with his IQ. Many wives are more fit to lead than their husbands in terms of worldly qualifications. The submission of the wife has everything to do with God.

This should make a single woman more cautious when considering whom to marry. She must ask herself, "Is this somebody I am willing to submit to spiritually, financially, socially, and in every other area of life?" Whom a woman marries is the second most important decision of her life, after choosing to follow Christ. This decision should not just be made emotionally; it must also be very practical.

The command also speaks to single men considering marriage. They must ask themselves, "Is the woman I'm considering faithfully submitting to Christ?" If she does not submit to the greater, neither will she submit to the lesser.

The wife must submit to her husband because it is her duty in following Christ.

2. The wife must submit to her husband because he is her head.

What does Paul mean by the term "head"? If we say that someone is the head of a company or an organization, it means he is the authority. Similarly, the husband is the head of the wife.

Interpretation Question: Is Paul's teaching of the headship of the husband over the wife cultural, or timeless (relevant for all times)?

Trinitarian Argument

Some say that Paul's reference to the man's headship was just cultural with no applications for today, but this is not true. Many Scriptures teach the man's position of authority as a universal concept—most notably 1 Corinthians 11:3, 1 Timothy 2:11-13, and the creation narrative in Genesis 2.

In 1 Corinthians 11:3, Paul describes the headship of man over the wife by comparing them to Christ and God. He says, "But I want you to know that Christ is the head of every man, and the man is the head of a woman, and God is the head of Christ." When God made Adam and Eve, he made them in his image and also one flesh—one body (Gen 2:24). But there is order in the body. The head leads the rest of the members. Paul says the headship of man over the wife is analogous to the headship of God over Christ. In the analogy, the woman pictures Christ, who is co-equal to God the Father, but submits to him. When God made man and woman in his image, he made the relationship to operate in perfect love and perfect submission as seen in the Trinity.

Order of Creation Argument

Similarly, in 1 Timothy 2:11-13, Paul states that women should not have the role of teacher over men (probably referring to the elder/pastor role, cf. 1 Tim 3:1-7, Titus 1:6-9). Here he does not make a cultural argument, but a creation one. Consider the text: "A woman must learn quietly with all submissiveness. But I do not allow a woman to teach or exercise authority over a man. She must remain quiet. For Adam was formed first and then Eve."

Paul tells us that the roles established in the New Testament do not stem from the fall or culture; they reflect the way God created man and woman in the Garden of Eden. The creation of Adam before Eve was significant. It meant that he was her head. She was made from his side to be his helper in ruling and subduing the world for God.

Adam Naming Eve

Further evidence of the husband's leadership role is seen in Adam naming his wife. Before creating Eve, God paraded all the animals before Adam and told him to name them (Genesis 2). This naming represented Adam's authority over the animals. Right after God created Eve from Adam's rib, Adam then named her "woman." After the fall, he named her "Eve" (Genesis 3). Again, this demonstrates Adam's headship over Eve. Naming has the same significance in our society.

The woman must submit to her husband not just because God commands, but because God made the husband to be the head of the wife. A home where the wife does not submit to her husband is like an arm that will not submit to its head. God made order in the body, and he made it in the home.

3. Wives must submit to their husbands because marriage symbolizes Christ's relationship to the church.

Paul says, "because the husband is the head of the wife as also Christ is the head of the church—he himself being the savior of the body" (Eph 5:23). In the same way the church submits to Christ, the wife is called to submit to her husband. From creation, God made marriage to model the present reality of Christ and the church. Paul deals further with this analog later in the text, calling it a "mystery" in Ephesians 5:32.

It is easy to understand the analogy of the husband being the head of the wife as Christ is the head of the church. But, how is the man the wife's savior? David Guzik's comments about Lloyd-Jones' views on this text are helpful:

> Lloyd-Jones thinks Paul used the wider understanding of the word Savior, which can simply mean preserver. 1 Timothy 4:10 speaks of Jesus being the Savior of all men, especially of those who believe. How can Jesus be the Savior of all men? In the sense that He preserves all men and blesses all men with good things from heaven above. It is in this way that husbands are to be their wife's savior... "What, then, is the doctrine? It is clearly this. The wife is the one who is kept, preserved, guarded, shielded, provided for by the husband.[194]

This is the third reason that the wife should submit to her husband— he is her savior in the sense that he guards, protects, and provides for her, even as Christ does his church. A Christian marriage is called to be a gospel message that evangelizes everyone around. The husband sacrificially loves his wife like Christ, and she submits to him like the church. The union itself is meant to model and glorify God.

But believers are not just called to model God in a good marriage, but even in a bad marriage. God commanded Hosea to marry a woman that would eventually cheat on him. After she did so, God commanded Hosea to take her back, just as Israel cheated on God and God took her back.

This teaches us that a Christian marriage is more about God and his glory than our own happiness, and when we understand this, it should radically change how we act in marriage. We should continually ask ourselves, "Are my actions reflecting God's forgiveness, patience, and love?" "Am I honoring God through my actions?" There is a sense in which we cannot control the actions of our spouse, but we can control how we respond to those actions. We must bring every thought and response before the litmus test of God's Word and his character. Lord, we are here to glorify you. Our life is not about our happiness, but about your happiness. Lord, help us be faithful reflections of you.

Interpretation Question: What is the extent of the wife's submission?

In Ephesians 5:24, Paul says, "But as the church submits to Christ, so also wives should submit to their husbands in everything." Essentially, the extent of the woman's submission is "in everything."

However, "in everything" must be qualified by his original command, "Wives, submit to your husbands as to the Lord" (v. 22). The wife must not do anything that would dishonor God. If the husband commands her to lie on taxes, she must refuse. If he commands her not to go to church, read her Bible, or worship, she must refuse. Her first priority is to follow God. And following God should ultimately make her a better wife to her husband.

This principle is very important, especially when it comes to arguments and fighting. The woman is not to be a doormat. She is made in the image of God and her input is important and valuable; a godly husband will recognize and cherish this reality. However, when the husband asks her to do something that is not sinful, she should submit. Yes, it may seem foolish. In such cases she should respectfully make her opinion known and pray for her husband, but ultimately she must submit to him, trusting God to work in his life. This also includes situations where a believing wife is married to an unbeliever. First Peter 3:1-2 says:

> In the same way, wives, be subject to your own husbands. Then, even if some are disobedient to the word, they will be won over without a word by the way you live, when they see your pure and reverent conduct.

Now, both the husband and wife are called to submit to Christ as Lord. When this happens in a marriage, typically the husband and wife will at some point be on the same page about decisions. Agreement may come in stages, and couples must be patient and prayerful as they wait. In fact, this is part of

God's sanctification process in couples as they seek him together to discern his will.

Application Questions: Why is the submission of the wife to her husband so important? What are some common reactions to this teaching in society and often in the church? How should a single woman apply this principle in seeking a future mate?

In a Spirit-filled Marriage, the Husband Loves His Wife

> Husbands, love your wives just as Christ loved the church and gave himself for her to sanctify her by cleansing her with the washing of the water by the word, so that he may present the church to himself as glorious—not having a stain or wrinkle, or any such blemish, but holy and blameless. In the same way husbands ought to love their wives as their own bodies. He who loves his wife loves himself. For no one has ever hated his own body but he feeds it and takes care of it, just as Christ also does the church, for we are members of his body. For this reason a man will leave his father and mother and will be joined to his wife, and the two will become one flesh. This mystery is great—but I am actually speaking with reference to Christ and the church.
> Ephesians 5:25-32

What about the role of the husband? First, let us notice God does not call the husband to make the wife submit to him. Submission must be voluntary. The abuse of wives by husbands seen throughout the ages is not God's will. It is a result of the curse. In Genesis 3:16, one of the results of the curse was that the woman would desire her husband (meaning desire to control him), and the husband would rule over his wife (an oppressive, forceful rule). However, Christ came to restore God's original design for marriage, and he gives us his Spirit to equip us for this.

Paul calls for the husband to love his wife. He uses the word agape, which is often used of God's love. This is not an emotional love; it is an act of the will. Believers are called to agape their enemies (Matt 5:44). And if this is possible, husbands can certainly agape their wives no matter the situation. I really struggle when Christian husbands or wives tell me they just don't "feel" like they "love" their spouse any more. In response, I say, "What does feelings have to do with it? God commanded you to love your spouse. He commands it and empowers it (cf. Rom 5:5, Gal 5:22). This is an obedience issue, not a feeling issue."

With that said, it should be remembered that in the ancient world Paul's command was pretty radical. Husbands had very little regard for their wives, and the idea of loving them would have sounded ridiculous.

In the Jewish and Greek cultures, the woman had few to no rights. She was a piece of property meant to serve her husband. Paul's teaching that the husband was to love his wife as Christ loves the church was profoundly counter-cultural.

It must be remembered that the husband is given an impossible standard here. No one can love just like Christ. This means that no husband will ever be able to say, "I made it!" nor should he feel satisfied with the love he shows his wife. Every husband falls woefully short of this impossible standard, but he must continually seek to reach it.

Interpretation Question: What characteristics of the husband's love can be discerned from Ephesians 5:25–28?

1. The husband's love must be realistic.

The man should have no unrealistic fantasies about the woman he married. Christ loved the church and died for her while she was still a sinner and an enemy of God (Rom. 5:8). Christ knew she was sinful and disobedient. Yet, he still gave his life for her while knowing her faults. His love was realistic.

In marriage, both partners should understand this reality. In fact, much of pre–marital counseling consists of destroying the false expectations set up by romantic comedies and other Hollywood productions. The husband must love realistically; his wife has been infected by sin just as he has. She must be reformed daily by God's grace, and she must be loved despite her faults. Scripture says, "Love covers a multitude of sins" (1 Peter 4:8). However, a realistic love is important for both partners to prevent disillusionment. I have no doubt that the reason the highest number of divorces happen in the first year of marriage is because most romantic love is unrealistic.

2. The husband's love must be sacrificial.

The husband is to love his wife as Christ loved the church, and thus be willing to die for her. If anyone feels that the wife's role is unfair, they should give more thought to that of the husband. Surely it is much easier to submit to someone than to give one's life for that person. Indeed, such love is impossible without the grace of God.

To love sacrificially means the husband must at times forgo his free time, entertainment, friendships, and sometimes even career in order to love his wife. It is sad to see how many husbands, because of their careers, are not even home to love their wives or their children.

3. The husband's love must be sanctifying.

Christ's love makes the church holy by cleansing her with the Word; his purpose is to make her the perfect bride. Similarly, the husband must help and encourage his wife to learn Scripture, and to get involved in a Bible-believing church and with small groups and ministries where she can grow and serve. He must help her cultivate not only her character but also her calling so she can fulfill God's plans for her life.

He must discern her gifts and talents, and encourage her to use them for the glory of God. This love may also mean admonishing his wife through the Word at times so that she might know and serve Christ better. It is a sanctifying love. Before getting married, every man should consider whether he is ready and willing to love a woman this way. Is he ready to be a spiritual leader?

4.   The husband's love must be humble.

The phrase "washing of the water" (Eph 5:26) seems to picture the job of a servant. It may specifically reflect Christ washing the feet of his disciples— the job of a slave, or the lowest ranking person in a house (John 13). Christ humbles himself and cleans his disciples. This is also the job of the husband. Though he is the head, he does not use his position to dominate or command his wife, but to humbly serve her. He must continually be concerned about her emotional, physical, social, and spiritual needs, and work to meet them. The husband's love must be humble and serving.

5.   The husband's love must be personal.

He must love her as his own body. Ephesians 5:28 says, "In the same way husbands ought to love their wives as their own bodies. He who loves his wife loves himself." David Guzik says this about Paul's command:

> The single word as is important. Paul did not say, "So ought men to love their wives in the same way as they love their bodies." That would be an improvement in many cases, but that is not the meaning. The meaning is, "So ought men to love their wives because they are their own bodies." … A man must love his wife as he would his body, as a part of himself. As Eve was a part of Adam, taken out of his side, so the wife is to the man because she is a part of him.[195]

Martyn Lloyd-Jones adds:

> The husband must realize that his wife is a part of himself. He will not feel this instinctively; he has to be taught it; and the Bible in all its parts teaches it. In other words, the husband must understand that he and his wife are not two: they are one.[196]

In fact, it seems as though Paul is appealing to man's selfish nature when he says, "He who loves his wife loves himself" (v. 28). In reality, this is a motivation that many of us men need. When we love our wives, we actually bless ourselves. And when we don't, it hurts us. Like a person who neglects a fractured leg and ends up being crippled by it, a husband who does not minister to his wife hurts himself both at the time and over the long term.

The husband's love must be realistic, sacrificial, sanctifying, humble, and personal. Husbands must love their wives and take time daily to cultivate a Christ-centered home.

Application Questions: Which aspects of the husband's love do you find most challenging, and why? For singles, how will you apply these principles in your preparation for marriage?

In a Spirit-filled Marriage, the Husband and Wife Meet Each Other's Deepest Need

> Nevertheless, each one of you must also love his own wife as he loves himself, and the wife must respect her husband.
> Ephesians 5:33

Interpretation Questions: Why does Paul focus on the husband's need for respect and the wife's need for love? Don't they both need love and respect?

Finally, Paul gives a summary statement of the husband's and wife's duties: The husband must love his wife and the wife must respect her husband. To respect her husband means to esteem and honor him, even when he doesn't deserve it.

It's interesting that Paul doesn't call the woman to love her husband. It's certainly assumed, but respect is the chief thing a man needs. If a wife talks down to her husband, she cuts him down at his place of greatest need. In the same way, when a husband doesn't love his wife, when he doesn't speak words of encouragement and make sacrifices for her, he cuts her down at her place of greatest need. The woman needs love and the man needs respect. When the house is out of order, they deprive one another of these blessings.

Dr. Emerson Eggerichs, in his book Love and Respect, cites research showing that when husbands and wives are in conflict, 83% of the men feel disrespected and 70% of the women feel unloved. This seems to support the necessity of a husband demonstrating love for his wife, and the need for a wife to always respect her husband.[197]

In a Spirit-filled marriage, the wife certainly loves her husband and the husband respects his wife, but they also meet each other's core needs in a special way. Wives especially need love and husbands especially need respect. Scripture seems to emphasize this and so does research.

Application Questions: Do you think there is a major difference in the psychology of men and women with respect to their needs for love and respect? If not, why not? If so, in what way have you seen or experienced this difference?

Conclusion

As we consider the characteristics of a Spirit-filled marriage, we must remember that they come only through a work of God. A marriage needs God to function correctly—it needs the Spirit of God to empower both partners.

Marriage has often been compared to a triangle with God at the peak and the husband and the wife on the sides. As the husband and the wife get closer to God, they get closer to one another. As we abide in the Spirit through prayer, time in the Word, and fellowship, the fruits of the Spirit are born in our marriages.

What are characteristics of a Spirit-filled marriage?

1. In a Spirit-filled marriage, the wife submits to her husband.
2. In a Spirit-filled marriage, the husband loves his wife.
3. In a Spirit-filled marriage, the husband and wife meet each other's deepest needs.

Characteristics of a Spirit-filled Home

Children, obey your parents in the Lord for this is right. "Honor your father and mother," which is the first commandment accompanied by a promise, namely, "that it may go well with you and that you will live a long time on the earth." Fathers, do not provoke your children to anger, but raise them up in the discipline and instruction of the Lord. Ephesians 6:1-4 (NET)

What are characteristics of a Spirit-filled home, as seen in the relationship between parents and children?

In Ephesians 6:1-4, Paul gives instructions to children and parents. Since the word "fathers" in verse 4 can be translated as "parents," in this study we will address both parents.

It must be remembered that this passage is connected to Ephesians 5:18, where Paul calls the Ephesians to be filled with the Spirit. To be "filled" means to be empowered and controlled by the Spirit of God. In Ephesians 5:19-22, he gives the results of the Spirit's filling. Believers worship, give thanks, and submit to one another out of reverence to Christ. Paul then talks about the Spirit-filled relationship between a husband and wife, and then between children and parents.

In a Spirit-filled home, children obey their parents, and parents raise their children in the Lord and do not exasperate them. If this is true of a Spirit-filled home, then in a worldly home, children are disobedient and parents neglect training them in the Lord.

Romans 1 describes the results of society denying God, and one of them is disobedient children (v. 30). Furthermore, Isaiah describes how in a society under God's judgment, children rule and oppress the people. Isaiah 3:12-13 (ESV) says, "My people—infants are their oppressors, and women rule over them. O my people, your guides mislead you and they have swallowed up the course of your paths."

Sadly, this is happening all over the world. The Duke of Windsor once quipped, "The thing that impresses me most about America is the way parents obey their children."[198] Instead of children submitting to their parents, parents often do whatever it takes to make children happy, even to their demise. In many places, youth run wild and people are scared to walk the streets because of theft, murder, and gang violence.

In many families there is oppression by either the parents or the children, instead of love and obedience to God's Word. John MacArthur shares a quote from the Minnesota Crime Commission, which demonstrates the truthfulness of Scripture on this topic:

> Every baby starts life as a little savage. He is completely selfish and self–centered. He wants what he wants when he wants it: his bottle, his mother's attention, his playmate's toys, his uncle's watch, or whatever. Deny him these and he seethes with rage and aggressiveness which would be murderous were he not so helpless. He's dirty, he has no morals, no knowledge, no developed skills. This means that all children, not just certain children but all children, are born delinquent. If permitted to continue in their self–centered world of infancy, given free reign to their impulsive actions to satisfy each want, every child would grow up a criminal, a thief, a killer, a rapist.[199]

Every child is infested with a sin nature, and if not trained, he or she will live a life of rebellion towards parents, God, and ultimately all authority. Children are a blessing, but they need godly instruction and ultimately the new birth.

Parents need Spirit empowerment to train their children, and children need Spirit empowerment to obey and honor their parents. In this study, we will consider characteristics of a Spirit-filled home.

Big Question: What characteristics of a Spirit-filled home can be discerned from Ephesians 6:1-4?

In a Spirit-filled Home, Children Obey and Honor Their Parents

> Children, obey your parents in the Lord for this is right. "Honor your father and mother," which is the first commandment accompanied by a promise, namely, "that it may go well with you and that you will live a long time on the earth."
> Ephesians 6:1-3

Interpretation Question: Who is Paul referring to when he says "children"?

When Paul commands "children" to obey and honor their parents, he is not only referring to small children; tekna (children) is a general term referring to all offspring.[200] Biblically, it denotes those who are unmarried and still financially dependent on their parents. Genesis 2:24 says this about the marriage relationship: "For this reason a man will leave his father and mother and be united to his wife, and they will become one flesh." God must still come first, but then the wife must be devoted to her husband and the husband to his wife. Obedience to parents is no longer the priority.

However, the responsibility to honor parents, which at times includes obedience, never changes. Obedience refers primarily to our actions and honor refers primarily to our attitude. We should always honor our parents, even if we are no longer under their supervision.

Sadly, aging parents are often not honored in our culture. They are seen as a burden instead of a blessing, and are often neglected. Conversely, Scripture teaches that sons and daughters owe parents and grandparents special honor when they age and cannot provide for themselves. First Timothy 5:4 and 8 says,

> But if a widow has children or grandchildren, they should first learn to fulfill their duty toward their own household and so repay their parents what is owed them. For this is what pleases God... But if someone does not provide for his own, especially his own family, he has denied the faith and is worse than an unbeliever.

Now this teaching would have been especially hard for children in the ancient culture of Ephesus to receive. Many held a deep animosity towards their father. The patriarch of the family held unlimited power and was typically excessively strict. He owned all the property, and even adult children could not own anything in their own name until he died. Even a forty-five-year-old senator could not own property if his father was still alive.[201] This unlimited power commonly resulted in lording over the children and creating a deep animosity within them. Sometimes this anger even resulted in patricide, for which Romans reserved one of their worst punishments—being stripped, whipped, and drowned in a bag, along with live animals to scratch at the flesh.[202]

In Ephesians 6:1, Paul says, "Children, obey your parents in the Lord for this is right." In this text, we can discern how they are to obey their parents. "The Greek word translated 'obey' is very helpful because it comes from two words, under and to listen — so that it literally means to listen under."[203] From this we can learn two qualities of the child's obedience.

Observation Question: How are children to obey and honor their parents?

1. In order to obey their parents, children must listen to them.

The book of Proverbs is primarily about a father teaching his son wisdom. He constantly calls the child to listen and to hear. Proverbs 4:10 says, "Listen, my child, and accept my words, so that the years of your life will be many."

In the same way, children should listen to their parents. Parents are not perfect, but they have lived more years than their children. Even adult children should constantly seek the advice and wisdom of their parents, for it will bless their souls.

2.   In order to obey their parents, children must submit to them.

To "listen under" has the connotation of submitting to authority and responding positively when spoken to. Often this is not the normal reaction of children. Instead of responding positively to parental instruction, children tend to respond negatively because they want their own way.

As long as children are under their parents' authority, they must recognize that this authority is God-given. Romans 13:1 says there is no authority but that which comes from God.

A powerful story of submitting to parental authority comes from the life of Dr. Martyn Lloyd-Jones. While in college, Martyn Lloyd-Jones felt a call to pastoral ministry; however, his parents really wanted him to be a doctor. After praying about the matter, he felt that he should first become a doctor to honor his parents and then become a pastor in obedience to God. And he did. He became one of the top doctors in his field, and then left the medical field to go to seminary and became one of the most well-known pastors in history.

3.   In order to obey their parents, children must be faithful to the Lord.

The command for children to obey their parents "in the Lord" has several implications.

* First, it means children must submit to their parents as their duty to God; it is one of the ways they obey and honor God.

* Second, children must cultivate their relationship with God (and be filled with the Spirit) in order to obey their parents.

We see children cultivating a deep relationship with God throughout the Scriptures. Samuel came to know God at a very young age. God spoke to him and he replied, "Speak, for your servant is listening" (1 Sam 3:10b). Similarly, David, though marginalized by his parents for his age, had a deep relationship with God, and God used him at a young age. God enabled him to kill a lion and a bear, and one day God used him to defeat Israel's enemy,

Goliath. In order to faithfully obey, especially when things are difficult with parents, children must cultivate their relationship with God and be filled with the Spirit.

- Finally, it describes the sphere of children's obedience.

Children should obey their parents in everything except when their parents tell them to disobey God. If their parents tell them to lie, steal, or cheat, they should disobey because their allegiance is to God first.

Application Questions: What type of relationship did/do you have with your parents? As a child, were you generally obedient or disobedient, and why? How does this relationship affect you today?

In a Spirit-filled Home, Children Understand the Importance of Obeying and Honoring Their Parents

Children, obey your parents in the Lord for this is right. "Honor your father and mother," which is the first commandment accompanied by a promise, namely, "that it may go well with you and that you will live a long time on the earth."
Ephesians 6:1-3

In a Spirit-filled home, children don't just obey because they have to—they also understand why. When Paul says, "for this is right," he begins to lay reasons for obedience and honor. This also is an important parenting practice. Often children ask the question, "Why?" after being told to do something by their parents. And often the response is, "Because I told you so." There is a place for this, but if it's the primary way parents respond to their children, it's not healthy. Children need to understand why in order to learn to make wise decisions on their own.

Like a wise parent, Paul explains why children should obey and honor their parents.

Observation Question: What reasons does Paul give children for obeying and honoring their parents in Ephesians 6:1-3?

1. Children should obey and honor their parents because it is ethical.

The first reason Paul gives is simply because it is right. "Dikaios (right) refers to that which is correct, just, righteous—to that which is exactly as it should be."[204] This is the way God meant for families to function, and therefore it is righteous and pleasing to him.

If children want to please their heavenly Father, they must obey their parents. It doesn't matter how mean, rude, or unspiritual the parents are. What matters is obeying and pleasing God.

2. Children should obey and honor their parents because it brings prosperity.

Next, Paul quotes the fifth commandment in Exodus 20:12. He says, "Honor your father and your mother, that you may live a long time in the land the Lord your God is giving to you."

In this commandment, God promised Israel that it would go well with a child who obeyed his parents. Even though we are not under Old Testament law (cf. Rom 6:14), the fact that Paul repeats this in the New Testament means that this promise is still true for us today.

God promises to bless the life of a child who obeys his parents. Certainly, we can see this happening around us: An obedient child develops healthy patterns and character traits like honesty, hard work, and generosity that often lead to a prosperous life. His integrity and diligence lead to blessing from teachers, employers, spouses, and ultimately God.

In contrast, a child that rebels against his parents will rebel against teachers, bosses, and ultimately every other authority, including God. This leads to pain. Commonly, rebellious children get caught up in hazardous practices like alcohol and drug abuse and dishonest dealings, which will affect them for the rest of their lives. They will constantly deal with the consequences of their sins and ultimately God's discipline.

Interpretation Question: In what way is this "the first commandment with a promise, as Paul says?

Pastor Steve Cole's comments are helpful here. He says,

But, Paul's comment, that this is "the first commandment with a promise," is a bit puzzling. Scholars point out that the second commandment, not to make any idols, promises that God will show lovingkindness to those who love Him and keep His commands (Exod. 20:4-6). But, as Calvin explains (The Institutes of the Christian Religion [Westminster Press], ed. by John McNeill, 2:8:37), that promise was not confined to that particular command, but extends to the whole law. So the promise attached to the fifth commandment was the first specific promise among the ten and the first of many promised blessings for obedience.[205]

3. Children should obey and honor their parents because it promotes a long life.

Now, when God promises a long life to Israel and the church for obedience to parents, this probably refers to a full life—however long God planned for a person to live. It must be remembered that God has an allotted amount of time for each believer on the earth. As David says in Psalm 139:16, "Your eyes saw me when I was inside the womb. All the days ordained for me were recorded in your scroll before one of them came into existence." God ordained all the days of David before he was born.

However, some experience untimely deaths because of their disobedience. This is seen with Ananias and Sapphira (Acts 5:5-10), and certain members of the church at Corinth (1 Cor 11:30).[206] Today lack of respect for authorities, substance abuse, and crime shorten lives, as the disobedience perpetuated in childhood continues into adulthood.

Obeying and honoring parents is so important that in the Old Covenant, God commanded that a child who struck or cursed his parents be put to death (Ex 21:15, 17; Lev 20:9). To physically or verbally abuse a parent was a capital offense because this type of behavior would not only dishonor the parents and God, but ultimately destroy society. A society where children rule is a society under God's curse and is headed for destruction (cf. Is 3:11-12).

Application Questions: What are your thoughts about God's promise of prosperity and long life to obedient children, and the lack of these blessings for the rebellious? How have you seen this promise play out in your life or the lives of others?

In a Spirit-filled Home, Parents Do Not Exasperate Their Children

Fathers, do not provoke your children to anger
Ephesians 6:4

The next aspect of a Spirit-filled home is that parents do not exasperate their children—provoking them to anger and rebellion.

Pateres, the Greek word Paul uses here, typically referred to male parents but at times referred to parents in general. We see it used this way in Hebrews 11:23, when referring to Moses' parents. Since Paul calls for children to obey both parents in the previous three verses, he is most likely still referring to both parents in this verse.[207]

With that said, the father was the most dominant figure in the home and the one most likely to exasperate the children, or provoke them to wrath. Certainly, mothers did this as well, but fathers were more inclined to it.

MacArthur shares why the father's love would be hard to even imagine in this ancient context.

> By the Roman law of patria potestas a father had virtual life and death power not only over his slaves but over his entire household. He could cast any of them out of the house, sell them as slaves, or even kill them—and be accountable to no one. A newborn child was placed at its father's feet to determine its fate. If the father picked it up, the child was allowed to stay in the home; if the father walked away, it was simply disposed of—much as aborted babies are in our own day. Discarded infants who were healthy and vigorous were collected and taken each night to the town forum, where they would be picked up and raised to be slaves or prostitutes.[208]

As we consider this command, we must ask, "How do parents provoke their children to wrath?" By understanding how this happens, parents can avoid it.

Interpretation Question: How do parents exasperate their children, or provoke them to wrath?

1. Parents exasperate their children by not disciplining them.

This is one of the quickest ways to develop bitter children. A spoiled child is a thankless and bitter child. Because they get their way all the time, they are bitter whenever any authority does not submit to them or when life becomes difficult. Solomon said, "Folly is bound up in the heart of a child, but the rod of discipline will drive it far from him" (Prov. 22:15).

Parents embitter their children by never driving the foolishness—the sin—out of their hearts through good discipline. Parents who do not discipline their children but instead give them everything they want often become surprised when the children eventually rebel later in life. These spoiled kids want nothing to do with their parents. Sadly, this happens too much, even in the church.

2. Parents exasperate their children by abusing them, or applying improper discipline.

Verbal and physical abuse sow seeds of anger—and even hatred—into children's hearts. Such anger is difficult to overcome, and often results in these children abusing others.

However, this happens not only as a result of abuse, but also because of improper discipline. Parents who do not manage their anger wisely train their children to react in the same manner. A parent who curses, criticizes, or even harshly disciplines a child—even if the punishment is just—teaches him that cursing, uncontrolled hitting, and "going crazy" are acceptable ways to express anger. This child does not learn how to manage his anger, and therefore struggles with it throughout his life. He grows up doing what he has been trained to do—fight others, and hold grudges against those he feels failed him.

Listen parents, telling your children to go to their rooms while you are angry can be a wise tactic. It gives you a chance to evaluate their sin, their motives, and your own heart. It allows you to teach them how to respond to anger, and it also allows you to discipline them appropriately.

3.   Parents exasperate their children by neglecting them.

Many children lack love and affection because of parental neglect and therefore grow bitter. Some parents neglect their children for work; they put in long hours to achieve secular success, but this pursuit keeps them away from home. Ultimately, this hurts children both emotionally and spiritually.

Sadly, many parents in our society neglect their children by sending them away to extensive education programs often to compensate for their lack of being around. However, it is not God's will for teachers, coaches, or babysitters to raise children. That is why he gave them parents. These people certainly play a role, but it is important for parents to be the primary influence on their children's lives.

We see the tragic consequences of neglect in the account of David and his son Absalom. When one of David's sons raped his half-sister, David did nothing. When Absalom killed the rapist, David did nothing. When Absalom ran away from the kingdom, David did nothing. When Absalom came back after murdering his brother, David refused to see him. This neglect created such anger in Absalom that he eventually usurped his father's authority in the kingdom and essentially tried to kill him. David neither disciplined Absalom nor encouraged him to make right choices, with drastic and far-reaching consequences.

Many children have tremendous anger at a father or mother who neglected them. Parents, do not embitter your children. Prioritize them over your work, your church, your entertainment, and your social life. Let only God and your spouse come before them.

4. Parents exasperate their children by never encouraging them and showing them affection.

We see this in the story of Martin Luther, whose father never encouraged him or showed him love. Listen to what commentator William Barclay said:

> It is one of the tragic facts of religious history that Martin Luther's father was so stern to him that, all his life, Luther found it difficult to pray: 'Our Father.' The word father in his mind represented nothing but severity. The duty of the parent is discipline, but it is also encouragement. Luther himself said: 'Spare the rod and spoil the child. It is true. But beside the rod keep an apple to give him when he does well.'[209]

Healthy parents not only discipline their children, but also reward them. As they reward their children when they do well and discipline them when they do wrong, children learn fairness by this balanced approach.

5. Parents exasperate their children by showing favoritism toward other siblings.

We get a good picture of this in the story of Jacob and Joseph. Jacob gave Joseph a robe of many colors, showing his favor of this son above the other eleven. In anger, the embittered older siblings later kidnapped Joseph and sold him into slavery.

How often do siblings become embittered against one another because of unwise parenting practices? These children grow up disliking one another: "Mother always thought you were the prettiest." "Dad always liked you because you were the smartest and most athletic." This happens all too often.

6. Parents exasperate their children by neglecting or deriding their God-given bent or disposition.

Proverbs 22:6 says, "Train a child in the way that he should go, and when he is old he will not turn from it." "In the way that he should go" can also be translated as "his way," or "his bent." The Amplified Bible translates it this way: "Train up a child in the way he should go [and in keeping with his individual gift or bent], and when he is old he will not depart from it." The word "way" comes from a Hebrew verb used of a bow launching an arrow.[210] When a person shoots an arrow, the tension must align with the natural bend in the bow or it will break. This is also true in raising children.

Some parents damage their children by trying to train them in a way God didn't wire them. They may do this by pushing their them into the medical field, athletics, or music, even though the children show no aptitude or passion in those areas. God gives us children who are already uploaded with a unique and specific program, like a computer. We can't use software uniquely made for an Apple with a PC. It's the same with children. Some will be wired towards the arts, technology, or serving ministries. It is the job of parents to get to know the way God wired their children so they can encourage them in those areas.

This can be difficult for parents, especially if their child's wiring doesn't fit their expectations or what might be considered successful in society. However, we are called to train a child according to "his way"—according to his own bent (Prov 22:6)—not ours or others'. His "way" may not appeal to us, but we are to raise our children to live for God and fulfill his calling on their lives.

7. Parents exasperate their children by pushing them to achieve beyond reasonable bounds.

Parents often exasperate their children by unrealistic academic, athletic, social, or career expectations. No matter how well the child does, it is never good enough. Eventually the child learns that nothing will ever please his parents—pushing him towards rebellion. Some parents do this because they are trying to live out their unfulfilled dreams through their children, or trying to meet society's expectations instead of God's. Many children are exasperated even to the point of suicide by these types of expectations.

Instead of their own expectations or those of the world, Spirit-filled parents seek God's expectations for their children's lives.

Application Questions: In what other ways do parents provoke their children to wrath? How can the church play a role in remedying unwise parenting?

In a Spirit-filled Home, Parents Lovingly Raise Their Children in the Lord

> Fathers, do not provoke your children to anger, but raise them up in the discipline and instruction of the Lord.
> Ephesians 6:4

Finally, Paul calls for parents to train their children in the Lord. Sadly, in many homes, only culture and secular wisdom are taught—often creating secular, worldly children. But in a Spirit-filled home, parents raise their children in the training and instruction of the Lord.

Interpretation Question: How should parents raise their children in the Lord?

1. Parents raise their children in the Lord by providing for their needs.

"The words 'bring them up' means 'to nourish or feed,' as in 5:29 which says that a man 'feeds and cares' for his own body. Calvin translates 'bring them up' with the words, 'let them be kindly cherished.'"[211]

Spirit-filled parents should meet their children's needs. This includes providing food and shelter, and also caring for them emotionally. To neglect them and not spend time with them is to damage them emotionally, physically, or spiritually. "Bring them up" has the sense of being kind and loving, as seen in Calvin's translation, "let them be kindly cherished." Parents must care for their children with kindness instead of treating them harshly.

2. Parents raise their children in the Lord by training them.

The word "discipline" (also translated "training" in the NIV) means "discipline, even by punishment."[212] Because children have a sin nature—a propensity to sin—they must be disciplined. Many Scriptures teach the necessity of discipline such as:

> The one who spares his rod hates his child, but the one who loves his child is diligent in disciplining him.
> Proverbs 13:24

> Discipline your child, for there is hope, but do not set your heart on causing his death.
> Proverbs 19:18

> Now all discipline seems painful at the time, not joyful. But later it produces the fruit of peace and righteousness for those trained by it.
> Hebrews 12:11

Application Question: What are some principles for disciplining children correctly?

- Discipline should never be administered in anger.

Scripture says that "human anger does not accomplish God's righteousness" (James 1:20). As mentioned earlier, when parents yell at their children or spank them in anger, they abuse them. This will not produce the righteous life that God desires in children. Parents should be calm and measured when disciplining their children.

- Discipline should fit the sin.

In the Mosaic law, civil discipline had to fit the crime; it was to be "eye for eye, tooth for tooth, hand for hand, foot for foot" (Ex 21:24). This is also true in disciplining children. Parents must wisely consider the consequences for each infraction. If discipline is unfair, it may result in rebellion.

Parents must also discern the difference between childishness and foolishness. Small children are going to spill their milk; that is childishness. But when they spill the milk, are they doing it to be rebellious? Foolishness should be punished, but childishness should be corrected.

- Discipline should be consistent.

When parents say, "If you do this, I will discipline you when we get home," but then do nothing, children learn that their parents don't always mean what they say. They then conclude that they don't always have to obey. Also, it confuses children when they can turn on the TV when they should be sleeping on one occasion, but are disciplined for it on another occasion. Discipline must be consistent. In addition, the administration of discipline should be consistent between the parents. They must present a unified front; otherwise, it will encourage manipulation by the children and can cause discord in the marriage.

- Discipline should create intimacy instead of distance.

When children disobey their parents, distance is created in the relationship. However, parental discipline shouldn't create greater distance—it should restore intimacy. This is how God's discipline functions with us. Sin separates us from God, but his discipline is meant to draw us back into intimacy with him. This is another reason why parents shouldn't discipline unfairly or in anger; it further alienates children instead of drawing them closer.

How else should parents raise their children in the Lord?

3. Parents raise their children in the Lord by instructing them.

"Instruction" can also be translated as "admonition," "correction," or "advice." It refers to verbal instruction or a verbal warning, with the literal meaning of "to place before the mind"[213] or "putting in mind."[214] Again, this is what we see in Proverbs: a father instructing his son about life—warning him about the adulterous woman, the practice of sin and dishonesty, and encouraging him to fear the Lord and to find a godly wife. Parents should not only train their children through discipline but also through godly instruction.

The primary instructions that parents should give their children come from God's Word. Consider what Moses taught the parents in Israel to do with their children in Deuteronomy 6:4-9:

> Listen, Israel: The Lord is our God, the Lord is one! You must love the Lord your God with your whole mind, your whole being, and all your strength. These words I am commanding you today must be kept in mind, and you must teach them to your children and speak of them as you sit in your house, as you walk along the road, as you lie down, and as you get up. You should tie them as a reminder on your forearm and fasten them as symbols on your forehead. Inscribe them on the doorframes of your houses and gates.

MacArthur says this about the instructions to parents in Deuteronomy 6:

> Parents were to continually speak about the things of God, so that knowledge and love of Him would become a matter of life and breath for the family. When the parents were not speaking the testimony would continue. "And you shall bind them as sign on your hand and they shall be as frontals on your forehead" (v. 8). Even when the parents were gone, the testimony remained, because it was to be written "on the doorposts of your house and on your gates" (v. 9). In other words, there was always to be both verbal and visible commitment to the Word of God in the home. It is God's plan for His Word to be passed on from one generation to the next. And His primary agent is the family.[215]

In a Spirit-filled home, the parents raise their children in the Lord by tenderly providing for them, disciplining them, and instructing them in the Lord.

Application Question: What are some other wise principles or practices for raising children in the Lord?

Conclusion

What are characteristics of a Spirit-filled home?

1. In a Spirit-filled home, children obey and honor their parents.

2. In a Spirit-filled home, children understand the importance of obeying and honoring their parents.

3. In a Spirit-filled home, parents do not exasperate their children.

4. In a Spirit-filled home, parents lovingly raise their children in the Lord.

How to Glorify Christ in the Workplace

Slaves, obey your human masters with fear and trembling, in the sincerity of your heart as to Christ, not like those who do their work only when someone is watching—as people-pleasers—but as slaves of Christ doing the will of God from the heart. Obey with enthusiasm, as though serving the Lord and not people, because you know that each person, whether slave or free, if he does something good, this will be rewarded by the Lord. Masters, treat your slaves the same way, giving up the use of threats, because you know that both you and they have the same master in heaven, and there is no favoritism with him.
Ephesians 6:5-9 (NET)

How can we glorify Christ in the workplace? What should a Christian worker look like?

Each person is called to work. Some work as students, some as teachers, some as mothers, some in business, etc. Everybody works for a living. The primary difference is pay. Some don't get paid at all, some get paid a little, and some get paid a lot. What should the Christian's work life look like?

Often, people think of work as a bad thing. Some may even think it is a result of the fall (Gen 3:17–18). However, work was given before the fall. It was Adam's responsibility to till the ground and take care of the Garden of Eden (Gen 2:15).

In fact, Scripture teaches that we will work in heaven. Luke 19:17 tells us that those who are faithful with their gifts and talents on earth will be rewarded with overseeing cities in the coming kingdom.

Also, in Revelation 21:2, we see the holy city of Jerusalem coming out of heaven to the earth. Just the fact that heaven is called a city implies many characteristics about eternity. A city has commerce, education, and government. Heaven will not be sitting on a cloud doing nothing. It will be worshiping and serving the Lord together in the heavenly city forever. It has always been God's will for man to work.

Moreover, our God is a worker too! He creates and sustains the world by the power of his Word (Heb 1:2-3). He is not idle! Christ, God the Son, prays for his saints in order to save them to the uttermost (Heb 7:25). We serve a God who neither sleeps nor slumbers (Ps. 121:4). He is always active in his creation.

Work is something we do here on earth and something we will also do in heaven. It is a way that we imitate God and bring honor to him. If work is something we will do throughout eternity, we must ask ourselves, "How can we work in such a way that God is glorified?"

In Ephesians 6:5-9, Paul speaks to slaves, who constituted much of the workforce in the ancient world, and to their masters. He tells them how to work to glorify Christ. We see this in the number of times "Christ," "Lord," and "Master" are mentioned in this passage. It is mentioned in every verse. In verse 5, it says, "as to Christ." In verse 6, "but as slaves of Christ doing the will of God from the heart." In verse 7, "as though serving the Lord." In verse 8, "rewarded by the Lord." In verse 9, "you and they have the same master in heaven." As this is connected to Paul's call to be Spirit-filled in Ephesians 5:18, Paul is saying that a Spirit-filled worker glorifies Christ in the workplace, even as Christ is glorified in a Spirit-filled marriage (Eph 5:22-33) and a Spirit-filled household (Eph 6:1-4).

The Christian's workplace is supposed to be a place of worship to the Lord—no matter how corrupt and ungodly the environment. Christian employees must remember this. As 1 Corinthians 10:31 says, "So whether you eat or drink, or whatever you do, do everything for the glory of God."

In light of this reality, John Stott says:

> It is possible for the housewife to cook a meal as if Jesus Christ were going to eat it, or to spring-clean the house as if Jesus Christ were to be the honoured guest. It is possible for teachers to educate children, for doctors to treat patients and nurses to care for them, for solicitors to help clients, shop assistants to serve customers, accountants to audit books and secretaries to type letters as if in each case they were serving Jesus Christ.[216]

No doubt, this is why some Christian housewives have this motto over their kitchen sink: 'Divine service held here three times daily.'—it is a form of worship.[217]

A Word about Slavery

It is important to remember that slavery was universal in the ancient world. There were about sixty million slaves in the Roman Empire, an estimated third or half of the population.[218] They constituted the majority of the workforce. This "included not only domestic servants and manual labourers but educated people as well, like doctors, teachers and administrators. Slaves could be inherited or purchased, or acquired in settlement of a bad debt, and prisoners of war commonly became slaves."[219] In addition, "selling oneself into slavery was commonly used as a means of obtaining Roman citizenship and gaining an entrance into society."[220]

Although, Scripture does not condemn slavery, it clearly speaks against kidnapping and enslaving people. Exodus 21:16 says, "Whoever kidnaps someone and sells him, or is caught still holding him, must surely be put to death." In addition, 1 Timothy 1:9-10 addresses how the law condemns "slave traders."

However, Scripture does condone some beneficial forms of slavery. MacArthur's comments on this are helpful:

> Certain types of nonabusive and beneficial slavery were permitted, or even advocated, in the Old Testament. For example, a thief who could not make restitution could be indentured until repayment was worked out—a plan far superior to the modern prison sentence which provides for no restitution of property or money to the victim or restoration of dignity for the thief. Israelites were allowed to buy slaves from the pagan nations around them (Lev. 25:44), but fellow Israelites could not be bought or sold, although they could voluntarily indenture themselves until the year of jubilee (v. 39–40). During their time of service they were to be treated as hired workers, not as slaves (v. 40–41, 46). Even pagan slaves were not to be abused and were given their freedom if seriously injured by their master (Ex. 21:26–27). A slave who fled from an oppressive master was to be given asylum and protection (Deut. 23:15–16). A fellow Israelite could not be used as a slave for more than six years, at the end of which he was to be given liberal provisions as a form of severance pay (Ex. 21:2; Deut. 15:13–14). Every fiftieth year, the year of jubilee, all slaves were to be freed and returned to their families (Lev. 25:10). A slave who loved his master and preferred to remain with him could voluntarily indenture himself for life by having his ear pierced by his master (Ex. 21:5–6). The kind of slavery controlled by scriptural teaching was a blessing to both employer and employee and was a rewarding and fulfilling relation between them.[221]

Voluntary slavery was often a way for a person or family to eat and to receive protection. It was not unusual for there to be great love between a master and a slave, as seen with Abraham and his chief servant, Eliezer. Before Abraham had his first child, Eliezer was the heir to his household (Gen 15:3). Unfortunately, the institution of slavery was not always pleasant and was commonly abused, especially in the Greco-Roman culture, where slaves were simply property. To that culture, Paul wrote about Spirit-filled conduct between slaves and masters that glorified Christ.

With all that said, though Scripture doesn't focus on reforming ungodly systems like slavery, it does focus on reforming the root of these systems—the heart. Where Scripture and the gospel have spread, it has changed the hearts of the greedy, the prideful, and the racist—leading to the abolishment of ungodly systems. It has often led to the abolishment of slavery, of unfair treatment of women, and of the murder of the unborn.

In this text Paul speaks to slaves and masters, calling them to glorify Christ in the workplace. Since slaves constituted much of the ancient workforce, these principles apply directly to employees and employers today. Sadly, our workplaces are often not honoring to God; they are filled with complaining, bitterness, unrest, and even dishonesty, even by believers. However, this was never God's will. Let's consider Paul's exhortations on how to honor and glorify Christ in the workplace.

Big Question: How can employees and employers glorify Christ in the workplace?

To Glorify Christ in the Workplace, Employees Must Obey Their Employers

> Slaves, obey your human masters with fear and trembling, in the sincerity of your heart as to Christ, not like those who do their work only when someone is watching—as people-pleasers—but as slaves of Christ doing the will of God from the heart. Obey with enthusiasm, as though serving the Lord and not people, because you know that each person, whether slave or free, if he does something good, this will be rewarded by the Lord.
> Ephesians 6:5-8

Though many worked for non-Christian masters who were harsh and abusive, Paul calls for slaves to obey them as they would obey Christ. The word "obey" is "in the present tense in the Greek, indicating uninterrupted obedience."[222] The only time they should disobey is when called to do something sinful (cf. Col 3:22, Acts 4:18, 19).

In verses 5-8, Paul gives principles of how slaves should bring glory to Christ through obedience to their earthly masters. Again, this applies directly to Christian employees.

Observation Question: In what ways should employees obey their employers in order to glorify Christ, according to Ephesians 6:5-8?

1. To glorify Christ, employees must obey with the right perspective.

Interpretation Question: Why does Paul refer to "earthly masters" in Ephesians 6:5, and what are some implications?

When Paul says, "Slaves, obey your human masters," he reminds slaves that their work and submission to their masters is temporary. Our current jobs and careers are temporary because we can only work at a certain place or do certain jobs for a limited period of time. More importantly, they are temporary because we were made for eternity. And one day, we will be in heaven with our Heavenly Master.

This is important to remember for many reasons. (1) One person finds himself depressed and unsatisfied because he doesn't enjoy his career and it is extremely difficult. This worker must remember that his career or job is earthly and temporary. Our final destination and workplace is heaven. We must live with a proper perspective of this.

(2) Another person becomes consumed with his job to the point of idolatry. He focuses on his work to the exclusion of God and often family. Again, this is wrong. Our primary job is to serve and honor God. Those who focus entirely on their earthy job and earthly employers to the exclusion of God will live worldly lives. Again, we must remember that we have a heavenly employer. First Corinthians 3:9 calls us "coworkers" with God. We work for him and with him to build his kingdom on this earth, and we will work for him and with him in heaven. This must be our primary focus wherever God places us.

Christian workers, remember that your job is temporary! You are really serving the Heavenly Master. Don't let work become your life, which will lead to either discouragement or idolatry—it is only temporary. Live for eternity.

Do you work with the right perspective? Our careers are temporary, but our calling to work for God is eternal.

Application Questions: Why is it important to keep the right perspective in the workplace—that our work is temporary? How have you struggled with this?

2.   To glorify Christ, employees must obey with respect and fear.

Interpretation Question: What does Paul mean when he calls slaves to serve their masters with "fear and trembling"?

He does not mean a cowering fright, but he does mean to serve with an honor and respect that makes them anxious to please their masters. Obviously, this was hard at times, especially when serving a master that was difficult and ungodly. However, in such cases the slave's—or for us the employee's--fear and trembling must be for the higher authority that their master represented.

Romans 13:1-2 says,

Let every person be subject to the governing authorities. For there is no authority except by God's appointment, and the authorities that exist have been instituted by God. So the person who resists such authority resists the ordinance of God, and those who resist will incur judgment

All authorities are established by God, even evil ones. Spirit-filled Christians must recognize the God-given authority of their employers. We see this with David and Saul. Even though King Saul tried to kill David, David continued to say, "I will not touch God's anointed" (1 Sam 26:9, paraphrase). Even though Saul was an evil authority, David always honored and respected him in recognition of God's authority behind Saul's position.

Paul probably was also addressing the situation of Christian slaves serving Christian masters. No doubt some masters attended churches where their slaves attended and even pastored. As a result, some slaves, in focusing on their spiritual equality with their masters, were beginning to show them less respect. Paul addresses this problem in 1 Timothy 6:1-2:

Those who are under the yoke as slaves must regard their own masters as deserving of full respect. This will prevent the name of God and Christian teaching from being discredited. But those who have believing masters must not show them less respect because they are brothers. Instead they are to serve all the more, because those who benefit from their service are believers and dearly loved. Teach them and exhort them about these things.

For Christian employees, there is no place for insubordination or disrespect of employers. Although our culture readily accepts complaining and dishonoring leaders, Christians should be struck with fear and trembling. Why? It's because they recognize God's authority, even over the ungodly. Like David, they declare, "Who can touch God's chosen one and remain guiltless?"

Do you work with fear and trembling to honor God? Is there a reverence to your work?

Application Questions: How can employees honor an unfair or unjust employer/authority? Have you ever encountered this situation? How did you respond?

3. To glorify Christ, employees must obey with sincerity of heart.

Next, Paul calls for believers to serve "in the sincerity of your heart as to Christ" (Eph 6:5). "'Sincerity' literally means singleness of heart, the idea being that we ought to obey and serve with an undivided mind—with no ulterior motive or hypocrisy."223

It means that Spirit-filled employees serve with a heart that pleases God—not one full of pride, bitterness, selfish ambition, or anything that could be disruptive—because they are focused on their Heavenly Master. Like David they cry out, "May the words of my mouth and the meditation of my heart be pleasing to you, O Lord, My rock and my redeemer" (Psalm 19:14, NLT). They want their hearts and their actions to honor God in whatever place God has called them to serve.

Do you work with singleness of heart as unto the Lord?

Application Questions: How can employees keep a sincere heart in the workplace? What are some distractions from this type of heart?

4.   To glorify Christ, employees must obey without eye service.

Paul says, "[obey] not like those who do their work only when someone is watching" (Eph 6:6). This can also be translated as, "Not with eyeservice, as menpleasers" (KJV). The Spirit-filled employee doesn't only work hard when the employer is watching.

The picture Paul paints here is reminiscent of a contemporary gym class. While doing push-ups, the students stay in the up position while the gym teacher is not looking. Many are like that in the workplace. When the boss is around they work diligently, but when he is not, they play video games, crack jokes, and play on social media. Believers should endeavor to deliver sixty minutes of work for every hour of pay.

Do you work without eye service—delivering a day's work whether your boss is around or not?

Application Questions: In what ways have you seen or experienced workers that render eye service instead of faithful service in the workplace? How have you struggled with this?

5.   To glorify Christ, employees must obey with a good attitude.

Paul says, "Obey with enthusiasm, as though serving the Lord and not people" (Eph 6:7). This can also be translated as "with good will," "eagerly," or "with a good attitude."

The Spirit-filled believer works eagerly, with a positive attitude instead of a bitter and complaining one. Just as Scripture says God loves a cheerful giver (2 Cor 9:7), God loves a cheerful worker. Colossians 3:23 says, "Whatever you are doing, work at it with enthusiasm, as to the Lord and not for people."

Now, you can imagine the normal attitude of slaves in that difficult environment. Why work hard? They often didn't receive pay or incentives. For most, other than fear of their masters, there really wasn't a reason to be motivated. However, Christian slaves had many reasons to be motivated, the greatest one being that they were in fact serving God.

Do you work with a good attitude—eager and enthusiastically? Or are you a complainer?

Application Questions: How can employees maintain a good attitude in a bad work situation? Have you ever experienced a work environment where it was hard to maintain joy?

6. To glorify Christ, employees must obey with an expectation of God's judgment and reward.

Finally, Paul says, "because you know that each person, whether slave or free, if he does something good, this will be rewarded by the Lord" (Eph 6:8). Christian employees should work with an expectation of God's judgment. God will reward each one for what he does, and this should be a tremendous motivation for us.

Do you work with a view of God's judgment and reward?

John MacArthur tells the story of two missionaries returning home to the United States. It is a helpful reminder of the importance of having an expectation of God's judgment and reward.

The story is told of an elderly missionary couple who were returning home on a ship after many years of sacrificial service in Africa. On the same ship was Theodore Roosevelt, who had just completed a highly successful big game hunt. As the ship docked in New York harbor, thousands of well-wishers and dozens of reporters lined the pier to welcome Roosevelt home. But not a single person was there to welcome the missionaries. As the couple rode to a hotel in a taxi, the man complained to his wife, "It just doesn't seem right. We give forty years of our lives to Jesus Christ to win souls in Africa, and nobody knows or cares when we return. Yet the president goes over there for a few weeks to kill some animals and the whole world takes notice." But as they prayed together that night before retiring, the Lord seemed to say to them, "Do you know why you haven't received your reward yet, My children? It is because you are not home yet."[224]

If we forget that he is the one who rewards us, it is easy to become discouraged and apathetic. Although there is certainly a sense in which God rewards us on earth, as promotion and exaltation come from the Lord (cf. Ps 75:6-7), he will especially reward us in heaven (cf. 1 Cor 3:11-15, Luke 19:17).

Desire for reward and fear of God's discipline would also be a motivation for lazy or evil slaves to repent. They would not want to experience loss of heavenly reward (cf. 1 Cor 3:14-15) and God's discipline (cf. 1 Cor 11:31-32; Heb 12:6). Fear of God's judgment should also motivate us to be faithful employees.

Application Questions: In what ways are fear of God's judgment and anticipation of his reward motivators to faithful service in the workplace? Are they motivators for you?

Because of practicing these truths, Christian slaves were often sold for a higher price than pagan slaves.[225] When Spirit-filled, they worked respectfully, with the right attitude, without eye service, and with many other godly traits. They did this because they were serving God and not men. Being a Christian should make us better at whatever God calls us to do, including our jobs.

Application Questions: Which principles about glorifying Christ in the workplace are most challenging to you and why? In what ways has your faith affected your performance in the workplace?

To Glorify Christ in the Workplace, Employers Must Care for Their Employees

> Masters, treat your slaves the same way, giving up the use of threats, because you know that both you and they have the same master in heaven, and there is no favoritism with him.
> Ephesians 6:9

Interpretation Question: What does Paul mean by "masters, treat your slaves in the same way"?

Many believe "the same way" refers primarily to verse 6, where Paul says, "doing the will of God from the heart."[226] Masters must have the same motivation and goal as the Christian slave: to obey, please, and glorify the Lord. Again, this is really an application of being filled with the Spirit and of submitting to one another out of reverence to Christ (Eph 5:18-21).

Paul expands further on how masters should treat their slaves throughout Eph 6:9, and these truths can be applied directly to Christian employers and managers.

Observation Question: In what ways should masters treat their slaves in order to glorify Christ according to Ephesians 6:9, and how does this apply to Christian employers today?

1. To glorify Christ, employers must treat workers the way they want to be treated.

Another interpretation of "masters, treat your slaves the same way," is that it essentially refers to the golden rule. "If the employer expects the workers to do their best for him, he must do his best for them. The master must serve the Lord from his heart if he expects his servants to do the same. He must not exploit them."[227] Kent Hughes comments are also helpful:

> What Paul is telling those in authority is, treat your slaves/employees the way you want to be treated. If you want respect, show respect. If you want sincerity, be sincere. If you want conscientiousness, you be the same. If you want pleasantness, model pleasantness. "Promote the welfare of your slaves as you expect them to promote yours. Show the same interest in them and in their affairs as you hope they will show in you and your affairs."[228]

This is the Golden Rule of managers and employers: Treat employees the way you would want to be treated.

When in leadership, do you treat people the way you want to be treated?

Application Questions: How have you seen the Golden Rule modeled by those in leadership? How do you want to be treated as an employee?

2. To glorify Christ, employers must focus on positive reinforcement rather than threats or punishment.

When Paul says, "giving up the use of threats," he is not saying that masters should never use their authority. They should—their authority is from God. However, it should not be the primary way they lead. A manager who continually says, "Do this or I will fire you," will destroy employee morale. No doubt, this type of demanding leadership was common to slave masters. Under Roman law slaves were property, and masters had the right to kill them if they so desired. Although this rarely happened since slaves were so expensive, many masters led by abusing their authority.

A Spirit-filled master or employer "uses his authority and power as little as possible and does not throw his weight around or lord it over those under him. He is never abusive or inconsiderate."[229] "In other words, 'Let your approach be positive, not negative.' Hence, not, 'Unless you do this, I will do that to you,' but rather, 'Because you are a good and faithful servant, I will give you a generous reward.'"[230]

This is how Christ deals with us—his servants. He promises that if we are faithful, he will reward us. In the Parable of the Talents, Christ says, "Well done, good and faithful slave! You have been faithful in a few things. I will put you in charge of many things. Enter into the joy of your master" (Matt 25:21). Similarly, good employers use positive verbal reinforcement such as, "Thank you" or "Good job." They do this both privately and publicly when it is warranted. And when they can, they also reward their employees with tangible benefits such as promotions, higher wages, and extra vacation days.

Spirit-filled employers focus on positive reinforcement rather than threats and punishment.

Is your leadership style positive or negative?

Application Questions: What are some positive ways that employers can motivate their employees? What is your experience with these motivational strategies? How have you seen or experienced the opposite, and what were its effects?

3. To glorify Christ, employers must remember the lordship of Christ.

Paul says, "Masters, treat your slaves the same way, giving up the use of threats, because you know that both you and they have the same master in heaven, and there is no favoritism with him" (Eph 6:9). He calls for slave masters to always remember that they are under the authority and lordship of Christ. They are essentially stewards of God's authority and resources, and one day they will be held accountable for their stewardship. And this accountability will be without partiality—masters and slaves, employers and employees, are equal before God. Leaders must ask themselves every day, "Would God approve?" If the answer is no or they are unsure, they must ask, "How can I do better?"

Application Questions: How can employers and employees keep their focus on the lordship of Christ? How have you applied this when in leadership positions? How are you going to apply it in the future?

4. To glorify Christ, employers must not show favoritism.

As Paul reminds masters that with God there is no favoritism, the implication is that they should not show favoritism either. Earthly masters and employers are just representatives of their Heavenly Master.

Wiersbe says, "One of the fastest ways for a leader to divide his followers and lose their confidence is for the leader to play favorites and show partiality." [231] Giving unfair favor or discipline can often be hazardous to cohesion and unity in the workplace. Christian employers must avoid this. Paul says something similar to Timothy, who later pastored the Ephesian church, "Before God and Christ Jesus and the elect angels, I solemnly charge you to carry out these commands without prejudice or favoritism of any kind" (1 Timothy 5:21). Christian employers must lead without partiality or favoritism.

Application Question: How have you seen or experienced favoritism destroying the workplace?

Christian employers must work and care for their employees as unto the Lord. This is something that God gives his Spirit to enable (Eph 5:18). Employees should see the power and wisdom of God in the leadership of Christian employers, and it should inspire them to follow Christ.

Application Questions: Who was your favorite manager/employer and why? What are some other good managerial principles that Christians should employ in the workplace?

Conclusion

How can believers glorify Christ in the workplace?

1. To glorify Christ, employees must obey with the right perspective.
2. To glorify Christ, employees must obey with respect and fear.
3. To glorify Christ, employees must obey with sincerity of heart.
4. To glorify Christ, employees must obey without eye service.
5. To glorify Christ, employees must obey with a good attitude.
6. To glorify Christ, employees must obey with an expectation of God's judgment and reward.
7. To glorify Christ, employers must treat workers the way they want to be treated.
8. To glorify Christ, employers must focus on positive enforcement rather than negative.
9. To glorify Christ, employers must remember the lordship of Christ.
10. To glorify Christ, employers must not show favoritism.

Again, we must be filled with the Spirit to fulfill these commands—meaning our primary focus must be abiding in Christ so these fruits can be born in our lives for his glory.

Standing Firm in Spiritual Warfare

Finally, be strengthened in the Lord and in the strength of his power. Clothe yourselves with the full armor of God so that you may be able to stand against the schemes of the devil. For our struggle is not against flesh and blood, but against the rulers, against the powers, against the world rulers of this darkness, against the spiritual forces of evil in the heavens. For this reason, take up the full armor of God so that you may be able to stand your ground on the evil day, and having done everything, to stand.
Ephesians 6:10-13 (NET)

How can we stand firm in spiritual warfare?

In this text, Paul talks about the spiritual war every Christian is engaged in. When a person accepts Christ as Savior, he crosses over from the realm of darkness to the realm of light. He enters a spiritual war that includes demons and angels battling over the souls of men.

Sadly, many Christians live without any real awareness of this battle, and are therefore losing it. There are two wrong views of this battle: some see Satan and his demons in every cough, problem at work, or difficulty with their car. He gets far too much credit in many Christian circles. However, in other circles, Christians act as if Satan doesn't really exist. They know he is there, but they live without any true awareness of his activity in their lives.

We must recognize that Satan is real. He is an enemy of God and an enemy of the church. He tempts, traps, deceives, and kills, and nobody is exempt from his wrath. In light of this, Paul exhorts us to live the Spirit-filled life. In Ephesians 5:18, he calls believers to be filled with the Spirit, and then in the following verses, he looks at the results of the filling, including the Spirit-filled marriage, home, and workplace (v. 19-33, 6:1-9). A believer who is living a life of power—one that affects and changes people—will receive special attention from the evil one. He doesn't waste his best resources on those far away from God, but the closer a person gets to God and the more faithful he or she is, the more the enemy attacks.

It is not uncommon for me to talk to men and women who experience more problems the closer they get to God. The more they read their Bible, the more involved they get in church or ministry, the more problems they encounter.

In fact, I remember one young man sharing the constant problems he experienced when faithfully reading his Bible, and it made him not want to read it at all. This is exactly how our enemy works.

As seen with Satan's temptation of Adam and Eve in the Garden, he wants people to doubt God and to turn away from following him. There is no greater joy for the enemy than when a believer is angry at God or cursing him. That was his objective when attacking Job—he wanted Job to curse God (Job 1:11), and he wants us to do so as well.

In Ephesians 6, Paul talks about standing firm in spiritual warfare. The word "stand," or it can be translated "stand firm," (from histēmi), when used in a military sense, had the idea of holding a critical position while under attack."[232] He mentions our need to stand four times (v.11,13-14). Essentially, he says the wobbly Christian—the one not serious about God and trapped in sin—cannot stand in this war. He will be destroyed. Sadly, many fail to stand in this battle. MacArthur's comments are helpful in considering this reality:

> Countless men and women have faithfully taught Sunday school for years, led many people to Jesus Christ, pastored a church, led Bible studies, ministered to the sick, and done every sort of service in the Lord's name—only to one day give up, turn their backs on His work, and disappear into the world. The circumstances differ, but the underlying reason is always the same: they took God's armor off and thereby lost the courage, the power, and the desire to stand firm.[233]

How can we stand in this treacherous war and not miss our calling, be taken captive, or be destroyed? We'll consider three ways to stand firm in this spiritual war.

Big Question: How can believers stand firm in spiritual warfare according to Ephesians 6:10-13?

Believers Stand Firm by Being Prepared

> Finally, be strengthened in the Lord and in the strength of his power.
> Clothe yourselves with the full armor of God...
> Ephesians 6:10-11

In order to stand firm, believers must prepare for battle. This is true for any warfare—a soldier cannot be successful without preparation. Governments invest billions of dollars into training their soldiers both mentally and physically, and such commitment should be similar for Christians—no corners should be cut in becoming spiritually prepared. Many lose this battle simply because of failure to prepare.

Paul says to "be strengthened in the Lord and in the strength of his power. Clothe yourselves with the full armor of God." Essentially, Paul wants believers to understand that this battle cannot be won through human strength, but in God's strength alone. He talks about God's power throughout Ephesians. In Ephesians 1:18-21, he prays for the believers to know this power.

> – since the eyes of your heart have been enlightened so that you may know what is the hope of his calling, what is the wealth of his glorious inheritance in the saints, and what is the incomparable greatness of his power toward us who believe, as displayed in the exercise of his immense strength. This power he exercised in Christ when he raised him from the dead and seated him at his right hand in the heavenly realms far above every rule and authority and power and dominion and every name that is named, not only in this age but also in the one to come.

This power raised Christ from the dead and put Satan and his demons under his feet (and therefore also under ours according to Ephesians 2:6). We must know that this power is in us. But also in Ephesians 3:16, Paul prays for the believers to be strengthened by it. He says, "I pray that according to the wealth of his glory he may grant you to be strengthened with power through his Spirit in the inner person." Finally, in Ephesians 5:18, he calls for us to be filled with the Spirit—meaning to be controlled and empowered by him.

A powerless Christianity is a vulnerable Christianity—in danger of being enslaved and destroyed by the enemy. This is what we see in most churches and in most Christians' lives—a powerless Christianity. We must constantly pray to know the power that is in us, to be strengthened by it, and to be continually filled with it. That is what Paul again calls for in Ephesians 6:10. "Be strong in the Lord and in his mighty power"—the same power that raised Christ from the dead and seated him in heavenly places over the enemy. We must put on the full armor of God so we can take our stand.

Since the verb "be strengthened" is passive present, the verse could also be rendered, "Strengthen yourselves in the Lord" or (NEB) "Find your strength in the Lord." It is the same construction as in 2 Timothy 2:1 where Paul exhorts Timothy to "take strength from the grace of God which is ours in Christ Jesus" (NEB).[234]

In considering the armor of God, we must realize that throughout Scripture clothing often refers to attitudes and actions (cf. Col 3:12-14, Eph 4:24-25). The armor is God's clothing, as it essentially represents his character. Isaiah 59:17 says, "He wears his desire for justice like body armor, and his desire to deliver is like a helmet on his head. He puts on the garments of vengeance and wears zeal like a robe." Therefore, we prepare for battle by putting on God's power and God's character.

Interpretation Question: How can we be strong in the Lord (God's power) and put on his armor (God's character)?

1. We must recognize our weakness.

If we don't recognize our insufficiency for this battle, we won't put on God's strength and character. Therefore, to prepare us for a lifetime of battle, God often allows us to go through pain, trials, and failure first to show us our weakness. Paul said this in 2 Corinthians 12:9-10 about God's response to his request to take away the thorn in the flesh:

> But he said to me, "My grace is enough for you, for my power is made perfect in weakness." So then, I will boast most gladly about my weaknesses, so that the power of Christ may reside in me. Therefore I am content with weaknesses, with insults, with troubles, with persecutions and difficulties for the sake of Christ, for whenever I am weak, then I am strong.

Often trials are meant to reveal our weakness so we can see our need for more of God's power and character.

2. We must be dependent.

Again, Ephesians 6:10 can be translated, "Find your strength in the Lord." We need to depend on God to stand in this battle. Sadly, too many Christians are independent. You can see this in their lack of desire to read the Bible, pray, or fellowship with other believers. Why is this so common? It is because they are too independent. They believe that they can make it on their own.

However, the very opposite is true. We can do nothing without Christ. We are like sheep without a shepherd. We are like branches apart from the vine. John 15:5 says, "I am the vine; you are the branches. The one who remains in me – and I in him – bears much fruit, because apart from me you can accomplish nothing."

Are you abiding in Christ? Are you drawing near him daily? Or are you independent, and therefore losing this spiritual battle?

3. We must be disciplined.

The present tense of the verb "be strengthened" means that it is not a once and for all event—be strong—but a constant strengthening through God.[235] The implication of this is that we need discipline. If it were a one-time event we could stop working, but it is not. We need to continue to strengthen ourselves in the Lord.

Discipline is not only necessary to be empowered by God, but also to put on his character—his armor. First Timothy 4:7 says, "train yourself for godliness" or, as it can also be translated, "exercise yourself unto godliness." We need to practice spiritual disciplines—prayer, Bible reading, fellowship, serving, solitude, and giving—daily in order to become holy.

The Christian with poor spiritual discipline is like the soldier without discipline—unprepared and therefore vulnerable to attack.

4. We must be thorough.

Paul says to clothe ourselves with the "full" armor of God (Eph 6:11). Partial preparation will not do. If there are any chinks in our armor—which symbolizes our character—that is exactly where the enemy will attack. If we commonly struggle with unforgiveness, lust, anger, or lack of self-control, the enemy will attack in those areas. We must be thorough in this battle. In physical warfare, little compromises can get someone captured or killed, and it is the same in spiritual warfare. We must constantly repent of our sins and seek to get right with God. We must be thorough—putting on the full armor of God.

If we are going to stand in this battle, we must be prepared by knowing our weakness, depending on God, being disciplined, and being thorough.

Application Question: How is God calling you to seek his power and character in your life? What are your spiritual disciplines like? How can you strengthen them?

Believers Stand Firm by Knowing the Enemy

> Clothe yourselves with the full armor of God so that you may be able to stand against the schemes of the devil. For our struggle is not against flesh and blood, but against the rulers, against the powers, against the world rulers of this darkness, against the spiritual forces of evil in the heavens.
> Ephesians 6:11-12

A crucial part of every army is the intelligence branch. Those who work in intel gather information about the enemy so the army can be equipped and prepared. In Ephesians 6:11-12, Paul gives intel about our enemy so we can be equipped to stand firm in this war.

Paul mentions the devil's schemes (v.11). The word "schemes" in the Greek is methodia, from which we get the English word "method." It carries the idea of craftiness, cunning, and deception. It was used of a "wild animal who cunningly stalked and then unexpectedly pounced on its prey. Satan's evil schemes are built around stealth and deception."[236]

Paul refers to awareness of the devil's schemes in 2 Corinthians 2:11: "so that we may not be exploited by Satan (for we are not ignorant of his schemes)." In order for believers to not be outwitted and to stand firm, they must know their enemy and his schemes.

Interpretation Question: What are some of the devil's schemes—his methods?

1. The devil uses accusation.

The name "devil" actually means "accuser." One of the devil's primary tactics against believers is to accuse and condemn. He accuses God to our ears—slandering his goodness and his faithfulness. Many people struggle with worship because they have accepted the enemy's accusations of God. As in Satan's attack on Eve, the enemy tempts us to doubt God's goodness so we will fall into sin.

But Satan also accuses us. He does this primarily through condemnation. After he successfully tempts us to sin, he then says, "Feel bad—feel really bad!" in order to further pull us away from God. Because of their stumbles, many Christians don't feel worthy to read the Bible, go to church, or serve. In contrast, the Holy Spirit convicts us of sin so we will draw near to God; he doesn't condemn us and push us away from God.

Finally, Satan accuses other people. He continually brings up the failures of others and seeks to draw us into anger, discord and unforgiveness. Many Christians have left the church because they listened to the devil's accusations.

One of his methods is accusation. He accuses God, us, and others.

2. The devil uses deception.

Very similar to accusation is the devil's tactic of deception. Jesus says the devil is a liar and the father of lies (John 8:44). He lied to Eve about God's Word and God's intentions. Since the devil oversees the world system, it is a system built on lies. He lies about what humanity is, what success is, what beauty is, and many other things. Satan lies in order to lead people away from God and his best for their lives.

He wants people to think they are an accident of evolution instead of the purposeful creation of God. He wants people to think that something is wrong with them—they are not pretty enough, smart enough, tall enough, tan enough, light enough, etc. We live in a world full of discouragement and depression because it is based on Satan's lies.

He also deceives people about the Word of God. The church is full of false teachings and cults because of the lies of the devil. First Timothy 4:1 calls these lies "demonic teachings." Second Corinthians 11:14-15 says, "And no wonder, for even Satan disguises himself as an angel of light. Therefore it is not surprising his servants also disguise themselves as servants of righteousness, whose end will correspond to their actions." He and his servants twist God's Word—creating false teachings or leading people to doubt the accuracy and inerrancy of the Word. He ultimately does this to lead people away from believing in Christ and God all together.

3. The devil uses persecution and fear of persecution.

Though the devil's favorite tactic is to use deception like a serpent, he often shows up as a lion to incite fear and to destroy. First Peter 5:8 says, "Be sober and alert. Your enemy the devil, like a roaring lion, is on the prowl looking for someone to devour."

In many nations around the world, he works to quiet believers or turn them away from God through fear and persecution. He roars so believers will be quiet about their faith instead of being the bold witnesses they are called to be. Christ describes the end times as a time of persecution, and a time when many will fall away from the faith because of it. In Matthew 24:9-10, he says:

"Then they will hand you over to be persecuted and will kill you. You will be hated by all the nations because of my name. Then many will be led into sin, and they will betray one another and hate one another. And many false prophets will appear and deceive many."

4. The devil uses the world.

Since the devil is not omnipresent, he uses the world system to draw believers away from God. It is essentially a system without God—meant to lead and corrupt people. Satan uses this system to deceive and to conform people to his image. First John 5:19 says, "We know that we are from God, and the whole world lies in the power of the evil one."

We must be aware that Satan is over the fashion industry, the entertainment industry, education, government, and religion. When he offered Jesus the kingdoms of this world, it was a literal offer (Matt 4:8-9).

When Christians are aware of this reality, they keep themselves from befriending the world (James 4:4), loving the world (1 John 2:15), being spotted or polluted by it (James 1:27), and ultimately being conformed to it (Rom 12:2)—where they look just like the world (1 Cor 3:3).

5. The devil works through our flesh.

Our flesh is the unredeemed part of our bodies—it desires to sin and rebel against God. Though saved, we still carry this part of our nature, which came from Adam. When we give in to the flesh, we open the door for the enemy to work in our lives. Ephesians 4:26-27 talks about how anger gives the devil a foothold. But this is also true of lying, stealing, lust, unforgiveness, corrupt talk, and worldly thoughts. The devil works through our flesh.

We get a good picture of this in the account of Christ rebuking Satan while talking to Peter. Matthew 16:21-23 says:

> From that time on Jesus began to show his disciples that he must go to Jerusalem and suffer many things at the hands of the elders, chief priests, and experts in the law, and be killed, and on the third day be raised. So Peter took him aside and began to rebuke him: "God forbid, Lord! This must not happen to you!" But he turned and said to Peter, "Get behind me, Satan! You are a stumbling block to me, because you are not setting your mind on God's interests, but on man's."

What gave Satan the door into Peter's life? It was his secular, worldly thinking. He was mindful of the things of men and not the things of God. Man doesn't want to sacrifice—he wants prosperity, wealth, and health. Acceptance of death and sacrifice are not part of his old nature. Therefore, many people open doors to the enemy simply because their minds are still secular—their thinking has not been transformed through the Word of God (Rom 12:2).

6. The devil works through an army of demons.

Paul says this in Ephesians 6:12: "For our struggle is not against flesh and blood, but against the rulers, against the powers, against the world rulers of this darkness, against the spiritual forces of evil in the heavens."

Scripture teaches that demons are fallen angels. Revelation 12:4 says that at Satan's fall a third of the angels fell with him.

How many demons are there? We don't know. But we do know that Satan could spare up to 6,000 of them to focus on one person. In the story of the demoniac in Mark 5:9, the demons said their name was Legion. As a Roman legion consisted of up to 6,000 men, [237] the fallen angels appear to be innumerable. Satan has no shortage of allies, and all of them are seeking to destroy the people of God and the plans of God.

Paul doesn't teach us everything about demons, but there are many things that can be discerned from this passage.

Observation Question: What characteristics of demons can be discerned from Paul's teaching in Ephesians 6:12?

- Demons are supernatural.

Paul says we don't battle against flesh and blood. This means that demons are supernatural, and that our primary opponents are not evil people, but the power that works behind them. Wiersbe's comments are helpful here:

> The important point is that our battle is not against human beings. It is against spiritual powers. We are wasting our time fighting people when we ought to be fighting the devil who seeks to control people and make them oppose the work of God... The advice of the King of Syria to his soldiers can be applied to our spiritual battle: "Fight neither with small nor great, save only with the king" (1 Kings 22:31).[238]

- Demons are wicked.

Again, Paul says our struggle is against "the world rulers of this darkness, against the spiritual forces of evil in the heavens." Darkness symbolizes evil in the Bible. That is the demons' character—there is nothing good in them. They are the spiritual forces of evil. John Stott says this about demons:

> If we hope to overcome them, we shall need to bear in mind that they have no moral principles, no code of honour, no higher feelings. They recognize no Geneva Convention to restrict or partially civilize the weapons of their warfare. They are utterly unscrupulous, and ruthless in the pursuit of their malicious designs.[239]

- Demons are organized.

The demonic categories that Paul uses are not explained, but they seem to represent "differing degrees of authority, such as presidents, governors, mayors, and aldermen, on the human scale."[240]

"Word rulers" in the Greek is the word kosmokratoras or, with an anglicized rendering, "cosmocrats."[241] It can als be translated "cosmic powers" as in the ESV. This probably refers to demons that are set over nations or regions. In Daniel, we see powerful demons called "princes" over Persia and Greece (Daniel 10:20). The angel who spoke with Daniel was involved in a battle with two of these demons. In the same way, there are demons that rule like princes and generals over nations and cities—seeking to turn the people and the culture away from God. It is very interesting to consider that when Christ cast the demons out of the demoniac (Mark 5), they begged him not to send them out of the country. It seems that even the minions are territorial—focused on whatever territory or person they are assigned to.

Rulers, powers, and spiritual forces of evil also seem to reflect varying ranks. MacArthur says this about the "spiritual forces of evil":

> The spiritual forces of wickedness are possibly those demons who are involved in the most wretched and vile immoralities—such as extremely perverse sexual practices, the occult, Satan worship, and the like.[242]

What else can we discern about our enemy?

7. The devil wants to kill us.

Paul says our "struggle is not against flesh and blood." The word "struggle" was used of hand to hand combat—especially wrestling. However, wrestling in the ancient world was often a fight to the death.[243] This wrestling wasn't just for sport; it was deadly combat. The devil and his demons don't want to just tempt us and lead us into sin; they ultimately want to kill and destroy us. Jesus says this about Satan in John 10:10: "The thief comes only to steal and kill and destroy; I have come so that they may have life, and may have it abundantly."

When Satan leads people into ungodly language, secular thinking, selfishness, or compromise, though they may seem harmless at the time, he ultimately wants to lead them to their destruction. The devil is nobody to play with—he is a destroyer.

The only reason he has not killed us is that God is the ultimate sovereign. As in the story of Job, God sets boundaries on how far the enemy can go. If Satan cannot kill us, he is content to attack our bodies, our sleep, our joy, our peace, our testimonies, our callings, and our relationships—with the hope of destroying them. Our enemy is a murderer, and our only hope is our Shepherd—Jesus.

8. The devil often attacks in an overwhelming manner.

Paul says for us to put on the full armor of God so that we may stand on the "evil day" (Eph 6:13). MacDonald says this about the evil day:

> The evil day probably refers to any time when the enemy comes against us like a flood. Satanic opposition seems to occur in waves, advancing and receding. Even after our Lord's temptation in the wilderness, the devil left Him for a season (Luke 4:13).[244]

Job experienced the "evil day" when the devil attacked his body, his family, his finances, and his friends for a season. This happens with many believers. Satan desires to make people give up, get angry at God, and turn away from him. A believer that is not being filled with the Spirit, who is not strong in the Lord, will fall prey to our enemy on this day.

Application Questions: What are some other characteristics of our enemy? What is a healthy perspective for Christians to have regarding the devil and spiritual warfare? What is an unhealthy one?

Believers Stand Firm by Fighting

> For this reason, take up the full armor of God so that you may be able to stand your ground on the evil day, and having done everything, to stand.
> Ephesians 6:13

Paul writes of the need to stand firm four times in Ephesians 6; however, it must be remembered that this standing is not a passive, defensive stance. It is, in fact, active and offensive. Ephesians 6:17 and 19 tell us so.

> And take the helmet of salvation and the sword of the Spirit, which is the word of God... Pray for me also, that I may be given the message when I begin to speak – that I may confidently make known the mystery of the gospel

The sword was not primarily a defensive weapon, but an offensive one. As we share the Word of God with others, we are on the offensive. In fact, Paul prays for grace in sharing the gospel with others (v. 19).

It has been said that the best defense is a great offense. When the enemy is constantly being attacked, it is hard for him to mount an effective offense. Similarly, when Paul was going throughout the Gentile world spreading the gospel, he was fighting against the darkness. He was setting captives of Satan free by leading them to Christ. He was exposing the Roman world to light so that the darkness began to flee, and it must be the same for us.

We also see this in Christ's words about building his church in Matthew 16:18. He says, "And I tell you that you are Peter, and on this rock I will build my church, and the gates of Hades will not overpower it." The gates of Hades not prevailing is a picture of the church on the offensive. Believers are taking the battering ram of the gospel and breaking down the gates of Hades in communities, cities, and nations. This is a proper picture of God's battle plan for the church in this war.

Application Question: How can believers fight this spiritual battle?

1. We must know what we are fighting for.

In a war, a soldier fights to protect his home, his family, his country, and his freedom. These things motivate him, and it must be the same for believers. If we don't know what we're fighting for, our spiritual lives often become dreary and lifeless.
What do believers fight for?

*   Believers fight for the souls of the lost.

Jesus says this to Paul about his calling as an apostle in Acts 26:17-18:

"I will rescue you from your own people and from the Gentiles, to whom I am sending you to open their eyes so that they turn from darkness to light and from the power of Satan to God, so that they may receive forgiveness of sins and a share among those who are sanctified by faith in me."

Similarly, Christians must recognize that they are on a rescue mission to save the lost from eternal darkness.

*   Believers fight to please God and be rewarded by him.

Consider these verses:

Watch out, so that you do not lose the things we have worked for, but receive a full reward.
2 John 1:8

Instead I subdue my body and make it my slave, so that after preaching to others I myself will not be disqualified.
1 Corinthians 9:27

John calls Christians to be careful to not lose their reward, but rather to seek a full reward from God. Similarly, Paul was not afraid of losing his salvation, but he feared losing his reward and ultimately his usefulness. We fight to please God and to be rewarded by him. Believers with no desire to please God will not fight—they will remain spiritually lethargic.

*   Believers fight to glorify God with their lives.

First Corinthians 10:31 says, "So whether you eat or drink, or whatever you do, do everything for the glory of God." Even our fighting in this war is for the glory of God. When Christ went into the temple and turned over tables, he was consumed with zeal for God's house (John 2:17), and with the glory of God. Similarly, we fight because we are consumed with the glory of God. A person not consumed with God's glory—God being exalted throughout the world—will not fight.

How else can believers fight this battle?

2. We must know that the war has already been won, and we must fight with Christ's authority.

Another important reality that every believer must understand when fighting this battle is that the war is already won. Therefore, we are not fighting to win, but because we've won. We see this taught in many texts, including the following:

> – since the eyes of your heart have been enlightened – so that you may know what is the hope of his calling, what is the wealth of his glorious inheritance in the saints, and what is the incomparable greatness of his power toward us who believe, as displayed in the exercise of his immense strength. This power he exercised in Christ when he raised him from the dead and seated him at his right hand in the heavenly realms far above every rule and authority and power and dominion and every name that is named, not only in this age but also in the one to come. And God put all things under Christ's feet, and he gave him to the church as head over all things. Now the church is his body, the fullness of him who fills all in all.
> Ephesians 1:18-22

> Disarming the rulers and authorities, he has made a public disgrace of them, triumphing over them by the cross.
> Colossians 2:15

This is important to understand so that we don't become discouraged and quit. Christ has already won this battle on the cross. Satan—the serpent—bit his heel, but Jesus crushed the serpent's head by his own death and resurrection (cf. Gen 3:15). He disarmed the evil powers and authorities, and was raised up in authority over them. Christians must remember this.

This is why when Paul encountered those possessed with demons, he cast them out in the "name of Jesus" (Acts 16:18). He declared Christ's authority over them. We must walk in this reality as well. Christ is seated in authority over the demonic powers; he disarmed them and has placed us in authority over them as well—because we are in Christ (Eph 2:6).

As Paul did, there may be times where you need to rebuke the devil in "the name of Jesus"—declaring Christ's authority. You may have to pray in authority over people stuck in spiritual depression (cf. 1 Sam 16:15), habitual sin (cf. Eph 4:26-27), or some type of demonic illness (cf. Lk 13:11). You may need to speak and stand on this reality in your own life, as you feel assaulted by the enemy emotionally, physically, and socially. Yes, the flesh and the world tempt and attack us, but we also must recognize this very real evil force—the devil and his demons—and the authority Christ has given us in his name (cf. Matt 28:18-19).

Application Questions: Why is it important to be on the offensive in spiritual warfare? What is your motivation to fight?

Conclusion

How can believers stand firm in this spiritual war?

1. Believers Stand Firm by Being Prepared (with God's Power and Character)
2. Believers Stand Firm by Knowing the Enemy
3. Believers Stand Firm by Fighting

The Belt of Truth and the Breastplate of Righteousness

> Stand firm therefore, by fastening the belt of truth around your waist,
> by putting on the breastplate of righteousness,
> Ephesians 6:14 (NET)

How can we stand firm in spiritual warfare? In Ephesians 6:12, Paul tells us to be strong in the Lord and in his might and to put on the full armor of God. This is not a battle that can be won in our own strength. It is a battle against the devil and innumerable spiritual forces all set on opposing God and his people.

In Ephesians 6:14, Paul begins to talk about the armor Christians should put on. Commonly in Scripture, clothing is used symbolically of actions and attitudes. For example, Colossians 3:12 says, "Therefore, as the elect of God, holy and dearly loved, clothe yourselves with a heart of mercy, kindness, humility, gentleness, and patience." In this passage, a heart of mercy, kindness, humility, etc., are symbolized by clothing. It is the same with the armor of God. Each part of the soldier's armor represents an action or attitude needed for the believer to stand in spiritual warfare.

As we consider each piece of armor, it tells us something about Satan's attacks. No piece of armor can be excluded in our warfare—for Satan and his demons will always attack the vulnerable area. In this text, Paul focuses on the belt of truth and the breastplate of righteousness.

Big Question: How can believers stand firm in spiritual warfare by using the belt of truth and the breastplate of righteousness?

Believers Stand Firm by Putting On the Belt of Truth

> Stand firm therefore, by fastening the belt of truth around your waist...
> Ephesians 6:14

A Roman soldier wore a tunic under his armor, and a large leather belt "was used to gather his garments together as well as hold his sword."[245] The belt was the first part of the armor put on, and it held everything else together. It was crucial. Similarly, truth is a crucial component for every believer in this spiritual battle—without it believers are not prepared to stand and fight.

Interpretation Question: What does the belt of truth represent, how do we put it on, and how does it protect us from the enemy?

Commentators are divided on the exact meaning of the belt of truth. It could represent several things.

1. The belt of truth represents knowing the content of truth as revealed in Scripture.

Jesus said this in John 17:17: "Set them apart in the truth; your word is truth." The Word of God is truth, and it is through knowing and applying this truth that we are sanctified—daily made holy and righteous.

With that said, we can clearly discern Satan's attacks during this age. We can see it in the post-modern concept of relativism. We live in an age of no absolutes. It is the predominant philosophical thought taught in our education system today. Peter Singer, an ethics professor at Princeton and arguably the most influential modern philosopher, teaches that bestiality is not morally wrong (as long as it doesn't hurt the animal),[246] and neither is killing infants with disabilities.[247] Ironically, he teaches at the same seminary where Jonathan Edwards served as president!

Because of teachings like this, we are raising up a generation that is increasingly vulnerable to the devil. In their world-view, there are no absolute rights or wrongs. Therefore, sexual immorality, homosexuality, the murder of innocent infants, assisted suicide, and sometimes even gross injustices like pedophilia are not wrong. The only thing "wrong" is to declare the existence of absolute truth—for that you will be persecuted. We live in a system that is based on the lies of the devil, and if you don't know the truth, you will fall into the temptation of the day.

But Satan is not just attacking the culture with relativism and other fashionable lies, he is also attacking the church—the pillar and foundation of truth (1 Tim 3:15)—and specifically, the Word of God. With Eve in the Garden, he attacked God's Word. "Did God really say?" he asked. In the Parable of the Sower, the devil removed the seed on the wayside before it could produce any fruit (Matt 13:4). Our enemy always attacks the Word of God. In 1 Timothy 4:1, Paul talks about doctrines of demons that will lead some away from the faith. The enemy of our souls constantly assaults the church by twisting or denying Scripture—pulling many away from God. It is increasingly common for people to call themselves Christians and yet not believe that the Bible is true and without error, even though Scripture refers to itself as true, perfect, inspired, and enduring (cf. John 17:17, Ps 19:7, 2 Tim 3:16, 1 Peter 1:23). Jesus says man shall not live by bread alone but by "every word" that comes from the mouth of God (Matt 4:4). He does not say "SOME" words, as many in the church today would teach, but "EVERY" word.

When believers accept the lie that not all Scripture is true, they are on a slippery slope. It is not too soon after that they throw out the virgin birth, the resurrection, the judgment, the miracles of Christ—soon leading them to discard the gospel and salvation altogether.

Saints, if you do not know the Word of God, you are not prepared to stand in this spiritual war. An ancient soldier couldn't even fight without cinching his belt—all his clothing would have hindered him. And neither can we fight without knowing the truth. Ephesians 4:11-14 talks about God giving the church pastors and teachers so his children would no longer be tossed to and fro by every wind of teaching, and by deceitful men. The enemy feasts on believers who don't know the Word of God, but at the same time, he is defeated by those who do know it. Consider John's description of spiritual young men in the church in 1 John 2:14. He says, "I have written to you, young people, that you are strong, and the word of God resides in you, and you have conquered the evil one." Spiritual young men overcome the devil because the Word of God is strong in them. Therefore, they are conquering their lusts, confronting false teachings, and helping set others free.

It is no wonder that many of the great warriors in church history have been men and women of the Word of God. It was said of Martin Luther that he essentially memorized the entire Bible in Latin. John Wesley memorized almost the entire Greek New Testament.[248] If we are going to win this battle, we must know the great doctrines of the Word of God.

In considering this, I would especially recommend that young believers systematically study the major doctrines of Scripture. It is harder to understand Scripture verse by verse in a short time, but easier to understand it systematically. Wayne Grudem's Systematic Theology, for example, addresses the doctrines of Christ, the Holy Spirit, salvation, end times, etc. Know what the Bible teaches on major doctrines so you won't be led astray by all the false teachings circulating in the church.

Application Questions: How is the enemy attacking truth throughout the world and the church today? How is God challenging you to hide God's truth in your heart to better stand against the attacks?

2.   The belt of truth represents living a life of honesty and integrity.

The belt of truth does not represent just knowing the content of the truth, but also living out the truth practically in our daily lives. Ephesians 4:25-27 says:

Therefore, having laid aside falsehood, each one of you speak the truth with his neighbor, for we are members of one another. Be angry and do not sin; do not let the sun go down on the cause of your anger. Do not give the devil an opportunity.

Practicing falsehood and hypocrisy opens the door to the devil in our lives—it gives him a foothold. Wiersbe says, "Once a lie gets into the life of a believer, everything begins to fall apart. For over a year, King David lied about his sin with Bathsheba, and nothing went right."[249] When David repented, he wrote this (Psalm 32:2-5):

How blessed is the one whose wrongdoing the Lord does not punish, in whose spirit there is no deceit. When I refused to confess my sin, 9 my whole body wasted away, while I groaned in pain all day long. For day and night you tormented me; you tried to destroy me in the intense heat of summer. (Selah) Then I confessed my sin; I no longer covered up my wrongdoing. I said, "I will confess my rebellious acts to the Lord." And then you forgave my sins. (Selah).

While David was living a hypocritical, dishonest life, he lost the blessing of God. He experienced sickness, depression, and physical weakness until he confessed his sins. As he said in Psalm 51:6, "Look, you desire integrity in the inner man; you want me to possess wisdom."

Lies and deception open the door to the devil; therefore, we must put off falsehood and practice transparency before God and others as we confess our sins (cf. 1 John 1:9, James 5:16). Satan likes to work in the shadows—he wants people to keep their sins in the dark instead of confessing them before God and man. It gives him a base from which to attack us. But the light of confession enables God to work in those dark places and set us free.

In what ways are you giving the enemy a foothold by practicing dishonesty? Is it through cheating on tests, lying on taxes, illegal downloading, or telling little fibs at work? In what ways are you practicing transparency—confession before God and man—in order to close the door on the devil?

In order to put on the belt of truth, we must practice honesty and get rid of all deception in our lives.

Application Question: In what ways have you seen or experienced dishonesty opening the door for Satan to attack a believer personally?

3. The belt of truth represents total commitment and zeal for Christ.

The metaphor of buckling or girding is often used in Scripture to describe the preparatory action of gathering one's flowing garments in order to work, run a race, or fight a battle.[250] Luke 12:35 says, "Let your loins be girded about, and your lights burning" (KJV). First Peter 1:13 says, "Wherefore gird up the loins of your mind" (KJV). These texts both refer metaphorically to the action of tightening one's belt so as not to hinder action.

Since buckling or girding is often used to describe preparation, some commentators think the belt of truth refers to serving the Lord wholeheartedly, with total commitment, as a soldier going into battle. John MacArthur says this:

> I believe that being girded ... with truth primarily has to do with the self–discipline of total commitment. It is the committed Christian, just as it is the committed soldier and the committed athlete, who is prepared. Winning in war and in sports is often said to be the direct result of desire that leads to careful preparation and maximum effort. It is the army or the team who wants most to win who is most likely to do so—even against great odds...To be content with mediocrity, lethargy, indifference, and half–heartedness is to fail to be armored with the belt of God's truth and to leave oneself exposed to Satan's schemes.[251]

Christ says that in order to follow him one must hate his father, mother, brothers, sisters, and even his own life (Lk 14:26). He requires total commitment—anything less is to not be his disciple. Everything that might hinder our walk with Christ must be removed. Uncommitted Christians are fodder for the enemy. He uses them to scatter people from Christ instead of gathering people to Christ (Matt 12:30).

Application Questions: Is there anything in your life keeping you from being fully committed to Christ? If so, how can you get on fire for God—totally committed to him?

Are you putting on the belt of truth? Are you daily seeking to know the full counsel of Scripture, or are you neglecting God's Word? Are you practicing truth, or are you practicing hypocrisy and deception? Are you fully committed to Christ, or are you half-hearted? We must put on the belt of truth to stand against Satan's attacks.

Application Question: Which aspect of the belt of truth stood out most to you and why?

Believers Stand Firm by Putting On the Breastplate of Righteousness

Stand firm therefore, by fastening the belt of truth around your waist,
by putting on the breastplate of righteousness,
Ephesians 6:14

The Roman soldier wore a tough, sleeveless piece of armor that covered the whole torso, front and back, from neck to waist. It was often made of leather, metal, or chains. The primary purpose of the armor was "to protect the heart, lungs, intestines, and other vital organs." [252]

Interpretation Question: What does the breastplate of righteousness represent, how do we put it on, and how does it protect us from the enemy?

As with the belt of truth, commentators are divided on what the breastplate of righteousness symbolizes. It could represent several things.

1.The breastplate of righteousness represents recognition of the imputed righteousness of Christ.

Second Corinthians 5:21 says, "God made the one who did not know sin to be sin for us, so that in him we would become the righteousness of God." Essentially, Christ took our sin at the cross and gave us his righteousness. This is the very reason we can come into the presence of God and worship him. When he sees us, he sees the righteousness of Christ. This is probably symbolized in Zechariah 3:1-7, where Joshua, the high priest, comes into God's presence wearing filthy clothes. Satan stands by Joshua's side to accuse him—and no doubt to declare him unfit to be in God's presence. However, God rebukes Satan and places clean clothes on Joshua, which probably represents imputing to him the righteousness of Christ. The Angel of the Lord says, "Remove his filthy clothes." Then he says to Joshua, "I have freely forgiven your iniquity and will dress you in fine clothing" (v.4).

It's the same for us. Our clothes—representing our character and works—are unclean to God. Even our righteousness is like filthy rags to him (Is 64:6). Even our best works are full of bad intentions—to be known, exalted, etc. However, God rebukes the devil and gives us clean clothes—the righteousness of Christ. This is the only reason we can stand in the presence of God.

Because the imputation of Christ's righteousness happens at salvation, many commentators say the breastplate of righteousness cannot represent Christ's work. How can we put it on if we are already wearing it positionally? However, we still need to recognize this work in order to stand against the accusations and condemnation of the devil.

Many believers, though they assent to salvation by grace, think it is their daily works that continue to justify them before God. When they fail to fully satisfy God's righteous requirements, the enemy quickly comes to condemn them and pull them away from God. By not recognizing Christ's work, they are agreeing with the devil. "You are right, Satan. I should not go to church; I should not read my Bible—that would be hypocritical." They agree with the devil's lies—opening the door for him into their hearts and minds.

However, we must not do that. We must continually declare the righteousness of Christ. "I am justified by grace—the unmerited favor of God—through Christ's righteousness. I can do nothing to justify myself before God. Every day I must throw myself upon God's gracious provisions. He provided the perfect Lamb that was slain so I could come into his presence."

Are you still depending on the perfection of the Lamb? If not, you will accept the lies and condemnation of the devil and allow him to pull you away from God. We must daily recognize the perfect righteousness of Christ to put on the breastplate of righteousness.

Application Question: How does one recognize the difference between condemnation from the devil and conviction from the Holy Spirit? How can we practically apply the righteousness of Christ in our warfare?

2.The breastplate of righteousness represents our practical righteousness.

But the breastplate is not just imputed righteousness; it is also practical righteousness. When we are living a righteous life, we are protected from Satan. However, when we fall into sin, we give Satan an open door to attack and defeat us. Again, Ephesians 4:26-27 indicates this, as it says, "Be angry and do not sin; do not let the sun go down on the cause of your anger. Do not give the devil an opportunity."

The Parable of the Unforgiving Servant in Matthew 18 also represents this truth. In the parable, a master forgave a servant a great debt, but the servant did not forgive his fellow servant a much lesser debt. Because of this, the master handed the servant over to torturers. Matthew 18:32-35 shares the master's judgment:

> "Then his lord called the first slave and said to him, 'Evil slave! I forgave you all that debt because you begged me! Should you not have shown mercy to your fellow slave, just as I showed it to you?' And in anger his lord turned him over to the prison guards to torture him until he repaid all he owed. So also my heavenly Father will do to you, if each of you does not forgive your brother from your heart."

Obviously, the master reflects God and the servants reflect believers, but who are the torturers? No doubt, they are Satan and his demons. We see this throughout Scripture. When Saul was in unrepentant sin, who did God hand him over to? A tormenting spirit (1 Sam 16:14)! In the Corinthian church, when an unrepentant man was fornicating with his stepmother, who did Paul call for the church to hand him over to? Satan (1 Cor 5:5)! They would do this by putting him out of the church.

Sin opens the door for the devil into our lives. No doubt there are many Christians who, as a result of unrepentance, have psychological problems which are demonic in origin. There are Christians being tormented in their minds, bodies, emotions, work, and relationships because they have been handed over by God to the enemy until they repent.

Ephesians 2:2 says Satan works in those who are "disobedient"; however, a righteous life is a protection.

Application Questions: What doors are still open in your life for the enemy? In what ways is God calling you to turn away from sin so you can put on the breastplate of righteousness?

3.The breastplate of righteousness represents guarding our mind and emotions.

As mentioned, the Roman soldier's breastplate was used to protect the vital organs such as the heart and intestines. In the Hebrew mindset, the heart represented the mind and will. The bowels, or intestines, represented emotions and feelings (cf. Col 3:12, KJV). [253] Therefore, the breastplate probably represents guarding our mind and emotions. Solomon says, "Guard your heart with all vigilance, for from it are the sources of life" (Prov 4:23).

Satan realizes that if he can get our minds and emotions, that will affect our worship and our obedience to God. That's why he always works to implant wrong teachings and lies into our minds through books, music, TV, and conversation. Our minds affect our walk—how we live. But he also wants to get our emotions. Many Christians are emotionally all over the place, and part of that is a result of spiritual warfare. Satan stirs up people to criticize and condemn. He stirs up little romances with the opposite sex to distract us from focusing on God. He works to make believers worry and fret about the future so that they lose their joy. The enemy is cunning and keen. Therefore, we must guard our hearts above all else.

Application Question: How can believers put on the breastplate of righteousness by guarding their hearts?

• Believers guard their hearts by recognizing wrong thoughts and emotions, taking them captive, and making them obedient to Christ.

Second Corinthians 10:4-5 says,

for the weapons of our warfare are not human weapons, but are made powerful by God for tearing down strongholds. We tear down arguments and every arrogant obstacle that is raised up against the knowledge of God, and we take every thought captive to make it obey Christ.

Here we see that a major part of our fight is recognizing wrong thoughts and emotions, taking them captive, and making them obedient to Christ. For example, Scripture teaches us to "not be anxious about anything" (Phil 4:6) and "in everything give thanks" (1 Thess 5:18). When we are struggling with anxiety or complaining, our hearts and minds are not being obedient to Christ. We need to confront wrong thoughts and emotions with the truth, confess them to God, and submit them to Christ.

Are you taking your thoughts and emotions captive? Scripture calls us to control our emotions. God says, "Rejoice in the Lord always. Again I say, rejoice!" (Phil 4:4). I must choose to obey even when I don't feel like it; I must bring my heart into submission to Christ.

- Believers guard their hearts by filling their minds with Scripture.

    Philippians 4:8-9 says this:

    Finally, brothers and sisters, whatever is true, whatever is worthy of respect, whatever is just, whatever is pure, whatever is lovely, whatever is commendable, if something is excellent or praiseworthy, think about these things. And what you learned and received and heard and saw in me, do these things. And the God of peace will be with you.

If we fill our minds with truth and righteousness, then the devil will have less opportunity to tempt us. Every day we must fill our minds with truth by thinking on Scripture through our reading, worshiping, and even entertainment, if at all possible.

Application Question: In what ways does Satan commonly attack your mind and emotions? How do you take rogue thoughts and emotions captive and make them obedient to Christ?

Are you putting on the breastplate of righteousness? Are you recognizing Christ's imputed righteousness, living a life, and guarding your heart and emotions? Without these practices, you are opening the door to the devil.

Application Question: Which aspect of the breastplate of righteousness stood out most to you and why?

Conclusion

How can believers stand firm in spiritual warfare—the attacks of Satan and his demons?

1. Believers Stand Firm by Putting on the Belt of Truth

- through knowing the content of truth as revealed in Scripture
- through living a life of honesty and integrity
- through being fully committed to God

2. Believers Stand Firm by Putting on the Breastplate of Righteousness

- through recognizing the imputed righteousness of Christ
- through living a righteous life
- through guarding their hearts

The Footwear of Peace and the Shield of Faith

> By fitting your feet with the preparation that comes from the good news of peace, and in all of this, by taking up the shield of faith with which you can extinguish all the flaming arrows of the evil one.
> Ephesians 6:15-16 (NET)

How can we stand firm in spiritual warfare? When we became Christians, we gained an enemy. Satan and his demons desire to steal our peace and joy, kill our physical bodies, and destroy our witness and callings. In this final section of Ephesians, Paul addresses this war and how Christians must stand firm. We stand firm in the strength and power of the Lord—apart from this, we will be destroyed (Eph 6:10). But we also stand firm by putting on the full armor of God (Eph 6:11). Each piece must be firmly put in place. The armor of God refers to righteous character traits (cf. Col 3:12). Therefore, sin in the life of believers gives the devil a foothold to destroy us and others.

Previously, we looked at the belt of truth and the breastplate of righteousness. Each piece of armor not only represents character traits but also, through implication, how Satan attacks. The belt of truth reminds us that Satan is a liar and that he constantly uses deception. The breastplate of righteousness reminds us that Satan attacks our vital organs representing our mind and emotions and also that sin in general opens a door for him.

In Ephesians 6:15-16, we will consider the footwear of peace and the breastplate of righteousness, as well as its implications about Satan's schemes.

Big Questions: How can believers stand firm by putting on the footwear of peace and the breastplate of righteousness? What do these two pieces of armor represent?

Believers Stand Firm by Putting On the Footwear of Peace

> By fitting your feet with the preparation that comes from the good news of peace,

Ephesians 6:15

When Paul talks about "fitting your feet with the preparation that comes from the good news of peace," he is picturing the footwear of a Roman soldier. They typically wore a half-boot with the toes uncovered and spikes coming out of the soles. The boots allowed "the soldier to be ready to march, climb, fight, or do whatever else is necessary."[254] The spikes specifically helped when hiking or on slippery surfaces.

Without the right shoes, the soldier's feet were prone to blisters, cuts, and other problems which put him at a disadvantage in battle. The soldier's shoes were very important—without them, he wasn't ready to fight.

Similarly, there is appropriate footwear for believers to wear in spiritual battles. It is the readiness that comes from the gospel of peace. As with the other pieces of armor, commentators are not unanimous on what this represents. It could represent several things, as outlined below.

Interpretation Question: What does feet fitted with the readiness that comes from the gospel of peace represent?

1. The readiness that comes from the gospel of peace represents appropriating the believer's peace with God.

Romans 5:1 says, "Therefore, since we have been declared righteous by faith, we have peace with God through our Lord Jesus Christ."

This is important because the enemy always aims to separate believers from God. It is God who gives believers the strength to put on God's armor and the power to conquer the devil. Therefore, the enemy always seeks to separate Christians from the source of all that is good. Sometimes he uses lies to foster anger at God. He often begins by cultivating a wrong view of God. Believers start to believe that God doesn't love them or want what's best for them—that he just doesn't care. Satan creates a caricature of God—a God of wrath but not a God of love, a God of judgment but not a God of mercy. However, God is all of these.

We must put on the gospel of peace by remembering that Christ died to bridge the chasm between us and God. He paid the penalty for our sins and gave us his righteousness so that we could know God and come into his presence. Jesus says, "Now this is eternal life – that they know you, the only true God, and Jesus Christ, whom you sent" (John 17:3). Christ died so we could come near God and have an intimate relationship with him.

In fact, Christ always strove to correct the disciples' thinking about God. In Luke 11:13, he said, "If you then, although you are evil, know how to give good gifts to your children, how much more will the heavenly Father give the Holy Spirit to those who ask him!" Christ wanted the disciples to know that their Abba desired to give them the greatest gifts—and it's the same for us. Do you know that our God wants to bless us, and that if we're in Christ we're at peace with him?

What is your view of God? Is he unloving, removed, strict, and overbearing? If so, you need to put on the footwear of peace—by recognizing that Christ removed the barrier between God and us. A wrong image of God destroys our footing. We cannot fight if we don't see God as he is: our Father, our Abba, our friend, and our spouse.

Are you wearing the footwear of peace?

2. The readiness that comes from the gospel of peace represents having the peace of God.

Not only has God given each of us peace with himself, but we also have the peace of God. In John 14:27, Jesus says, "Peace I leave with you; my peace I give to you; I do not give it to you as the world does. Do not let your hearts be distressed or lacking in courage." The peace Christ had while asleep in the boat during the storm, the peace that enabled him to go to the cross, he has given to us. It is not God's will for us to live in anxiety, fear, and worry. Scripture says, "Do not be afraid," "Do not worry," and "Do not be anxious about anything" (Phil 4:6). Christ has given us the promise of his peace.

If you are worried, anxious, and fearful, you have the wrong footwear for this battle. Our enemy is a roaring lion seeking whom he may devour (1 Peter 5:8). The lion roars to incite fear in his prey. Some believers are fearful about their future; others are fearful about what others think or say. Others are afraid of failure. These fears undermine the footing of Christians—our readiness for battle comes from God's peace.

Therefore, God commands us to put on his peace. Colossians 3:15 says, "Let the peace of Christ be in control in your heart (for you were in fact called as one body to this peace), and be thankful." Paul also refers to the peace of Christ as clothing to be worn (cf. Col 3:12). As believers, we must let God's peace rule in our hearts—not fear of failure, losing our jobs, or rejection. Satan wants to lead us as slaves through fear, but God guides us as children through his peace (cf. Rom 8:15).

Do you have peace in your heart? Or are you tormented by fear?

First John 4:18 says, "There is no fear in love, but perfect love drives out fear, because fear has to do with punishment. The one who fears punishment has not been perfected in love." A good earthly father doesn't want his children worried about food, drink, and clothing. He doesn't want his children worried about their future. As much as he can control events, he does so for their good. It's the same with our heavenly Father—except that, unlike our earthly fathers, he is all-wise and all-powerful. He wants us to know that he loves us and that he works all things for our good (cf. Rom 8:28).

Are you wearing the footwear of peace, or are you wearing fear, anxiety, and torment?

Application Question: How can we put on the peace of God instead of fear and anxiety?

Philippians 4:6-7 says,

Do not be anxious about anything. Instead, in every situation, through prayer and petition with thanksgiving, tell your requests to God. And the peace of God that surpasses all understanding will guard your hearts and minds in Christ Jesus.

- If we are going to have God's peace, we must reject anxiety and fear. They are not God's will for us, and they are sinful. They say, "God, you are not to be trusted," or "You are not in control."

- If we are going to have God's peace, we must learn to pray about everything. Prayer must become the atmosphere we live in. When we are not living in prayer (i.e. God's presence), the storms of life will constantly frighten and overwhelm us.

- If we are going to have God's peace, we must learn to give thanks in everything. When we complain, murmur, and criticize, we lose the peace of God.

3. The readiness that comes from the gospel of peace represents spreading the gospel.

The association of feet with the gospel is not uncommon in Scripture. Isaiah 52:7 says, "How delightful it is to see approaching over the mountains the feet of a messenger who announces peace, a messenger who brings good news, who announces deliverance, who says to Zion, "Your God reigns!" In Romans 10:15 (ESV), Paul says, "And how are they to preach unless they are sent? As it is written, 'How beautiful are the feet of those who preach the good news!'" One of our responsibilities in this war is to share the gospel with others. It is each person's assignment. Second Corinthians 5:18-20 says:

And all these things are from God who reconciled us to himself through Christ, and who has given us the ministry of reconciliation. In other words, in Christ God was reconciling the world to himself, not counting people's trespasses against them, and he has given us the message of reconciliation. Therefore we are ambassadors for Christ, as though

God were making His plea through us. We plead with you on Christ's behalf, "Be reconciled to God!"

In hand to hand combat, if one side is only playing defense, he will eventually be defeated. He must also attack. Our battle as believers is not just defensive; it is, in fact, primarily offensive. We are called to advance the kingdom of God by spreading the gospel everywhere in the name of Jesus. If you are not doing so, you won't stand firm. The enemy's offensive will eventually swallow you up.

Are you spreading the gospel? Is that your purpose at school, work, and home, and with family and friends?

Our feet must always be ready with the gospel. First Peter 3:15-16 says, "But set Christ apart as Lord in your hearts and always be ready to give an answer to anyone who asks about the hope you possess. Yet do it with courtesy and respect."

I think this also shows us how Satan attacks. He wants to attack our zeal for the gospel. He wants to quiet us. If we have lost our zeal, then we no longer are wearing the footwear of peace.

4. The readiness that comes from the gospel of peace represents peace in our relationships with others.

This is one of the major themes of Ephesians. Paul teaches the mystery of the gospel that God makes the Jew and Gentile one in Christ. Consider Ephesians 2:12-14:

> that you were at that time without the Messiah, alienated from the citizenship of Israel and strangers to the covenants of promise, having no hope and without God in the world. But now in Christ Jesus you who used to be far away have been brought near by the blood of Christ. For he is our peace, the one who made both groups into one and who destroyed the middle wall of partition, the hostility

Animosity between Jew and Gentile was a major issue for the early church. In Acts 6, the Jews neglected the Greek widows in the daily distribution while providing for the Hebrew widows. However, Paul said Christ is our peace—he has made us one.

Surely disunity is one of the major weapons the enemy uses against our churches. Sometimes he brings disunity through racism, as seen with the Jews and Gentiles in the early church. Sometimes he uses doctrine. What God means to equip and strengthen us, the enemy uses to bring division and discord. Most times, he just uses pride. Pride says, "My way is the only way, and it can't be done any other way." Churches divide over changing the color of the carpet, the music, the flow of worship services, and any other thing. The root of this is pride—"my way is the only way."

In attacking the church, Satan seeks to bring division. Remember, Paul says in Ephesians 4:26-27 not to let the sun go down while we are angry, and not to give the devil a foothold. Christ is our peace.

Are you living in peace with those around you? As much as depends on you, live at peace with all men (Rom 12:18).

Application Question: In what ways have you experienced Satan's attacks through division in your relationships—friends, family, co-workers, and church members? How have those experiences affected you and your relationship with God?

Are you wearing the right footwear for our spiritual war? Are you recognizing our peace with God? He loves us and cares for us. Are you being filled with the peace of God in your circumstances? Are you sharing the gospel—always prepared to give a defense of the hope that is in you? Finally, are you living at peace with all men, as much as depends on you?

Application Question: In what ways does the enemy constantly attack your readiness from the gospel of peace? How is God calling you to put on his footwear?

Believers Stand Firm by Taking Up the Shield of Faith

and in all of this, by taking up the shield of faith with which you can extinguish all the flaming arrows of the evil one.
Ephesians 6:16

The Greek word "thureos," translated "shield," referred to a large shield about two and half feet wide and four and a half feet high. It was designed to protect the entire body of a soldier. The shield was like a door—made of solid wood and covered with metal or leather. It was often dipped in water to extinguish the fiery arrows of the enemy.[255]

Armies often wrapped pieces of cloth around arrows, soaked them in pitch, set them on fire, and then shot them at the enemy. Upon contact an arrow would often "spatter burning bits for several feet, igniting anything flammable it touched."[256]

Our enemy also shoots flaming arrows at us. He shoots the arrows of criticism, fear, covetousness, anger, depression, doubt, lust, and every other temptation. In order to stand firm, we must take up the shield of faith.

Interpretation Question: What is the shield of faith and how can believers take it up?

1. The shield of faith refers to trust in God's person.

When Abram was struggling with fear, God said to him, "Fear not, Abram! I am your shield and the one who will reward you in great abundance" (Gen 15:1). Essentially, God said, "Trust me. I will protect you and reward you." Our protection is God himself and we must trust in him.

Putting on the shield of faith means running to God when life is difficult, when life is good, and when life is mundane. Believers without the shield of faith will run to everything else before God. When in a trial, they will run to coffee, to cigarettes, to relationships, to pity parties, etc. However, when we're wearing the shield of faith, we'll run to God. He is our shield—therefore we must trust him.

Application Question: How can we learn to trust God more?

•   Believers learn to trust God by knowing his character.

Proverbs 18:10 says, "The name of the Lord is like a strong tower; the righteous person runs to it and is set safely on high." In the ancient world, a person's name was not simply what he was called; it referred to his character. The writer of the proverb says that knowing God's character is a tremendous protection for us. The more we know God and who he is, the stronger we can stand in spiritual warfare.

At the same time, the less we know God and his character, the more prone we'll be to believe Satan's lies and stumble.

We must understand that God is perfect, all-knowing, all-present, and all-powerful. We must know that he loves us, cares for us, and wants the best for us. We must understand that he is sovereign and in control of all events—nothing happens apart from his watchful eye. If we don't understand this, we will be prone to anxiety, fear, and anger. God works all things according to the purpose of his will (Eph 1:11).

•   Believers learn to trust God by knowing his promises.

God has given us many promises to help us stand in spiritual warfare. Second Peter 1:3-4 says,

> I can pray this because his divine power has bestowed on us everything necessary for life and godliness through the rich knowledge of the one who called us by his own glory and excellence. Through

these things he has bestowed on us his precious and most magnificent promises, so that by means of what was promised you may become partakers of the divine nature, after escaping the worldly corruption that is produced by evil desire.

When tempted to fear, we take hold of Philippians 4:6-7—if we pray and give thanks in everything, the peace of God will guard our hearts and minds. When we feel like giving up, we hold on to Isaiah 40:31— those who wait on the Lord shall renew their strength. When burnt out, we take courage in Proverbs 11:25—those who refresh others shall themselves be refreshed. When weak, we hold on to 2 Corinthians 12:9—God's power is made perfect in our weakness; therefore, we will boast in our infirmities and trials. When God seems distant, we hold on to James 4:8—if we draw near God, he will draw near us.

Are you taking up the shield of faith by holding on to God's promises? God has given us many promises to help us to stand in the day of evil.

- Believers learn to trust God by faithfully walking with him.

The longer we walk with God, the more we will trust him. As we watch God part our Red Seas, defeat our Goliaths, close the mouths of lions, and use the evil intentions and actions of others for good, it enables us to trust him more.

Are you spending time with God—being in his presence? The less you are with a person, the less you will trust them. In order to be ready for this battle, you must live in the presence of God—walking faithfully with him.

What else does the shield of faith refer to?

2. The shield of faith refers to dependence on the body of Christ.

In ancient times, the edges of this shield were "so constructed that an entire line of soldiers could interlock shields and march into the enemy like a solid wall. This suggests that we Christians are not in the battle alone."[257]

The enemy attacks from every direction, and we need one another to stand firm. Yes, doing so is a struggle since the church is not perfect, as God is. However, it is the means through which God chooses to impart his grace. He works through an imperfect body. If we don't avail ourselves of the body's resources, we leave ourselves more vulnerable to the devil's attacks.

For this reason, Satan works overtime to pull people away from the church by accusing and condemning it. Yes, the church is full of sinners; in fact, it is full of both weeds and wheat (cf. Matt 13:24-30). However, every army is full of people with flaws, but without trust in one another, no army can stand.

Therefore, in order to put on the shield of faith, we must depend upon the body of Christ—just like Roman soldiers depended on one another.

Are you depending on the body of Christ? Are you confessing your sins to one another and praying for one another (James 5:16)? Are you speaking the truth in love to one another (Eph 4:15)?

3.   The shield of faith refers to living a life of faith—a life of serving God.

In ancient Roman armies, the people holding the thureos—the large shields—were always at the front of the army. They were the front line. When they lifted their shields, they protected those behind them. This also allowed the archers to shoot arrows while under their protection. Therefore, to put on the shield of faith means to live a life of faith—serving God.

It means stepping out of our comfort zone to serve in a ministry. It means using our gifts to serve the church. When we do so, we'll be criticized by others, and we'll be attacked emotionally, physically and spiritually by the enemy. But as we stand firm against these attacks with the shield of faith, we protect others and help them grow as they benefit from our faith.

To never get involved, use our spiritual gifts, or build others up means to not use the shield of faith. In fact, those not serving, not involved, often aren't the focus of the enemy. Why waste resources on somebody who's not fighting?

However, the more serious we get about God—the more we pursue God and serve others—the more Satan will attack us. In some ways, we should find encouragement from being attacked—this means we are a threat. And if we are not being attacked by the enemy, we should be alarmed. Maybe, we are not in the battle.

Application Question: In what ways have you experienced more spiritual attacks when pursuing and serving God?

Are you daily taking up the shield of faith? Are you living a life of faith or a life of fear? Are you depending on the body of Christ, or are you independent? Are you on the front line or the sidelines? If we are going to stand firm, we must take up the shield of faith.

Application Question: What aspects of the shield of faith stood out most and why? How is God calling you to take up his shield?

Conclusion

How can we stand firm in spiritual warfare?

1.   Believers Stand Firm by Putting on the Footwear of Peace

- As they appropriate the believers' peace with God

- As they appropriate the peace of God
- As they share the gospel with others
- As they walk in peace with others

2. Believers Stand Firm by Taking up the Shield of Faith

- As they trust in God's person
- As they depend on the body of Christ
- As they pursue and serve God

The Helmet of Salvation and the Sword of the Spirit

And take the helmet of salvation and the sword of the Spirit, which is the word of God.
Ephesians 6:17 (NET)

In studying the armor of God and our need to stand in spiritual warfare, we must remember that each piece of armor not only represents an action or attitude that we need to daily practice, but it also represents ways our enemy attacks us.

We need the belt of truth because Satan is a liar who tries to deceive us and keep us from God's best. We need the breastplate of righteousness because Satan continually attacks our vital organs which represent our mind and emotions. In addition, when believers sin, we become vulnerable to our enemy. Believers need the footing of peace because Satan is always trying to attack our relationship with God and our relationships with others. The gospel, truly understood and applied, produces peace with God, the peace of God, and peace with others. The last piece of armor considered was the shield of faith. Our enemy always encourages us to doubt God and his promises. However, it is by believing in God and his promises that we can stand in the war.

In today's study, we will consider two more pieces of armor—the helmet of salvation and the sword of the Spirit. We will consider what they represent, why we need them, and how to put them on.

Big Questions: How can we stand firm in spiritual warfare with the helmet of salvation and the sword of the Spirit? What do they represent, why do we need them, and how do we put them on?

Believers Stand Firm by Putting On the Helmet of Salvation

And take the helmet of salvation and the sword of the Spirit, which is the word of God.
Ephesians 6:17

Here, Paul pictures the Roman soldier's helmet. James Boice's comments are helpful:

> The helmet had a band to protect the forehead and plates for the cheeks, and extended down in back to protect the neck. When the helmet was strapped in place, it exposed little besides the eyes, nose, and mouth. The metal helmets, due to their weight, were lined with sponge or felt. Virtually the only weapons which could penetrate a metal helmet were hammers or axes.[3]

In warfare, the enemy commonly attacked the head since the solder's mind controlled his decisions and reactions in a fight. To harm the head was to gain an advantage in combat. Our enemy, Satan, does the same.

Interpretation Question: What does the helmet of salvation represent?

1. The helmet of salvation represents assurance of salvation.

As with every other piece of armor, the helmet of salvation shows us how the enemy attacks. Here we see how he attacks the believer's assurance of salvation. Satan's use of assurance is actually two pronged. He seeks to assure professed believers who are not truly saved that they are, in fact, "safe," and he plants seeds of doubt in those who are truly saved, leading to discouragement and depression. Personally, I've noticed it is often the Christians who are walking faithfully with God that struggle the most with assurance. And those who are not walking faithfully with him are not very concerned about their salvation at all, even though they should be.

When true believers are constantly worried about their salvation, they are not much use to the kingdom of God. They typically don't evangelize or serve. They essentially stop growing because they are too concerned with themselves. This is why attacking the head is a common tactic of Satan—it makes a Christian unprofitable.

Application Question: How can believers be assured of their salvation?

• Believers must recognize their need for assurance.

In many churches, pastors never teach on the need for assurance of salvation. It's almost a forgotten doctrine. However, this is unwise. Christ says this about the last days:

On that day, many will say to me, 'Lord, Lord, didn't we prophesy in your name, and in your name cast out demons and do many powerful deeds?' Then I will declare to them, 'I never knew you. Go away from me, you lawbreakers!'
Matthew 7:22-2

Many in the church profess Christ but are not saved. Jesus explains this in the Parable of the Weeds and Wheat (Matt 13:36-43). God plants wheat—true believers—and Satan plants weeds—false believers. Because of this reality, we must consider if we are truly saved.

Paul and Peter both taught the need for assurance. Second Corinthians 13:5 says this: "Put yourselves to the test to see if you are in the faith; examine yourselves! Or do you not recognize regarding yourselves that Jesus Christ is in you – unless, indeed, you fail the test!" Similarly, 2 Peter 1:10 says: "Therefore, brothers and sisters, make every effort to be sure of your calling and election. For by doing this you will never stumble into sin."

All believers must examine themselves to see if their salvation is real. This is not something to put off; we must eagerly pursue such assurance. The first step is to recognize our need for it in light of the fact that Scripture commands us to seek it.

- Believers must use the tests in Scripture to confirm their salvation.

Several portions of Scripture are written specifically for this purpose. The primary text is the book of 1 John. John says, "I have written these things to you who believe in the name of the Son of God so that you may know that you have eternal life" (1 John 5:13). In the book, he gives a series of tests so we can know that we have eternal life.

Application Question: What are some of these tests?

✓ The test of obedience.

First John 2:3-5 says,

Now by this we know that we have come to know God: if we keep his commandments. The one who says "I have come to know God" and yet does not keep his commandments is a liar, and the truth is not in such a person. But whoever obeys his word, truly in this person the love of God has been perfected. By this we know that we are in him.

Faithful obedience to God and his Word is a proof of true salvation. Christ says, "If you abide in my words, then you are truly my disciples" (John

8:31, ESV). If we don't love his Word and continually follow it, we have no reason to call ourselves Christians in the first place.

Are you abiding in his Word?

✓ The test of love for Christians.
First John 3:14-15 says,

We know that we have crossed over from death to life because we love our fellow Christians. The one who does not love remains in death. Everyone who hates his fellow Christian is a murderer, and you know that no murderer has eternal life residing in him.

Similarly, Jesus says, "Everyone will know by this that you are my disciples – if you have love for one another" (John 13:35). If we are lacking a supernatural love for other believers, then we are not his disciples. At spiritual birth, the love of God is shed abroad in our hearts by the Holy Spirit (Romans 5:5).

I really struggle when I meet people who profess Christ but say they don't need to attend church. If they are true Christians, they will want to attend church. Why? Not just out of love for God, but also out of love for other believers. They will want to be with believers and use their gifts to build them up. They will want to pray with them and serve them. This is a natural fruit of love. If a person doesn't even want to be around the church, then they don't love the believers and surely they are not saved.

Do you love your brothers?

✓ The test of doctrine.

First John 4:15 says, "If anyone confesses that Jesus is the Son of God, God resides in him and he in God." This is a proper acknowledgment of Christ's humanity and deity. (The name "Jesus" represents his humanity and "Son of God" represents his deity). This is what keeps many cult members out of heaven—they have bad Christology. To them, Christ was either not a man or not God. He was an angel or something else. In the above statement John was refuting the doctrine of the Gnostic cult, which was attacking the Ephesian church. It's also a problem in many cults today and for many professing "Christians." They believe Christ was a good man and a good religious teacher, but not the Son of God.

Do you pass the doctrinal test?

✓ The test of not loving the World.

First John 2:15 says, "Do not love the world or the things in the world. If anyone loves the world, the love of the Father is not in him."

True believers are different from the world and the culture around them. Where the rich man was not willing to leave his riches to follow Christ (Matt 19:16-22), the true believer is willing to leave the praise, adoration and riches of this world for the kingdom of God (cf. Lk 14:26-27).

It is sobering to consider that the rich man was highly spiritual. We know he appeared righteous-because he kept the law; he also desired eternal life. Since we can't see the heart, we would have quickly taught him the Four Spiritual Laws, then had him say the Sinner's Prayer and join the church. Because he was an upright person and a successful businessman, he would soon have been an elder in most churches. However, he had never been born again. He was living for the riches of the world and not for God.

Many professed believers are kept out of the kingdom because they don't truly love God. They love him only for what they can get. They want the riches of this world—health and wealth—but they don't want a Lord and they don't want a cross. Sadly, this might be the majority of "Christians," especially because of the widespread influence of the prosperity gospel.

Are you willing to reject the world and the things of the world to follow Christ? Or—like the rich man—do you want both salvation and the things of this world?

✓ The test of decreasing sin.

First John 3:6,9 says,

Everyone who resides in him does not sin; everyone who sins has neither seen him nor known him... Everyone who has been fathered by God does not practice sin, because God's seed resides in him, and thus he is not able to sin, because he has been fathered by God.

John says, "everyone who has been fathered by God does not practice sin." This was the professing Christians' problem in Matthew 7:21-23. Jesus said to them, "'I never knew you. Go away from me, you lawbreakers!'" They professed Christ, but lived a life of sin. True salvation always changes the lifestyle of believers (2 Cor 5:17). They still sin, but the direction and pattern of their lives will be different. They will practice living for God and yet stumble—sometimes repeatedly. However, the direction of their lives will have changed—they will be trying to serve and honor God.

Is there a pattern of decreasing sin in your life? Or do you profess Christ, but not live for him?

✓ The test of persecution for righteousness.

First John 3:12-13 says,

> ...not like Cain who was of the evil one and brutally murdered his brother. And why did he murder him? Because his deeds were evil, but his brother's were righteous. Therefore do not be surprised, brothers and sisters, if the world hates you.

Because of their changed lives and values, believers will often be hated and persecuted by society. Jesus gives persecution as a test of salvation. In Matthew 5:10, he says, "Blessed are those who are persecuted for righteousness, for the kingdom of heaven belongs to them."

He essentially says that those who are persecuted for their faith are part of the kingdom of heaven. This doesn't necessarily mean that we will all be beaten, stoned, or jailed. Persecution often shows up in more subtle ways, like verbal abuse or being considered strange. First Peter 4:3-4 says,

> For the time that has passed was sufficient for you to do what the non-Christians desire. You lived then in debauchery, evil desires, drunkenness, carousing, drinking bouts, and wanton idolatries. So they are astonished when you do not rush with them into the same flood of wickedness, and they vilify you.

Do others find you strange because you don't get drunk like everybody else? Do people find you strange because you have chosen to practice chastity until marriage? This is normal for a Christian. You will receive some type of persecution from the world.

✓ The test of perseverance.

First John 2:19 says, "They went out from us, but they did not really belong to us, because if they had belonged to us, they would have remained with us. But they went out from us to demonstrate that all of them do not belong to us." In talking about those leaving the Ephesian church to join the Gnostic cult, John says that they left because they were never truly saved. This is the final truth that we will consider. Those who are truly born again will continue to walk with Christ and will never ultimately turn their backs on him (cf. Matt 24:13).

Similarly, Paul says this in Colossians 1:22-23:

> but now he has reconciled you by his physical body through death to present you holy, without blemish, and blameless before him – if indeed you remain in the faith, established and firm, without shifting from the hope of the gospel that you heard. This gospel has also been

preached in all creation under heaven, and I, Paul, have become its servant.

Our reconciliation to God is proved by a faith that endures and continues in the hope of the gospel.

Are you still following Christ? Is your faith enduring?

These are just a few of the tests. All the Beatitudes are essentially tests of salvation, and the book of James has many as well. James says, "Faith without works is dead" (2:26). If our faith doesn't change us, it won't change our eternal destiny either.

Are you continually examining yourself? Has God given you a love for the saints and for his Word? Do you believe that Jesus is the perfect God-man?

Again, this challenge to test our salvation has almost been lost in the church. Therefore, we are amassing professing believers who are not really saved. And many who are saved don't know how to put on the helmet of salvation—referring to assurance—which makes them an easy target for the accusations of the devil.

Paul often teaches assurance side by side with the need to respond to the gospel. In Acts 26:20 he says, "but I declared to those in Damascus first, and then to those in Jerusalem and in all Judea, and to the Gentiles, that they should repent and turn to God, performing deeds consistent with repentance." Essentially, we prove our salvation by growing and producing the fruit of righteousness (cf. 2 Peter 1:10, 5-9).

It should be noted that salvation is eternal. Eternal security is an objective reality based on what Christ has done for us. He gives us eternal life and he keeps us (cf. John 6:37-39, John 10:27-30, Rom 8:38-39). Those who are truly saved will never lose their salvation. They will persevere in following Christ to the end.

However, assurance is not eternal. It is a subjective experience given by the Holy Spirit, and it can be temporary. Romans 8:15-16 says,

> For you did not receive the spirit of slavery leading again to fear, but you received the Spirit of adoption, by whom we cry, "Abba, Father." The Spirit himself bears witness to our spirit that we are God's children.

The Holy Spirit assures our hearts primarily by changing us into the Father's image—making us holy. Therefore, when believers are faithfully walking with God, they can clearly discern the Holy Spirit's assurance that they are children of God. But when believers are living in sin, they commonly start to lose that assurance.

Do you have assurance? Do you have on the helmet of salvation? Satan wants to steal the joy of your salvation. He wants to steal your calling and the good works God has called you to. If you don't know you're saved, then your head is vulnerable and you're not prepared to fight.

What else could the helmet of salvation represent?

2. The helmet of salvation represents anticipation of our future salvation.

First Thessalonians 5:8 says, "But since we are of the day, we must stay sober by putting on the breastplate of faith and love and as a helmet our hope for salvation." Paul calls the helmet the hope of salvation. James Boice's comments are helpful here:

> If that is what he is thinking of here, then he is looking to our destiny rather than our present state. He is saying that our anticipation of that end will protect our heads in the heat (and often confusion) of the battle.[258]

Therefore, if we have lost the hope of our future salvation, we will not be able to stand in this spiritual battle. The luxuries of the world will draw us into idolatry and spiritual lethargy; the trials and persecutions in this world will draw our hearts away from God and our heavenly home. However, when believers hope in their salvation, that hope keeps them from living for the world and/or fearing persecution by the world.

Consider what Paul says in 2 Corinthians 4:16-18:

> Therefore we do not despair, but even if our physical body is wearing away, our inner person is being renewed day by day. For our momentary, light suffering is producing for us an eternal weight of glory far beyond all comparison because we are not looking at what can be seen but at what cannot be seen. For what can be seen is temporary, but what cannot be seen is eternal.

Paul says he and the other apostles did not lose heart during their trials because their eyes were fixed on eternity. His trials seemed like light afflictions because he was focused on the glory of heaven. This focus kept him from becoming unraveled when going through temporary trials. He was wearing the helmet of salvation. In Philippians 1:21, Paul says, "For to me, living is Christ and dying is gain." He was ready to die a martyr for Christ because of his hope in salvation.

And surely this is true of many great missionaries who go into foreign territories and wage war against the powers and principalities for the souls of men. They do not hold their lives or comfort dear because their hope is eternal. Their eyes are fixed on the unseen and not on the seen. And this must be true for us as well.

Here we can discern one of Satan's most effective modes of attack. He attacks our heads by drawing our attention away from the eternal to the temporary. If our hope is on earth and earthly things—jobs, promotions, wealth, health, and the applause of men—we will be ineffective soldiers in this spiritual war. We will be unstable—up and down with the events of life. The enemy will continually attack our heads because they are unprotected—they are focused on the world instead of eternity.

Is death really gain for you, or is it the loss of all you live for? Can you rejoice while going through a trial, not getting promoted, or going through criticism—because your hope is on heavenly things and not on earthly things? If so, you are ready for war—you are ready to stand firm in this spiritual battle.

Application Questions: What is your belief about eternal security? Can believers lose their salvation or is it eternally kept by Christ? Briefly support your view. How can believers develop assurance of their salvation and why is it important? If the helmet of salvation refers to our hope of salvation, how can we keep our eyes on the eternal instead of the earthly?

Believers Stand Firm by Taking Up the Sword of the Spirit

> And take the helmet of salvation and the sword of the Spirit, which is the word of God.
> Ephesians 6:17

Interpretation Question: What is the sword of the Spirit?

The sword Paul refers to is not the broadsword (rhomphaia) but the dagger (machaira), which varied in length from six to eighteen inches. It was the common sword used by Roman soldiers in hand-to-hand combat, and was carried in a sheath attached to the belt.[259]

A skillful soldier used it to deflect the blows of his enemy, and the Word of God must be used in this fashion. We get a picture of this when Satan attacked Christ in the wilderness (Matt 4). To each of Satan's temptations, Christ responded with Scripture. Therefore, the Christian who does not know the Word of God well will have problems defending against the attacks of the devil.

What's interesting about Paul's description of the sword as the "word" of God is the Greek term used. John MacArthur says:

> The term Paul uses here for word is not logos, which refers to general statements or messages, but is rhēma, which refers to individual words or particular statements. The apostle is therefore not talking here about

general knowledge of Scripture, but is emphasizing again the precision that comes by knowledge and understanding of specific truths.[260]

James Boice adds:

While logos embraces nearly everything, rhēma has a slighter weight. It really means "a saying," in this case, a particular, specific portion of God's written revelation. John 3:16 is a rhēma. Romans 3:23 is a rhēma, and so on for all the other specific portions of the written "Word of God." It is important to see this, as I said, because according to Paul's teaching we are to overcome Satan by the particular words or portions of Scripture.[261]

This emphasizes the extreme power of each Scripture verse. Christ said that man shall not live by bread alone but by "EVERY" word that comes from the mouth of God (Matt 4:4). Scripture is God-inspired and powerful. It can translate a person from darkness to light and defeat the attacks of the devil. Therefore, we must know and love God's Word.

However, even though most Christians would say they believe this, in practice they deny it. Though they know Scripture equips the man of God for all righteousness and that each saying is powerful (cf. 2 Tim 3:16-17), they largely neglect it. Sadly, this is also seen in most preaching today. Instead of messages that drive the sword home, setting people free from sin and sharpening their consciences, most sermons are a chain of illustrations to support the pastor's thoughts, which may or may not come from Scripture.

For some preachers, this happens because of laziness. It takes hard work to really preach God's Word. But for many, it probably happens simply because they don't really believe how powerful each Word from God is. Each rhema—each verse of Scripture—is a surgical scalpel—needed to save and heal lives. We cannot fend off Satan with stories and illustrations, no matter how much people enjoy them. They need the Word of God.

Both in the pulpit and in the pew, people profess to believe in the power and necessity of the Word of God, yet they deny it by their actions.

Moses tells the Jews to talk about the Word of God at home, when walking along the road, when lying down, and when getting up (Deut 6:7). At that time, the Jews had only a few books of the Bible to talk about, but we have the whole written counsel of God. However, we probably talk about it much less than they did.

Application Question: How do we take up the sword of the Spirit?

The word "take" is a command. If we are going to fight this spiritual battle, we must take the sword of the Spirit—the Word of God.

1. We take up the sword of the Spirit by reading Scripture.

Most Christians have never completely read the Bible. By reading 3.25 chapters a day, or slightly over twelve minutes a day, one can complete the Bible in a year. Or, if a person reads only thirteen chapters a day, they can complete the Bible in three months. Isn't it do-able to read six or seven chapters in the morning and six or seven at night to complete the Bible in three months?

Are you taking up your sword by reading Scripture daily?

2. We take up the sword of the Spirit by memorizing Scripture.

Again, the "word" of God Paul refers to in 2 Tim 3:17 is specific sayings—not the whole of Scripture. Christ defeated the devil with specific Scriptures committed to memory. Similarly, Psalm 119:11 says, "In my heart I store up your words, so I might not sin against you."

Each verse that we memorize is a dagger to help us in spiritual warfare. How many daggers do you have memorized? If we memorize one verse a week that equals fifty-two verses a year.

3. We take up the sword of the Spirit by meditating on Scripture.

Psalm 1:2 talks about the blessing on the man who meditates on the law of God day and night. The word "meditate" in the Hebrew was used of a cow chewing its cud. A cow has a chambered stomach with four compartments. It chews and swallows its food, then regurgitates it and repeats the process. This usage of the word "meditate" also has the connotation of muttering under the breath. The Hebrew word used can be translated "ponder" or "declare."[262] It means to speak God's Word over and over again, both audibly and inaudibly.

God blesses the person who thinks and speaks about the Word of God all day. This person is taking up the sword of the Spirit.

Are you meditating on Scripture all day long—pondering it and talking about it?

4. We take up the sword of the Spirit by studying Scripture.

Second Timothy 2:15 (KJV) says, "Study to shew thyself approved unto God, a workman that needeth not to be ashamed, rightly dividing the word of truth." "Study," which can also be translated "Be diligent" or "Do your best," obviously overlaps with reading, memorizing and meditating.

Application Question: How can we practice studying Scripture?

- We study by taking notes during sermons, Bible studies, and our devotions in order to help commit the truths to memory.

- We study by comparing portions of Scripture with other portions in order to better understand the meaning and application.

- We study by using tools to increase our understanding, such as a study Bible, concordance, commentary, or theological dictionary (cf. Eph 4:11-13).

- We study by writing the truths in a systematic manner to organize our thoughts.

- We study by teaching the truths we're learning to others, which is the most effective way to internalize something.

One of the problems in the church today is that people don't want to study the Bible. They are "sluggish in hearing," and have to be retaught the same truths over and over. Hebrews 5:11-12 says this:

> On this topic we have much to say and it is difficult to explain, since you have become sluggish in hearing. For though you should in fact be teachers by this time, you need someone to teach you the beginning elements of God's utterances. You have gone back to needing milk, not solid food.

I think it is especially important for parents to teach their children how to study the Bible and not just listen—otherwise they will continue to lose what they learn. Again, 2 Timothy 2:15 says those who study—those who do their best—will be approved by God. Those who do not study don't really care about the truths they hear, and will therefore forget them. These people will not be approved by God.

Since our churches are filled with people who don't study (or care to study), most pastors can't teach the depths of God's Word. The writer of Hebrews says he wants to teach them more, but he can't because the congregation is "sluggish in hearing." What's happened in our day is that the church no longer teaches doctrine, but has handed that sacred task over to Bible colleges and seminaries. Most church services are filled with the milk of God's Word instead of the meat.

Doctrine needs to be restored to God's church, but the church also needs to be prepared to receive it. It's inspiring to read the sermons of Martin Luther, John Calvin, Jonathan Edwards, and Martyn Lloyd-Jones—the content is amazingly deep. For example, Martyn Lloyd-Jones preached 232 sermons on the book of Ephesians over an 8-year period (1954-1962).[263] However, the only way people can receive such content is by studying it.

If you're going to stand against Satan's attacks, you must take up the Sword of the Spirit—the Word of God—by reading, meditating on, memorizing, and studying it.

Application Question: What is your Bible study routine like? How can it be improved?

Conclusion

How can we stand firm by taking up the helmet of salvation and the sword of the Spirit?

1.   Believers Stand Firm by Putting on the Helmet of Salvation

Do you have assurance of salvation? Are you proving your salvation by growing and producing fruit?

Do you have the hope of your final salvation? If not, you will become worldly, earthly, and vulnerable to the temptations of the devil.

2.   Believers Stand Firm by Taking up the Sword of the Spirit

Are you taking up the sword by reading the Word, memorizing it, meditating on it, and studying it?

Prayer in the Spirit

With every prayer and petition, pray at all times in the Spirit, and to this end be alert, with all perseverance and requests for all the saints. Pray for me also, that I may be given the message when I begin to speak – that I may confidently make known the mystery of the gospel, for which I am an ambassador in chains. Pray that I may be able to speak boldly as I ought to speak.
Ephesians 6:18-20 (NET)

Paul talks about spiritual warfare in this final section of Ephesians. In Ephesians 6:10-17, he details the believer's need to be filled with the power of God, and also to put on the full armor of God in order to stand against the attacks of the devil. The armor of God represents attitudes and actions that believers must practice to win on the spiritual battlefield. It includes the belt of truth, the breastplate of righteousness, the footwear of peace, the shield of faith, the helmet of salvation, and the sword of the Spirit. No Christian soldier can win without them; however, even these are not enough. We must pray in the Spirit.

We can see Paul's emphasis on the importance of prayer in two ways. First, he writes more about prayer than about any other piece of armor. He uses three verses to teach on prayer in the Spirit. Also, praying in the Spirit is the seventh piece of armor. In Scripture, seven is the number of completion. This means that one can be suited up with every other piece of armor and yet still lose the battle. Praying in the Spirit is a necessity.

Prayer is the energy and atmosphere in which we wage war. Believers must live in prayer at all times in order to win this spiritual battle. It is how we are strengthened in the power of God, and it is how we put on the full armor (cf. Eph 6:10-11).

I think we can discern the importance of prayer by considering the battle between Israel and Amalek in Exodus 17. Joshua led Israel's army into battle, but they only won while Moses prayed. When Moses became tired of lifting his hands in prayer, Israel began to lose. And this is true for us as well. We can read the Word, preach, evangelize, and live a moral life, but if we are not praying, we will be defeated.

Similarly, when Peter was going to be tempted by Satan right before Christ's death, the Lord told him that he needed to pray in order not to fall into temptation (Matt 26:41). Peter fell asleep and therefore did not stand in the evil day. We are often like this as well. We sleep when we should be praying. We fight when we should be waiting on the Lord. Prayer is essential. "Edward Payson said: 'Prayer is the first thing, the second thing, the third thing necessary to minister. Pray, therefore, my dear brother, pray, pray, pray.'"[264]

Again, Paul doesn't call us to just any type of prayer, but specifically prayer in the Spirit. What is prayer in the Spirit? Praying in the Spirit does not refer to speaking in tongues or any other charismatic experience. It simply means to pray according to God's Word and according to his promptings. Jude also commands us to do this in Jude 1:20. He says, "But you, dear friends, by building yourselves up in your most holy faith, by praying in the Holy Spirit."

As we consider praying in the Spirit, we must ask, "What are the characteristics of this type of prayer?" It is important to know the answer so we can tell if we are indeed praying in the Spirit.

In this study, we will consider the characteristics of praying in the Spirit as seen in Ephesians 6:18-20. We will give more attention to this piece of armor than the others, even as Paul does.

Big Question: What are some aspects of prayer in the Spirit?

Prayer in the Spirit Is Constant

> With every prayer and petition, pray at all times in the Spirit …
> Ephesians 6:18

Paul says that in this spiritual war, we must pray at "all times"—we must live in constant prayer. This is how the early church prayed right before Pentecost. Acts 1:14 says, "All these continued together in prayer with one mind, together with the women, along with Mary the mother of Jesus, and his brothers." The 120 remaining followers of Christ met daily and devoted themselves to constant prayer. This was necessary for God to use them to turn the world upside down, as seen throughout the book of Acts. Similarly, 1 Thessalonians 5:17 says, "constantly pray," which can also be translated, "Pray without ceasing."

Interpretation Question: How do we pray without ceasing—on all occasions?

Does "pray without ceasing" mean we need to have a running dialogue with the Lord throughout the day? Not necessarily. Steve Cole shares helpful insight about the phrase "without ceasing":

> The Greek word translated without ceasing was used of a hacking cough and of repeated military assaults. Someone with a hacking cough does not cough every second, but rather he coughs repeatedly

and often. He never goes very long without coughing. In the case of repeated military assaults, the army makes an assault then regroups and attacks again and again until it conquers the city. In the same way, we should pray often and repeatedly until we gain the thing for which we are praying.[265]

"Prayer is not so much the articulation of words as the posture of the heart."[266] John MacArthur adds:

To pray at all times is to live in continual God consciousness, where everything we see and experience becomes a kind of prayer, lived in deep awareness of and surrender to our heavenly Father. To obey this exhortation means that, when we are tempted, we hold the temptation before God and ask for His help. When we experience something good and beautiful, we immediately thank the Lord for it. When we see evil around us, we pray that God will make it right and be willing to be used of Him to that end. When we meet someone who does not know Christ, we pray for God to draw that person to Himself and to use us to be a faithful witness. When we encounter trouble, we turn to God as our Deliverer. In other words, our life becomes a continually ascending prayer, a perpetual communing with our heavenly Father.[267]

If we are going to win this spiritual battle, we must learn how to pray without ceasing. We must return to it throughout the day like a hacking cough, and like an army launching continual military assaults. We must train ourselves to live in God's presence—bringing every thought and concern before the Lord. This is necessary in our spiritual battle.

Are you practicing prayer on all occasions?

Application Question: How do you aim to pray on all occasions? Are there any insights or disciplines that help you in this endeavor? How is God calling you to grow in constant prayer?

Prayer in the Spirit Is Varied

With every prayer and petition, pray at all times in the Spirit …
Ephesians 6:18

Praying in the Spirit includes "every prayer and petition." "Prayer" is a general term for various types of prayer, and "petition" is a specific type of prayer. Sadly, most Christians use only one type of prayer—petitions (or requests). They only come to God to ask for things. However, when the Spirit of God leads our prayer, he leads us into various types of prayer such as thanksgiving and worship, intercession, confession, lament, and corporate prayer, among others. All these types of prayer have the power to defeat the enemy.

When Israel shouted in worship while standing outside Jericho, the walls fell down (Joshua 6). When Jehoshaphat and the army worshiped while being attacked, God defeated the enemy (2 Chr 20). Many times when we are tempted to complain and worry, the Spirit of God calls us to praise in faith and God defeats our enemies.

In addition, the practice of corporate prayer carries much power. Consider what Jesus says in Matthew 18:19-20, "Again, I tell you the truth, if two of you on earth agree about whatever you ask, my Father in heaven will do it for you. For where two or three are assembled in my name, I am there among them." Jesus teaches that corporate prayer carries tremendous power, and that when it occurs, God is with us in a special way. Similarly, James 5:16 says, "So confess your sins to one another and pray for one another so that you may be healed. The prayer of a righteous person has great effectiveness."

Some Christians never access this type of prayer because they never share their burdens with others or carry others' burdens; therefore, they lack power. There are some things God does only when his people pray together.

When the Spirit of God is leading prayer, he leads us to pray in a variety of ways. A good picture of this is seen in the Lord's Prayer, which Christ gave as a pattern. Consider the following types of prayer:

- "Our Father in heaven, may your name be honored" (Matt. 6:9) calls us into worship, as we pray for others to worship as well.
- "May your kingdom come, may your will be done on earth as it is in heaven" (Matt. 6:10) calls us to pray for missions, evangelism, and discipleship.
- "Give us today our daily bread" (Matt. 6:11), calls us to pray for our personal needs and those of others.
- "And forgive us our debts, as we ourselves have forgiven our debtors" (Matt. 6:12), calls us to confess our sins and those of others.
- "And do not lead us into temptation, but deliver us from the evil one." (Matt. 6:13) calls us to pray for spiritual protection from temptation and the devil.

It is a good practice to pray often through the Lord's Prayer.

Application Question: What type(s) of prayer are you most prone to pray? How is God calling you to vary your prayers?

Prayer in the Spirit Is Watchful

> With every prayer and petition, pray at all times in the Spirit, and to this end be alert, with all perseverance and requests for all the saints.
> Ephesians 6:18

Another aspect of praying in the Spirit is being watchful. Paul says, "and to this end be alert." This is military terminology. It pictures a soldier on duty watching for signs of either infiltration by the enemy or advancement by his fellow soldiers. As Peter says in 1 Peter 5:8, "Be sober and alert. Your enemy the devil, like a roaring lion, is on the prowl looking for someone to devour."

Our enemy is like a prowling lion; therefore, we must always be alert. Christ warned his disciples right before he went to the cross in Matthew 26:41, "Stay awake and pray that you will not fall into temptation. The spirit is willing, but the flesh is weak." He called for the disciples to pray so they wouldn't fall into temptation. He called them to be aware of what the enemy was doing around them.

Application Question: How can Christian soldiers practice being alert in their prayer lives?

1. Christian soldiers practice being alert both by using their natural senses (like their eyes and ears), and by listening to the Spirit's promptings in order to discern the work of the evil one.

Is someone being unfaithful to the church or small group? Let us pray for God to draw them back. Is there discord in the body of Christ? Let us pray for unity. Is someone discouraged? Let us pray for joy.

What difficulties or attacks of the enemy are happening around you? How is God calling you to intercede?

2. Christian soldiers practice being alert by using their natural senses and listening to the Spirit's promptings to intercede on behalf of what God is doing.

We must understand that we are not just watching our enemy, but also our God. Is God changing somebody's heart? Let us give thanks and pray. Is he stirring a revival? Let us praise and intercede.

What is God doing around you? How is he calling you to intercede?

Application Question: What types of distractions commonly keep us from being spiritually alert? Are there any other practices that help with being spiritually alert?

Prayer in the Spirit Is Persevering

> With every prayer and petition, pray at all times in the Spirit, and to this end be alert, with all perseverance and requests for all the saints. Ephesians 6:18

Paul says that we must pray "with all perseverance." Prayer in the flesh is often short-lived, but Spirit-led prayer is persevering. This is especially important in spiritual warfare, because many of our blessings and victories come only through persevering prayer. Consider what Christ teaches in Luke 11:9-13:

> "So I tell you: Ask, and it will be given to you; seek, and you will find; knock, and the door will be opened for you. For everyone who asks receives, and the one who seeks finds, and to the one who knocks, the door will be opened. What father among you, if your son asks for a fish, will give him a snake instead of a fish? Or if he asks for an egg, will give him a scorpion? If you then, although you are evil, know how to give good gifts to your children, how much more will the heavenly Father give the Holy Spirit to those who ask him!"

"Ask, and it will be given to you; seek, and you will find; knock, and the door will be opened for you" (v. 9) can be translated literally, "Ask and keep asking, seek and keep seeking, knock and keep knocking." Christ says there must be perseverance in prayer to receive God's blessing. In addition, consider the promise in verse 13, "How much more will the heavenly Father give the Holy Spirit to those who ask him!" In the Greek, "the" does not precede "Holy Spirit"— it can be translated literally "give Holy Spirit." Many scholars say that when the article is missing, this term does not refer to the person of the Spirit, but rather the ministries of the Spirit.[268]

When you pray with perseverance, God will give you the strength you need, the wisdom and power to conquer habitual sins, and everything else you need to live a godly life. Don't give up! Spirit-led prayer perseveres.

Persevering prayer is also needed because of the spiritual forces we are fighting against. In Daniel 10:10-14, Daniel petitioned God for three weeks and then an angel appeared. The angel said that God had sent him with a response when Daniel first began to pray, but he was caught up in a war with the spiritual forces over Persia. While Daniel continued to pray, the angel Michael came to set the other angel free so he could answer Daniel's request. Yes, persevering prayer is needed because of the spiritual war we are engaged in. We must persevere in prayer for the salvation of a relative, revival in a church or a nation, and any other good work. We must pray at least until God removes the burden of prayer, as he did with Paul when he prayed for healing (2 Cor 12:8-9).

Are you persevering in prayer?

Application Question: Are there any answers to prayer you received after a long season of praying? If so, what were they? What are some things that you are still praying for?

Prayer in the Spirit Is Universal

> With every prayer and petition, pray at all times in the Spirit, and to this end be alert, with all perseverance and requests for all the saints.
> Ephesians 6:18

Prayer in the Spirit is also universal—we pray "for all the saints." I have often been taught to pray specifically and this is correct, but it is also important to pray generally. We are in this war with millions of other Christians we do not know. Does this lack of knowledge mean that we should not pray for them? Absolutely not! We must intercede according to the knowledge we have.

We intercede for the Christians in our church, our nation, and all the nations of the earth. We should remember both persecuted Christians and those living at ease (a temptation in itself). We must especially pray for our spiritual leaders such as missionaries, pastors, and teachers.

I once heard a story about the president of Taylor University in Indiana. While on a flight, he was seated next to a lady who was clearly fasting and praying—every time the food came, she refused it. As he watched her he became very convicted of his own need to pray, so he decided to ask if she was a Christian. However, when asked, the lady responded, "Why no! I am a Satanist, and I'm praying for Christian leaders throughout the world to fall into sin, to turn away from God, and for others to follow them." This is sobering! Certainly, it should encourage us to continually lift up our Christian leaders throughout the world, as they are the target of special attacks by the enemy.

This is a real war, and we are not in it by ourselves. Therefore, we must continually intercede for other believers.

Application Question: How can we be more faithful in praying for all saints?

1. Keep a prayer list. A list helps us pray faithfully for people we know, and it can also remind us to pray in general for believers in various parts of society and the world.

2. Use a prayer method—like the "Five-Finger Prayer."

Here is a description of it from a Daily Bread devotional:

- "When you fold your hands, the thumb is nearest you. So begin by praying for those closest to you—your loved ones (Philippians 1:3-5).
- The index finger is the pointer. Pray for those who teach—Bible teachers and preachers, and those who teach children (1 Thessalonians 5:25).
- The next finger is the tallest. It reminds you to pray for those in authority over you—national and local leaders, and your supervisor at work (1 Timothy 2:1-2).
- The fourth finger is usually the weakest. Pray for those who are in trouble or who are suffering (James 5:13-16).
- Then comes your little finger. It reminds you of your smallness in relation to God's greatness. Ask Him to supply your needs (Philippians 4:6, 19)."[269]

Prayer in the Spirit is universal—for all saints.

Application Question: Are there any other concepts or disciplines that help you faithfully intercede for others?

Prayer in the Spirit Is Gospel-Centered and Bible-Centered

> Pray for me also, that I may be given the message when I begin to speak – that I may confidently make known the mystery of the gospel, for which I am an ambassador in chains. Pray that I may be able to speak boldly as I ought to speak.
> Ephesians 6:19-20

Finally, prayer in the Spirit is always consumed with the spread of the gospel and God's Word. While Paul was in prison, he didn't ask the believers to pray for his release. Led by the Spirit, he sought prayer for God to give him the words to preach and the courage to preach them fearlessly. He essentially asked for prayer over the content of the message and the manner it was presented.

Interpretation Question: Why does Paul mention his need to be fearless in preaching twice in his prayer request?

The fact that he mentions the need for boldness (or to be "fearless") twice shows us his own struggle to preach God's Word faithfully. Such preaching could lead to his death or a longer prison term.

However, this does not just show Paul's great need for boldness in preaching, but also the church's. Most Christians struggle with fear in sharing God's Word. They feel inadequate. They fear the response of people. They fear persecution, for example, in the form of job loss. And therefore most remain quiet. This is also true for preachers. Often there is hesitation to preach the full counsel of God, especially in an age where his Word is widely rejected.

However, like Paul, when we are led by the Spirit, he leads us to pray about the proclamation of the Word (cf. Col 4:3-4, 2 Thess 3:1). We should pray for believers to properly interpret and understand God's Word, and for them to share it in their churches and workplaces, and with their families. In addition, we should pray for the gospel to be received. When this happens, the enemy is defeated as people are translated from darkness to light and set free from strongholds.

The Holy Spirit is the author of the Word of God, as Scripture was inspired by him (cf. 2 Tim 3:16, 2 Peter 1:21). Therefore, he continually encourages people to pray over the Word of God and for it to be shared. Let us continually call on the Holy Spirit to empower his people to share his Word with boldness, for God's kingdom to be built, and for the evil one's kingdom to be destroyed.

Lord, spread your Word throughout the world, bring glory to yourself, and destroy the evil one and all his forces! In Jesus name, we pray.

Application Questions: Do you struggle with boldness when witnessing? Why or why not? How can we overcome our fear in speaking for God? Why is it so important to pray for the preaching of the Word of God?

Conclusion

Before we close, let's consider some words on prayer from John Piper's book, *Desiring God*:

> Unless I'm badly mistaken, one of the main reasons so many of God's children don't have a significant life of prayer is not so much that we don't want to, but that we don't plan to. If you want to take a four-week vacation, you don't just get up one summer morning and say, "Hey, let's go today!" You won't have anything ready. You won't know where to go. Nothing has been planned.
>
> But that is how many of us treat prayer. We get up day after day and realize that significant times of prayer should be part of our life, but nothing's ever ready. We don't know where to go. Nothing has been planned. No time. No place. No procedure. And we all know that the opposite of planning is not a wonderful flow of deep, spontaneous experiences in prayer. The opposite of planning is the rut. If you don't plan a vacation you will probably stay home and watch TV! The natural unplanned flow of spiritual life sinks to the lowest ebb of vitality.

There is a race to be run and a fight to be fought. If you want renewal in your life of prayer you must plan to see it.

Therefore, my simple exhortation is this: Let us take time this very day to rethink our priorities and how prayer fits in. Make some new resolve. Try some new venture with God. Set a time. Set a place. Choose a portion of Scripture to guide you. Don't be tyrannized by the press of busy days. We all need mid-course corrections. Make this a day of turning to prayer — for the glory of God and for the fullness of your joy.[270]

How can we pray in the Spirit in order to stand in this spiritual war?

1. Prayer in the Spirit Is Constant
2. Prayer in the Spirit Is Varied
3. Prayer in the Spirit Is Watchful
4. Prayer in the Spirit Is Persevering
5. Prayer in the Spirit Is Universal
6. Prayer in the Spirit Is Gospel-Centered and Bible-Centered

Attributes of Godly Soldiers

Tychicus, my dear brother and faithful servant in the Lord, will make everything known to you, so that you too may know about my circumstances, how I am doing. I have sent him to you for this very purpose, that you may know our circumstances and that he may encourage your hearts. Peace to the brothers and sisters, and love with faith, from God the Father and the Lord Jesus Christ. Grace be with all of those who love our Lord Jesus Christ with an undying love.
Ephesians 6:21-24 (NET)

What are attributes of godly soldiers?

It is no accident that Paul mentions himself and Tychicus right after teaching about spiritual warfare and the armor of God. These men are models of war-torn, decorated soldiers from whom we can learn much. If we are going to fight this spiritual war well, we must model godly soldiers like Paul and Tychicus.

Tychicus is briefly mentioned only five times in Scripture.[271] His name actually means "lucky."[272] Many believe he was a convert from Paul's ministry in Ephesus because he is first mentioned in Acts 20:4, at the end of Paul's missionary work there.[273] From there, he accompanied Paul on many missionary journeys, and was sent to relieve Timothy as the pastor over Ephesus (2 Tim 4:12) during Paul's second imprisonment. He was probably also sent to Crete to relieve Titus (Tit 3:12).

In this text, Paul sends Tychicus on a mission to complete two duties. He was to deliver the Ephesian letter (Eph 6:21), and also the Colossian and Philemon letters (cf. Col 4:7-8). In addition, he was to inform the Ephesian church (and probably other Asian churches) of Paul's situation, and to encourage them (Eph 6:22).

Since Tychicus was probably an Ephesian convert, the church knew him well, just as they knew Paul well. No doubt, these two soldiers inspired the Ephesians to stand strong in spiritual warfare. As we study these two men in the final section of Ephesians, we will consider attributes of godly soldiers—ones worth modeling.

Big Questions: What attributes of godly soldiers can we discern from Paul's description of Tychicus, and from his benediction? How can we model these attributes in our spiritual lives?

Godly Soldiers Are Loving

> Tychicus, my dear brother and faithful servant in the Lord, will make everything known to you, so that you too may know about my circumstances, how I am doing.
> Ephesians 6:21

Paul describes Tychicus in many different ways, but the first way is with the word "dear" or it can be translated "beloved." He calls him a dear brother. This certainly means that Paul and the Ephesians loved Tychicus. However, it probably also means that his character was loving. Steve Cole's insight on this is helpful. He says,

> He could have called him just a "brother," but he adds this word, beloved. It shows that Tychicus was a warmly relational man. He wasn't cold and aloof. He wasn't brusque and insensitive. He wasn't grumpy and difficult to be around. He was beloved. When Paul used that word to describe Tychicus, everyone who knew him would have nodded and thought, "Yes, he is a dear, loving man. We love him dearly ourselves!"[274]

How would people describe you? Are you loving and relational? Do you take time to get to know people in the church and do they know you? If not, that probably says more about you than it does about the church.

Christian soldiers are not hardened like many other war veterans; they are deeply loving and relational. Hebrews 10:24-25 says this:

> And let us take thought of how to spur one another on to love and good works, not abandoning our own meetings, as some are in the habit of doing, but encouraging each other, and even more so because you see the day drawing near.

Godly soldiers are not only loving, but they also constantly seek to help others love as well. In fact, Jesus says, "Everyone will know by this that you are my disciples – if you have love for one another" (John 13:35).

Are you constantly considering how to stir others to love God and others more? Are you continually gathering with the saints out of sincere love for them? This is the character of a godly soldier—a beloved brother or sister.

Application Questions: How is God calling you to become more loving in your relationship with the body of Christ? In what ways should we demonstrate this love?

Godly Soldiers Are Faithful

> Tychicus, my dear brother and faithful servant in the Lord, will make everything known to you, so that you too may know about my circumstances, how I am doing.
> Ephesians 6:21

Paul calls Tychicus a "faithful servant" here, and a "dear brother, a faithful minister and fellow servant in the Lord" in Colossians 4:7, emphasizing just how faithful Tychicus was.

Interpretation Questions: What does the term "faithful" mean? How was this exemplified in Tychicus' character, and how should we model it?

1. To be faithful means to be honest.

Tychicus was a man whose "yes" meant yes and whose "no" meant no (cf. James 5:12). People could count on him. This is why Paul called him to relieve other pastors in ministry. He relieved Timothy at Ephesus and probably Titus at Crete. He also was entrusted with carrying the Scriptures to various churches.

Can people trust you? Does your "yes" mean yes and your "no" mean no? Are you honest? Godly soldiers are honest.

2. To be faithful means to faithfully use one's gifts to serve God and others.

No doubt, Tychicus had the gifts of helps—wherever there was a need, he lent a helping hand. He probably had the gift of teaching, as he relieved pastors, and probably the gift of encouragement, as he was sent to encourage the Ephesians. He was not one of those Christians who are content sitting on the bench and not getting in the game (cf. Matt 25:24-28). He was using every ounce of his person to serve Christ and to faithfully use his gifts.

Paul instructs Timothy to "rekindle God's gift that you possess through the laying on of my hands" (2 Timothy 1:6). We each have a responsibility to find out what our spiritual gifts are and to cultivate them to their maximum potential. Is your gift serving? Serve. Is it teaching? Teach. Is it evangelism? Evangelize.

Are you faithfully using your gifts? When Christ returns, he will reward those who have done so (Matt 25:21).

3.   To be faithful means to persevere through difficulties.

Tychicus was a man who did not give up easily. Not only did he accompany Paul on his missionary journeys, he was with Paul during his imprisonment in Rome even though it might have meant his own imprisonment and death. He was also with Paul during the second imprisonment, when Paul sent him to relieve Timothy (2 Tim 4:12). Tychicus was the kind of friend who would be right next to you while you were sick, or going through bankruptcy, divorce, or even death.

In fact, he was not only beside Paul, he no doubt often suffered with Paul, simply by being associated with him. Many of the difficulties that Paul recounts in 2 Corinthians 11:23-33—shipwreck, stoning, beatings, sleeplessness, hunger and more—must have also happened to Tychicus. He faithfully persevered through many difficulties while serving Christ and others.

Many Christians want to quit at the first sign of trouble. They got in a fight with their small group leader, their pastor hurt them, or the music director changed the worship music—so they abandon their church or ministry. These Christians are not faithful—they don't persevere. No doubt, Tychicus experienced all this (and some) and yet faithfully persevered.

Are you faithful when encountering difficulties, or are you a quitter?

Here is a great illustration that demonstrates the importance of faithfulness:

"In the eleventh century, King Henry III of Bavaria grew tired of court life and the pressures of being a monarch. He made application to Prior Richard at a local monastery, asking to be accepted as a contemplative and spend the rest of his life in the monastery.

"Your Majesty,' said Prior Richard, "do you understand that the pledge here is one of obedience? That will be hard because you have been a king."

"I understand," said Henry. "The rest of my life I will be obedient to you, as Christ leads you."

"Then I will tell you what to do," said Prior Richard. "Go back to your throne and serve faithfully in the place where God has put you."

When King Henry died, a statement was written: "The king learned to rule by being obedient."

When we tire of our roles and responsibilities, it helps to remember God has planted us in a certain place and told us to be a good accountant or teacher or mother or father. Christ expects us to be faithful where he puts us, and when he returns, we'll rule together with him." [275]

Godly soldiers are faithful—they are trustworthy, they use their gifts fully, and they persevere through difficulties. How about you?

Application Questions: In what ways is God calling you to grow in faithfulness? How is he calling you to persevere in your current situation? What gifts is he calling you to cultivate and use? Are there any current challenges to your integrity?

Godly Soldiers Are Servants

> Tychicus, my dear brother and faithful servant in the Lord, will make everything known to you, so that you too may know about my circumstances, how I am doing.
> Ephesians 6:21

Paul also describes Tychicus as a "servant." Godly soldiers faithfully serve Christ and others. It has been said that in every church there are two types of people. One type thinks, "Here I am church! Meet my needs!" These people often leave disheartened because the church failed them in some way. The second type asks, "How can I serve this church? What are the needs and how can I meet them?" Like Christ, they don't come to be served, but to serve others (Mark 10:45).[276]

Which type are you?

Tychicus did menial tasks like delivering letters to various churches. Many pastors would say, "I didn't go to seminary for this! Somebody else can do it!" However, Tychicus was willing to serve by performing small tasks, and also big tasks like pastoring a church when Titus or Timothy wasn't around.

I think that marks true servants—they essentially say, "What is the need? I'll do my best to meet it or find someone who can." And one day, Christ will say to them, "His master said to him, 'Well done, good and faithful servant. You have been faithful over a little; I will set you over much. Enter into the joy of your master'" (Matt 25:21 ESV).

Are you a servant? Godly soldiers serve God and others.

Application Questions: What are some other characteristics of good servants? How is God calling you to grow in servanthood?

Godly Soldiers Are Encouragers

> I have sent him to you for this very purpose, that you may know our
> circumstances and that he may encourage your hearts.
> Ephesians 6:22

The last characteristic we can discern about Tychicus is that he was an encourager. Paul sent him to Ephesus to encourage the saints. Again, he had been with Paul during his imprisonment—keeping him company, serving him, and encouraging him when he was feeling down. No doubt Paul knew from his own experience that Tychicus would be very helpful at encouraging the Ephesians, who were probably discouraged by Paul's sufferings (cf. Eph 3:13) and the persecution happening to them and other believers.

Application Questions: How would Tychicus encourage them? How can we encourage others when they are discouraged or going through trials?

1. We encourage others by coming alongside them.

Encourage is from the Greek word "parakaleo," which means "to come alongside for help."[277] It is related to the word Christ used for the Holy Spirit in John 14:16. The Holy Spirit is our paraclete—our counselor, our advocate, and our helper.

If we are going to encourage others, the first step is to simply come beside them. Often we are afraid because we don't know what to say or do when somebody is hurting or struggling—so we say and do nothing. We must remember that the first step is just to be there for them. When Job's friends just sat in silence with him while he mourned (cf. Job 2:11-13)—they did well.

How else should we encourage others?

2. We encourage others by listening to them.
3. We encourage others by praying for them.
4. We encourage others by sharing God's Word with them.

Application Question: Share a time God used somebody to really encourage you.

Godly Soldiers Are Disciplers

> Peace to the brothers and sisters, and love with faith, from God the
> Father and the Lord Jesus Christ. Grace be with all of those who love
> our Lord Jesus Christ with an undying love.
> Ephesians 6:23-24

It was the custom for correspondents in the ancient world to end their letters with a wish for the readers' health and happiness, typically invoking the names of the gods. Paul doesn't abandon this tradition, but he Christianizes it. Instead of a wish, he gives a benediction—a prayer for blessing.[278]

However, this benediction is more than just a benediction—it is a summary of many of the rich themes in the epistle.[279] Paul prays that God will enable the Ephesians to internalize these truths so that they can look more like Christ.

And this is true for all godly soldiers—one of their primary focuses in life is helping others know and look more like Christ. Again, as we look at the blessings, they demonstrate the major truths in Ephesians.

Observation Question: What blessings does Paul pray for the Ephesians and how are they demonstrated throughout the book?

1. Paul prays for Ephesians to have peace.

No doubt this pictures the believers' peace with God. However, it also pictures their peace with one another, a primary theme throughout the book of Ephesians, especially in chapter 2. Paul teaches that Christ made the Jew and Gentile one by breaking the dividing wall of the law to unite them and becoming their peace (cf. Eph 2:14-17).

Paul prays that the Ephesians will not be divided by race, ethnicity, or tradition, but that they will truly be one in Christ. This should be true of us as well.

Are you walking in peace with others?

2. Paul prays for the Ephesians to have love.

In Ephesians 1:15, Paul declares how he heard about the Ephesians' "love for all the saints." It's one thing to love some saints, but to love all the saints is special. Though they already excelled in love, he calls for them to imitate God and further live a life of love, just as Christ loved and died for us (Eph 5:1-2).

Are you loving others sacrificially?

3. Paul prays for the Ephesians to have faith.

This word is used seven other times in this small epistle.[280] Paul wants them to develop a deeper trust in God regardless of their circumstances, and also to trust in God's Word—believing his promises. Kent Hughes paraphrases the aspect of faith in Paul's benediction this way, "Ease back and rest on what you believe. Put your whole weight on it."[281]

Are you growing in your trust in God and his Word? Are you putting all your weight on Christ in every circumstance? First Peter 5:7 says, "by casting all your cares on him because he cares for you."

4. Paul prays for the Ephesians to have grace.

This is the twelfth occurrence of the word "grace" in the letter.[282] It is used in the introduction (Eph 1:2, 6), closing, and throughout the letter. Ephesians 2:8-9 says, "For by grace you are saved through faith, and this is not from yourselves, it is the gift of God; it is not from works, so that no one can boast."

However, we are not just saved by grace. John 1:16 says, "For we have all received from his fullness one gracious gift after another." God continually pours grace on believers, especially as we are obedient to him— grace upon our marriages, families, work, and churches. This should be our hope and prayer for all who call on Christ—grace upon grace—unmerited favor upon unmerited favor. As James 4:6 says, "he gives greater grace."

Are you daily seeking his renewed grace?

Godly soldiers are continually seeking the spiritual maturity of others. They desire other believers' lives to be full of peace, love, faith, and grace.

Application Questions: Why is discipleship so important? What spiritual leaders have most influenced your spiritual life in a positive manner? Who has God called you to disciple?

Godly Soldiers Are Intercessors

Peace to the brothers and sisters, and love with faith, from God the Father and the Lord Jesus Christ. Grace be with all of those who love our Lord Jesus Christ with an undying love.
Ephesians 6:23-24

Not only can we see Paul's heart for discipleship in his benediction, but also his heart for prayer. In Ephesians 6:18-20 Paul has just described the need to pray in the Spirit on all occasions with all types of prayer—and what he taught, he practiced. He prays for the Ephesians in chapters 1 and 3, and now again in closing. He prays for peace, love, faith and grace over the church. This is the practice of all godly soldiers—they are faithful intercessors.

Where worldly soldiers put confidence in their strength, training, and knowledge, godly soldiers understand they are unequipped even for mundane tasks—only God's grace and strength will do. Therefore, they are constant in prayer.

Are you praying and interceding for others in this battle? Ezekiel 22:30-31 says,

> "I looked for a man from among them who would repair the wall and stand in the gap before me on behalf of the land, so that I would not destroy it, but I found no one. So I have poured my anger on them, and destroyed them with the fire of my fury. I hereby repay them for what they have done, declares the sovereign Lord."

God seeks those who will faithfully intercede for others in order to preserve them from destruction and lead them into blessing. Isaiah 62:6-7 says,

> I post watchmen on your walls, O Jerusalem; they should keep praying all day and all night. You who pray to the Lord, don't be silent! Don't allow him to rest until he reestablishes Jerusalem, until he makes Jerusalem the pride of the earth.

Brothers and sisters, give our Lord no rest as you intercede for kings, presidents, business people, wives, mothers, children, churches, communities, and nations. Give him no rest until he makes our world fully his own. This is the heart and practice of godly soldiers—like Paul, they are intercessors.

Application Questions: How would you rate your prayer life on a scale of 1 to 10, and why? What are some good practices to help us grow in intercession?

Conclusion

What are attributes of godly soldiers—ones worth modeling—as revealed in Tychicus and Paul?

1. Godly soldiers are loving.
2. Godly soldiers are faithful.
3. Godly soldiers are servants.
4. Godly soldiers are disciplers.
5. Godly soldiers are Intercessors.

Study Group Tips

Leading a small group using the Bible Teacher's Guide can be done in various ways. One format is the "study group" model, where each member prepares and shares in the teaching. This appendix will cover tips for facilitating a weekly study group.

1. Each week the members of the study group read through a selected chapter of the guide, answer the reflection questions (see Appendix 2), and come prepared to share in the group.

2. Prior to each meeting, a different member is selected to lead the group and share his answer to Question 1 of the reflection questions, which is a short summary of the chapter read. This section of the gathering could last from five to fifteen minutes. This way, each member can develop his ability to teach and will be motivated to study harder during the week. Or, each week the same person could share the summary.

3. After the summary has been given, the leader for that week facilitates discussion of the remaining reflection questions and selected questions from the chapter.

4. After discussion, the group shares prayer requests and members pray for one another.

The strength of the study group is that the members are required to prepare their responses before the meeting, allowing for easier discussion. Another is that each member has the opportunity to further develop his ministry skills through teaching. These are distinct advantages.

Reflection Questions

Writing is one of the best ways to learn. In class, we take notes and write papers, and all these methods are used to help us learn and retain the material. The same is true with the Word of God. Obviously, all of the authors of Scripture were writers. This helped them better learn the Scriptures and also enabled them to more effectively teach it. In studying God's Word with the Bible Teacher's Guide, take time to write so you can similarly grow both in your learning and teaching.

1. How would you summarize the main points of the text/chapter? Write a brief summary.

2. What stood out to you most in the reading? Did any of the contents trigger any memories or experiences? If so, please share them.

3. What follow-up questions do you have about the reading? Are there parts you do not fully agree with?

4. What applications did you take from the reading, and how do you plan to implement them in your life?

5.   Write several goals: As a result of my time studying God's Word, I aspire to . . .

6.   What are some practical ways to pray as a result of studying the text? Spend some time in prayer.

Walking the Romans Road

How can a person be saved? From what is he saved? How can someone have eternal life? Scripture teaches that after death each person will spend eternity either in heaven or hell. How can a person go to heaven?

Paul said this to Timothy:

> You, however, must continue in the things you have learned and are confident about. You know who taught you and how from infancy you have known the holy writings, which are able to give you wisdom for salvation through faith in Christ Jesus.
> 2 Timothy 3:14-15

One of the reasons God gave us Scripture is to make us wise for salvation. This means that without it nobody can know how to be saved.

Well then, how can a people be saved and what are they being saved from? A common method of sharing the good news of salvation is through the Romans Road. One of the great themes, not only of the Bible, but specifically of the book of Romans is salvation. In Romans, the author, Paul, clearly details the steps we must take in order to be saved.

How can we be saved? What steps must we take?

Step One: We Must Accept that We Are Sinners

Romans 3:23 says, "For all have sinned and fall short of the glory of God." What does it mean to sin? The word sin means "to miss the mark." The mark we missed is looking like God. When God created mankind in the Genesis narrative, he created man in the "image of God" (1:27). The "image of God" means many things, but probably, most importantly it means we were made to be holy just as he is holy. Man was made moral. We were meant to reflect God's holiness in every way: the way we think, the way we talk, and the way we act. And any time we miss the mark in these areas, we commit sin.

Furthermore, we do not only sin when we commit a sinful act such as: lying, stealing, or cheating. Again, we sin anytime we have a wrong heart motive. The greatest commandments in Scripture are to "Love the Lord your

God with all your heart and to love your neighbor as yourself" (Matt 22:36-40, paraphrase). Whenever we don't love God supremely and love others as ourselves, we sin and fall short of the glory of God. For this reason, man is always in a state of sinning. Sadly, even if our actions are good, our heart is bad. I have never loved God with my whole heart, mind, and soul and neither has anybody else. Therefore, we have all sinned and fall short of the glory of God (Rom 3:23). We have all missed the mark of God's holiness and we must accept this.

What's the next step?

Step Two: We Must Understand We Are Under the Judgment of God

Why are we under the judgment of God? It is because of our sins. Scripture teaches God is not only a loving God, but he is a just God. And his justice requires judgment for each of our sins. Romans 6:23 says, "For the payoff of sin is death."

A wage is something we earn. Every time we sin, we earn the wage of death. What is death? Death really means separation. In physical death, the body is separated from the spirit, but in spiritual death, man is separated from God. Man currently lives in a state of spiritual death (cf. Eph 2:1-3). We do not love God, obey him, or know him as we should. Therefore, man is in a state of death.

Moreover, one day at our physical death, if we have not been saved, we will spend eternity separated from God in a very real hell. In hell, we will pay the wage for each of our sins. Therefore, in hell people will experience various degrees of punishment (cf. Lk 12:47-48). This places man in a very dangerous predicament—unholy and therefore under the judgment of God.

How should we respond to this? This leads us to our third step.

Step Three: We Must Recognize God Has Invited All to Accept His Free Gift of Salvation

Romans 6:23 does not stop at the wages of sin being death. It says, "For the payoff of sin is death, but the gift of God is eternal life in Christ Jesus our Lord." Because God loved everybody on the earth, he offered the free gift of eternal life, which anyone can receive through Jesus Christ.

Because it is a gift, it cannot be earned. We cannot work for it. Ephesians 2:8-9 says, "For by grace you are saved through faith, and this is not from yourselves, it is the gift of God; it is not from works, so that no one can boast."

Going to church, being baptized, giving to the poor, or doing any other righteous work does not save. Salvation is a gift that must be received from God. It is a gift that has been prepared by his effort alone.

How do we receive this free gift?

Step Four: We Must Believe Jesus Christ Died for Our Sins and Rose from the Dead

If we are going to receive this free gift, we must believe in God's Son, Jesus Christ. Because God loved us, cared for us, and didn't want us to be separated from him eternally, he sent his Son to die for our sins. Romans 5:8 says, "But God demonstrates his own love for us, in that while we were still sinners, Christ died for us." Similarly, John 3:16 says, "For this is the way God loved the world: He gave his one and only Son, so that everyone who believes in him will not perish but have eternal life." God so loved us that he gave his only Son for our sins.

Jesus Christ was a real, historical person who lived 2,000 years ago. He was born of a virgin. He lived a perfect life. He was put to death by the Romans and the Jews. And he rose again on the third day. In his death, he took our sins and God's wrath for them and gave us his perfect righteousness so we could be accepted by God. Second Corinthians 5:21 says, "God made the one who did not know sin to be sin for us, so that in him we would become the righteousness of God." God did all this so we could be saved from his wrath.

Christ's death satisfied the just anger of God over our sins. When God saw Jesus on the cross, he saw us and our sins and therefore judged Jesus. And now, when God sees those who are saved, he sees his righteous Son and accepts us. In salvation, we have become the righteousness of God.

If we are going to be saved, if we are going to receive this free gift of salvation, we must believe in Christ's death, burial, and resurrection for our sins (cf. 1 Cor 15:3-5, Rom 10:9-10). Do you believe?

Step Five: We Must Confess Christ as Lord of Our Lives

Romans 10:9-10 says,

> Because if you confess with your mouth that Jesus is Lord and believe in your heart that God raised him from the dead, you will be saved. For with the heart one believes and thus has righteousness and with the mouth one confesses and thus has salvation.

Not only must we believe, but we must confess Christ as Lord of our lives. It is one thing to believe in Christ but another to follow Christ. Simple belief does not save. Christ must be our Lord. James said this: "...Even the demons believe that – and tremble with fear" (James 2:19), but the demons are not saved—Christ is not their Lord.

Another aspect of making Christ Lord is repentance. Repentance really means a change of mind that leads to a change of direction. Before we met Christ, we were living our own life and following our own sinful desires. But when we get saved, our mind and direction change. We start to follow Christ as Lord.

How do we make this commitment to the lordship of Christ so we can be saved? Paul said we must confess with our mouth "Jesus is Lord" as we believe in him. Romans 10:13 says, "For everyone who calls on the name of the Lord will be saved."

If you admit that you are a sinner and understand you are under God's wrath because of them; if you believe Jesus Christ is the Son of God, that he died on the cross for your sins, and rose from the dead for your salvation; if you are ready to turn from your sin and cling to Christ as Lord, you can be saved.

If this is your heart, then you can pray this prayer and commit to following Christ as your Lord.

Dear heavenly Father, I confess I am a sinner and have fallen short of your glory, what you made me for. I believe Jesus Christ died on the cross to pay the penalty for my sins and rose from the dead so I can have eternal life. I am turning away from my sin and accepting you as my Lord and Savior. Come into my life and change me. Thank you for your gift of salvation.

Scripture teaches that if you truly accepted Christ as your Lord, then you are a new creation. Second Corinthians 5:17 says, "So then, if anyone is in Christ, he is a new creation; what is old has passed away – look, what is new has come!" God has forgiven your sins (1 John 1:9), he has given you his Holy Spirit (Rom 8:15), and he is going to disciple you and make you into the image of his Son (cf. Rom 8:29). He will never leave you nor forsake you (Heb 13:5), and he will complete the work he has begun in your life (Phil 1:6). In heaven, angels and saints are rejoicing because of your commitment to Christ (Lk 15:7).

Praise God for his great salvation! May God keep you in his hand, empower you through the Holy Spirit, train you through mature believers, and use you to build his kingdom! "He who calls you is trustworthy, and he will in fact do this" (1 Thess 5:24). God bless you!

About the Author

Greg Brown earned his MA in religion and MA in teaching from Trinity International University, a MRE from Liberty University, and a PhD in Theology from Louisiana Baptist University. He has served for over fourteen years in pastoral ministry, and currently serves as chaplain and professor at Handong Global University, teaching pastor at Handong International Congregation, and as a Navy Reserve chaplain.

Greg married his lovely wife, Tara Jayne, in 2006 and they have one daughter, Saiyah Grace. He enjoys going on dates with his wife, playing with his daughter, reading, writing, studying in coffee shops, working out, and following the NBA and UFC. His pursuit in life simply put is "to know God and to be found faithful by Him."

To connect with Greg, please follow at http://www.pgregbrown.com/

Coming Soon to the BTG Series

Praise the Lord for your interest in studying and teaching God's Word. If God has blessed you through the BTG series, please partner with us in petitioning God to greatly use this series to encourage and build his Church. Also, please consider leaving an Amazon review and signing up for free book promotions. By doing this, you help spread the "Word." Thanks for your partnership in the gospel from the first day until now (Phil 1:4-5).

Available:
First Peter
Theology Proper
Building Foundations for a Godly Marriage
Colossians
God's Battle Plan for Purity
Nehemiah
Philippians
The Perfections of God
The Armor of God
Ephesians
Abraham
Finding a Godly Mate
1 Timothy
The Beatitudes
Equipping Small Group Leaders
2 Timothy
Jacob

Coming Soon:
The Sermon on the Mount

Notes

[1] Boice, J. M. (1988). *Ephesians: an expositional commentary* (p. 2). Grand Rapids, MI: Ministry Resources Library.

[2] MacDonald, W. (1995). *Believer's Bible Commentary: Old and New Testaments*. (A. Farstad, Ed.) (p. 1903). Nashville: Thomas Nelson.

[3] (2014-03-12). The Moody Bible Commentary (Kindle Locations 76232-76235). Moody Publishers. Kindle Edition.

[4] MacArthur, John (2003-08-19). The MacArthur Bible Handbook (Kindle Locations 9706-9708). Thomas Nelson. Kindle Edition.

[5] Sproul, R. C. (1994). *The Purpose of God: Ephesians* (pp. 12–13). Scotland: Christian Focus Publications.

[6] Sproul, R. C. (1994). *The Purpose of God: Ephesians* (p. 12). Scotland: Christian Focus Publications.

[7] MacArthur, J. F., Jr. (1986). Ephesians (pp. 165–166). Chicago: Moody Press.

[8] Accessed 1/25/2016 from http://www.cowart.info/Ephesus/ephesus.html

[9] Boice, J. M. (1988). *Ephesians: an expositional commentary* (p. 3). Grand Rapids, MI: Ministry Resources Library.

[10] Boice, J. M. (1988). *Ephesians: an expositional commentary* (p. 3). Grand Rapids, MI: Ministry Resources Library.

[11] (2014-03-12). The Moody Bible Commentary (Kindle Locations 76235-76239). Moody Publishers. Kindle Edition.

[12] MacArthur, John (2003-08-19). The MacArthur Bible Handbook (Kindle Locations 9715-9717). Thomas Nelson. Kindle Edition.

[13] Sproul, R. C. (1994). *The Purpose of God: Ephesians* (p. 13). Scotland: Christian Focus Publications.

[14] MacArthur, John (2003-08-19). The MacArthur Bible Handbook (Kindle Locations 9725-9729). Thomas Nelson. Kindle Edition.

[15] Weaver, Paul (2015-01-04). Introducing the New Testament Books: A Thorough but Concise Introduction for Proper Interpretation (Biblical Studies Book 3) (Kindle Locations 1059-1061). Kindle Edition.

[16] MacArthur, John (2003-08-19). The MacArthur Bible Handbook (Kindle Locations 9759-9760). Thomas Nelson. Kindle Edition.

[17] MacDonald, W. (1995). *Believer's Bible Commentary: Old and New Testaments*. (A. Farstad, Ed.) (p. 1904). Nashville: Thomas Nelson.

[18] MacArthur, John (2003-08-19). The MacArthur Bible Handbook (Kindle Locations 9759-9760). Thomas Nelson. Kindle Edition.

[19] MacDonald, W. (1995). *Believer's Bible Commentary: Old and New Testaments*. (A. Farstad, Ed.) (p. 1904). Nashville: Thomas Nelson.

[20] Hughes, R. K. (1990). *Ephesians: the mystery of the body of Christ* (pp. 16–17). Wheaton, IL: Crossway Books.

[21] Wiersbe, W. W. (1996). *The Bible exposition commentary* (Vol. 2, p. 10). Wheaton, IL: Victor Books.

[22] Stott, J. R. W. (1979). *God's new society: the message of Ephesians* (p. 35). Downers Grove, IL: InterVarsity Press.

[23] MacArthur, J. F., Jr. (1986). *Ephesians* (p. 8). Chicago: Moody Press.

[24] Wiersbe, W. W. (1996). *The Bible exposition commentary* (Vol. 2, p. 9). Wheaton, IL: Victor Books.

[25] Hughes, R. K. (1990). *Ephesians: the mystery of the body of Christ* (p. 19). Wheaton, IL: Crossway Books.

[26] MacDonald, W. (1995). *Believer's Bible Commentary: Old and New Testaments*. (A. Farstad, Ed.) (p. 1413). Nashville: Thomas Nelson.

[27] MacDonald, W. (1995). *Believer's Bible Commentary: Old and New Testaments*. (A. Farstad, Ed.) (p. 1907). Nashville: Thomas Nelson.

[28] Stott, J. R. W. (1979). *God's new society: the message of Ephesians* (p. 34). Downers Grove, IL: InterVarsity Press.

[29] Wiersbe, W. W. (1996). *The Bible exposition commentary* (Vol. 2, p. 11). Wheaton, IL: Victor Books.

[30] Hughes, R. K. (1990). *Ephesians: the mystery of the body of Christ* (p. 25). Wheaton, IL: Crossway Books.

[31] Wiersbe, W. W. (1996). *The Bible exposition commentary* (Vol. 2, p. 11). Wheaton, IL: Victor Books.

[32] Guzik, David (2012-11-26). Galatians and Ephesians (Kindle Locations 3742-3745). Enduring Word Media. Kindle Edition.

[33] Wiersbe, W. W. (1996). *The Bible exposition commentary* (Vol. 2, pp. 11–12). Wheaton, IL: Victor Books.

[34] MacArthur, J. F., Jr. (1986). *Ephesians* (p. 21). Chicago: Moody Press.

[35] Accessed 3/24/15 http://biblehub.com/greek/1401.htm

[36] Wiersbe, W. W. (1996). *The Bible exposition commentary* (Vol. 2, p. 12). Wheaton, IL: Victor Books.

[37] MacArthur, J. F., Jr. (1986). *Ephesians* (p. 25). Chicago: Moody Press.

[38] Wiersbe, W. W. (1996). *The Bible exposition commentary* (Vol. 2, p. 12). Wheaton, IL: Victor Books.

[39] MacArthur, J. F., Jr. (1986). *Ephesians* (pp. 31–32). Chicago: Moody Press.

[40] MacArthur, J. F., Jr. (1986). *Ephesians* (p. 34). Chicago: Moody Press.

[41] MacArthur, J. F., Jr. (1986). *Ephesians* (pp. 34–35). Chicago: Moody Press.

[42] MacArthur, J. F., Jr. (1986). *Ephesians* (p. 30). Chicago: Moody Press.

[43] MacArthur, J. F., Jr. (1986). *Ephesians* (p. 36). Chicago: Moody Press.

[44] Wiersbe, W. W. (1996). *The Bible exposition commentary* (Vol. 2, p. 13). Wheaton, IL: Victor Books.

[45] MacDonald, W. (1995). *Believer's Bible Commentary: Old and New Testaments*. (A. Farstad, Ed.) (p. 1912). Nashville: Thomas Nelson.

[46] Cole, Steven. "Lesson 2: The Realities of Serving God (Nehemiah 2:1-20)". Retrieved 1/15/15 from https://bible.org/seriespage/lesson-2-realities-serving-god-nehemiah-21-20

[47] Hughes, R. K. (1990). *Ephesians: the mystery of the body of Christ* (p. 52). Wheaton, IL: Crossway Books.

[48] MacArthur, J. F., Jr. (1986). *Ephesians* (p. 44). Chicago: Moody Press.

[49] MacDonald, W. (1995). *Believer's Bible Commentary: Old and New Testaments*. (A. Farstad, Ed.) (p. 1913). Nashville: Thomas Nelson.

[50] Hughes, R. K. (1990). *Ephesians: the mystery of the body of Christ* (p. 53). Wheaton, IL: Crossway Books.

[51] Accessed December 31, 2015 from http://biblehub.com/ephesians/1-19.htm

[52] MacArthur, J. F., Jr. (1986). *Ephesians* (p. 46). Chicago: Moody Press.

[53] Hughes, R. K. (1990). *Ephesians: the mystery of the body of Christ* (pp. 53–54). Wheaton, IL: Crossway Books.

[54] Hughes, R. K. (1990). *Ephesians: the mystery of the body of Christ* (pp. 55–58). Wheaton, IL: Crossway Books.

[55] Stott, J. R. W. (1979). *God's new society: the message of Ephesians* (p. 61). Downers Grove, IL: InterVarsity Press.

[56] Stott, J. R. W. (1979). *God's new society: the message of Ephesians* (p. 62). Downers Grove, IL: InterVarsity Press.

[57] Hughes, R. K. (1990). *Ephesians: the mystery of the body of Christ* (pp. 62–63). Wheaton, IL: Crossway Books.

[58] Hughes, R. K. (1990). *Ephesians: the mystery of the body of Christ* (pp. 62–63). Wheaton, IL: Crossway Books.

[59] Stott, J. R. W. (1979). *God's new society: the message of Ephesians* (p. 65). Downers Grove, IL: InterVarsity Press.

[60] MacDonald, W. (1995). *Believer's Bible Commentary: Old and New Testaments*. (A. Farstad, Ed.) (p. 1916). Nashville: Thomas Nelson.

[61] MacArthur, J. F., Jr. (1986). *Ephesians* (p. 54). Chicago: Moody Press.

[62] MacArthur, J. F., Jr. (1986). *Ephesians* (pp. 54–55). Chicago: Moody Press.

[63] Wiersbe, W. W. (1996). *The Bible exposition commentary* (Vol. 2, pp. 17–18). Wheaton, IL: Victor Books.

[64] Stott, J. R. W. (1979). *God's new society: the message of Ephesians* (p. 73). Downers Grove, IL: InterVarsity Press.

[65] Stott, J. R. W. (1979). *God's new society: the message of Ephesians* (p. 73). Downers Grove, IL: InterVarsity Press.

[66] MacArthur, J. F., Jr. (1986). *Ephesians* (p. 57). Chicago: Moody Press.

[67] MacDonald, W. (1995). *Believer's Bible Commentary: Old and New Testaments*. (A. Farstad, Ed.) (pp. 1916–1917). Nashville: Thomas Nelson.

[68] Teacher's Outline and Study Bible - Commentary - Teacher's Outline and Study Bible – Ephesians: The Teacher's Outline and Study Bible.

[69] MacArthur, J. F., Jr. (1986). *Ephesians* (p. 61). Chicago: Moody Press.

[70] MacArthur, J. F., Jr. (1986). *Ephesians* (p. 61). Chicago: Moody Press.

[71] G. Kittel, G. W. Bromiley & G. Friedrich, Ed., *Theological Dictionary of the New Testament*, Electronic ed. (Grand Rapids, MI: Eerdmans, 1964), 6:175.

[72] Wiersbe, W. W. (1996). *The Bible exposition commentary* (Vol. 2, p. 19). Wheaton, IL: Victor Books.

[73] Accessed 4/25/15 from https://bible.org/seriespage/lesson-14-salvation-grace-through-faith-alone-ephesians-28-9

[74] Hughes, R. K. (1990). *Ephesians: the mystery of the body of Christ* (pp. 80–81). Wheaton, IL: Crossway Books.

[75] MacDonald, W. (1995). *Believer's Bible Commentary: Old and New Testaments*. (A. Farstad, Ed.) (p. 1919). Nashville: Thomas Nelson.

[76] Accessed 4/25/15 from https://bible.org/seriespage/lesson-14-salvation-grace-through-faith-alone-ephesians-28-9

[77] Wiersbe, W. W. (1996). *The Bible exposition commentary* (Vol. 2, p. 20). Wheaton, IL: Victor Books.

[78] MacDonald, W. (1995). *Believer's Bible Commentary: Old and New Testaments*. (A. Farstad, Ed.) (p. 1920). Nashville: Thomas Nelson.

[79] Stott, J. R. W. (1979). *God's new society: the message of Ephesians* (p. 91). Downers Grove, IL: InterVarsity Press.

[80] MacArthur, J. F., Jr. (1986). *Ephesians* (pp. 73–74). Chicago: Moody Press.

[81] MacArthur, J. F., Jr. (1986). *Ephesians* (p. 76). Chicago: Moody Press.

[82] Wiersbe, W. W. (1996). *The Bible exposition commentary* (Vol. 2, pp. 23–24). Wheaton, IL: Victor Books.

[83] Hughes, R. K. (1990). *Ephesians: the mystery of the body of Christ* (pp. 92–93). Wheaton, IL: Crossway Books.

[84] MacArthur, J. F., Jr. (1986). *Ephesians* (p. 79). Chicago: Moody Press.

[85] MacArthur, J. F., Jr. (1986). *Ephesians* (p. 80). Chicago: Moody Press.

[86] MacArthur, J. F., Jr. (1986). *Ephesians* (p. 80). Chicago: Moody Press.

[87] Barclay, W. (2002). *The Letters to the Galatians and Ephesians* (p. 136). Louisville, KY; London: Westminster John Knox Press.

[88] https://bible.org/seriespage/lesson-18-church-why-marry-it-ephesians-219-22

[89] Stott, J. R. W. (1979). *God's new society: the message of Ephesians* (p. 107). Downers Grove, IL: InterVarsity Press.

[90] Boice, J. M. (1988). *Ephesians: an expositional commentary* (p. 92). Grand Rapids, MI: Ministry Resources Library.

[91] MacArthur, J. F., Jr. (1986). *Ephesians* (p. 94). Chicago: Moody Press.

[92] Stott, J. R. W. (1979). *God's new society: the message of Ephesians* (p. 119). Downers Grove, IL: InterVarsity Press.

[93] Accessed 1/13/2016 from http://biblehub.com/greek/2097.htm

[94] MacDonald, W. (1995). *Believer's Bible Commentary: Old and New Testaments*. (A. Farstad, Ed.) (pp. 1927–1928). Nashville: Thomas Nelson.

[95] MacArthur, J. F., Jr. (1986). *Ephesians* (p. 100). Chicago: Moody Press.

[96] Hughes, R. K. (1990). *Ephesians: the mystery of the body of Christ* (p. 114). Wheaton, IL: Crossway Books.

[97] MacDonald, W. (1995). *Believer's Bible Commentary: Old and New Testaments*. (A. Farstad, Ed.) (p. 1929). Nashville: Thomas Nelson.

[98] Wiersbe, W. W. (1996). *The Bible exposition commentary* (Vol. 2, pp. 31–32). Wheaton, IL: Victor Books.

[99] Wiersbe, W. W. (1996). *The Bible exposition commentary* (Vol. 2, p. 32). Wheaton, IL: Victor Books.

[100] Wiersbe, W. W. (1996). *The Bible exposition commentary* (Vol. 2, p. 32). Wheaton, IL: Victor Books.

[101] Wiersbe, W. W. (1996). *The Bible exposition commentary* (Vol. 2, p. 32). Wheaton, IL: Victor Books.

[102] MacDonald, W. (1995). *Believer's Bible Commentary: Old and New Testaments*. (A. Farstad, Ed.) (p. 1930). Nashville: Thomas Nelson.

[103] Stott, J. R. W. (1979). *God's new society: the message of Ephesians* (p. 137). Downers Grove, IL: InterVarsity Press.

[104] MacDonald, W. (1995). *Believer's Bible Commentary: Old and New Testaments*. (A. Farstad, Ed.) (p. 1931). Nashville: Thomas Nelson.

[105] Teacher's Outline and Study Bible - Commentary - Teacher's Outline and Study Bible – Ephesians: The Teacher's Outline and Study Bible.

[106] MacDonald, W. (1995). *Believer's Bible Commentary: Old and New Testaments*. (A. Farstad, Ed.) (p. 1931). Nashville: Thomas Nelson.

[107] MacArthur, J. F., Jr. (1986). *Ephesians* (pp. 111–112). Chicago: Moody Press.

[108] MacArthur, J. F., Jr. (1986). *Ephesians* (pp. 112–113). Chicago: Moody Press.

[109] MacArthur, J. F., Jr. (1986). *Ephesians* (p. 119). Chicago: Moody Press.

[110] Teacher's Outline and Study Bible - Commentary - Teacher's Outline and Study Bible – Ephesians: The Teacher's Outline and Study Bible.

[111] MacArthur, J. F., Jr. (1986). *Ephesians* (p. 119). Chicago: Moody Press.

[112] Accessed 1/16/16 from http://www.christiansincrisis.net/

[113] Accessed 1/16/16 from http://www.charismamag.com/spirit/spiritual-growth/14683-10-basic-blessings-you-should-be-thankful-for

[114] MacDonald, W. (1995). *Believer's Bible Commentary: Old and New Testaments*. (A. Farstad, Ed.) (p. 1932). Nashville: Thomas Nelson.

[115] MacArthur, J. F., Jr. (1986). *Ephesians* (p. 120). Chicago: Moody Press.

[116] MacDonald, W. (1995). *Believer's Bible Commentary: Old and New Testaments*. (A. Farstad, Ed.) (p. 1932). Nashville: Thomas Nelson.

[117] Wiersbe, W. W. (1996). *The Bible exposition commentary* (Vol. 2, p. 35). Wheaton, IL: Victor Books.

[118] MacDonald, W. (1995). *Believer's Bible Commentary: Old and New Testaments*. (A. Farstad, Ed.) (pp. 1932–1933). Nashville: Thomas Nelson.

[119] Hughes, R. K. (1990). *Ephesians: the mystery of the body of Christ* (p. 125). Wheaton, IL: Crossway Books.

[120] Stott, J. R. W. (1979). *God's new society: the message of Ephesians* (pp. 153–154). Downers Grove, IL: InterVarsity Press.

[121] Stott, J. R. W. (1979). *God's new society: the message of Ephesians* (pp. 153–154). Downers Grove, IL: InterVarsity Press.

[122] Hughes, R. K. (1990). *Ephesians: the mystery of the body of Christ* (p. 124). Wheaton, IL: Crossway Books.

[123] MacDonald, W. (1995). *Believer's Bible Commentary: Old and New Testaments*. (A. Farstad, Ed.) (p. 1933). Nashville: Thomas Nelson.

[124] MacDonald, W. (1995). *Believer's Bible Commentary: Old and New Testaments*. (A. Farstad, Ed.) (p. 1933). Nashville: Thomas Nelson.

[125] MacArthur, J. F., Jr. (1986). *Ephesians* (p. 134). Chicago: Moody Press.

[126] Hughes, R. K. (1990). *Ephesians: the mystery of the body of Christ* (pp. 129–131). Wheaton, IL: Crossway Books.

[127] Hughes, R. K. (1990). *Ephesians: the mystery of the body of Christ* (p. 132). Wheaton, IL: Crossway Books.

[128] MacArthur, J. F., Jr. (1986). *Ephesians* (pp. 137–138). Chicago: Moody Press.

[129] MacArthur, J. F., Jr. (1986). *Ephesians* (p. 138). Chicago: Moody Press.

[130] Stott, J. R. W. (1979). *God's new society: the message of Ephesians* (pp. 158–159). Downers Grove, IL: InterVarsity Press.

[131] Stott, J. R. W. (1979). *God's new society: the message of Ephesians* (pp. 158–159). Downers Grove, IL: InterVarsity Press.

[132] MacArthur, J. F., Jr. (1986). *Ephesians* (p. 140). Chicago: Moody Press.

[133] Stott, J. R. W. (1979). *God's new society: the message of Ephesians* (pp. 158–159). Downers Grove, IL: InterVarsity Press. ,

[134] Accessed 1/18/2016 from http://www.churchleaders.com/pastors/pastor-articles/161343-tim_peters_10_common_reasons_pastors_quit_too_soon.html

[135] Stott, J. R. W. (1979). *God's new society: the message of Ephesians* (p. 168). Downers Grove, IL: InterVarsity Press.

[136] Stott, J. R. W. (1979). *God's new society: the message of Ephesians* (pp. 171–172). Downers Grove, IL: InterVarsity Press.

[137] MacArthur, J. F., Jr. (1986). *Ephesians* (p. 159). Chicago: Moody Press.

[138] MacArthur, J. F., Jr. (1986). *Ephesians* (p. 166). Chicago: Moody Press.

[139] MacArthur, J. F., Jr. (1986). *Ephesians* (p. 165). Chicago: Moody Press.

[140] Accessed 9/8/2015 from https://bible.org/seriespage/lesson-30-how-not-live-ephesians-417-19

[141] MacArthur, J. F., Jr. (1986). *Ephesians* (p. 168). Chicago: Moody Press.

[142] Accessed 9/8/2015 from https://bible.org/seriespage/lesson-30-how-not-live-ephesians-417-19

[143] Hughes, R. K. (1990). *Ephesians: the mystery of the body of Christ* (pp. 140–141). Wheaton, IL: Crossway Books.

[144] Hendriksen, W., & Kistemaker, S. J. (1953–2001). *Exposition of Ephesians* (Vol. 7, p. 210). Grand Rapids: Baker Book House.

[145] MacArthur, J. F., Jr. (1986). *Ephesians* (pp. 170–171). Chicago: Moody Press.

[146] Hughes, R. K. (1990). *Ephesians: the mystery of the body of Christ* (p. 141). Wheaton, IL: Crossway Books.

[147] MacArthur, J. F., Jr. (1986). *Ephesians* (pp. 171–172). Chicago: Moody Press.

[148] Accessed 9/8/2015 from http://abcnews.go.com/Primetime/story?id=132001

[149] Boice, J. M. (1988). *Ephesians: an expositional commentary* (p. 160). Grand Rapids, MI: Ministry Resources Library.

[150] Boice, J. M. (1988). *Ephesians: an expositional commentary* (p. 161). Grand Rapids, MI: Ministry Resources Library.

[151] MacArthur, J. F., Jr. (1986). *Ephesians* (p. 178). Chicago: Moody Press.

[152] Stott, J. R. W. (1979). *God's new society: the message of Ephesians* (p. 178). Downers Grove, IL: InterVarsity Press.

[153] MacDonald, W. (1995). *Believer's Bible Commentary: Old and New Testaments*. (A. Farstad, Ed.) (pp. 1938–1939). Nashville: Thomas Nelson.

[154] MacArthur, J. F., Jr. (1986). *Ephesians* (p. 185). Chicago: Moody Press.

[155] Wiersbe, W. W. (1996). *The Bible exposition commentary* (Vol. 2, p. 42). Wheaton, IL: Victor Books.

[156] Morris, L. (1984). *1 and 2 Thessalonians: An introduction and commentary* (Vol. 13, p. 86). Downers Grove, IL: InterVarsity Press.

[157] Wiersbe, W. W. (1996). *The Bible exposition commentary* (Vol. 2, p. 42). Wheaton, IL: Victor Books.

[158] MacArthur, J. F., Jr. (1986). *Ephesians* (p. 186). Chicago: Moody Press.

[159] MacDonald, W. (1995). *Believer's Bible Commentary: Old and New Testaments*. (A. Farstad, Ed.) (p. 1940). Nashville: Thomas Nelson.

[160] MacDonald, W. (1995). *Believer's Bible Commentary: Old and New Testaments*. (A. Farstad, Ed.) (p. 1940). Nashville: Thomas Nelson.

[161] Stott, J. R. W. (1979). *God's new society: the message of Ephesians* (p. 191). Downers Grove, IL: InterVarsity Press.

[162] MacArthur, J. F., Jr. (1986). *Ephesians* (p. 200). Chicago: Moody Press.

[163] Hughes, R. K. (1990). *Ephesians: the mystery of the body of Christ* (p. 156). Wheaton, IL: Crossway Books.

164 Hughes, R. K. (1990). *Ephesians: the mystery of the body of Christ* (p. 157). Wheaton, IL: Crossway Books.

165 Wiersbe, W. W. (1996). *The Bible exposition commentary* (Vol. 2, p. 45). Wheaton, IL: Victor Books.

166 Stott, J. R. W. (1979). *God's new society: the message of Ephesians* (p. 193). Downers Grove, IL: InterVarsity Press.

167 MacArthur, J. F., Jr. (1986). *Ephesians* (pp. 205–206). Chicago: Moody Press.

168 Hughes, R. K. (1990). *Ephesians: the mystery of the body of Christ* (p. 165). Wheaton, IL: Crossway Books.

169 Wiersbe, W. W. (1996). *The Bible exposition commentary* (Vol. 2, p. 45). Wheaton, IL: Victor Books.

170 MacArthur, J. F., Jr. (1986). *Ephesians* (p. 210). Chicago: Moody Press.

171 Stott, J. R. W. (1979). *God's new society: the message of Ephesians* (p. 200). Downers Grove, IL: InterVarsity Press.

172 Accessed 9/28/2015 from https://www.blueletterbible.org/lang/lexicon/Lexicon.cfm?Strongs=G1381&t=KJV

173 MacDonald, W. (1995). *Believer's Bible Commentary: Old and New Testaments.* (A. Farstad, Ed.) (p. 1943). Nashville: Thomas Nelson.

174 MacArthur, J. F., Jr. (1986). *Ephesians* (pp. 211–212). Chicago: Moody Press.

175 Hughes, R. K. (1990). *Ephesians: the mystery of the body of Christ* (p. 167). Wheaton, IL: Crossway Books.

176 MacArthur, J. F., Jr. (1986). *Ephesians* (pp. 212–213). Chicago: Moody Press.

177 Teacher's Outline and Study Bible - Commentary - Teacher's Outline and Study Bible – Ephesians: The Teacher's Outline and Study Bible.

178 MacArthur, J. F., Jr. (1986). *Ephesians* (pp. 213–214). Chicago: Moody Press.

179 MacArthur, J. F., Jr. (1986). *Ephesians* (p. 222). Chicago: Moody Press.

180 Stott, J. R. W. (1979). *God's new society: the message of Ephesians* (p. 202). Downers Grove, IL: InterVarsity Press.

181 MacArthur, J. F., Jr. (1986). *Ephesians* (p. 223). Chicago: Moody Press.

182 MacArthur, J. F., Jr. (1986). *Ephesians* (p. 223). Chicago: Moody Press.

183 MacDonald, W. (1995). *Believer's Bible Commentary: Old and New Testaments.* (A. Farstad, Ed.) (p. 1944). Nashville: Thomas Nelson.

184 Accessed10/3/2015 from http://www.merriam-webster.com/dictionary/debauchery

185 MacArthur, J. F., Jr. (1986). *Ephesians* (p. 233). Chicago: Moody Press.

186 Accessed 10/3//2015 from http://global.britannica.com/topic/Bacchanalia

187 Wiersbe, W. W. (1996). *The Bible exposition commentary* (Vol. 2, p. 48). Wheaton, IL: Victor Books.

[188] Wiersbe, W. W. (1996). *The Bible exposition commentary* (Vol. 2, p. 48). Wheaton, IL: Victor Books.

[189] MacDonald, W. (1995). *Believer's Bible Commentary: Old and New Testaments.* (A. Farstad, Ed.) (p. 1946). Nashville: Thomas Nelson.

[190] Evans, Tony (2009-01-01). Free at Last: Experiencing True Freedom Through Your Identity in Christ (Kindle Locations 1817-1819). Moody Publishers. Kindle Edition.

[191] MacArthur, J. F., Jr. (1986). *Ephesians* (p. 280). Chicago: Moody Press.

[192] Hughes, R. K. (1990). *Ephesians: the mystery of the body of Christ* (p. 190). Wheaton, IL: Crossway Books.

[193] W. W. Wiersbe, *The Bible Exposition Commentary.* (Wheaton, IL: Victor Books, 1996).

[194] Guzik, David (2012-11-26). Galatians and Ephesians (Kindle Locations 5895-5896). Enduring Word Media. Kindle Edition.

[195] Guzik, David (2012-11-26). Galatians and Ephesians (Kindle Locations 6140-6146). Enduring Word Media. Kindle Edition.

[196] Guzik, David (2012-11-26). Galatians and Ephesians (Kindle Locations 6150-6152). Enduring Word Media. Kindle Edition.

[197] Accessed 8/15/16 from http://loveandrespect.com/

[198] Cole, Steven, "The Spirit-filled Home Part 1", accessed 10/27/2015 from https://bible.org/seriespage/lesson-51-spirit-filled-home-part-1-ephesians-61-3

[199] MacArthur, J. F., Jr. (1986). *Ephesians* (p. 309). Chicago: Moody Press.

[200] MacArthur, J. F., Jr. (1986). *Ephesians* (p. 311). Chicago: Moody Press.

[201] Saller, Richard. "Family Values in Rome." Accessed 10/17/2015 from http://fathom.lib.uchicago.edu/1/777777121908/

[202] "Roman Punishment." Accessed 10/17/2015 from http://www.romae-vitam.com/roman-punishment.html

[203] Hughes, R. K. (1990). *Ephesians: the mystery of the body of Christ* (p. 199). Wheaton, IL: Crossway Books.

[204] MacArthur, J. F., Jr. (1986). *Ephesians* (p. 312). Chicago: Moody Press.

[205] Accessed 10/17/ 2015 on https://bible.org/seriespage/lesson-52-spirit-filled-home-part-2-ephesians-64

[206] MacArthur, J. F., Jr. (1986). *Ephesians* (p. 315). Chicago: Moody Press.

[207] MacArthur, J. F., Jr. (1986). *Ephesians* (p. 316). Chicago: Moody Press.

[208] MacArthur, J. F., Jr. (1986). *Ephesians* (pp. 315–316). Chicago: Moody Press.

[209] W. Barclay, *The New Daily Study Bible: The Letters to Philippians, Colossians, and Thessalonians*, 3rd ed. (Louisville, KY; London: Westminster John Knox Press, 2003), 190.

[210] Keathley, J. III. The Principle of Nature (Knowing Your Child), accessed 2/8/15 https://bible.org/seriespage/principle-nature-knowing-your-child .

[211] Hughes, R. K. (1990). *Ephesians: the mystery of the body of Christ* (p. 200). Wheaton, IL: Crossway Books.

[212] Hughes, R. K. (1990). *Ephesians: the mystery of the body of Christ* (pp. 200–201). Wheaton, IL: Crossway Books.
[213] Hughes, R. K. (1990). *Ephesians: the mystery of the body of Christ* (p. 201). Wheaton, IL: Crossway Books.
[214] MacArthur, J. F., Jr. (1986). *Ephesians* (p. 319). Chicago: Moody Press.
[215] MacArthur, J. F., Jr. (1986). *Ephesians* (p. 308). Chicago: Moody Press.
[216] Stott, J. R. W. (1979). *God's new society: the message of Ephesians* (p. 252). Downers Grove, IL: InterVarsity Press.
[217] MacDonald, W. (1995). *Believer's Bible Commentary: Old and New Testaments*. (A. Farstad, Ed.) (p. 1950). Nashville: Thomas Nelson.
[218] Accessed 10/24/2015 from https://bible.org/seriespage/lesson-54-working-god-ephesians-65-9
[219] Stott, J. R. W. (1979). *God's new society: the message of Ephesians* (p. 250). Downers Grove, IL: InterVarsity Press.
[220] Hughes, R. K. (1990). *Ephesians: the mystery of the body of Christ* (p. 206). Wheaton, IL: Crossway Books.
[221] MacArthur, J. F., Jr. (1986). *Ephesians* (p. 324). Chicago: Moody Press.
[222] MacArthur, J. F., Jr. (1986). *Ephesians* (p. 325). Chicago: Moody Press.
[223] Hughes, R. K. (1990). *Ephesians: the mystery of the body of Christ* (p. 208). Wheaton, IL: Crossway Books.
[224] MacArthur, J. F., Jr. (1986). *Ephesians* (p. 328). Chicago: Moody Press.
[225] MacDonald, W. (1995). *Believer's Bible Commentary: Old and New Testaments*. (A. Farstad, Ed.) (p. 1951). Nashville: Thomas Nelson.
[226] MacArthur, J. F., Jr. (1986). *Ephesians* (pp. 328–329). Chicago: Moody Press.
[227] Wiersbe, W. W. (1996). *The Bible exposition commentary* (Vol. 2, p. 55). Wheaton, IL: Victor Books.
[228] Hughes, R. K. (1990). *Ephesians: the mystery of the body of Christ* (p. 210). Wheaton, IL: Crossway Books.
[229] MacArthur, J. F., Jr. (1986). *Ephesians* (p. 329). Chicago: Moody Press.
[230] Hendriksen, W., & Kistemaker, S. J. (1953–2001). *Exposition of Ephesians* (Vol. 7, p. 265). Grand Rapids: Baker Book House.
[231] Wiersbe, W. W. (1996). *The Bible exposition commentary* (Vol. 2, p. 56). Wheaton, IL: Victor Books.
[232] MacArthur, J. F., Jr. (1986). *Ephesians* (pp. 337–338). Chicago: Moody Press.
[233] MacArthur, J. F., Jr. (1986). *Ephesians* (p. 344). Chicago: Moody Press.
[234] Stott, J. R. W. (1979). *God's new society: the message of Ephesians* (pp. 266–267). Downers Grove, IL: InterVarsity Press.
[235] Foulkes, F. (1989). *Ephesians: an introduction and commentary* (Vol. 10, p. 175). Downers Grove, IL: InterVarsity Press.
[236] MacArthur, J. F., Jr. (1986). *Ephesians* (p. 338). Chicago: Moody Press.
[237] Accessed 10/31/2015 from http://global.britannica.com/topic/legion

[238] Wiersbe, W. W. (1996). *The Bible exposition commentary* (Vol. 2, p. 57). Wheaton, IL: Victor Books.

[239] Stott, J. R. W. (1979). *God's new society: the message of Ephesians* (p. 264). Downers Grove, IL: InterVarsity Press.

[240] MacDonald, W. (1995). *Believer's Bible Commentary: Old and New Testaments*. (A. Farstad, Ed.) (p. 1952). Nashville: Thomas Nelson.

[241] Hughes, R. K. (1990). *Ephesians: the mystery of the body of Christ* (p. 215). Wheaton, IL: Crossway Books.

[242] MacArthur, J. F., Jr. (1986). *Ephesians* (p. 341). Chicago: Moody Press.

[243] MacArthur, J. F., Jr. (1986). *Ephesians* (p. 340). Chicago: Moody Press.

[244] MacDonald, W. (1995). *Believer's Bible Commentary: Old and New Testaments*. (A. Farstad, Ed.) (p. 1952). Nashville: Thomas Nelson.

[245] Boice, J. M. (1988). *Ephesians: an expositional commentary* (pp. 244–245). Grand Rapids, MI: Ministry Resources Library.

[246] Accessed 11/14/2015 from https://en.wikipedia.org/wiki/Peter_Singer#Bestiality

[247] Accessed 11/14/2015 from https://bible.org/seriespage/lesson-57-protected-truth-and-righteousness-ephesians-614

[248] Hughes, R. K. (1990). *Ephesians: the mystery of the body of Christ* (p. 224). Wheaton, IL: Crossway Books.

[249] Wiersbe, W. W. (1996). *The Bible exposition commentary* (Vol. 2, p. 58). Wheaton, IL: Victor Books.

[250] Foulkes, F. (1989). *Ephesians: an introduction and commentary* (Vol. 10, p. 179). Downers Grove, IL: InterVarsity Press.

[251] MacArthur, J. F., Jr. (1986). *Ephesians* (pp. 350–351). Chicago: Moody Press.

[252] MacArthur, J. F., Jr. (1986). *Ephesians* (p. 351). Chicago: Moody Press.

[253] MacArthur, J. F., Jr. (1986). *Ephesians* (p. 351). Chicago: Moody Press.

[254] MacArthur, J. F., Jr. (1986). *Ephesians* (p. 354). Chicago: Moody Press.

[255] MacArthur, J. F., Jr. (1986). *Ephesians* (pp. 358–359). Chicago: Moody Press.

[256] MacArthur, J. F., Jr. (1986). *Ephesians* (pp. 358–359). Chicago: Moody Press.

[257] Wiersbe, W. W. (1996). *The Bible exposition commentary* (Vol. 2, p. 58). Wheaton, IL: Victor Books.

[258] Boice, J. M. (1988). *Ephesians: an expositional commentary* (p. 248). Grand Rapids, MI: Ministry Resources Library.

[259] MacArthur, J. F., Jr. (1986). *Ephesians* (pp. 367–368). Chicago: Moody Press.

[260] MacArthur, J. F., Jr. (1986). *Ephesians* (p. 370). Chicago: Moody Press.

[261] Boice, J. M. (1988). *Ephesians: an expositional commentary* (p. 252). Grand Rapids, MI: Ministry Resources Library.

[262] Accessed 11/23/2015 from
http://www.biblestudytools.com/lexicons/hebrew/nas/hagah.html
[263] Accessed 11/23/2015 from http://www.mljtrust.org/sermons/
[264] Hughes, R. K. (1990). *Ephesians: the mystery of the body of Christ* (pp. 247–250). Wheaton, IL: Crossway Books.
[265] Accessed 11/28/2015 from https://bible.org/seriespage/lesson-62-how-fight-god-ephesians-618-20
[266] Hughes, R. K. (1990). *Ephesians: the mystery of the body of Christ* (p. 251). Wheaton, IL: Crossway Books.
[267] MacArthur, J. F., Jr. (1986). *Ephesians* (p. 380). Chicago: Moody Press.
[268] MacDonald, W. (1995). *Believer's Bible Commentary: Old and New Testaments.* (A. Farstad, Ed.) (p. 1413). Nashville: Thomas Nelson.
[269] Accessed 11/28/2015 from http://odb.org/2005/06/02/five-finger-prayers/
[270] John Piper, *Desiring God* (Portland, OR: Multnomah, 1986), pp. 150, 151.
[271] Hughes, R. K. (1990). *Ephesians: the mystery of the body of Christ* (p. 262). Wheaton, IL: Crossway Books.
[272] Accessed 12/05/2015 from https://bible.org/seriespage/lesson-63-caring-church-ephesians-621-24
[273] Hughes, R. K. (1990). *Ephesians: the mystery of the body of Christ* (p. 262). Wheaton, IL: Crossway Books.
[274] Accessed 8/17/16 from https://bible.org/seriespage/lesson-63-caring-church-ephesians-621-24
[275] Teacher's Outline and Study Bible - Commentary - Teacher's Outline and Study Bible – Ephesians: The Teacher's Outline and Study Bible.
[276] Accessed 12/06/2015 from https://bible.org/seriespage/lesson-63-caring-church-ephesians-621-24
[277] Accessed 12/05/2015 from https://bible.org/seriespage/lesson-63-caring-church-ephesians-621-24
[278] Stott, J. R. W. (1979). *God's new society: the message of Ephesians* (pp. 289–290). Downers Grove, IL: InterVarsity Press.
[279] MacArthur, J. F., Jr. (1986). *Ephesians* (p. 385). Chicago: Moody Press.
[280] Hughes, R. K. (1990). *Ephesians: the mystery of the body of Christ* (p. 266). Wheaton, IL: Crossway Books.
[281] Hughes, R. K. (1990). *Ephesians: the mystery of the body of Christ* (p. 266). Wheaton, IL: Crossway Books.
[282] Hughes, R. K. (1990). *Ephesians: the mystery of the body of Christ* (p. 266). Wheaton, IL: Crossway Books.

Made in the USA
Middletown, DE
12 April 2019